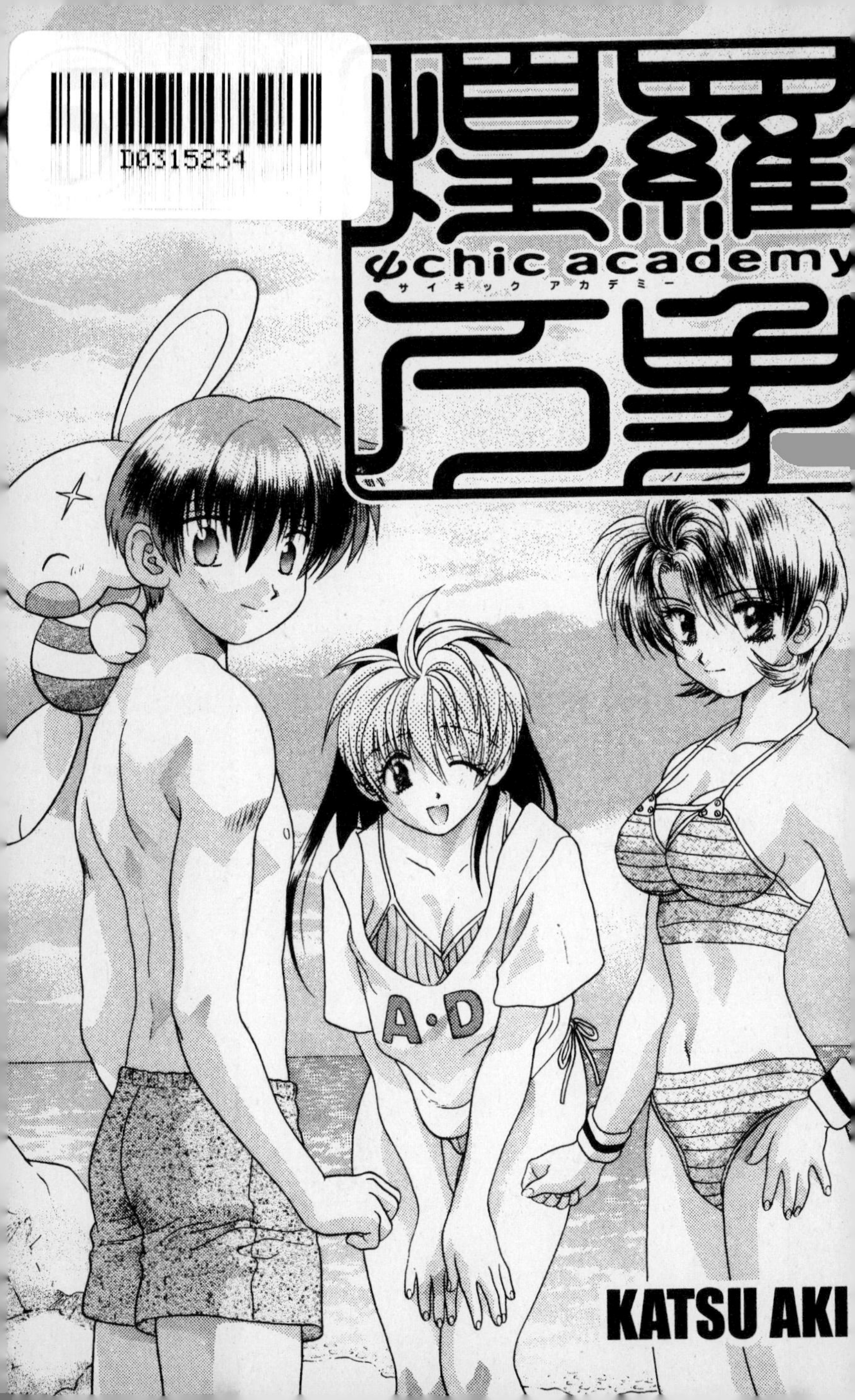
煌羅万象
ψchic academy
サイキックアカデミー
A·D
KATSU AKI

PSYCHIC ACADEMY

VOLUME 5

BY
KATSU AKI

HAMBURG // LONDON // LOS ANGELES // TOKYO

Psychic Academy Vol. 5

Created by Katsu Aki

Translation - Yuki N. Johnson
English Adaptation - Nathan Johnson
Associate Editor - Wendy Hunter
Retouch and Lettering - Erik Lervold
Graphic Design - James Lee
Cover Design - Anna Kernbaum

Editor - Luis Reyes
Digital Imaging Manager - Chris Buford
Pre-Press Manager - Antonio DePietro
Production Managers - Jennifer Miller and Mutsumi Miyazaki
Art Director - Matt Alford
Managing Editor - Jill Freshney
VP of Production - Ron Klamert
President and C.O.O. - John Parker
Publisher and C.E.O. - Stuart Levy

A  Manga

TOKYOPOP Inc.
5900 Wilshire Blvd. Suite 2000
Los Angeles, CA 90036

E-mail: info@TOKYOPOP.com
Come visit us online at www.TOKYOPOP.com

ISBN: 1-59182-625-X

First TOKYOPOP printing: November 2004
10 9 8 7 6 5 4 3 2 1
Printed in the USA

Story Thus Far...

In the near future, the discovery of psychic abilities has run congruously with the threat of evil forces. Luckily one man, Zerodyme Kyupura Pa Azalraku Vairu Rua Darogu, employing his incredible psychic power, has defeated the Dark Overlord and earned the venerable title, "Vanquisher of the Dark Overlord." The world is safe, but not complacent. Now, children who demonstrate a proclivity for psychic powers are separated from the common herd and placed in specialty schools designed to help them enhance their unique abilities. Of course, this separation has aroused suspicion and distrust among "normal" humans.

Ai Shiomi was perfectly happy NOT being so gifted. However, pressured by his parents, and with a filial reputation thrust upon him by his brother, the aforementioned Vanquisher of the Dark Overlord, Ai enrolled in the Psychic Academy. His life at the Academy has been a difficult one, dealing as he is with new powers, a new school and, perhaps worst of all, the onset of adolescence. Luckily he has the support of his old friend Sahra, his roommate Telda, the stern but caring Mew and a strange bunny, Master Boo, who vows to train the young buck in the psychic arts. And as luck would have it, his brother teaches at the school.

Having gotten through his first round of exams, and helping thwart a plot by a group of mortals to beat the hell out of every psychic they run across--a group, ironically enough, led by the Psychic Academy's very own schizophrenic student body president--and having actually gone so far as to tell Orina that he loves her, Ai Shiomi can really use a bit of a vacation. But two things might complicate matters: His increasing affection and mysterious connection to Mew, and a large rock creature that threatens to kill him, his brother and all of his friends in their little tropical paradise.

CONTENTS

煌羅万象
ψchic academy
サイキック アカデミー

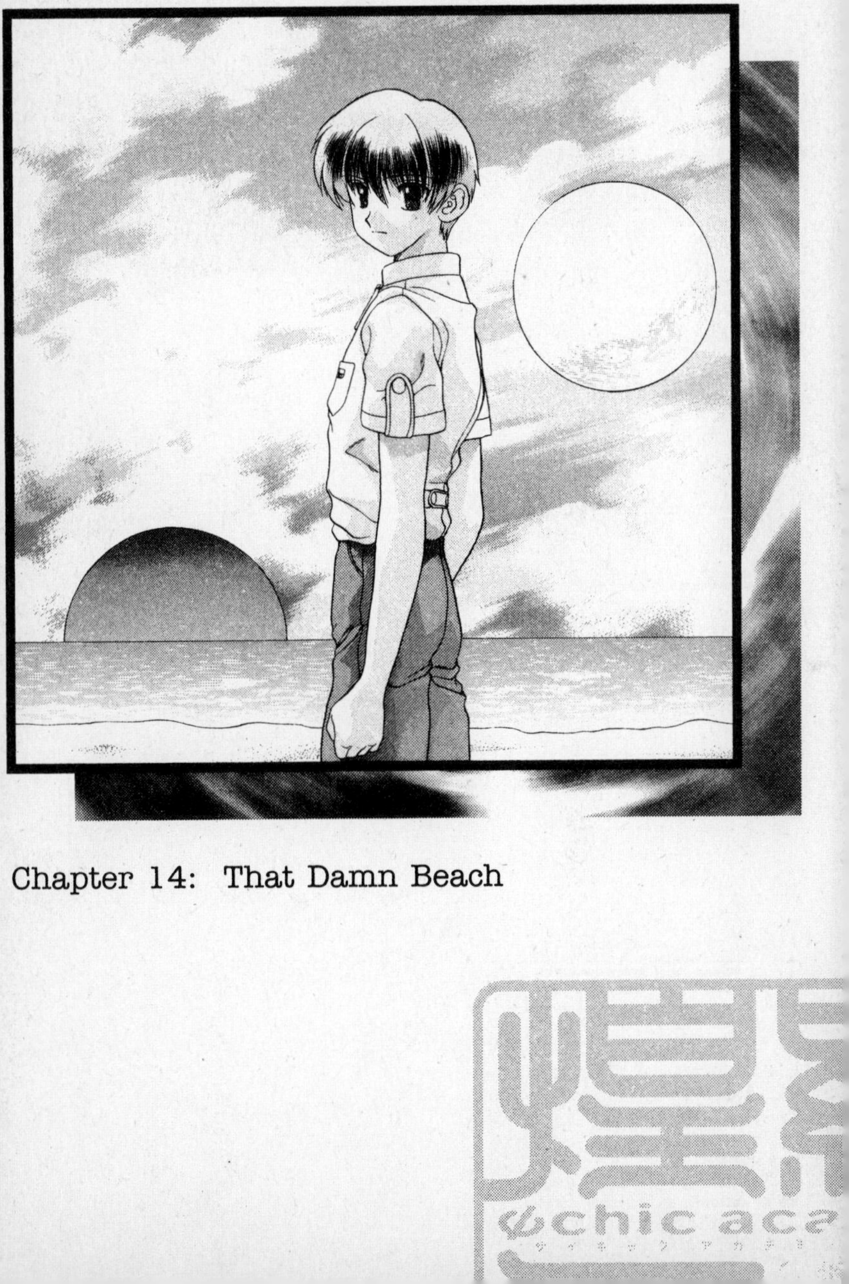

Chapter 14: That Damn Beach

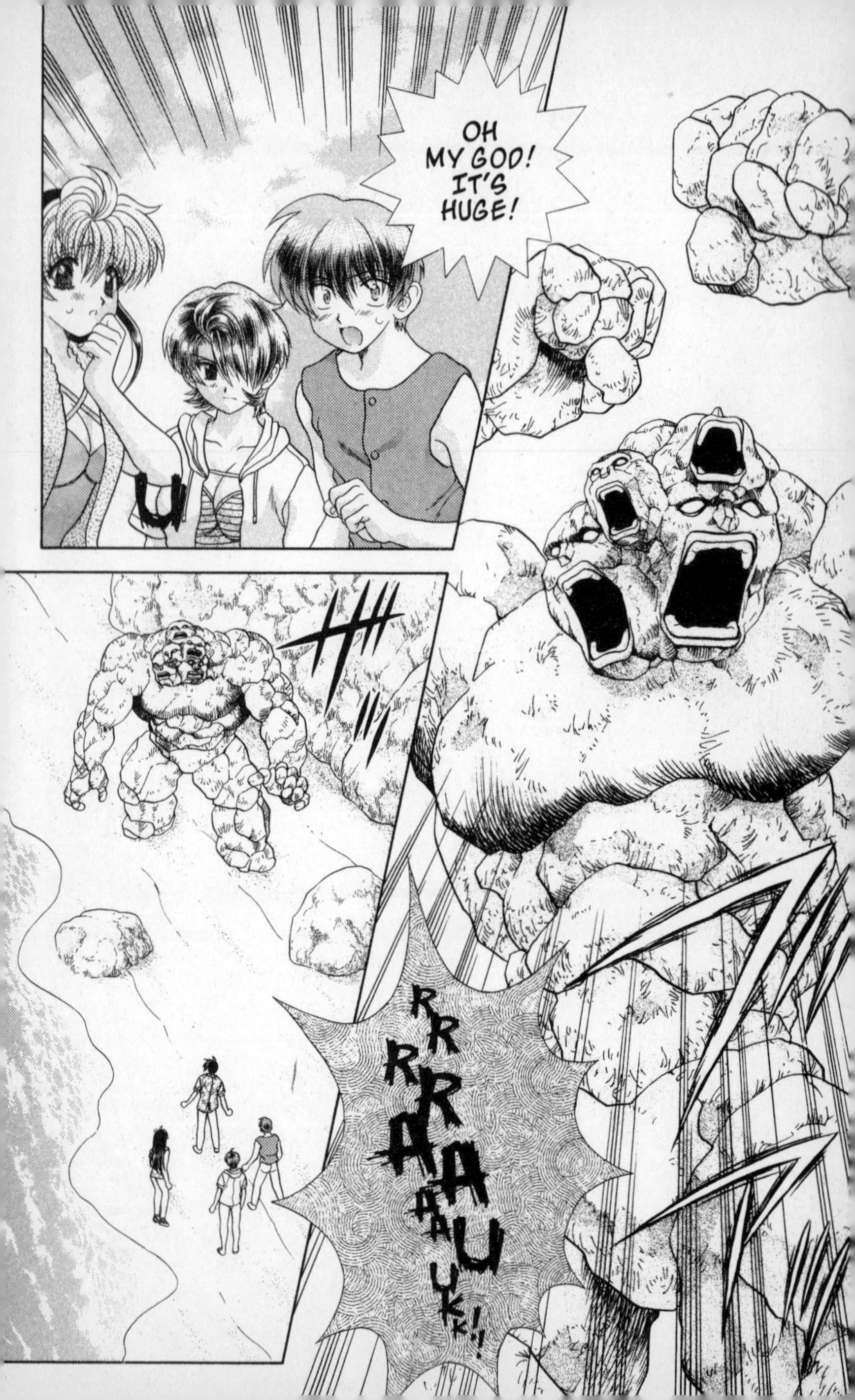
OH MY GOD! IT'S HUGE!
U
RRRRAAAAUUKK!!

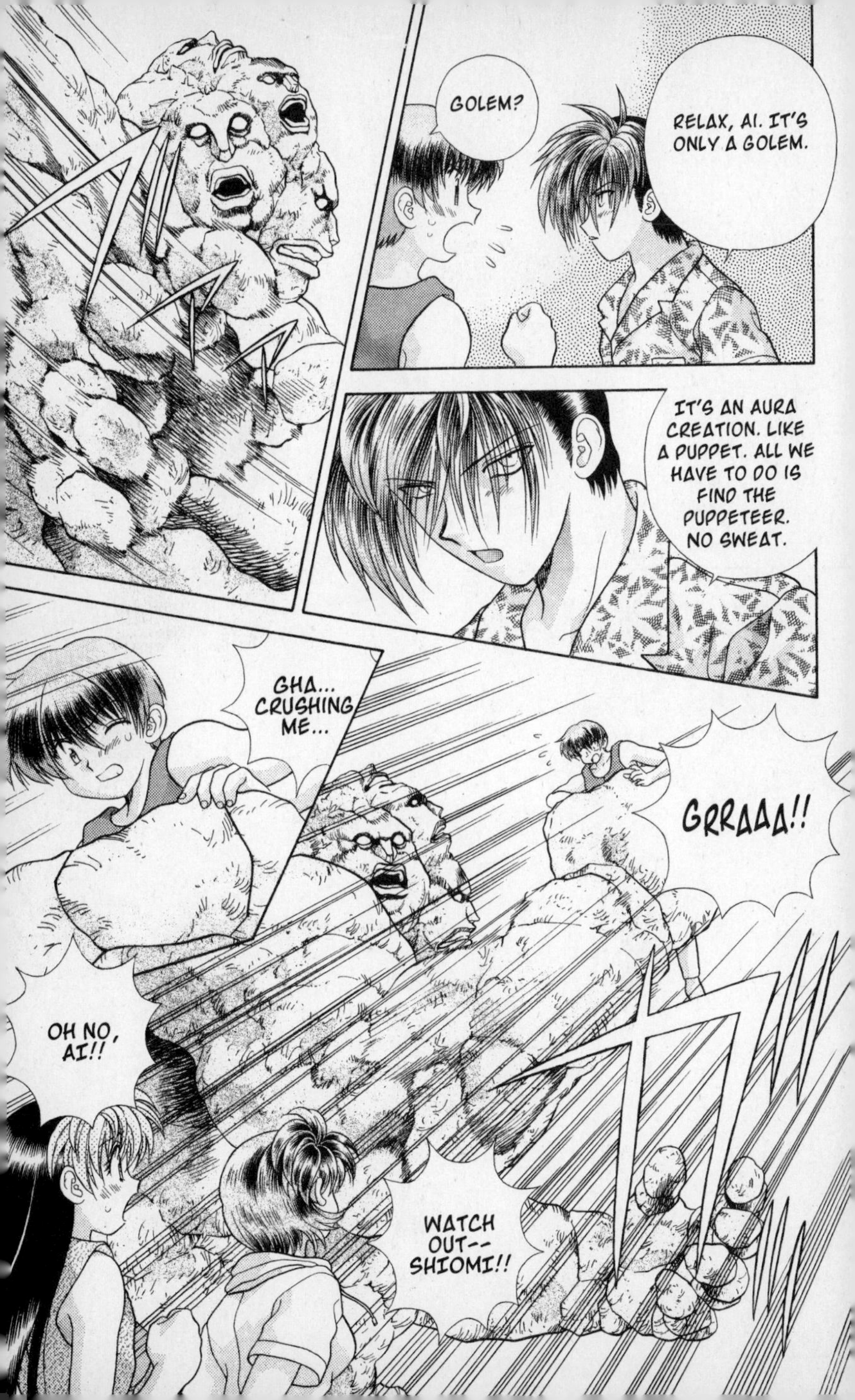
RELAX, AI. IT'S ONLY A GOLEM.
GOLEM?
IT'S AN AURA CREATION. LIKE A PUPPET. ALL WE HAVE TO DO IS FIND THE PUPPETEER. NO SWEAT.
GHA... CRUSHING ME...
GRRAAA!!
OH NO, AI!!
WATCH OUT-- SHIOMI!!

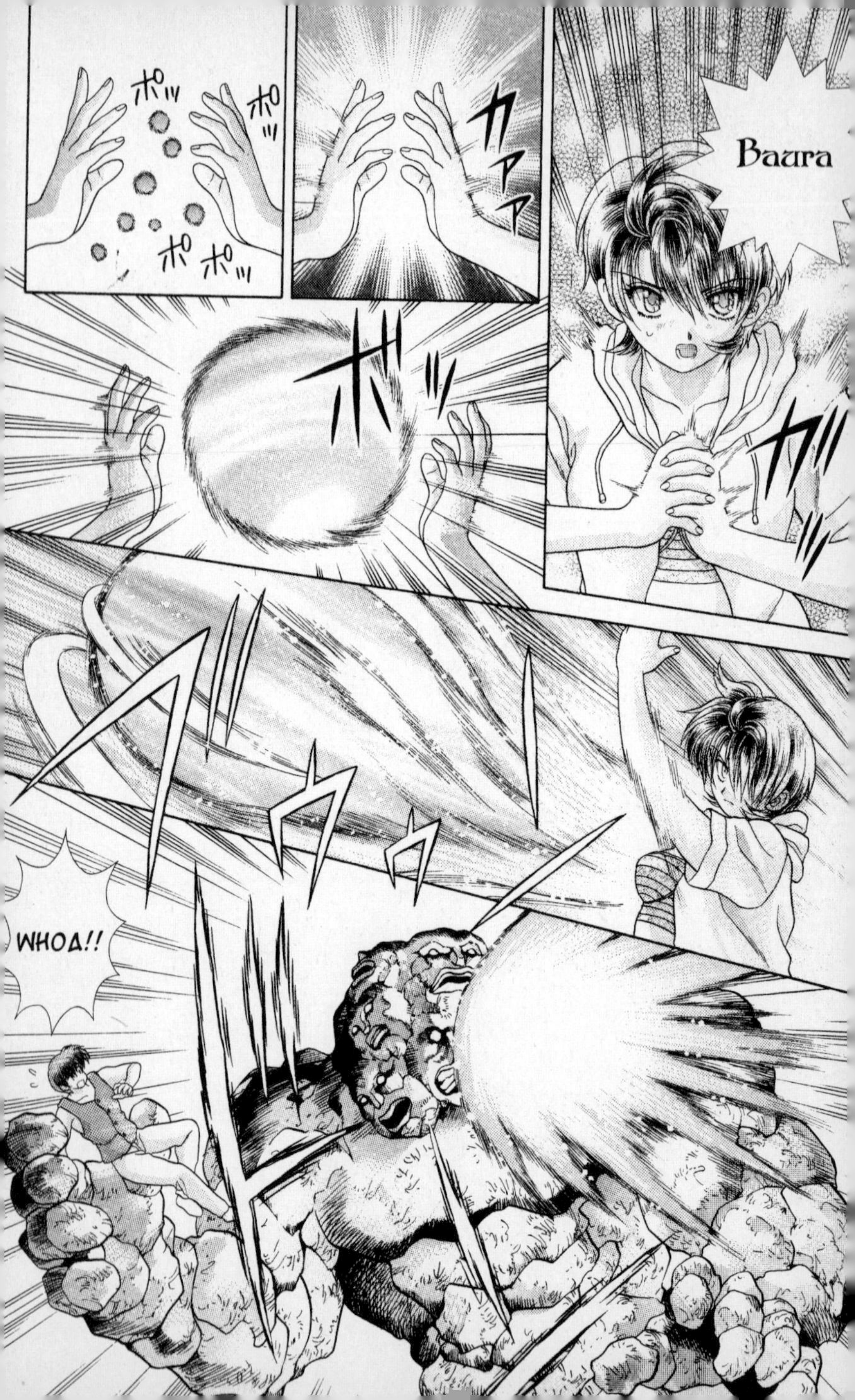
Baura
ガッ
カァァ
ポッ
ポッ
ポッ
ポッ
ボッ
ズウゥ
WHOA!!

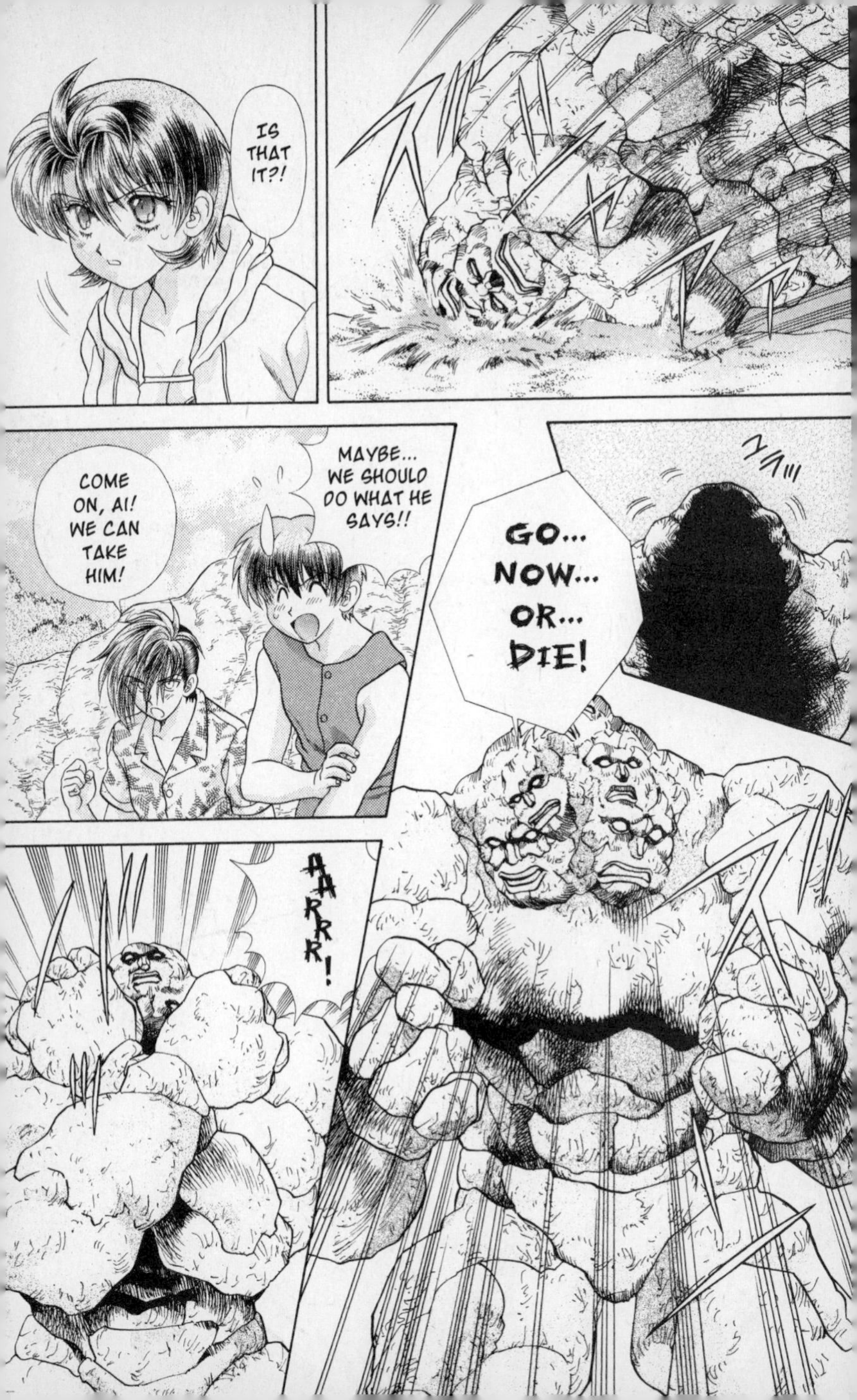
IS THAT IT?!
GO... NOW... OR... DIE!
MAYBE... WE SHOULD DO WHAT HE SAYS!!
COME ON, AI! WE CAN TAKE HIM!
AARRR!

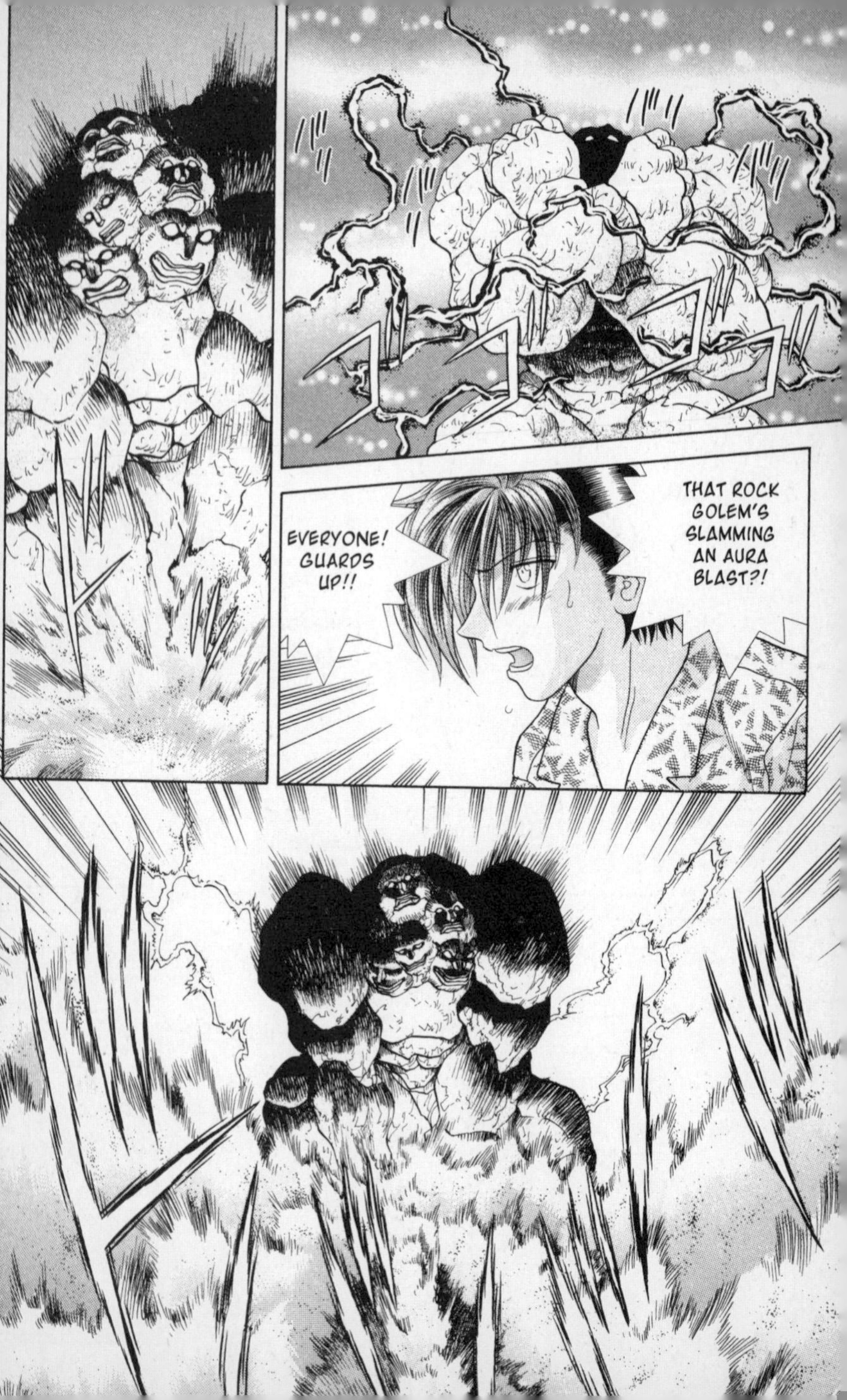
THAT ROCK GOLEM'S SLAMMING AN AURA BLAST?!
EVERYONE! GUARDS UP!!

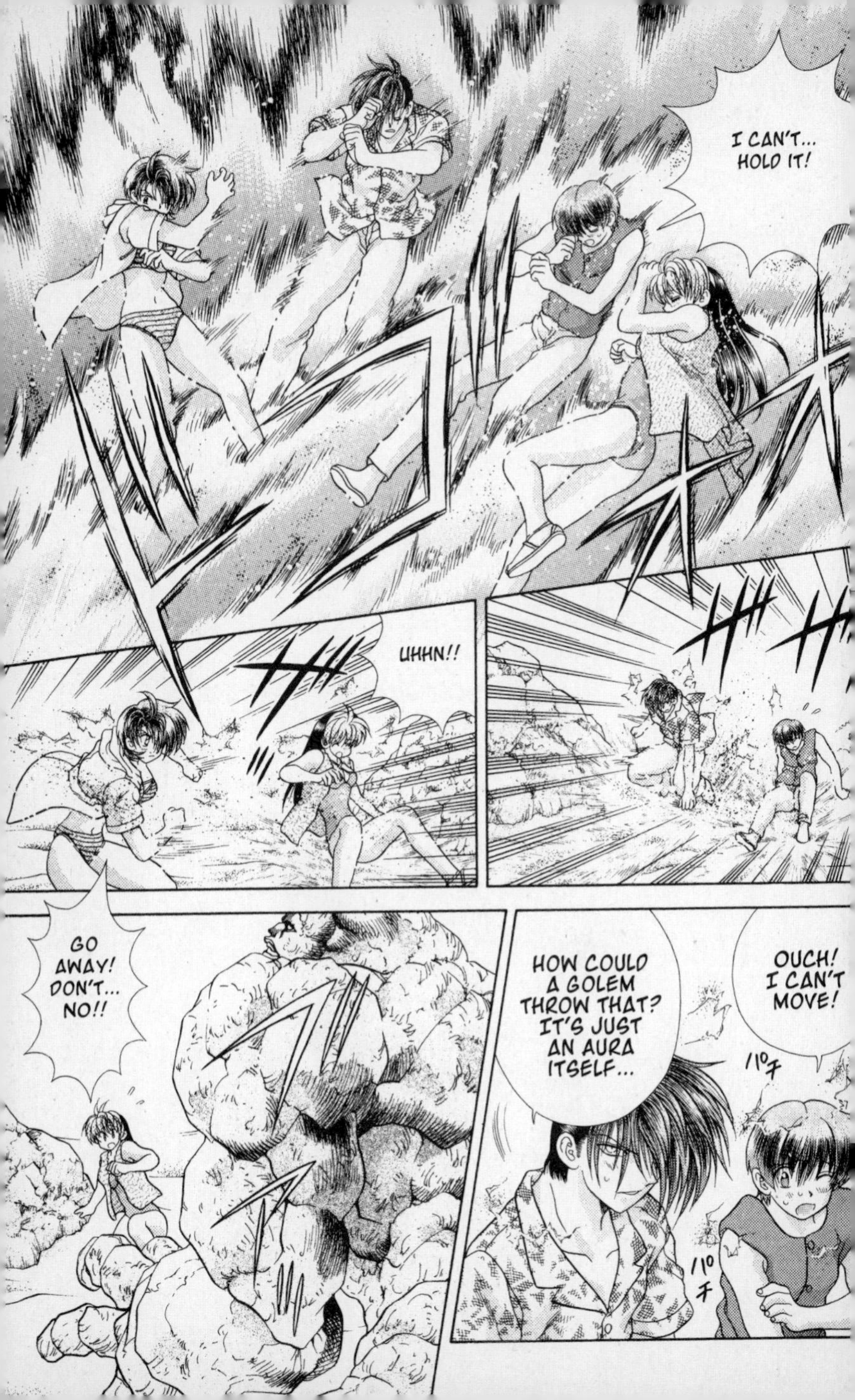

I CAN'T... HOLD IT!
UHHN!!
OUCH! I CAN'T MOVE!
パチ
HOW COULD A GOLEM THROW THAT? IT'S JUST AN AURA ITSELF...
パチ
GO AWAY! DON'T... NO!!

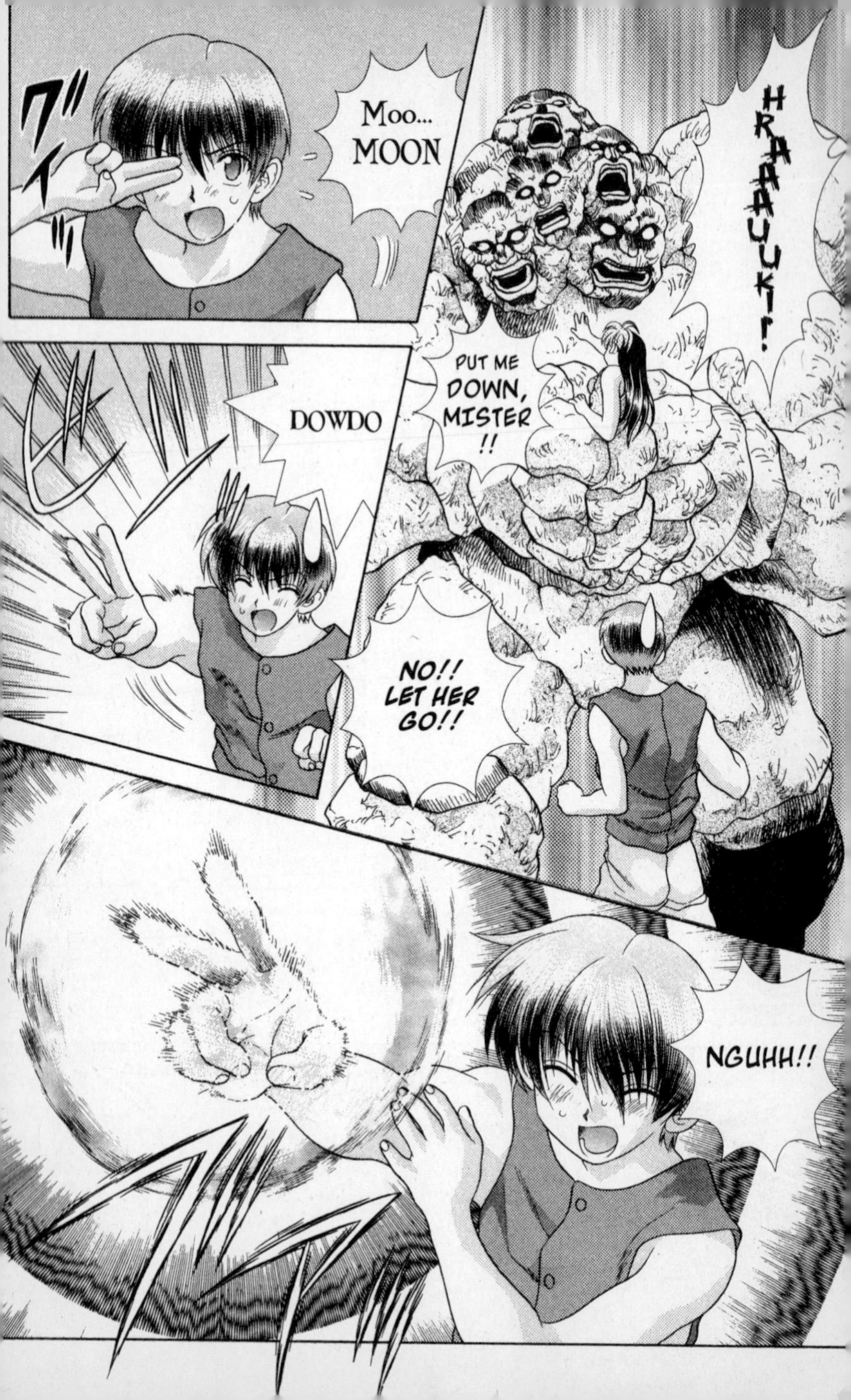
HRAAAUKI!!
PUT ME DOWN, MISTER!!
NO!! LET HER GO!!
Moo... MOON
DOWDO
NGUHH!!

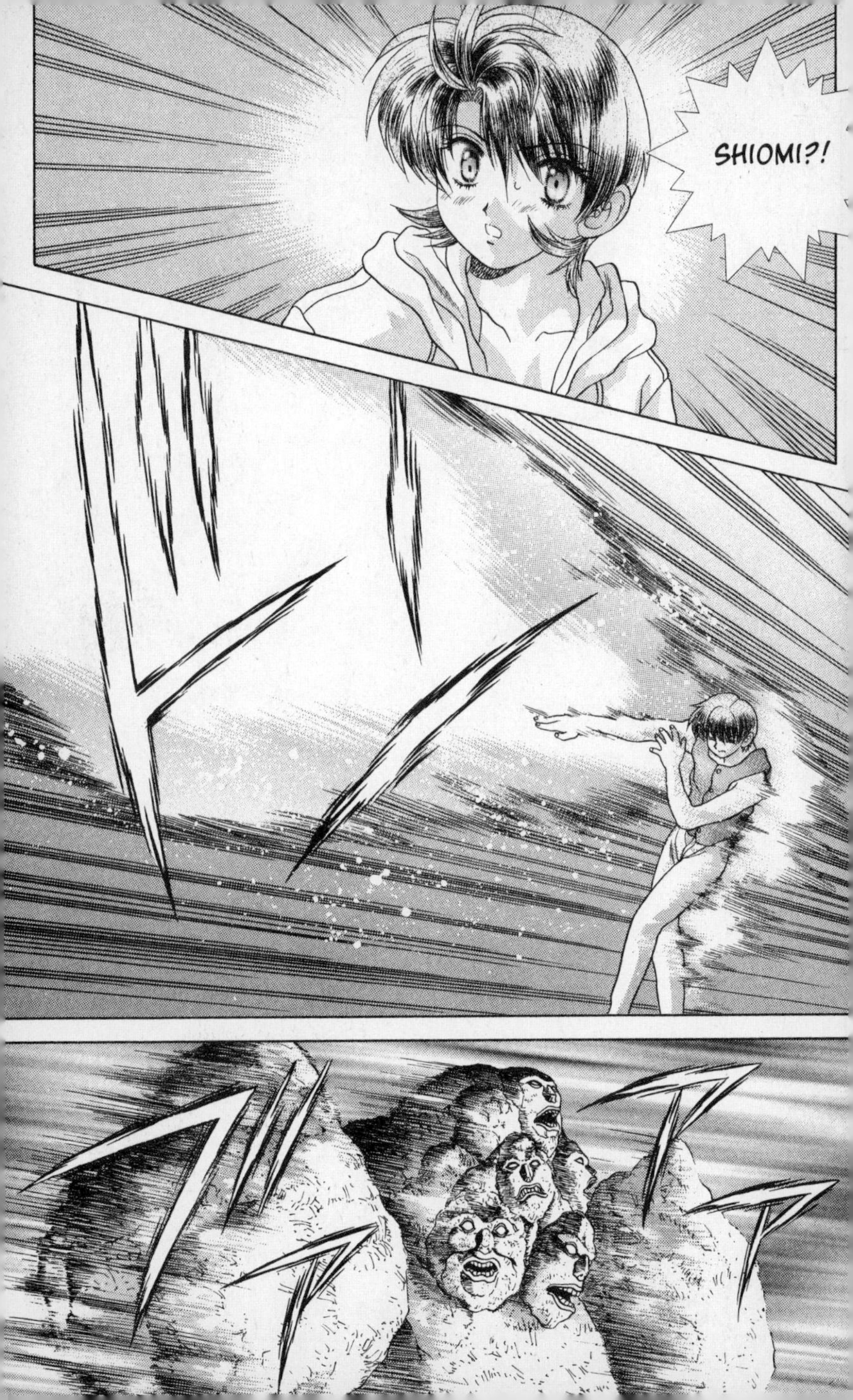
SHIOMI?!

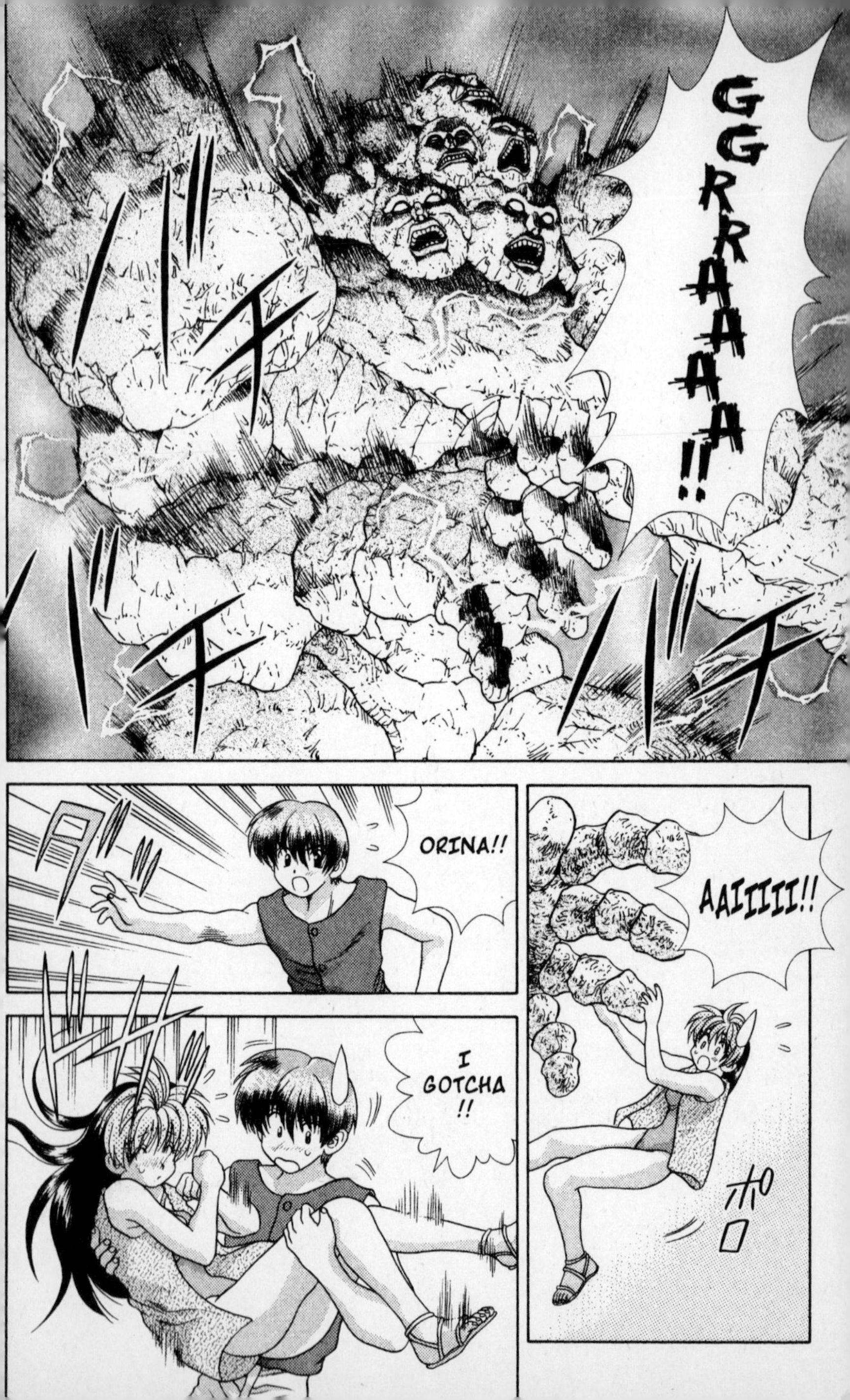
GGRRAAA!!
AAIIIII!!
ORINA!!
I GOTCHA!!

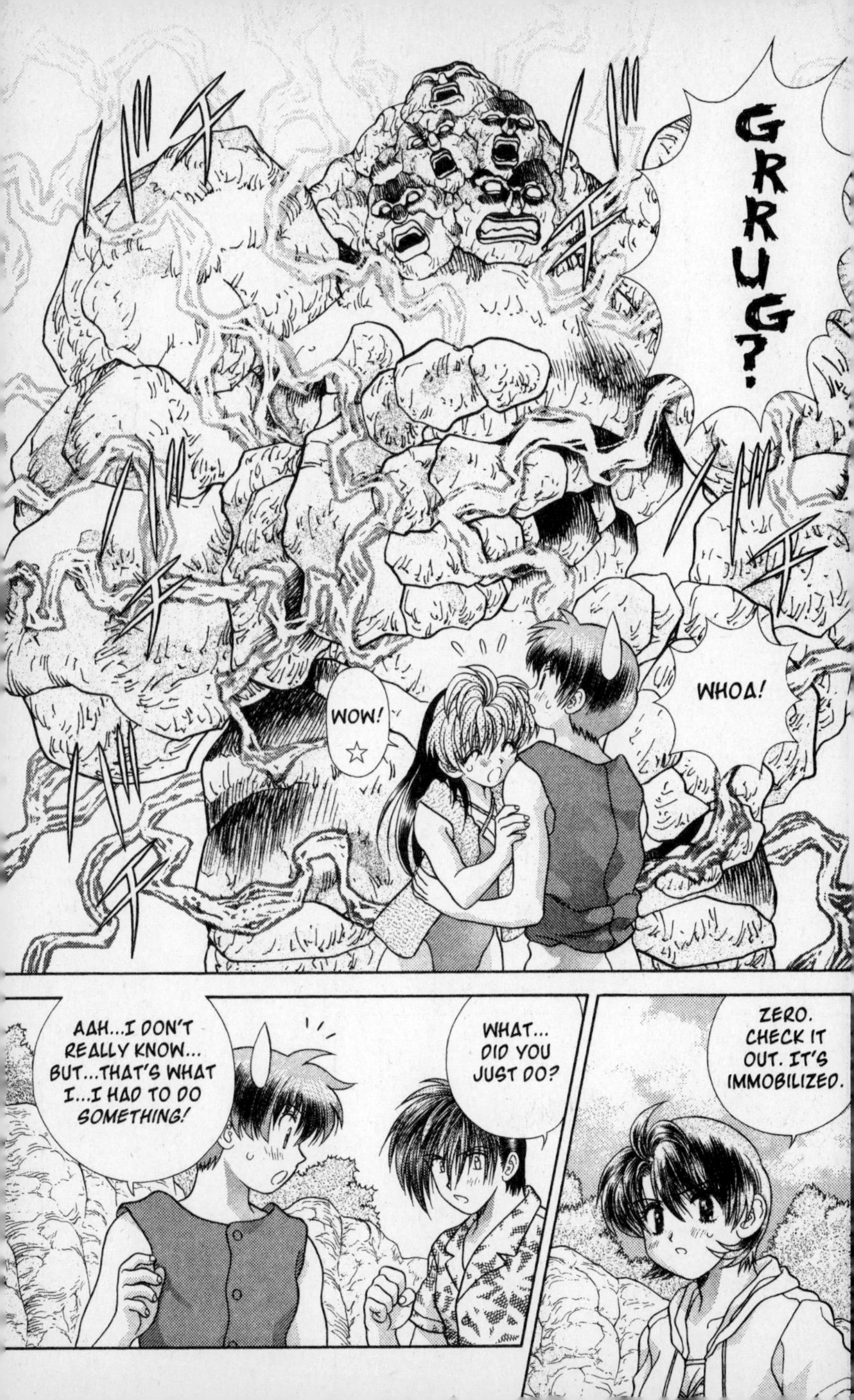
GRRUG?
WHOA!
WOW! ☆
ZERO. CHECK IT OUT. IT'S IMMOBILIZED.
WHAT... DID YOU JUST DO?
AAH...I DON'T REALLY KNOW... BUT...THAT'S WHAT I...I HAD TO DO SOMETHING!

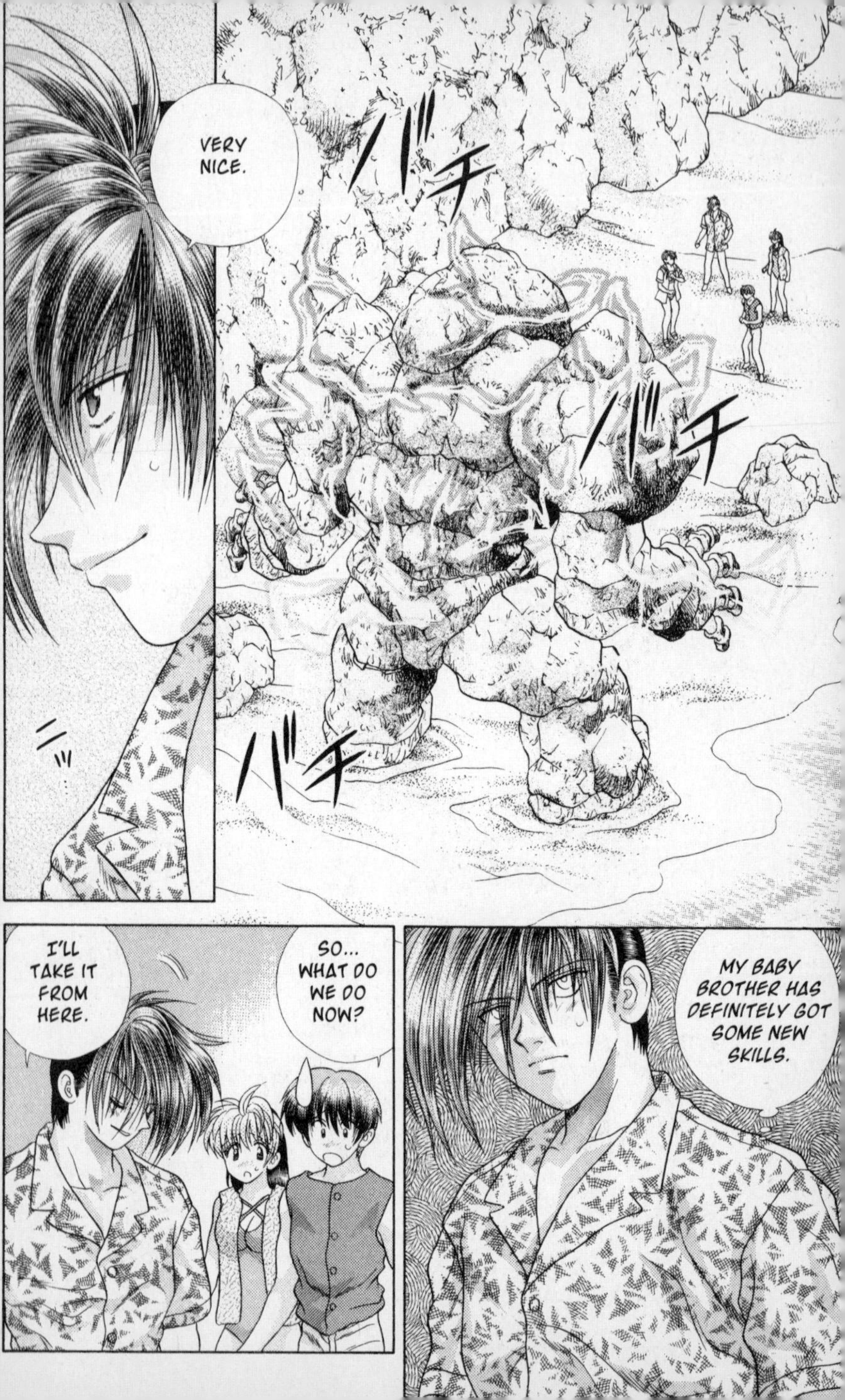
バチ
バチ
バチ
VERY NICE.
ニッ
MY BABY BROTHER HAS DEFINITELY GOT SOME NEW SKILLS.
SO... WHAT DO WE DO NOW?
I'LL TAKE IT FROM HERE.

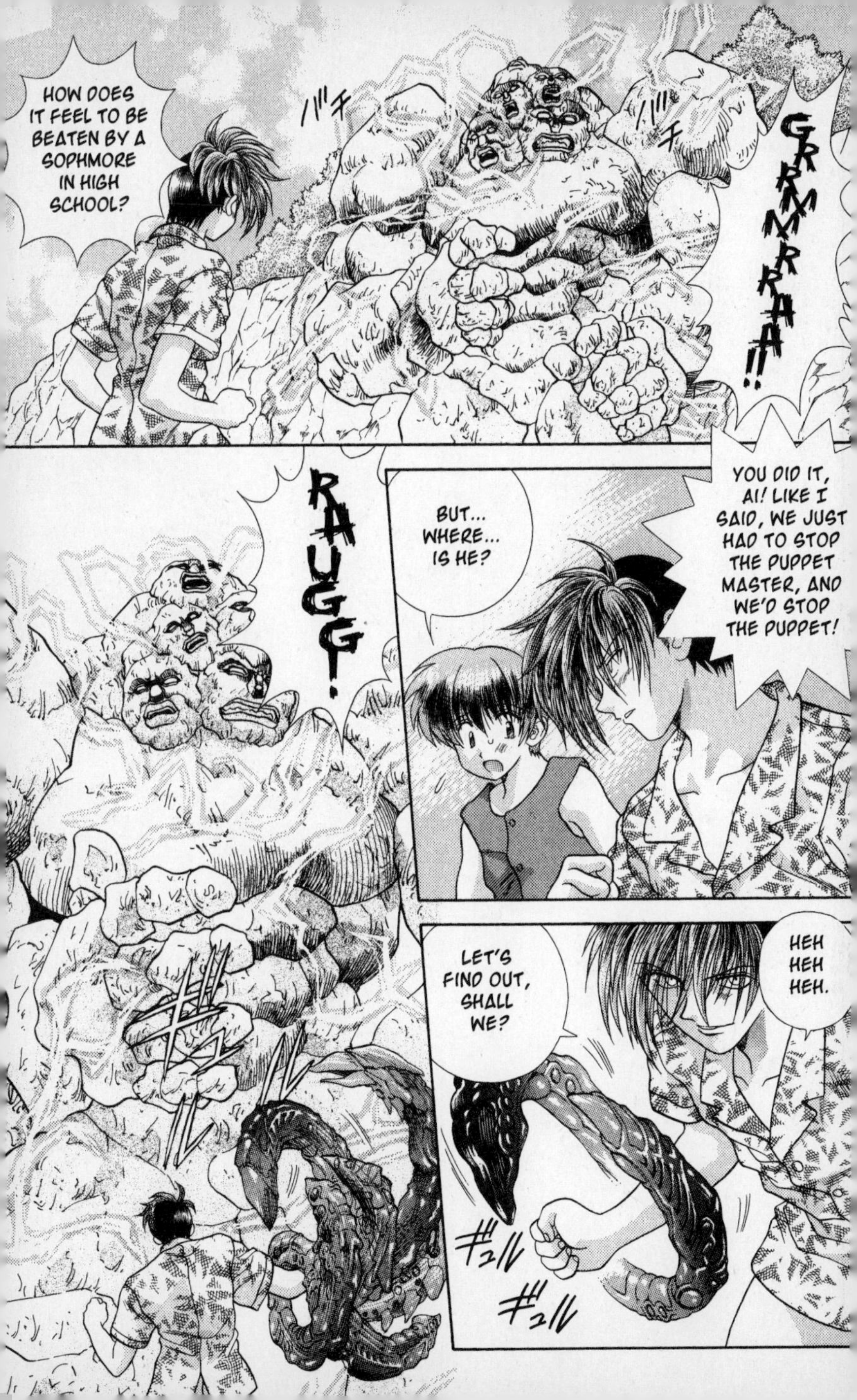
バチ
GRRMMRRAA!!
バチ
HOW DOES IT FEEL TO BE BEATEN BY A SOPHMORE IN HIGH SCHOOL?
YOU DID IT, AI! LIKE I SAID, WE JUST HAD TO STOP THE PUPPET MASTER, AND WE'D STOP THE PUPPET!
BUT... WHERE... IS HE?
HEH HEH HEH.
LET'S FIND OUT, SHALL WE?
ギュル
ギュル
RAUGG!

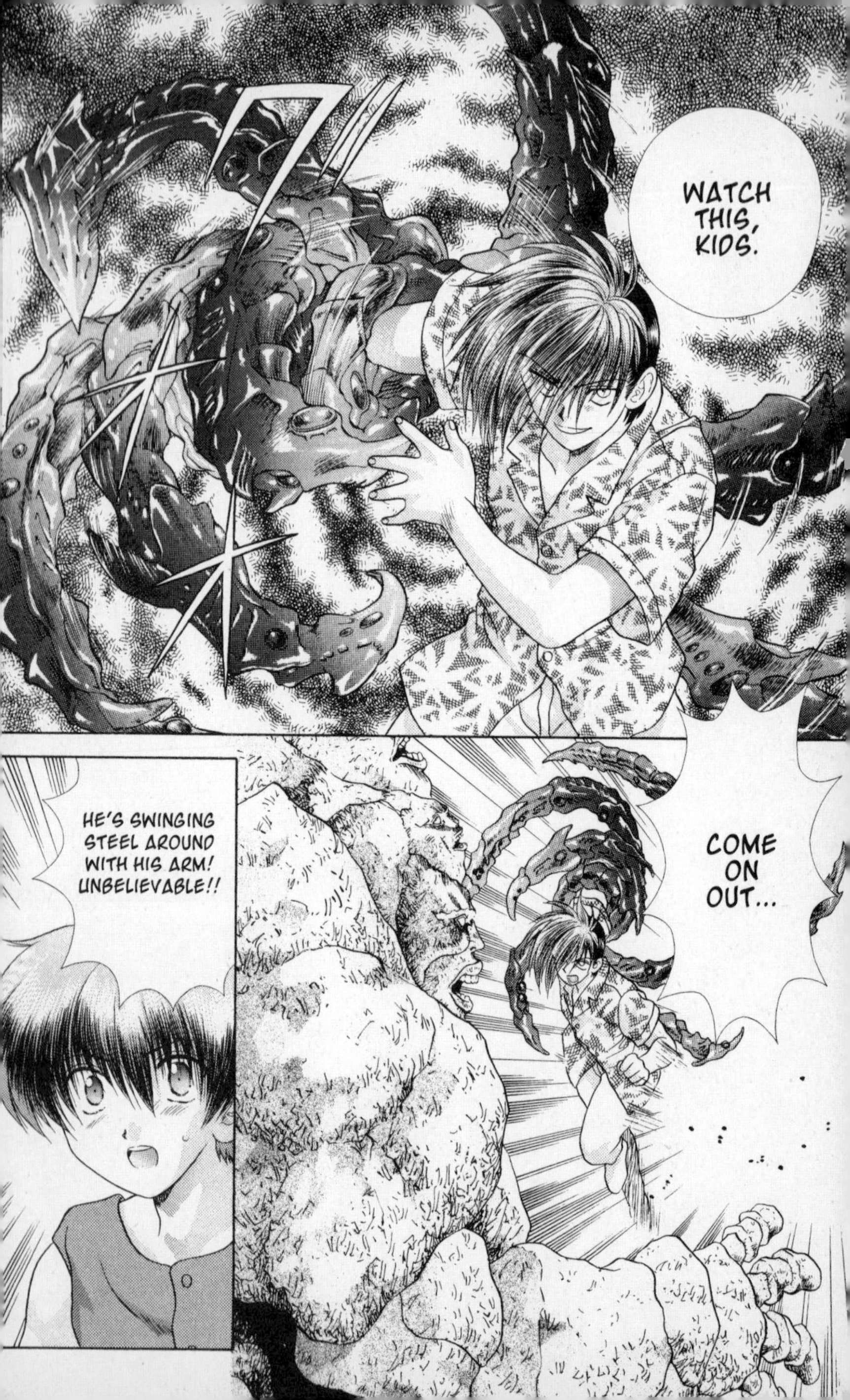
WATCH THIS, KIDS.
COME ON OUT...
HE'S SWINGING STEEL AROUND WITH HIS ARM! UNBELIEVABLE!!

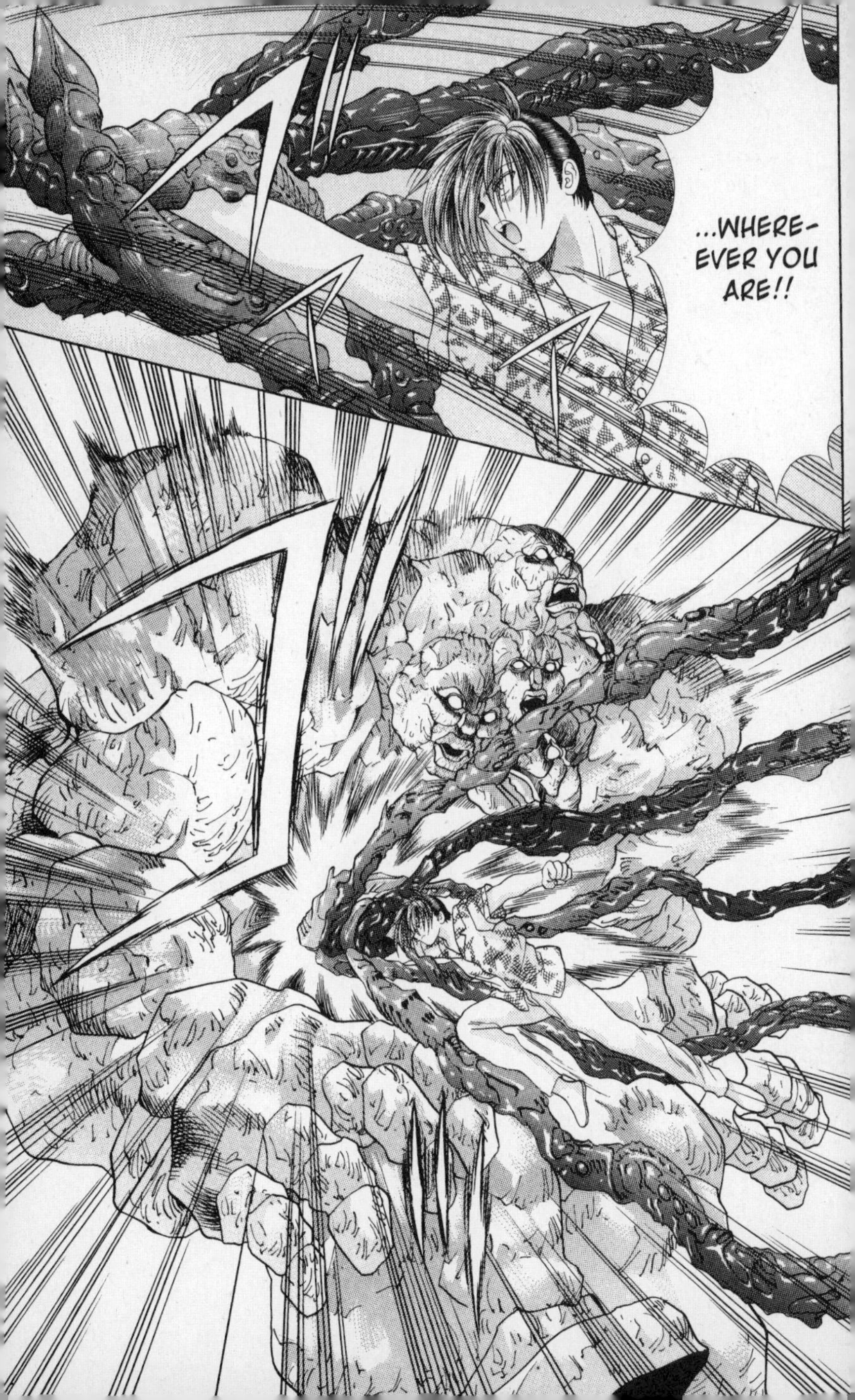
...WHERE-
EVER YOU
ARE!!

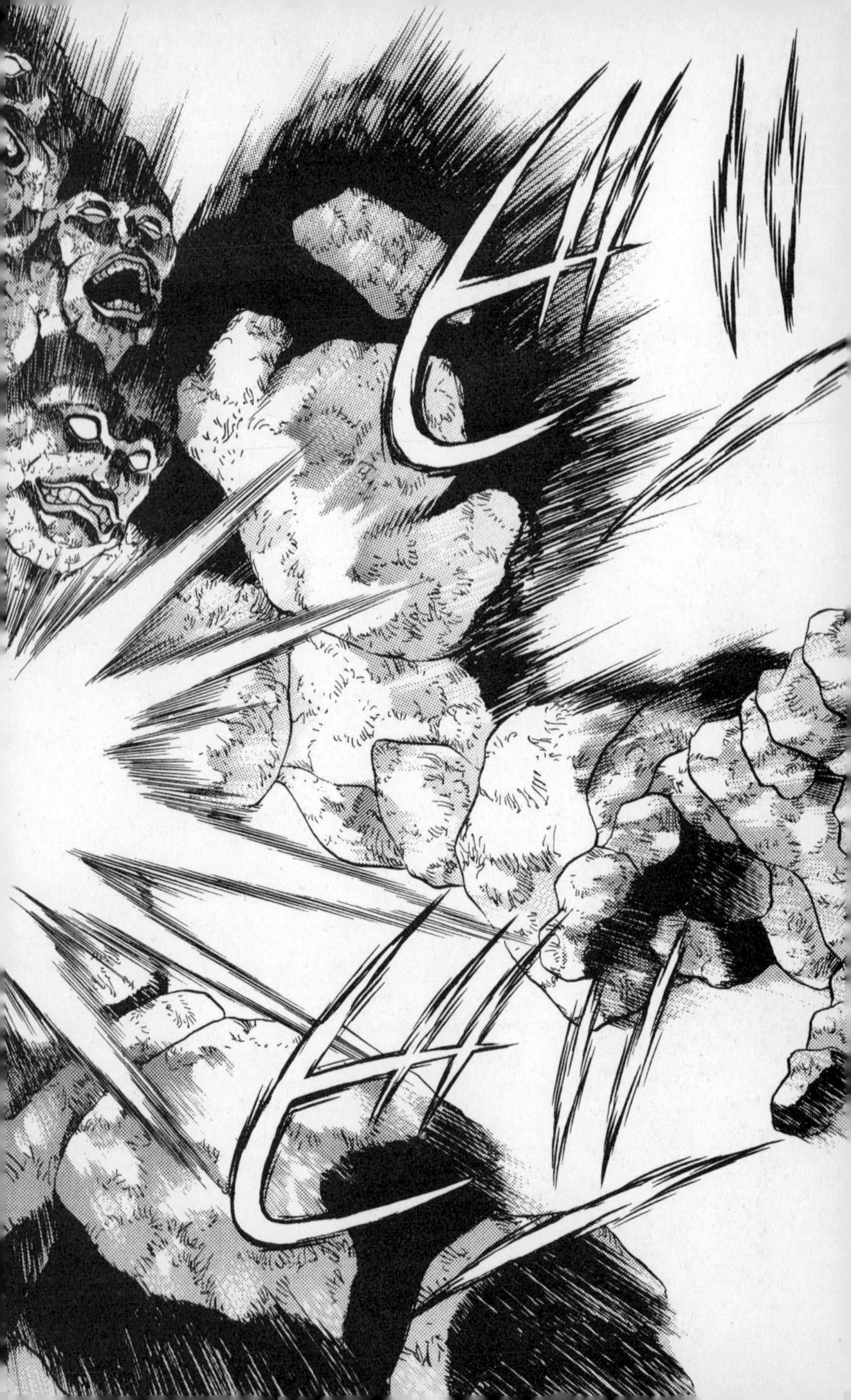

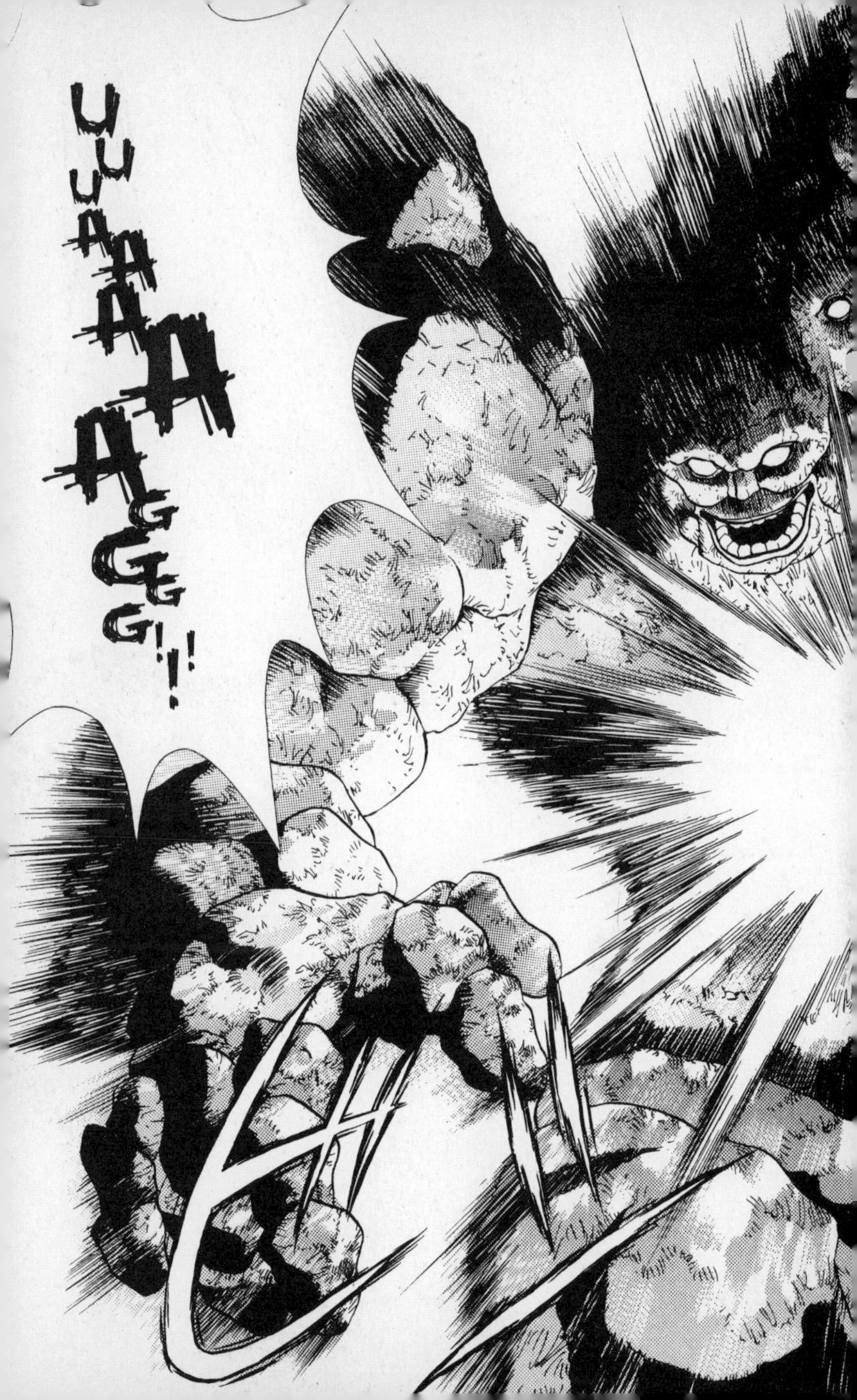
UUUAAAAAAAGGGG!!!

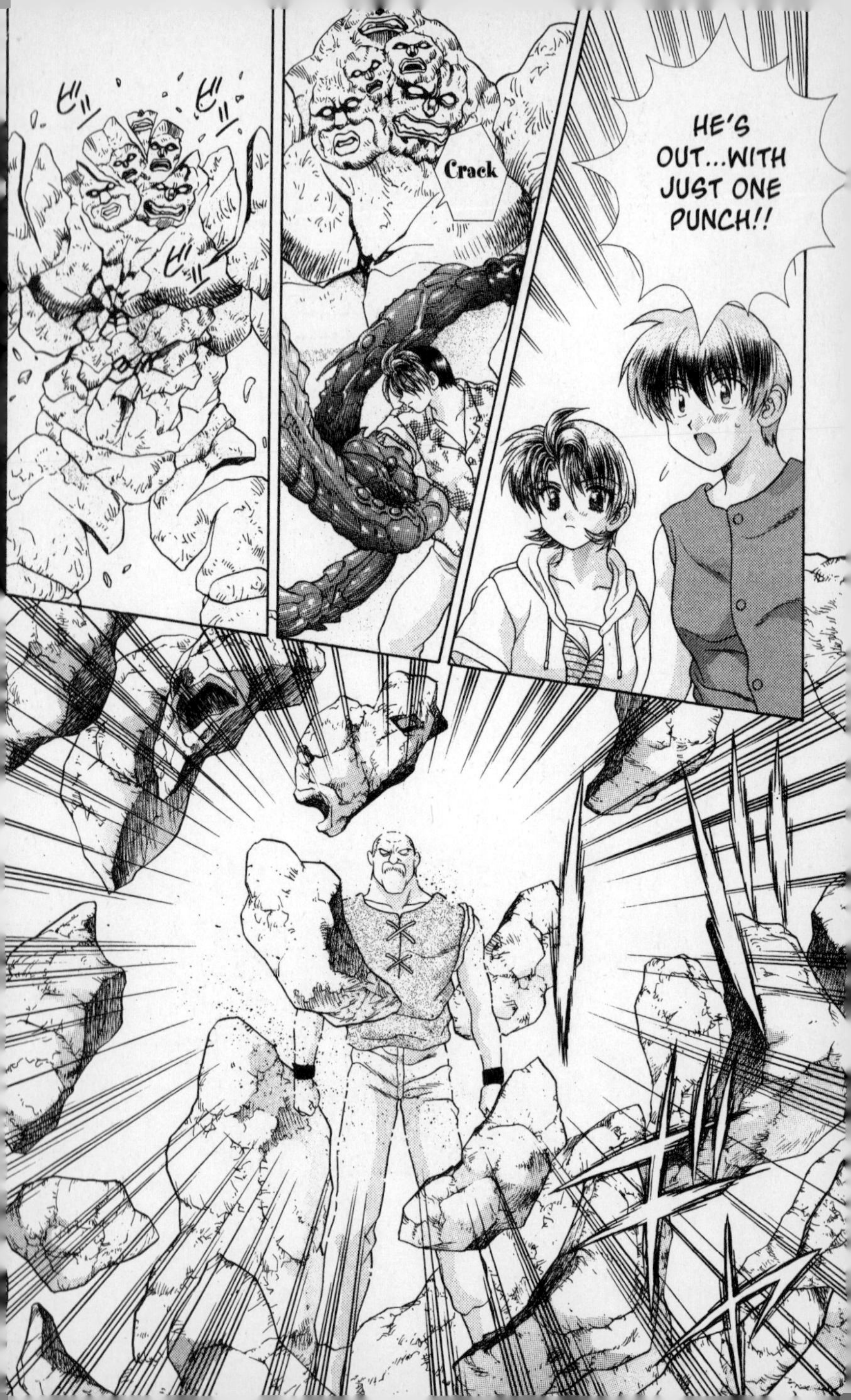
HE'S OUT...WITH JUST ONE PUNCH!!
Crack

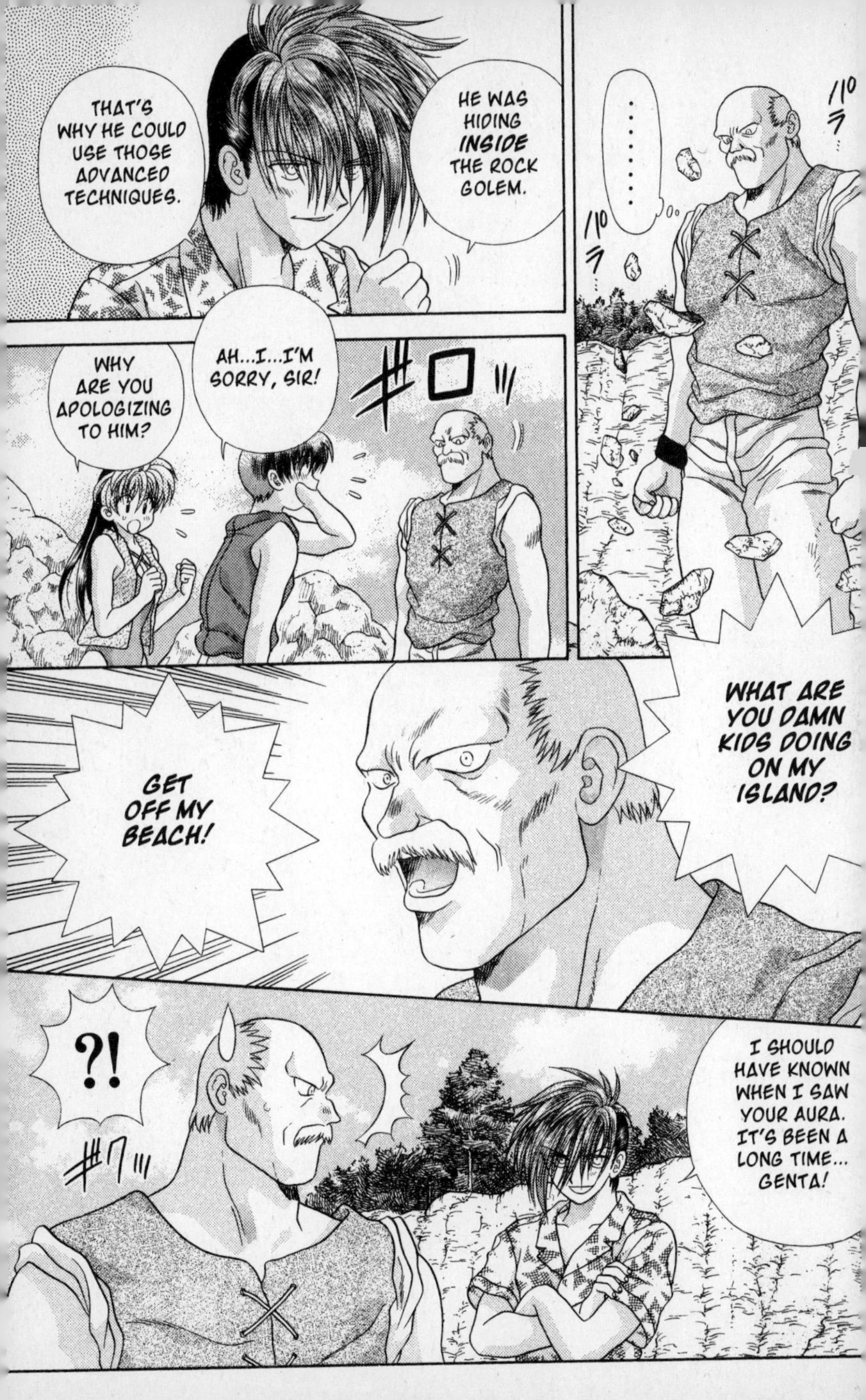
......
HE WAS HIDING INSIDE THE ROCK GOLEM.
THAT'S WHY HE COULD USE THOSE ADVANCED TECHNIQUES.
AH...I...I'M SORRY, SIR!
WHY ARE YOU APOLOGIZING TO HIM?
WHAT ARE YOU DAMN KIDS DOING ON MY ISLAND?
GET OFF MY BEACH!
I SHOULD HAVE KNOWN WHEN I SAW YOUR AURA. IT'S BEEN A LONG TIME... GENTA!
?!

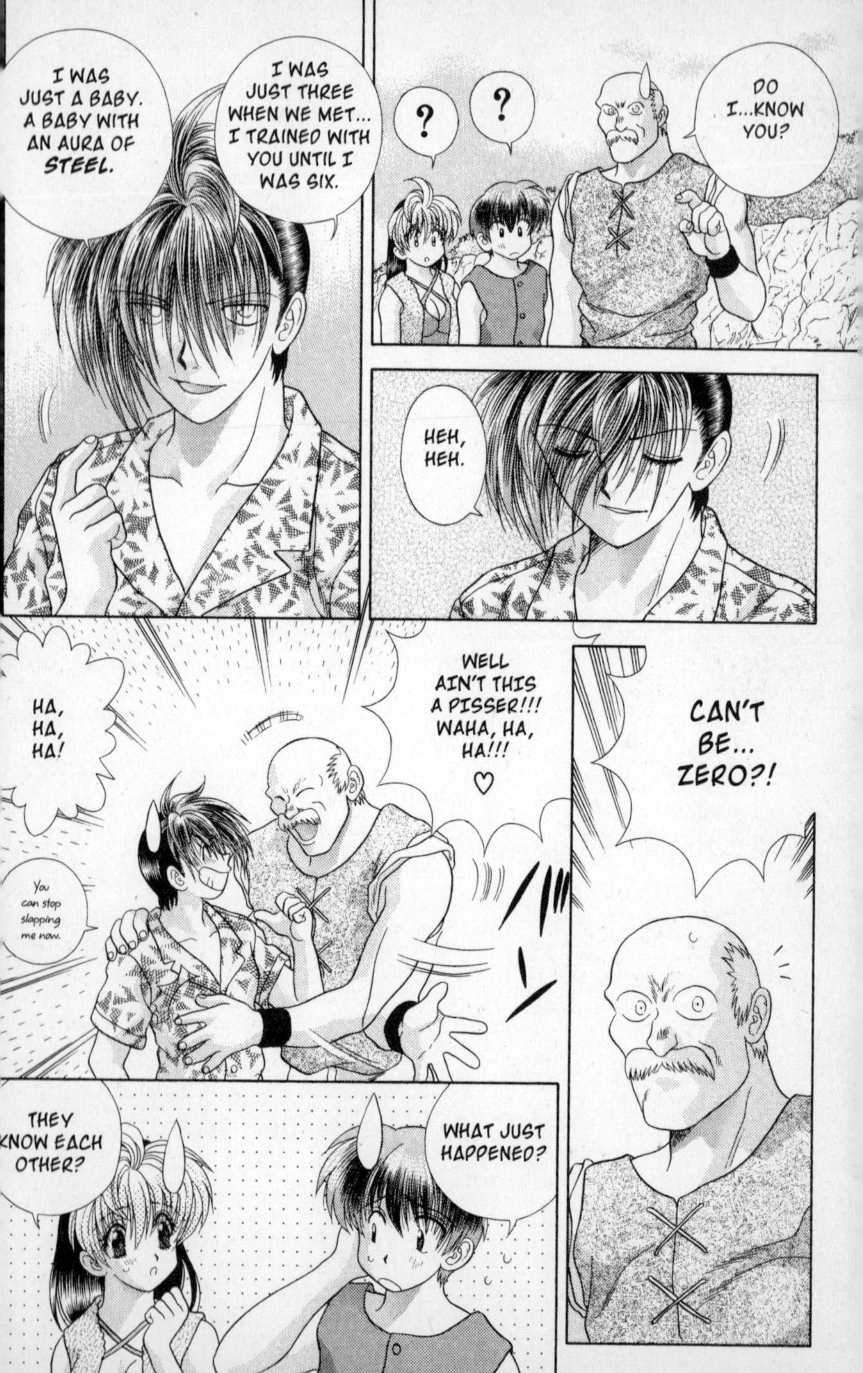
DO I...KNOW YOU?
?
?
HEH, HEH.
I WAS JUST THREE WHEN WE MET... I TRAINED WITH YOU UNTIL I WAS SIX.
I WAS JUST A BABY. A BABY WITH AN AURA OF STEEL.
CAN'T BE... ZERO?!
WELL AIN'T THIS A PISSER!!! WAHA, HA, HA!!! ♡
HA, HA, HA!
You can stop slapping me now.
WHAT JUST HAPPENED?
THEY KNOW EACH OTHER?

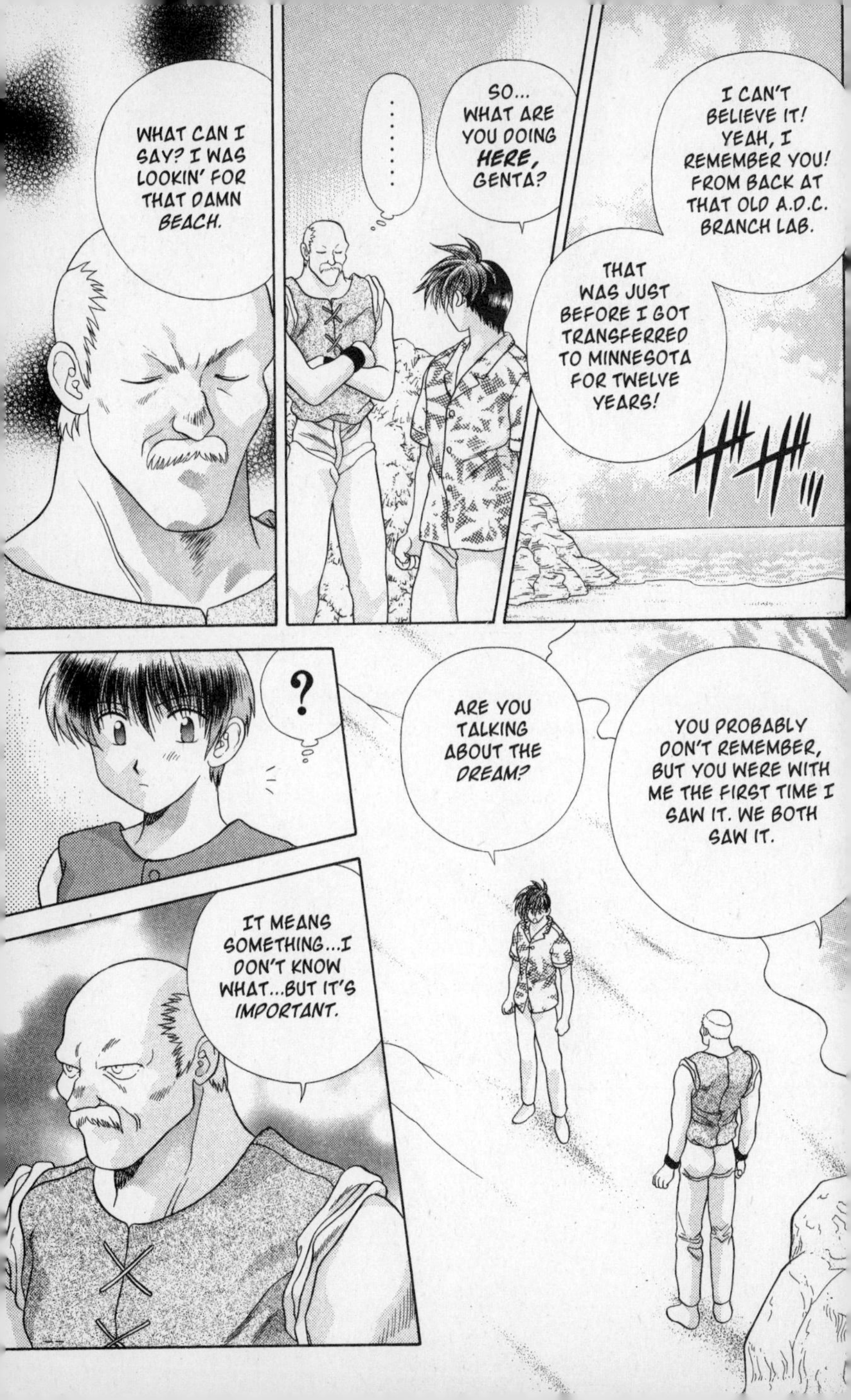
I CAN'T BELIEVE IT! YEAH, I REMEMBER YOU! FROM BACK AT THAT OLD A.D.C. BRANCH LAB.
THAT WAS JUST BEFORE I GOT TRANSFERRED TO MINNESOTA FOR TWELVE YEARS!
SO... WHAT ARE YOU DOING *HERE*, GENTA?
......
WHAT CAN I SAY? I WAS LOOKIN' FOR THAT DAMN *BEACH*.
YOU PROBABLY DON'T REMEMBER, BUT YOU WERE WITH ME THE FIRST TIME I SAW IT. WE BOTH SAW IT.
ARE YOU TALKING ABOUT THE *DREAM*?
?
IT MEANS SOMETHING...I DON'T KNOW WHAT...BUT IT'S *IMPORTANT*.

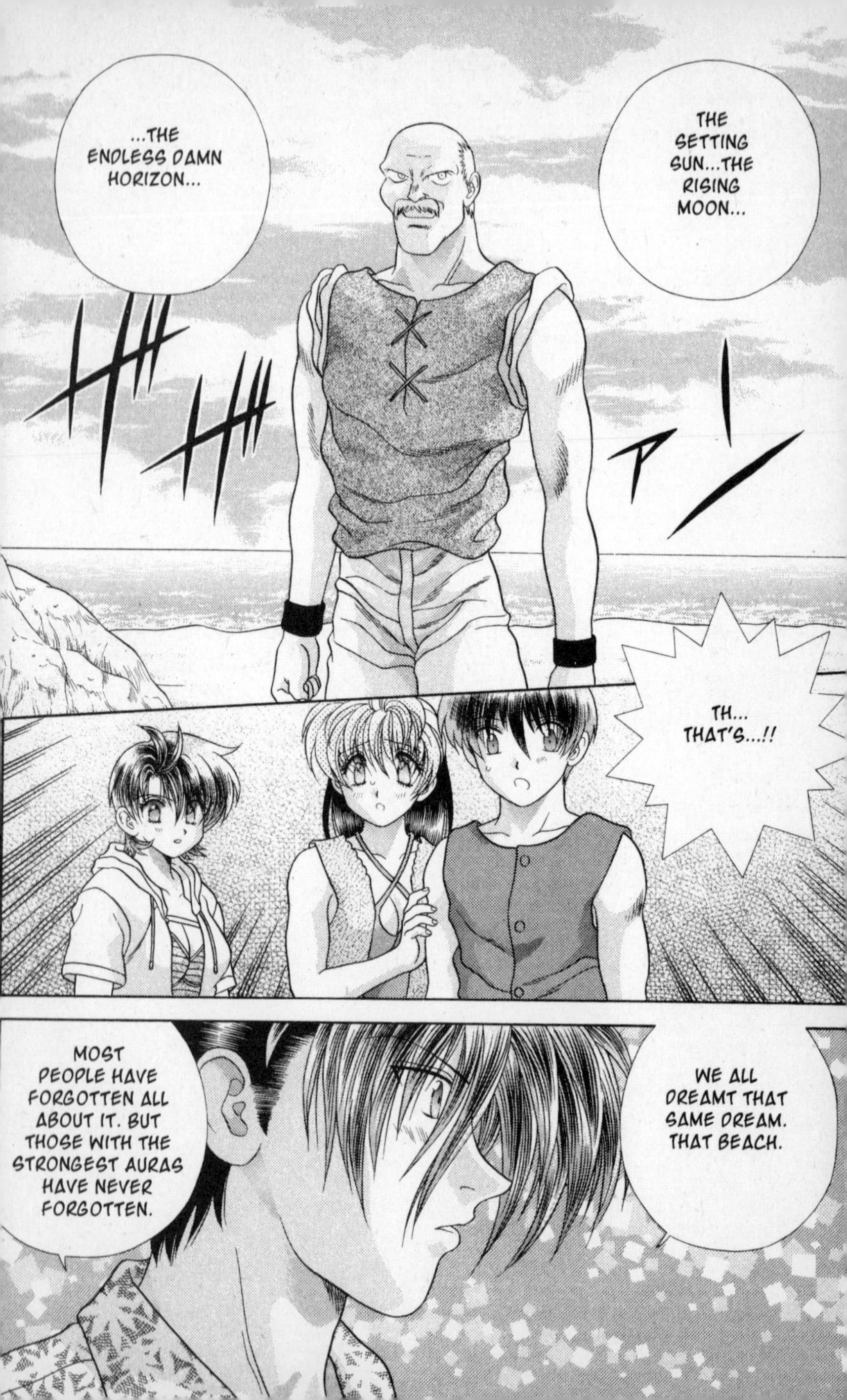
THE SETTING SUN...THE RISING MOON...
...THE ENDLESS DAMN HORIZON...
TH... THAT'S...!!
WE ALL DREAMT THAT SAME DREAM. THAT BEACH.
MOST PEOPLE HAVE FORGOTTEN ALL ABOUT IT. BUT THOSE WITH THE STRONGEST AURAS HAVE NEVER FORGOTTEN.

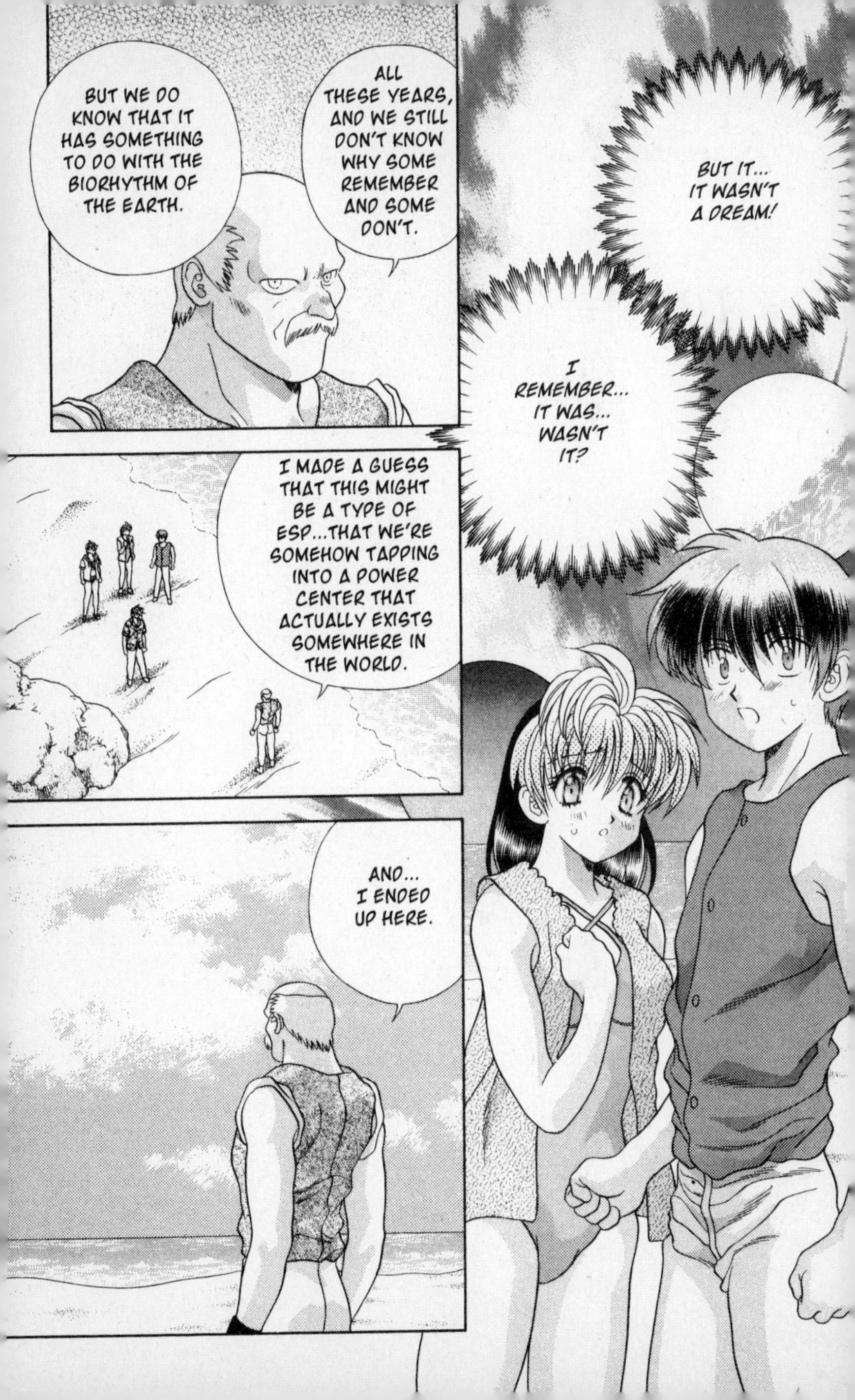
BUT IT... IT WASN'T A DREAM!
I REMEMBER... IT WAS... WASN'T IT?
ALL THESE YEARS, AND WE STILL DON'T KNOW WHY SOME REMEMBER AND SOME DON'T.
BUT WE DO KNOW THAT IT HAS SOMETHING TO DO WITH THE BIORHYTHM OF THE EARTH.
I MADE A GUESS THAT THIS MIGHT BE A TYPE OF ESP...THAT WE'RE SOMEHOW TAPPING INTO A POWER CENTER THAT ACTUALLY EXISTS SOMEWHERE IN THE WORLD.
AND... I ENDED UP HERE.

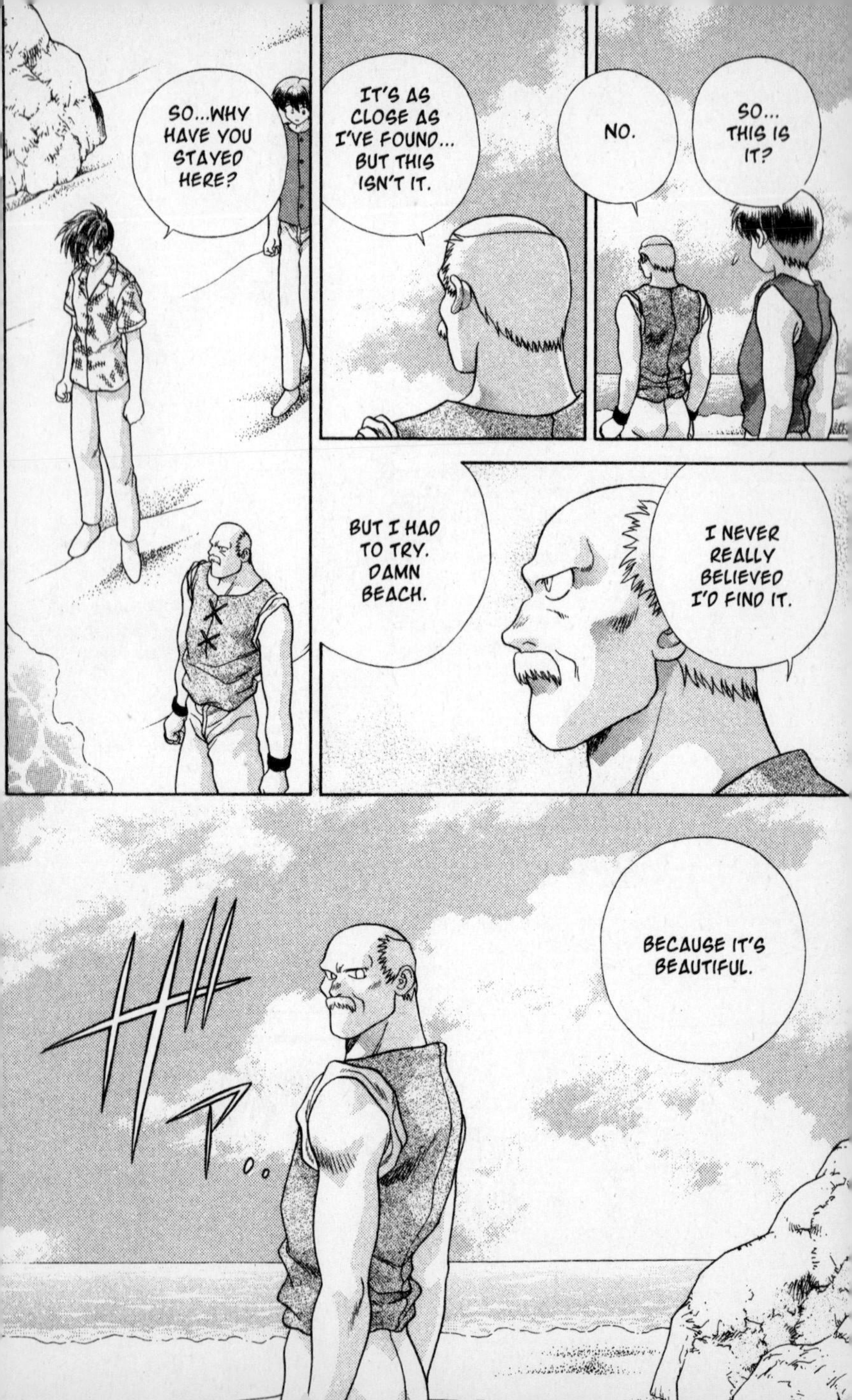
SO... THIS IS IT?
NO.
IT'S AS CLOSE AS I'VE FOUND... BUT THIS ISN'T IT.
I NEVER REALLY BELIEVED I'D FIND IT.
BUT I HAD TO TRY. DAMN BEACH.
SO...WHY HAVE YOU STAYED HERE?
BECAUSE IT'S BEAUTIFUL.

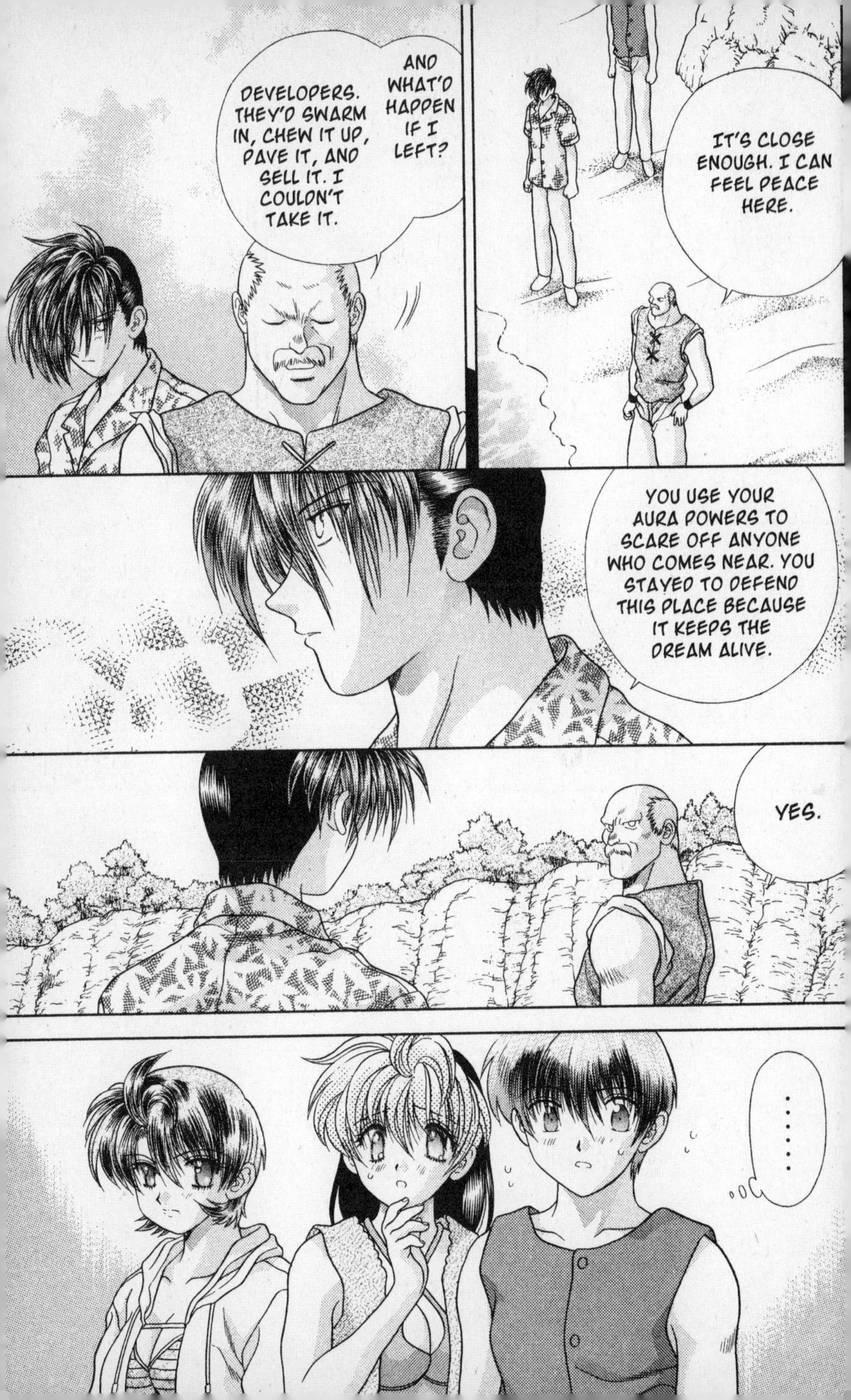
IT'S CLOSE ENOUGH. I CAN FEEL PEACE HERE.
AND WHAT'D HAPPEN IF I LEFT?
DEVELOPERS. THEY'D SWARM IN, CHEW IT UP, PAVE IT, AND SELL IT. I COULDN'T TAKE IT.
YOU USE YOUR AURA POWERS TO SCARE OFF ANYONE WHO COMES NEAR. YOU STAYED TO DEFEND THIS PLACE BECAUSE IT KEEPS THE DREAM ALIVE.
YES.
......

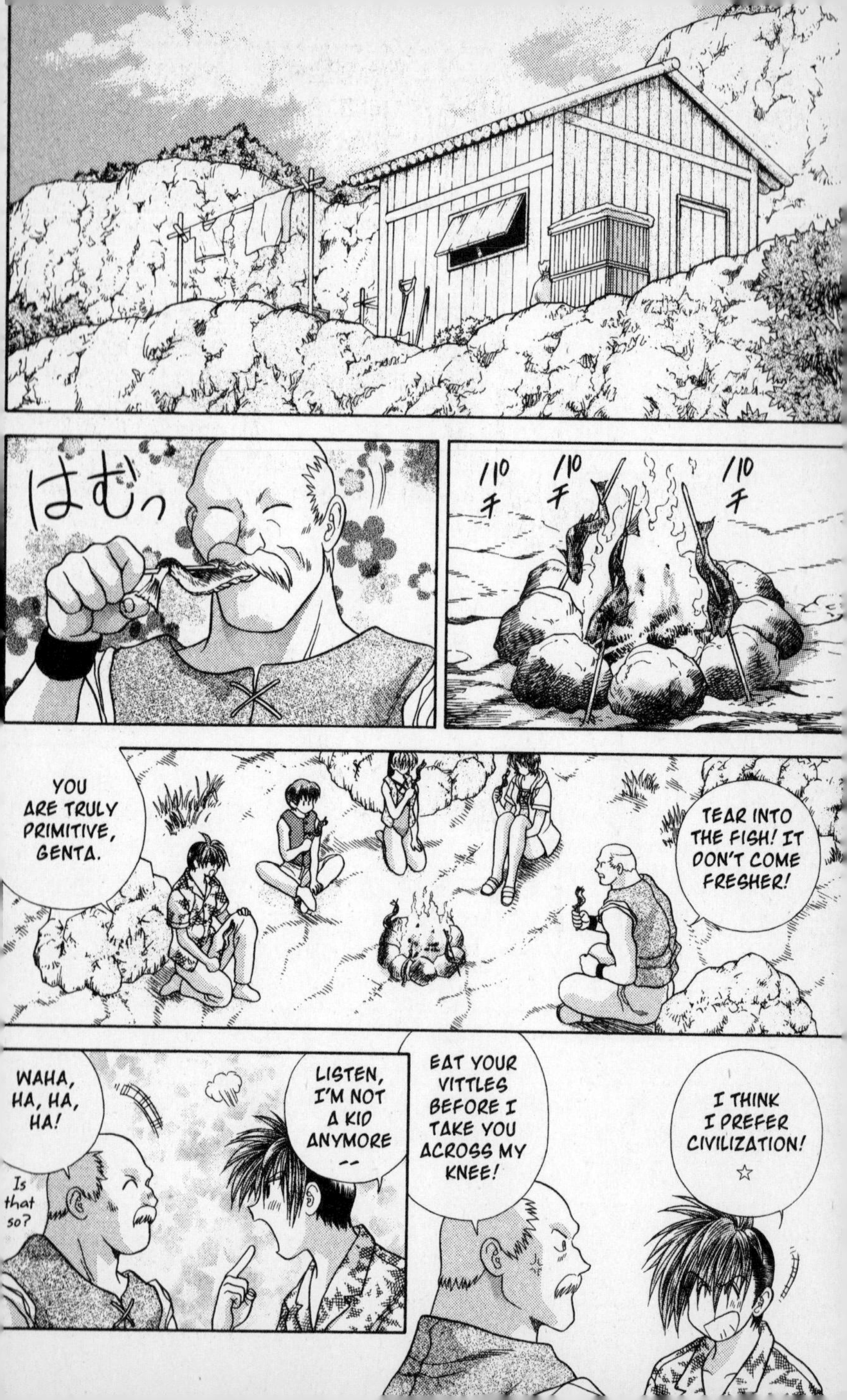
パチ
パチ
パチ
はむっ
TEAR INTO THE FISH! IT DON'T COME FRESHER!
YOU ARE TRULY PRIMITIVE, GENTA.
I THINK I PREFER CIVILIZATION! ☆
EAT YOUR VITTLES BEFORE I TAKE YOU ACROSS MY KNEE!
LISTEN, I'M NOT A KID ANYMORE --
WAHA, HA, HA, HA!
Is that so?

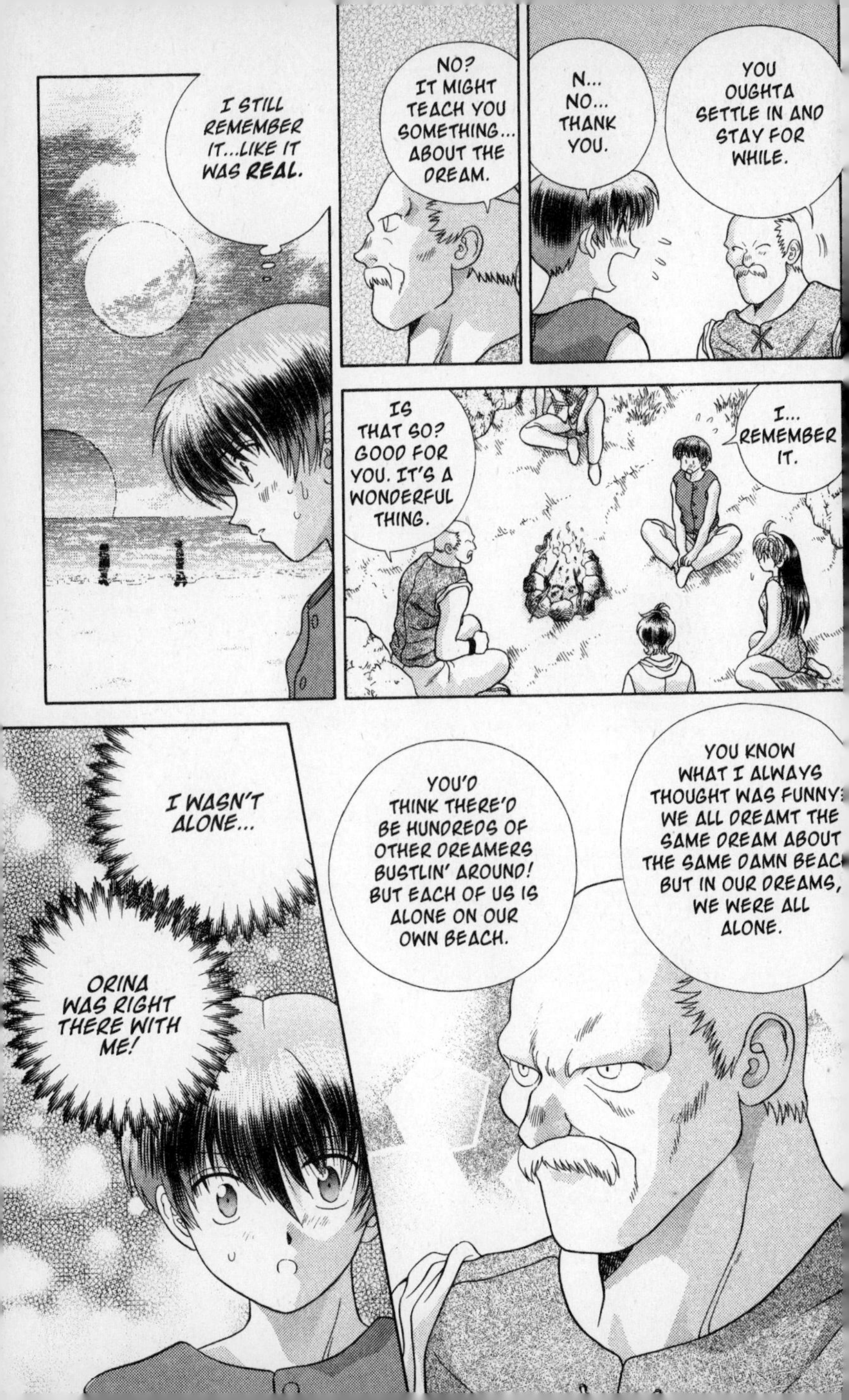

YOU OUGHTA SETTLE IN AND STAY FOR WHILE.
N... NO... THANK YOU.
NO? IT MIGHT TEACH YOU SOMETHING... ABOUT THE DREAM.
I... REMEMBER IT.
IS THAT SO? GOOD FOR YOU. IT'S A WONDERFUL THING.
I STILL REMEMBER IT...LIKE IT WAS REAL.
YOU KNOW WHAT I ALWAYS THOUGHT WAS FUNNY: WE ALL DREAMT THE SAME DREAM ABOUT THE SAME DAMN BEAC BUT IN OUR DREAMS, WE WERE ALL ALONE.
YOU'D THINK THERE'D BE HUNDREDS OF OTHER DREAMERS BUSTLIN' AROUND! BUT EACH OF US IS ALONE ON OUR OWN BEACH.
I WASN'T ALONE...
ORINA WAS RIGHT THERE WITH ME!

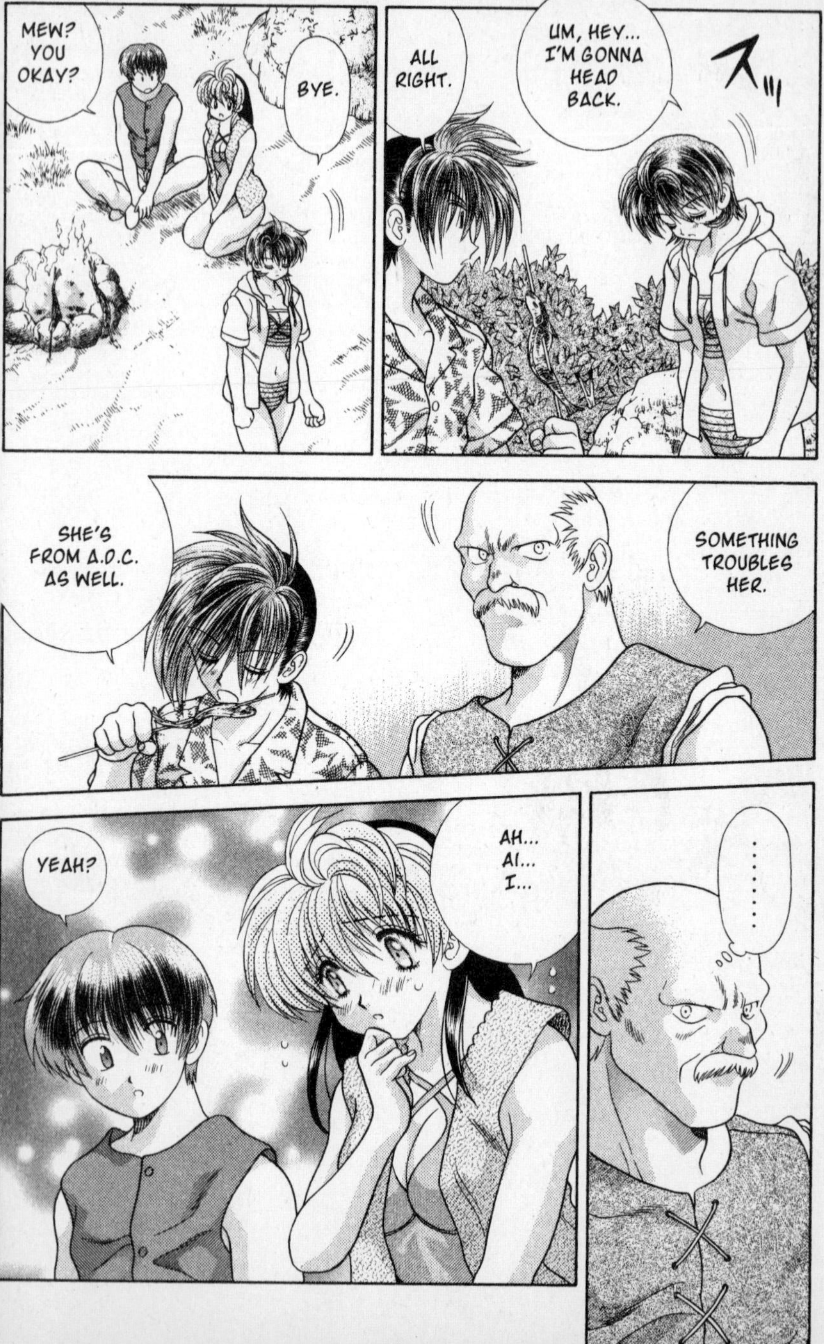

ス
UM, HEY... I'M GONNA HEAD BACK.
ALL RIGHT.
BYE.
MEW? YOU OKAY?
SOMETHING TROUBLES HER.
SHE'S FROM A.D.C. AS WELL.
......
AH... AI... I...
YEAH?

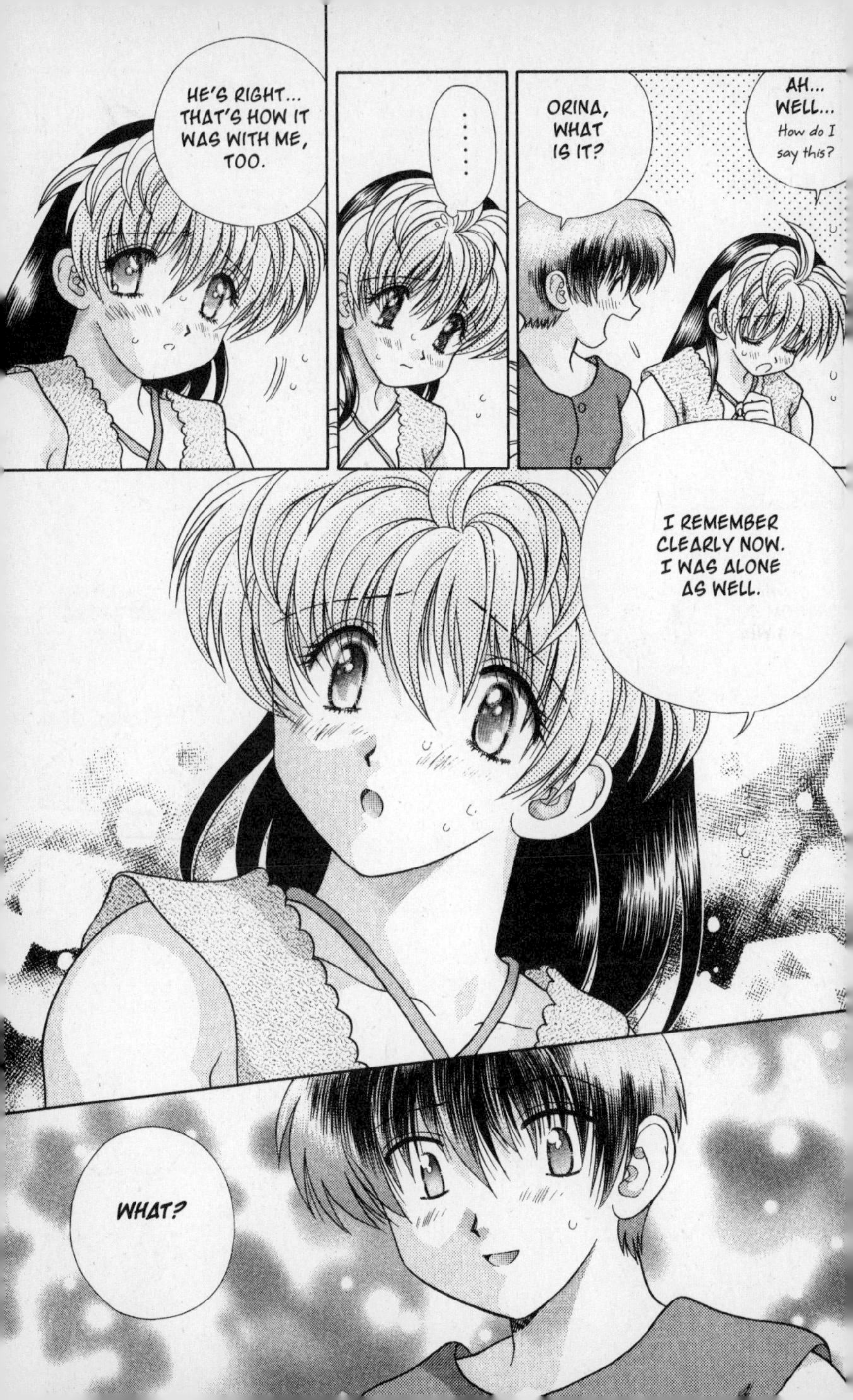
AH... WELL... How do I say this?
ORINA, WHAT IS IT?
......
HE'S RIGHT... THAT'S HOW IT WAS WITH ME, TOO.
I REMEMBER CLEARLY NOW. I WAS ALONE AS WELL.
WHAT?

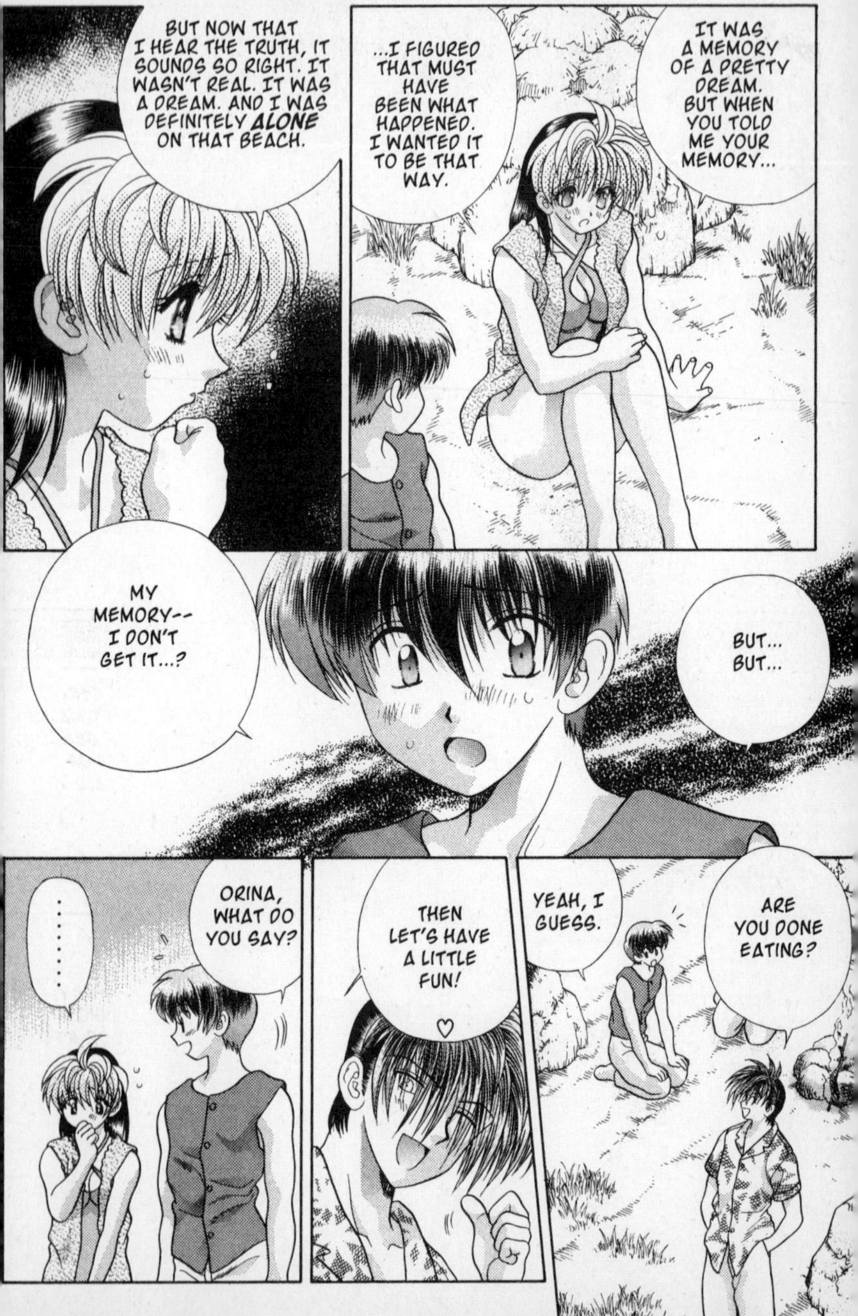
IT WAS A MEMORY OF A PRETTY DREAM. BUT WHEN YOU TOLD ME YOUR MEMORY...
...I FIGURED THAT MUST HAVE BEEN WHAT HAPPENED. I WANTED IT TO BE THAT WAY.
BUT NOW THAT I HEAR THE TRUTH, IT SOUNDS SO RIGHT. IT WASN'T REAL. IT WAS A DREAM. AND I WAS DEFINITELY ***ALONE*** ON THAT BEACH.
BUT... BUT...
MY MEMORY-- I DON'T GET IT...?
ARE YOU DONE EATING?
YEAH, I GUESS.
THEN LET'S HAVE A LITTLE FUN! ♡
ORINA, WHAT DO YOU SAY?
....

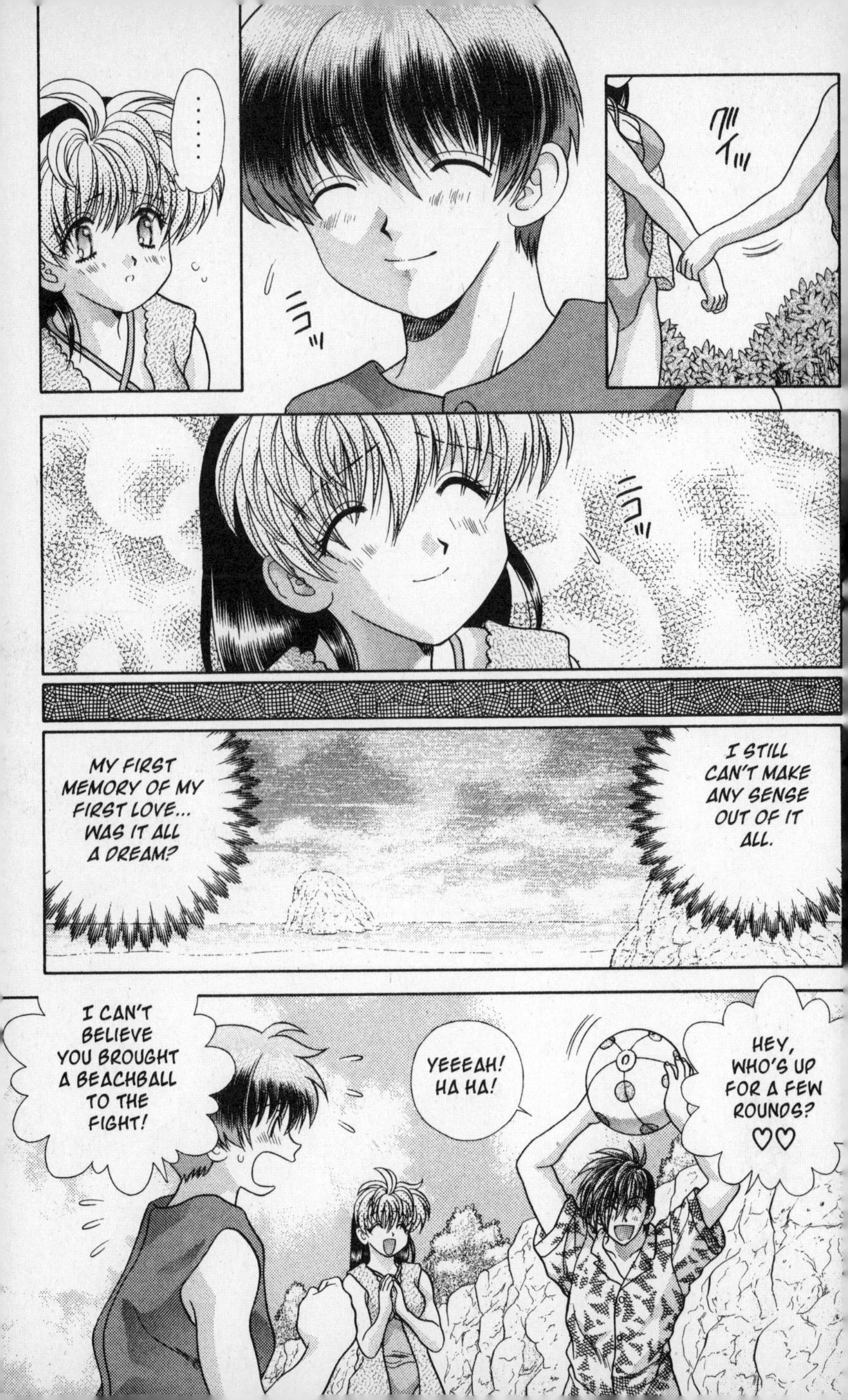
グイッ
ニコッ
......
ニコッ
I STILL CAN'T MAKE ANY SENSE OUT OF IT ALL.
MY FIRST MEMORY OF MY FIRST LOVE... WAS IT ALL A DREAM?
HEY, WHO'S UP FOR A FEW ROUNDS? ♡♡
YEEEAH! HA HA!
I CAN'T BELIEVE YOU BROUGHT A BEACHBALL TO THE FIGHT!

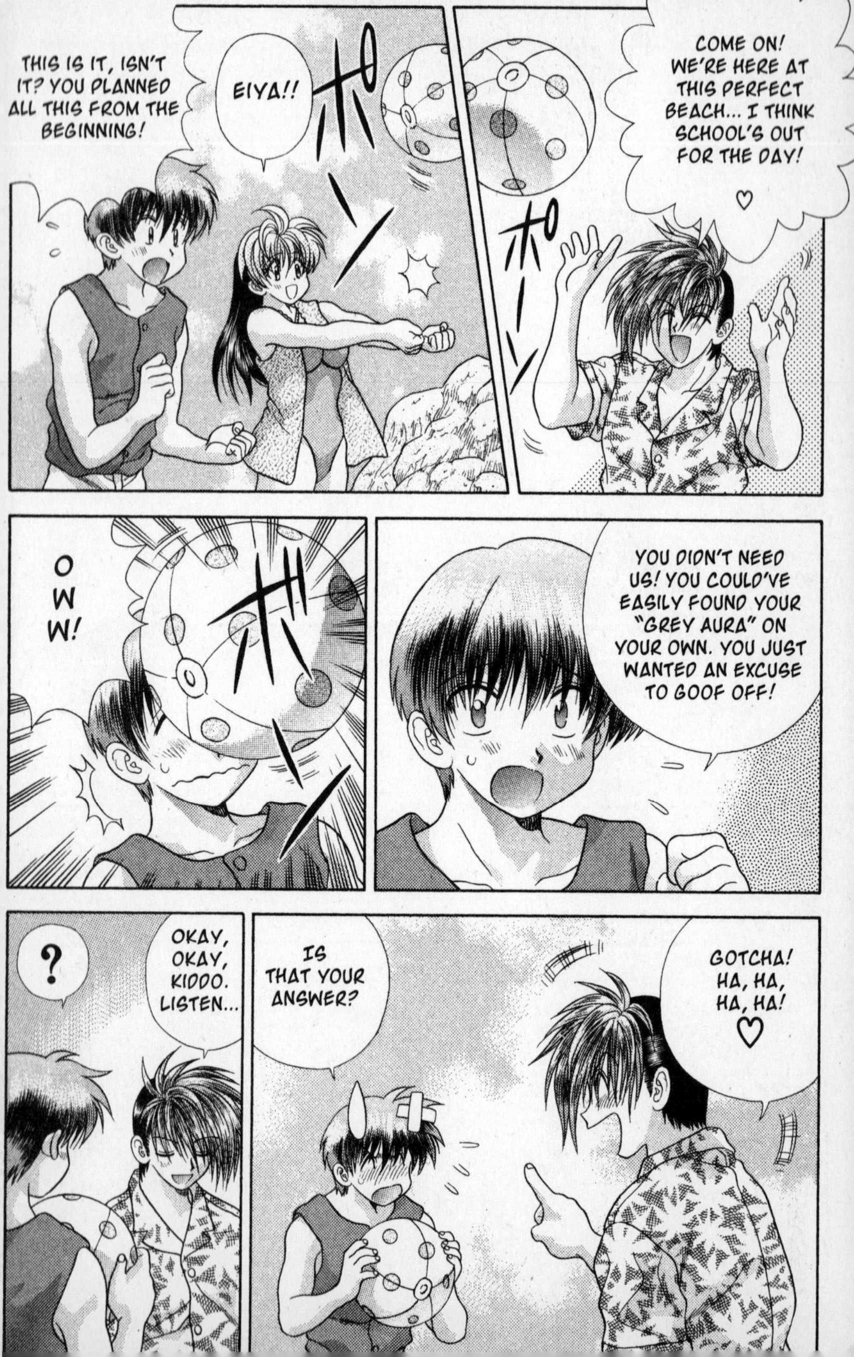
COME ON! WE'RE HERE AT THIS PERFECT BEACH... I THINK SCHOOL'S OUT FOR THE DAY! ♡
EIYA!!
THIS IS IT, ISN'T IT? YOU PLANNED ALL THIS FROM THE BEGINNING!
YOU DIDN'T NEED US! YOU COULD'VE EASILY FOUND YOUR "GREY AURA" ON YOUR OWN. YOU JUST WANTED AN EXCUSE TO GOOF OFF!
OWW!
GOTCHA! HA, HA, HA, HA! ♡
IS THAT YOUR ANSWER?
OKAY, OKAY, KIDDO. LISTEN...
?

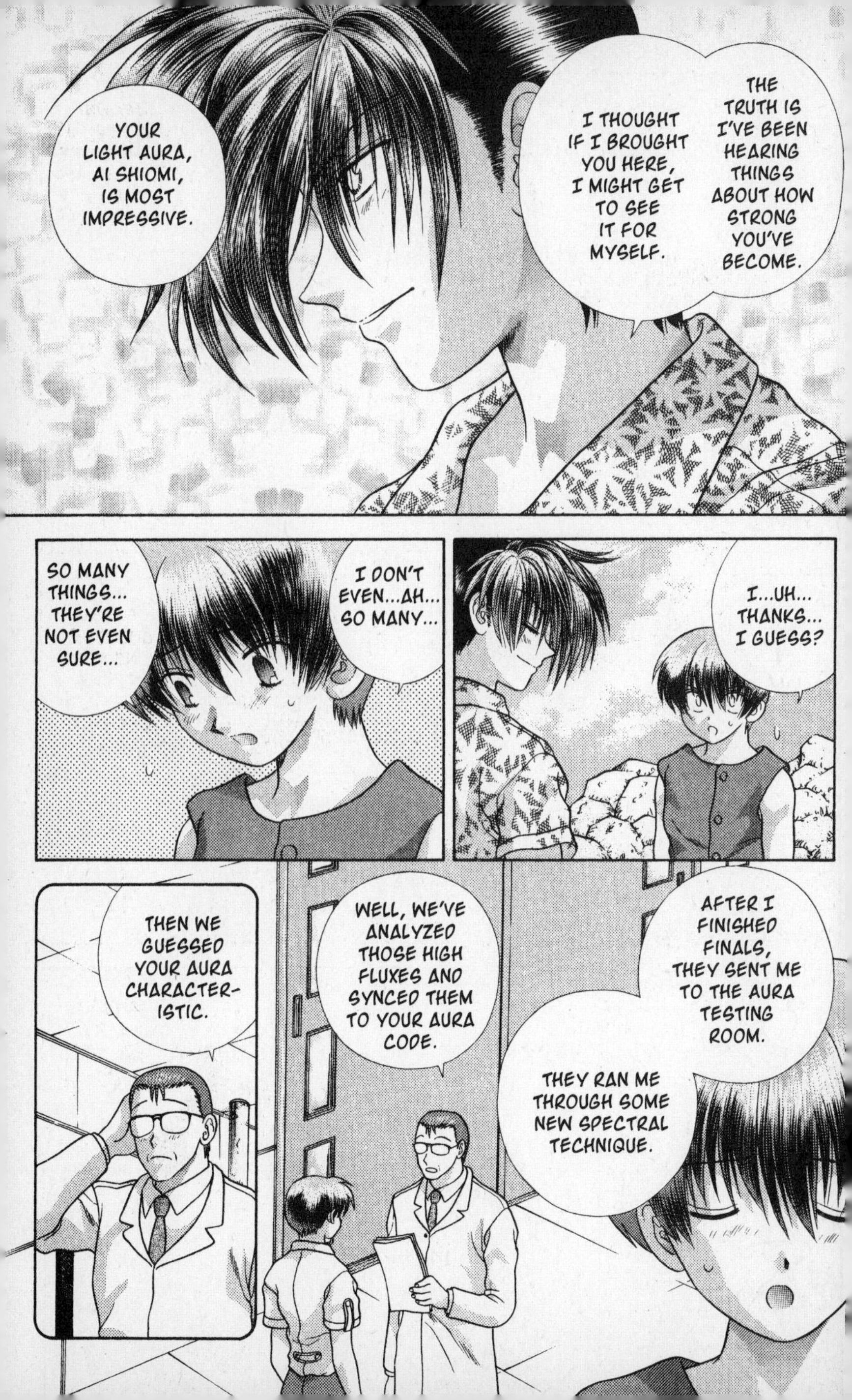
THE TRUTH IS I'VE BEEN HEARING THINGS ABOUT HOW STRONG YOU'VE BECOME.
I THOUGHT IF I BROUGHT YOU HERE, I MIGHT GET TO SEE IT FOR MYSELF.
YOUR LIGHT AURA, AI SHIOMI, IS MOST IMPRESSIVE.
I...UH... THANKS... I GUESS?
I DON'T EVEN...AH... SO MANY...
SO MANY THINGS... THEY'RE NOT EVEN SURE...
AFTER I FINISHED FINALS, THEY SENT ME TO THE AURA TESTING ROOM.
THEY RAN ME THROUGH SOME NEW SPECTRAL TECHNIQUE.
WELL, WE'VE ANALYZED THOSE HIGH FLUXES AND SYNCED THEM TO YOUR AURA CODE.
THEN WE GUESSED YOUR AURA CHARACTER-ISTIC.

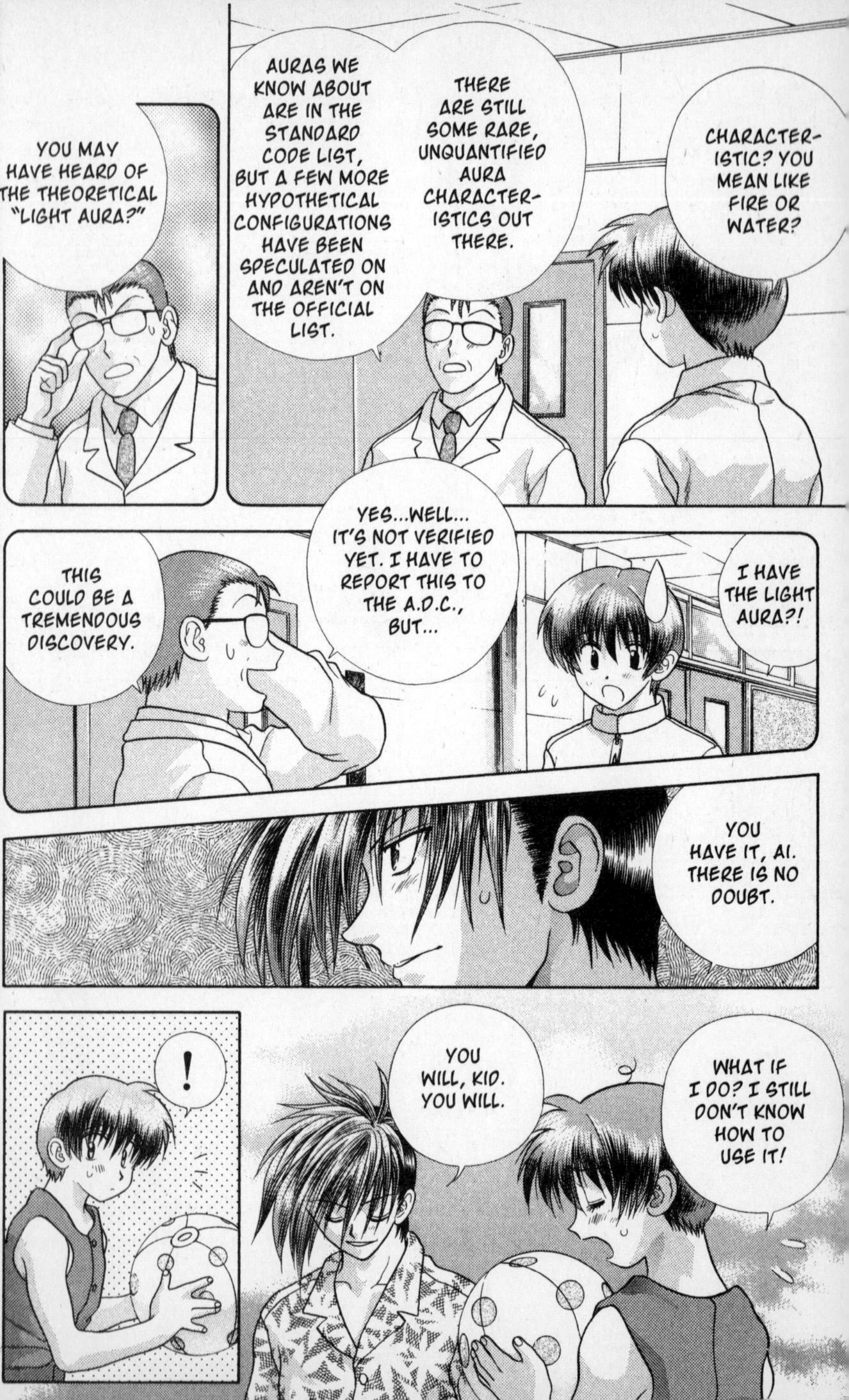
THERE ARE STILL SOME RARE, UNQUANTIFIED AURA CHARACTER-ISTICS OUT THERE.
CHARACTER-ISTIC? YOU MEAN LIKE FIRE OR WATER?
AURAS WE KNOW ABOUT ARE IN THE STANDARD CODE LIST, BUT A FEW MORE HYPOTHETICAL CONFIGURATIONS HAVE BEEN SPECULATED ON AND AREN'T ON THE OFFICIAL LIST.
YOU MAY HAVE HEARD OF THE THEORETICAL "LIGHT AURA?"
I HAVE THE LIGHT AURA?!
YES...WELL... IT'S NOT VERIFIED YET. I HAVE TO REPORT THIS TO THE A.D.C., BUT...
THIS COULD BE A TREMENDOUS DISCOVERY.
YOU HAVE IT, AI. THERE IS NO DOUBT.
WHAT IF I DO? I STILL DON'T KNOW HOW TO USE IT!
YOU WILL, KID. YOU WILL.
!

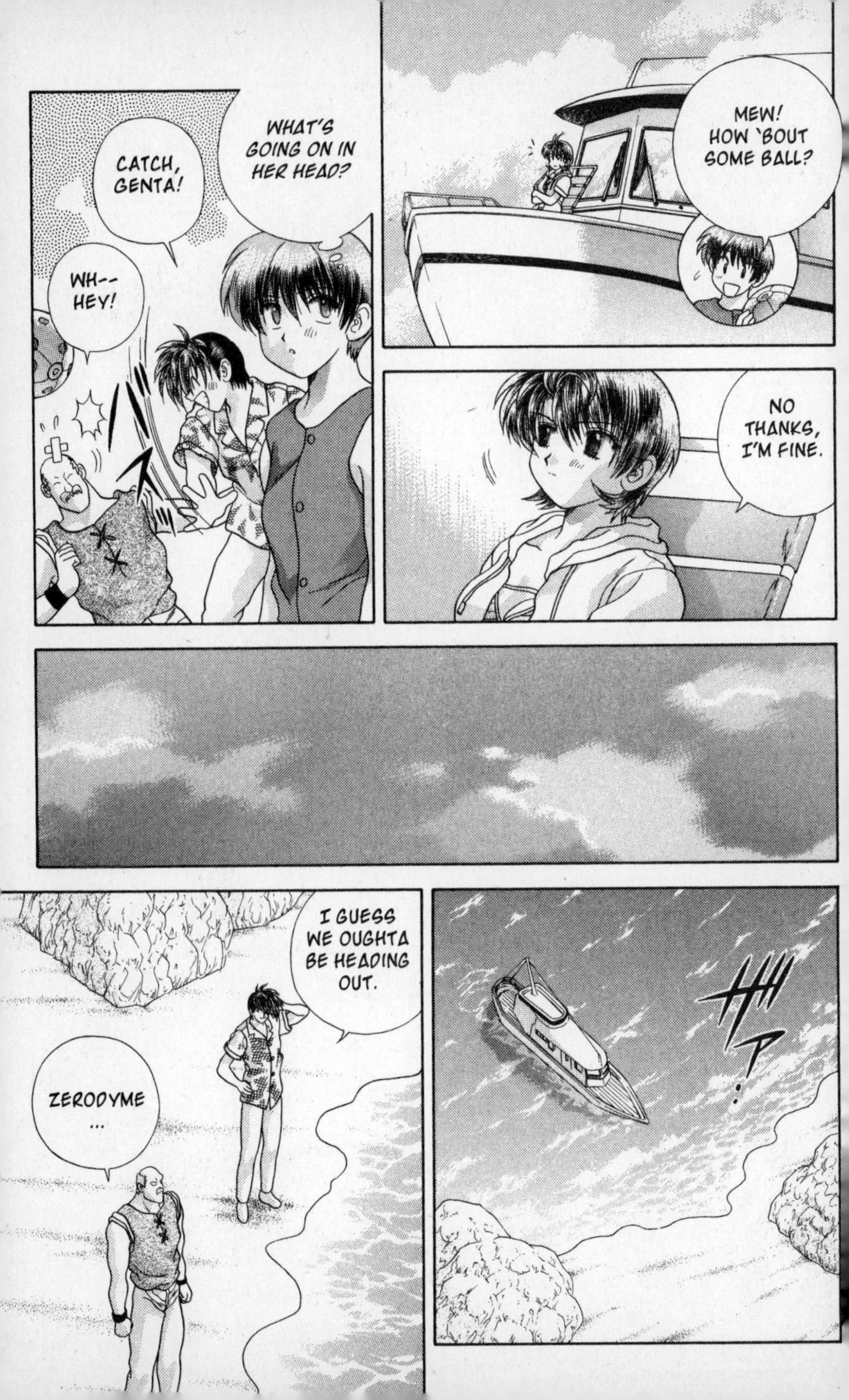
MEW! HOW `BOUT SOME BALL?
NO THANKS, I'M FINE.
WHAT'S GOING ON IN HER HEAD?
CATCH, GENTA!
WH-- HEY!
I GUESS WE OUGHTA BE HEADING OUT.
ZERODYME ...

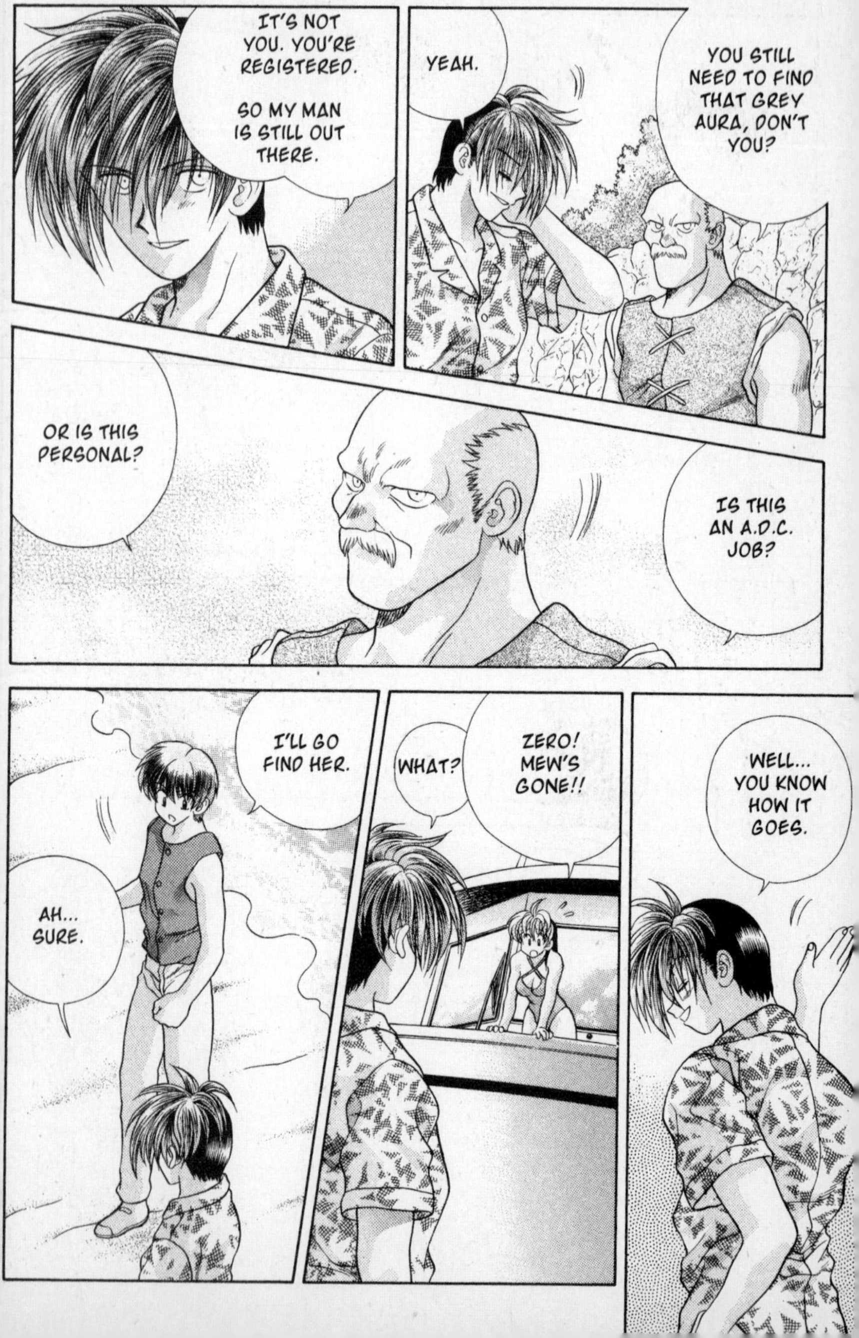
YOU STILL NEED TO FIND THAT GREY AURA, DON'T YOU?
YEAH.
IT'S NOT YOU. YOU'RE REGISTERED.
SO MY MAN IS STILL OUT THERE.
IS THIS AN A.D.C. JOB?
OR IS THIS PERSONAL?
WELL... YOU KNOW HOW IT GOES.
ZERO! MEW'S GONE!!
WHAT?
I'LL GO FIND HER.
AH... SURE.

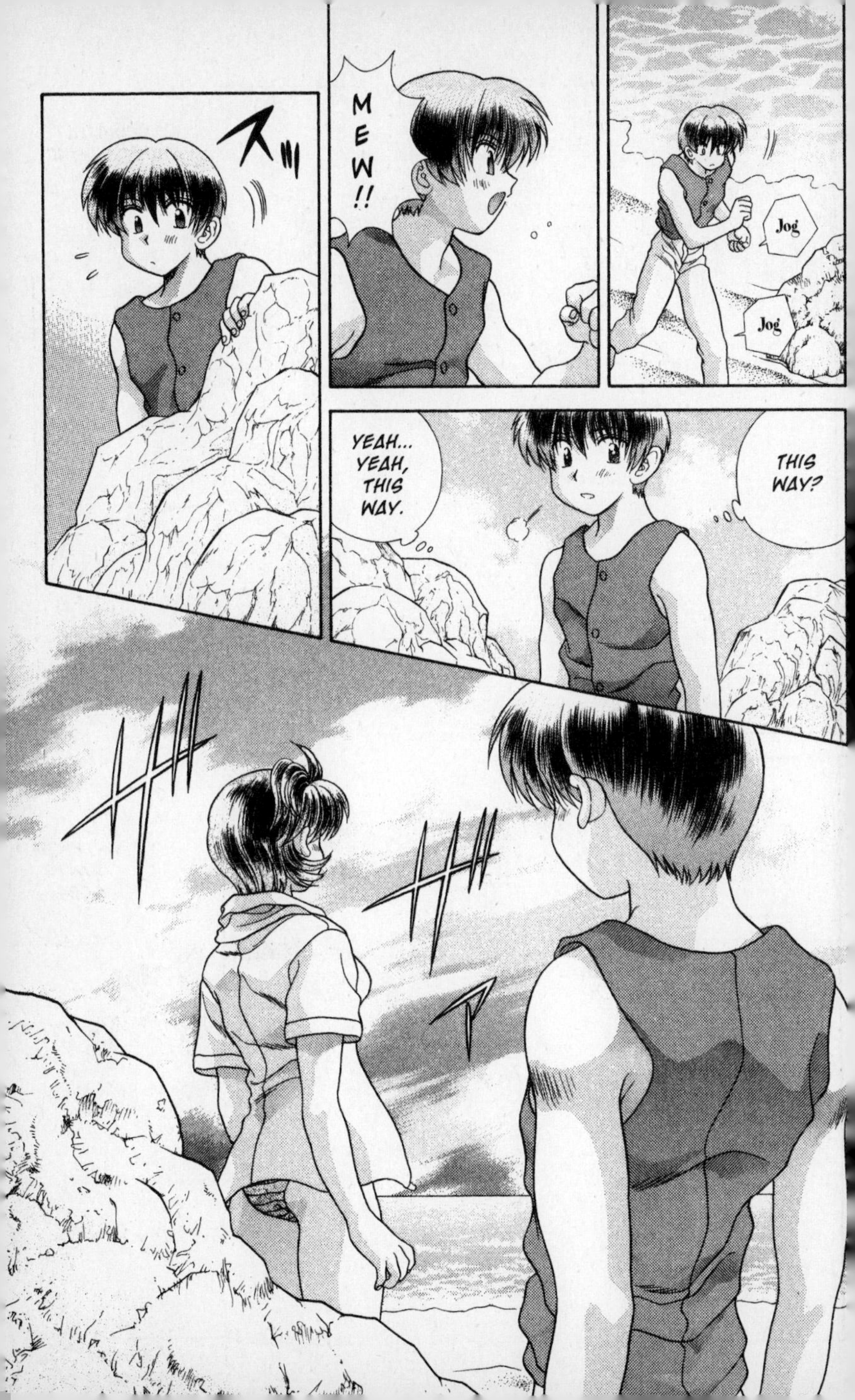
Jog
Jog
MEW!!
THIS WAY?
YEAH... YEAH, THIS WAY.

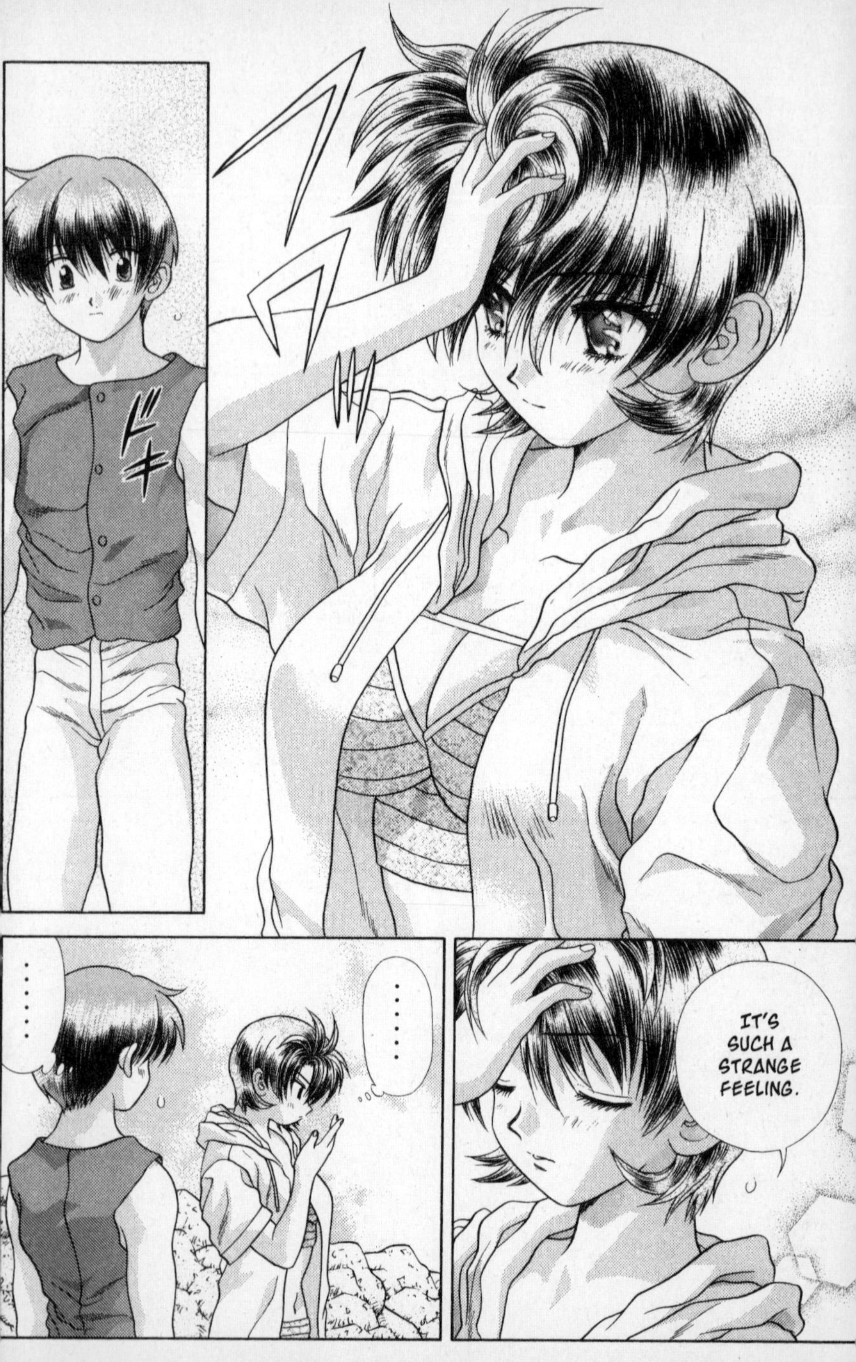
ドキ
IT'S SUCH A STRANGE FEELING.
......
......

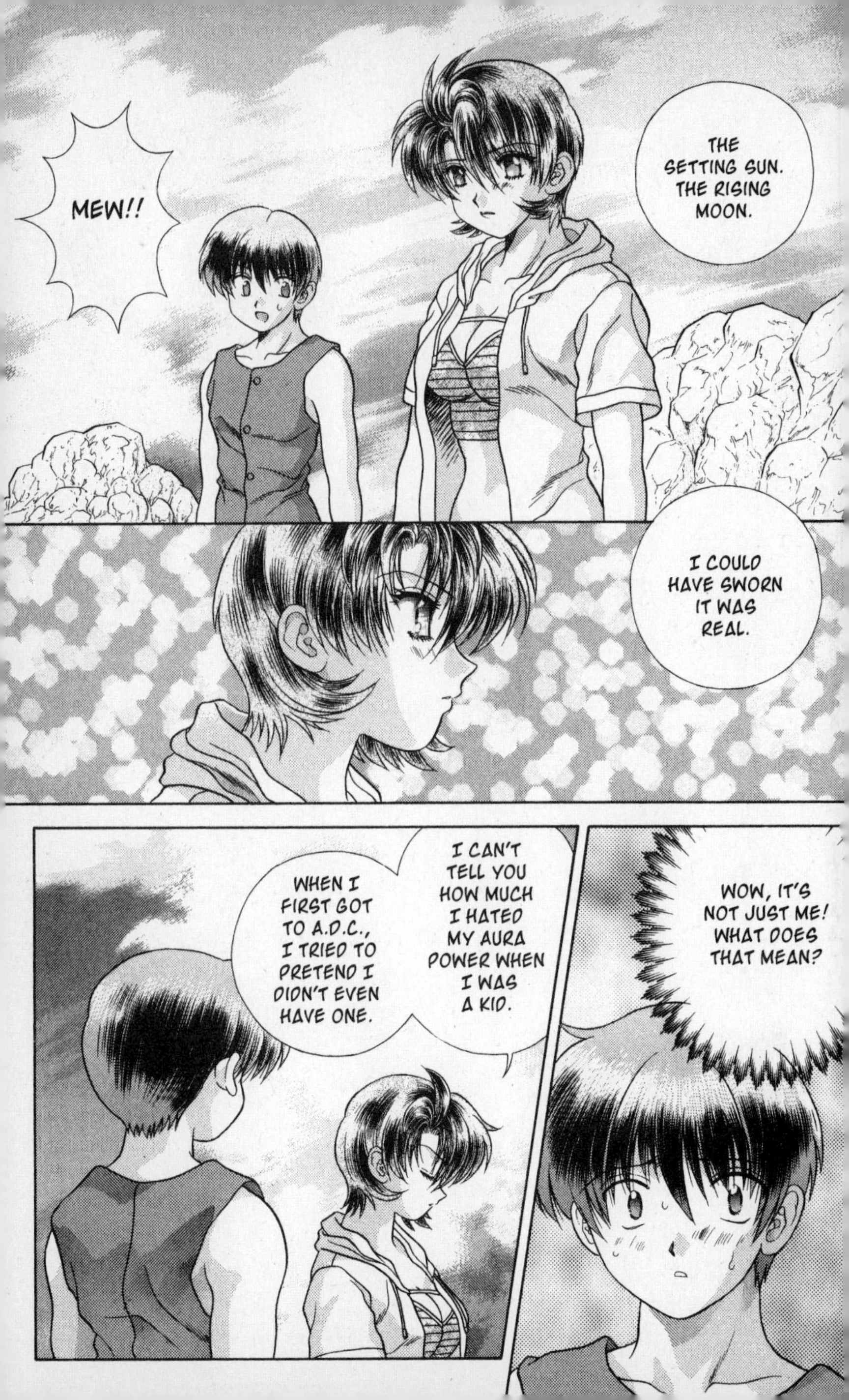
THE SETTING SUN. THE RISING MOON.
MEW!!
I COULD HAVE SWORN IT WAS REAL.
WOW, IT'S NOT JUST ME! WHAT DOES THAT MEAN?
I CAN'T TELL YOU HOW MUCH I HATED MY AURA POWER WHEN I WAS A KID.
WHEN I FIRST GOT TO A.D.C., I TRIED TO PRETEND I DIDN'T EVEN HAVE ONE.

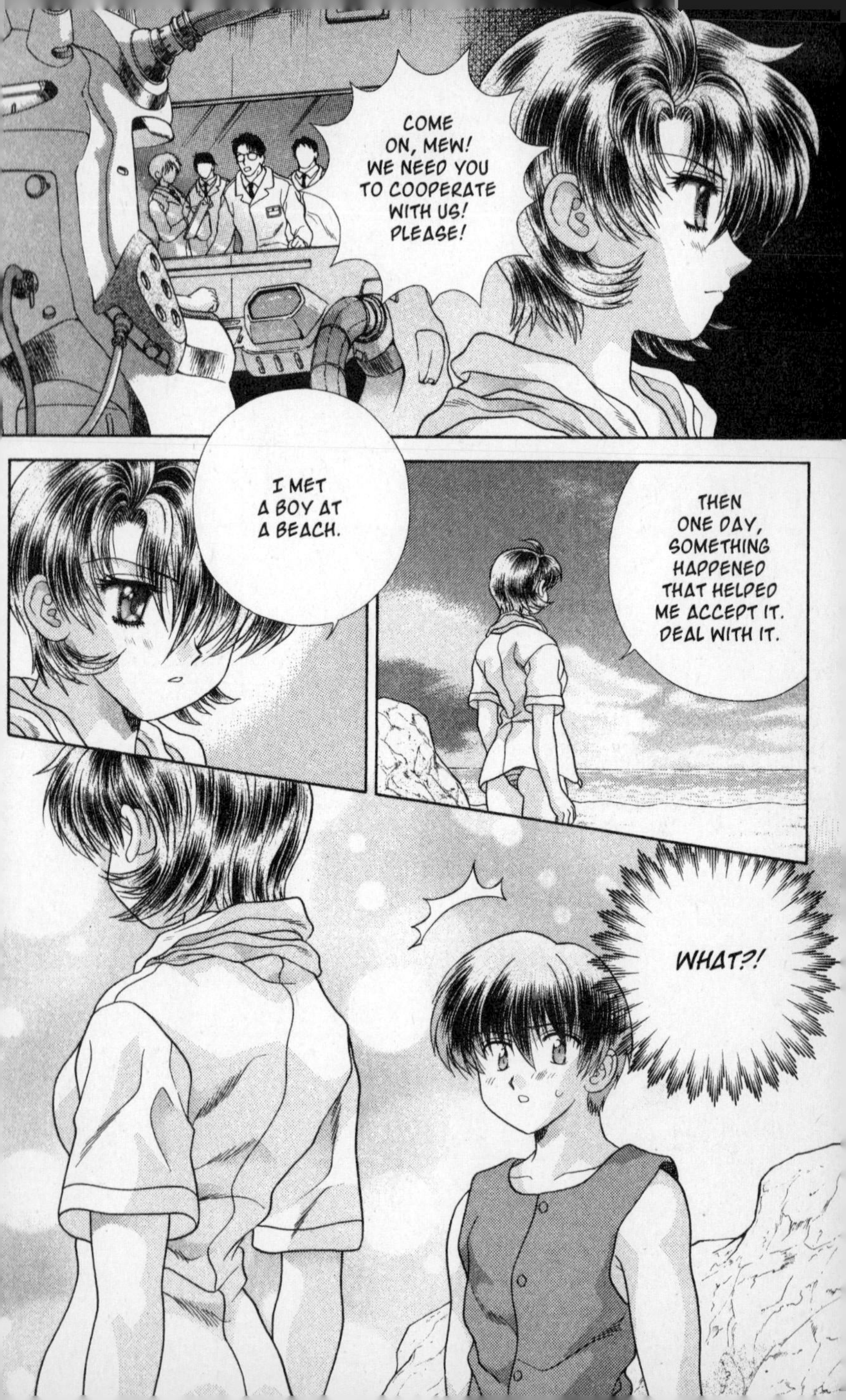
COME ON, MEW! WE NEED YOU TO COOPERATE WITH US! PLEASE!
THEN ONE DAY, SOMETHING HAPPENED THAT HELPED ME ACCEPT IT. DEAL WITH IT.
I MET A BOY AT A BEACH.
WHAT?!

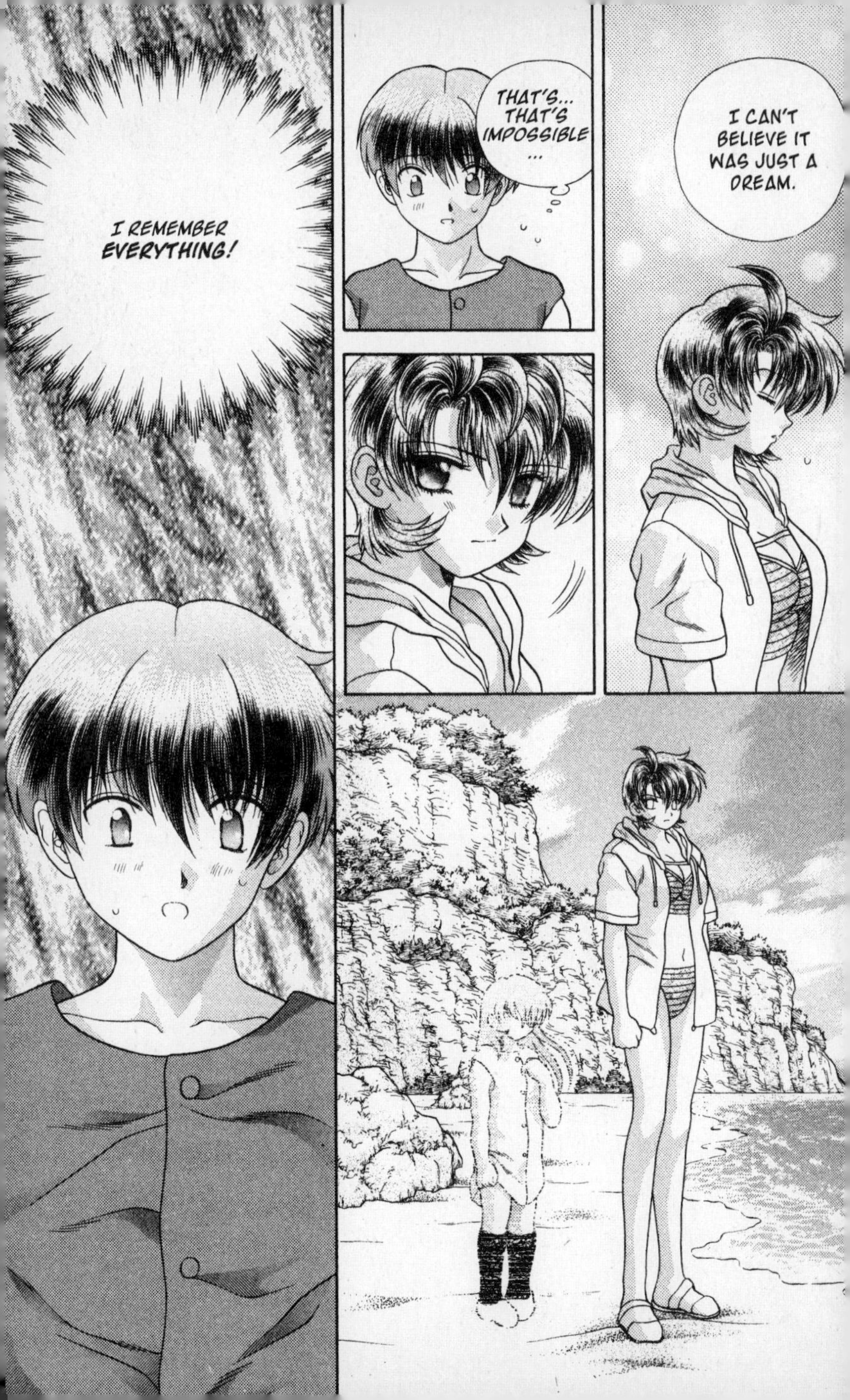
I CAN'T BELIEVE IT WAS JUST A DREAM.
THAT'S... THAT'S IMPOSSIBLE ...
I REMEMBER EVERYTHING!

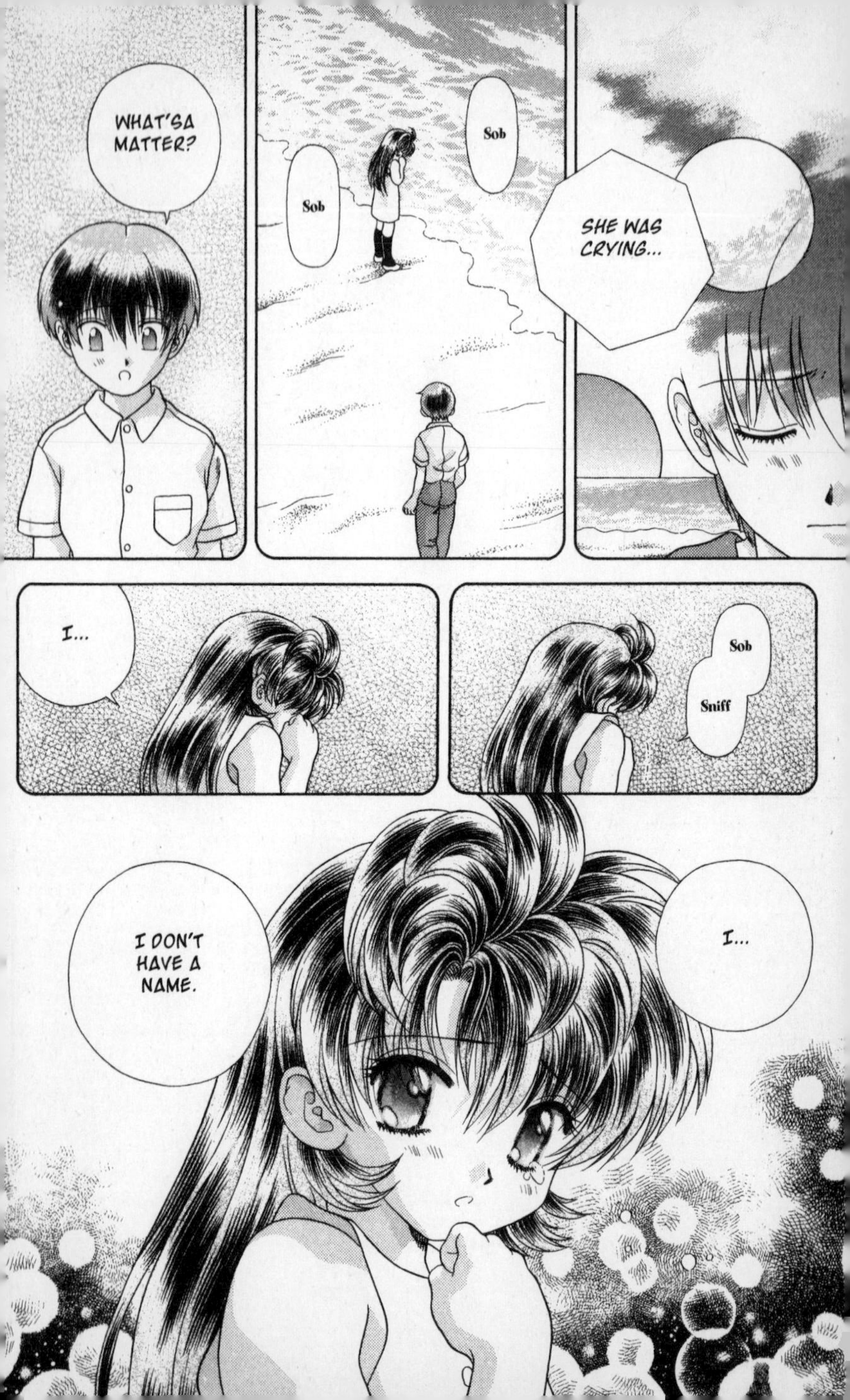
SHE WAS CRYING...
Sob
Sob
WHAT'SA MATTER?
Sob
Sniff
I...
I...
I DON'T HAVE A NAME.

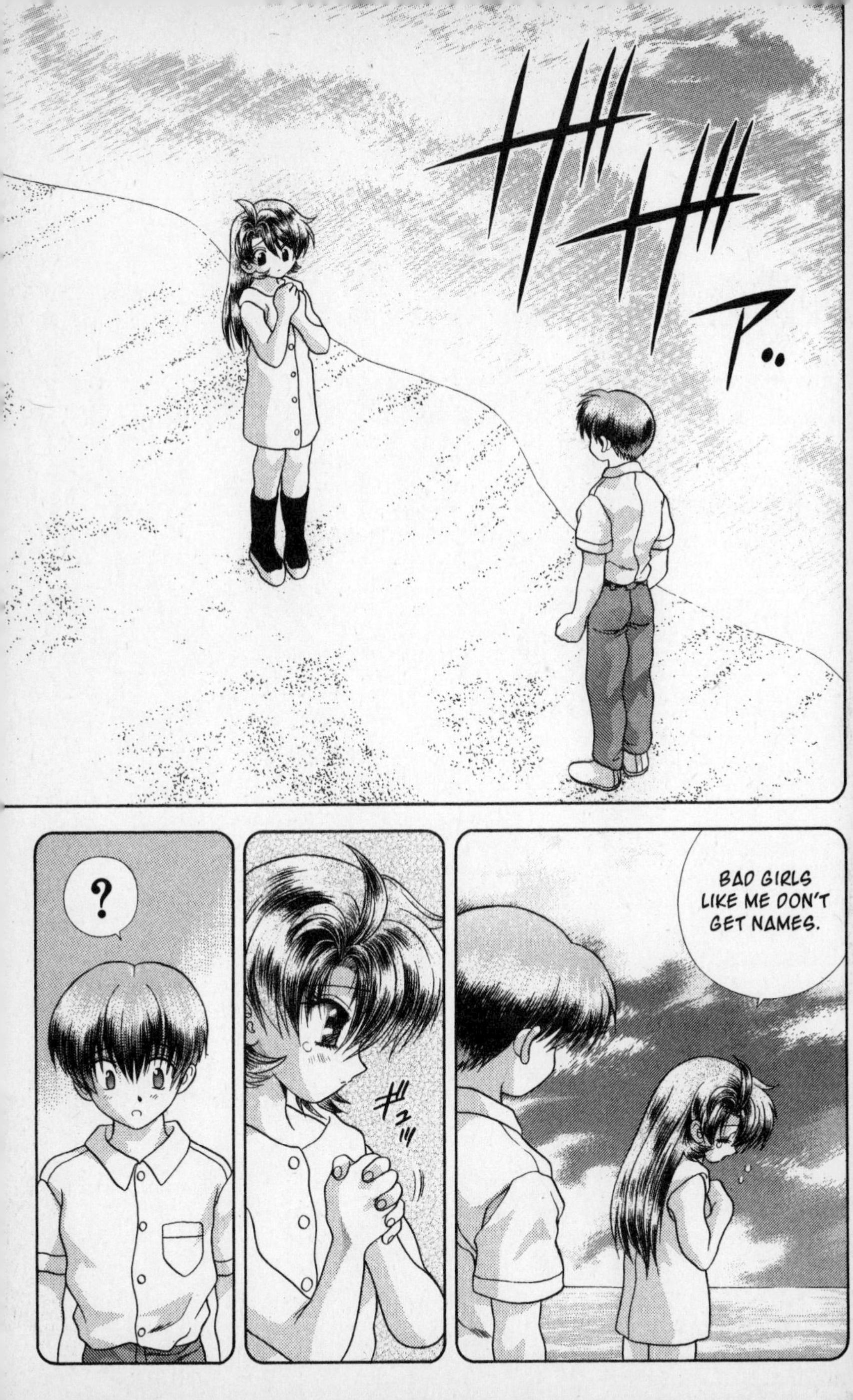
ザザザザァ..
BAD GIRLS LIKE ME DON'T GET NAMES.
ギュッ
?

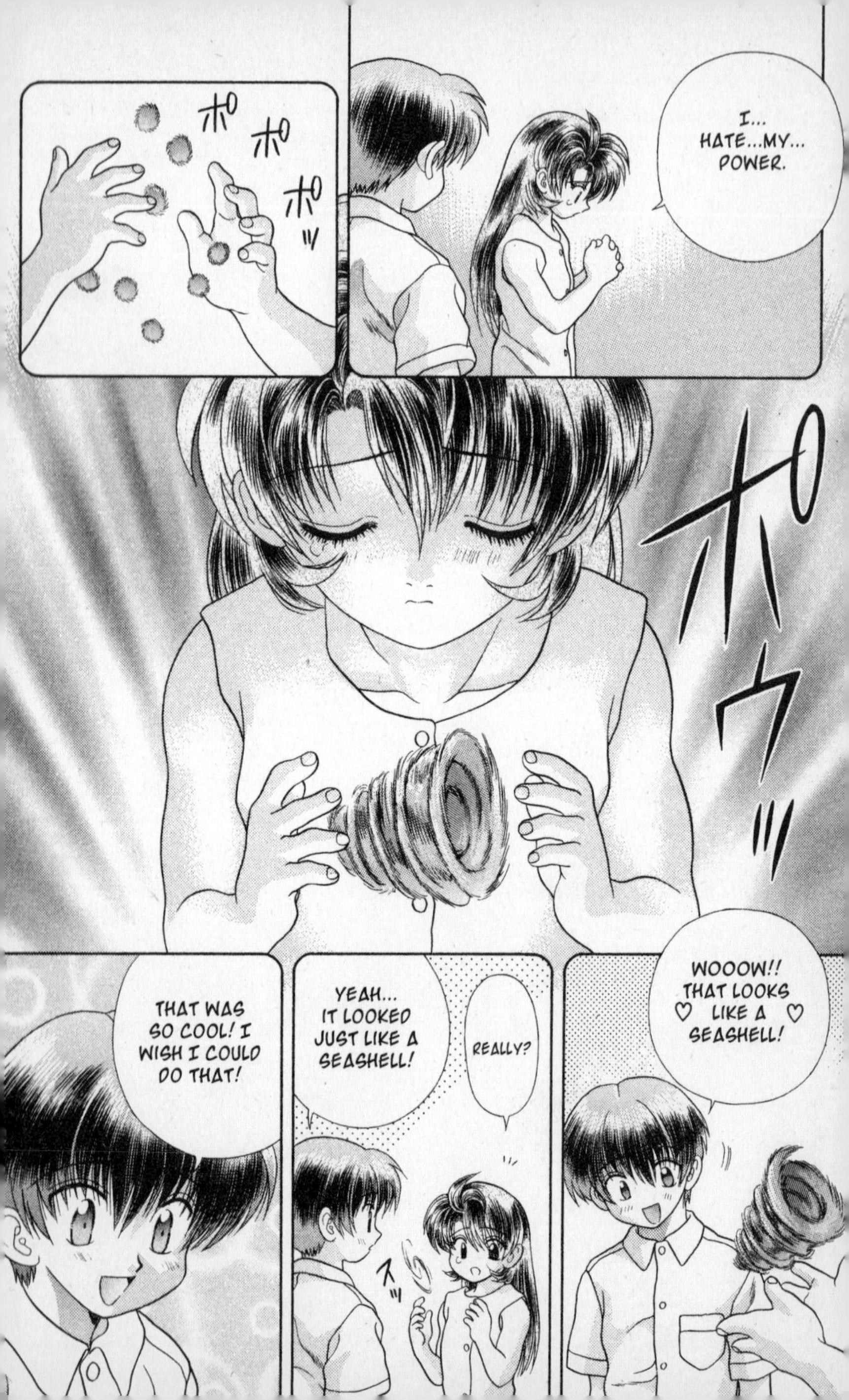
I... HATE...MY... POWER.
ポ ポ ポッ
ポウッ
WOOOW!! THAT LOOKS ♡ LIKE A ♡ SEASHELL!
REALLY?
YEAH... IT LOOKED JUST LIKE A SEASHELL!
スッ
THAT WAS SO COOL! I WISH I COULD DO THAT!

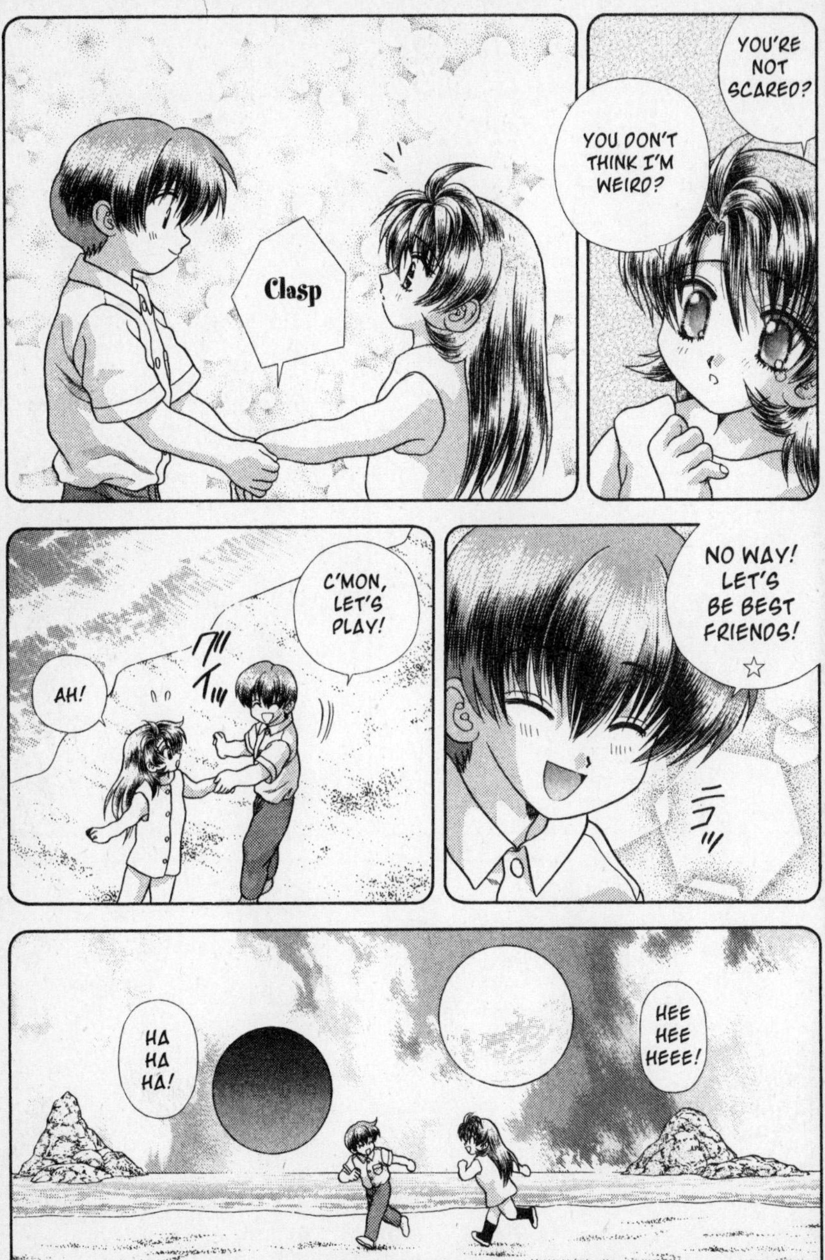
YOU'RE NOT SCARED?
YOU DON'T THINK I'M WEIRD?
Clasp
NO WAY! LET'S BE BEST FRIENDS! ☆
C'MON, LET'S PLAY!
AH!
HEE HEE HEEE!
HA HA HA!

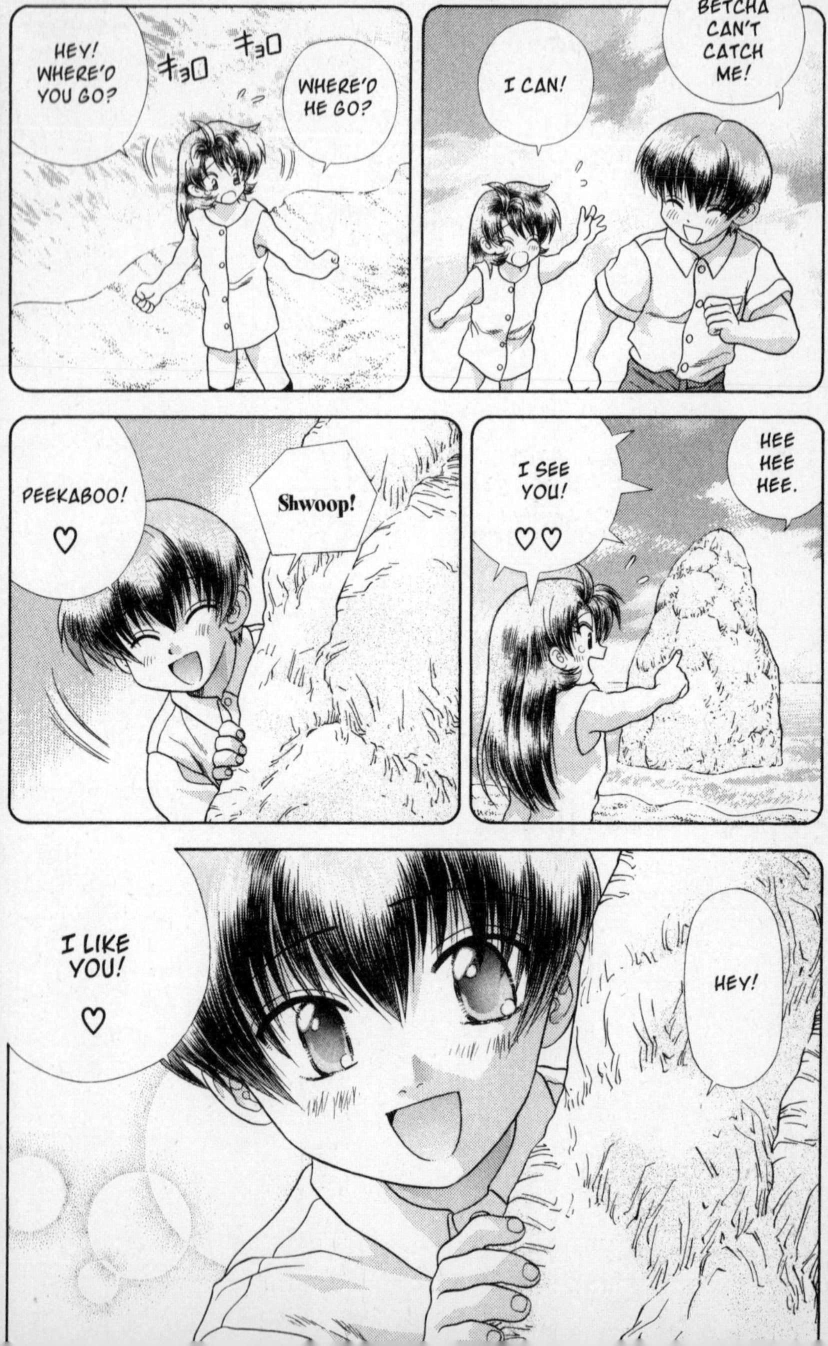
BETCHA CAN'T CATCH ME!
I CAN!
WHERE'D HE GO?
キョロ
キョロ
HEY! WHERE'D YOU GO?
HEE HEE HEE.
I SEE YOU! ♡♡
Shwoop!
PEEKABOO! ♡
HEY!
I LIKE YOU! ♡

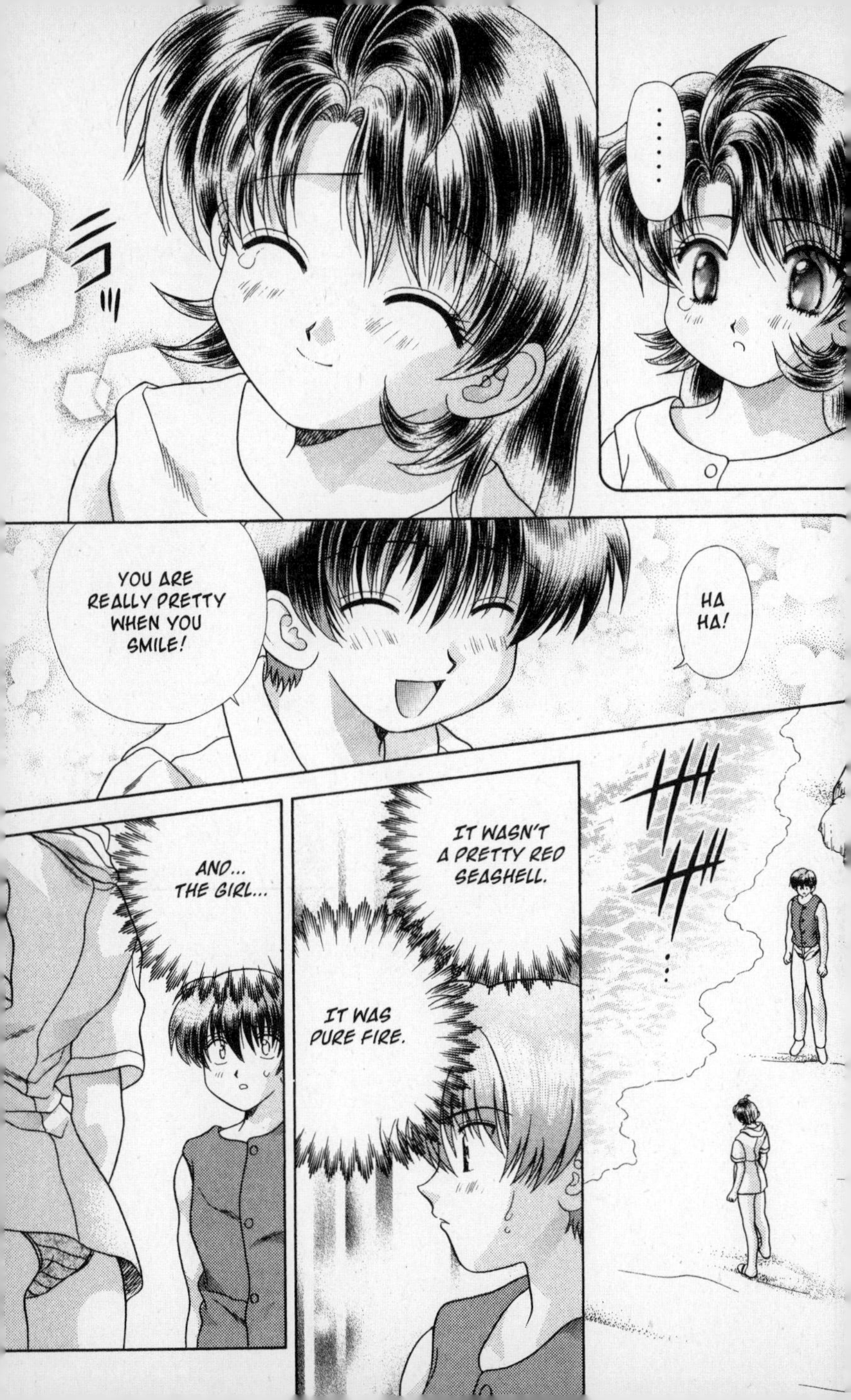
......
ニコッ
HA HA!
YOU ARE REALLY PRETTY WHEN YOU SMILE!
IT WASN'T A PRETTY RED SEASHELL.
IT WAS PURE FIRE.
AND... THE GIRL...

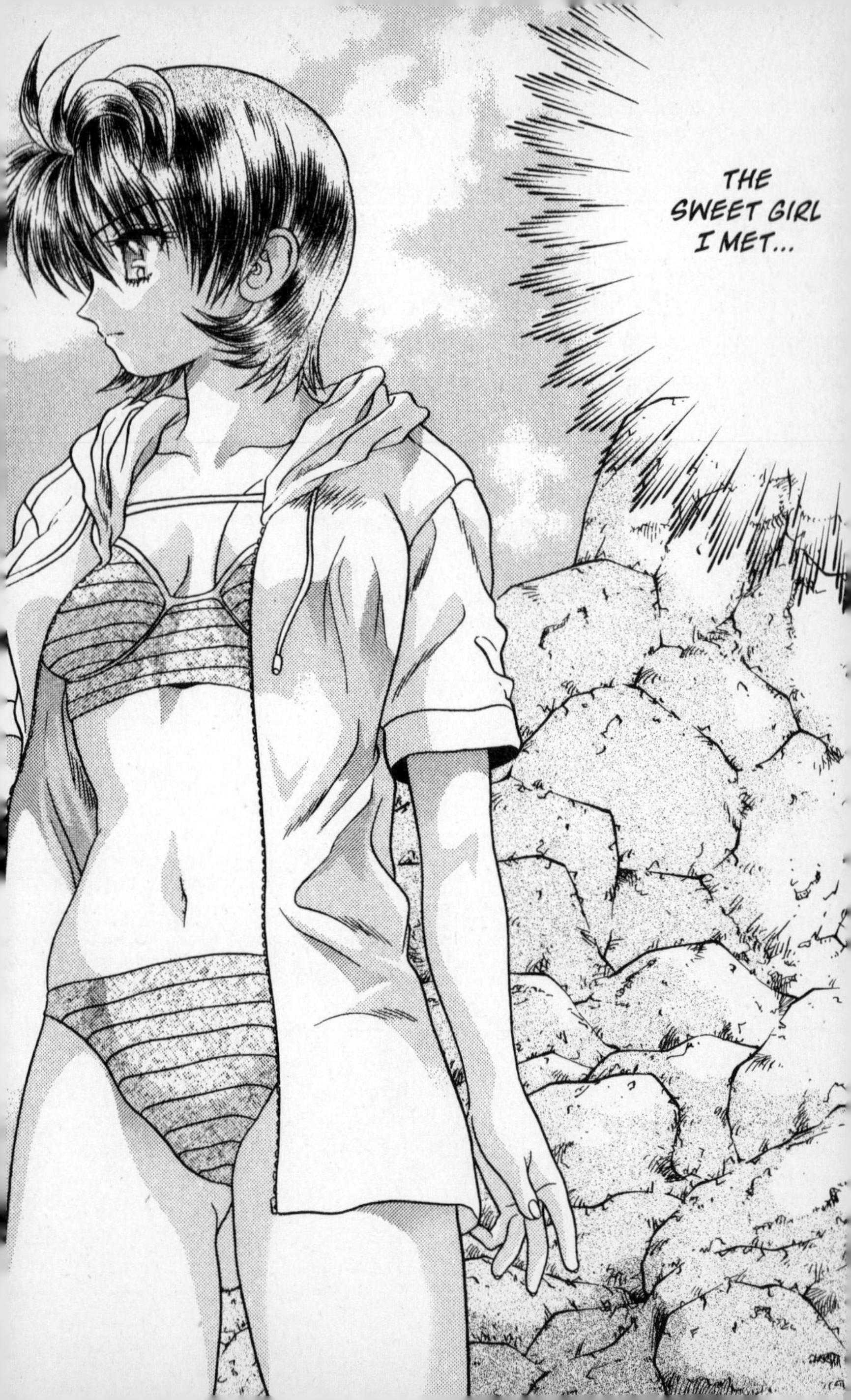
THE SWEET GIRL I MET...

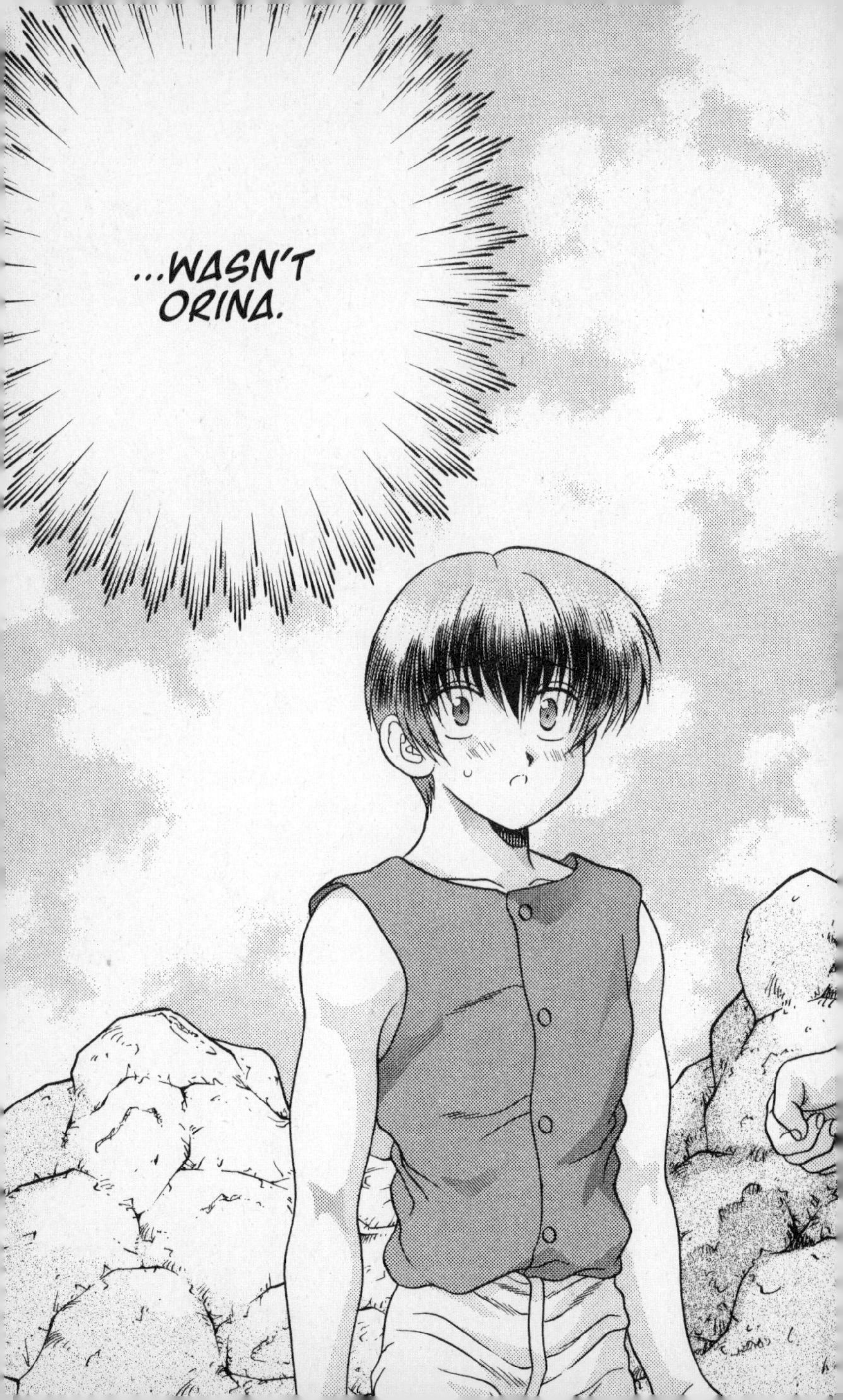
...WASN'T ORINA.

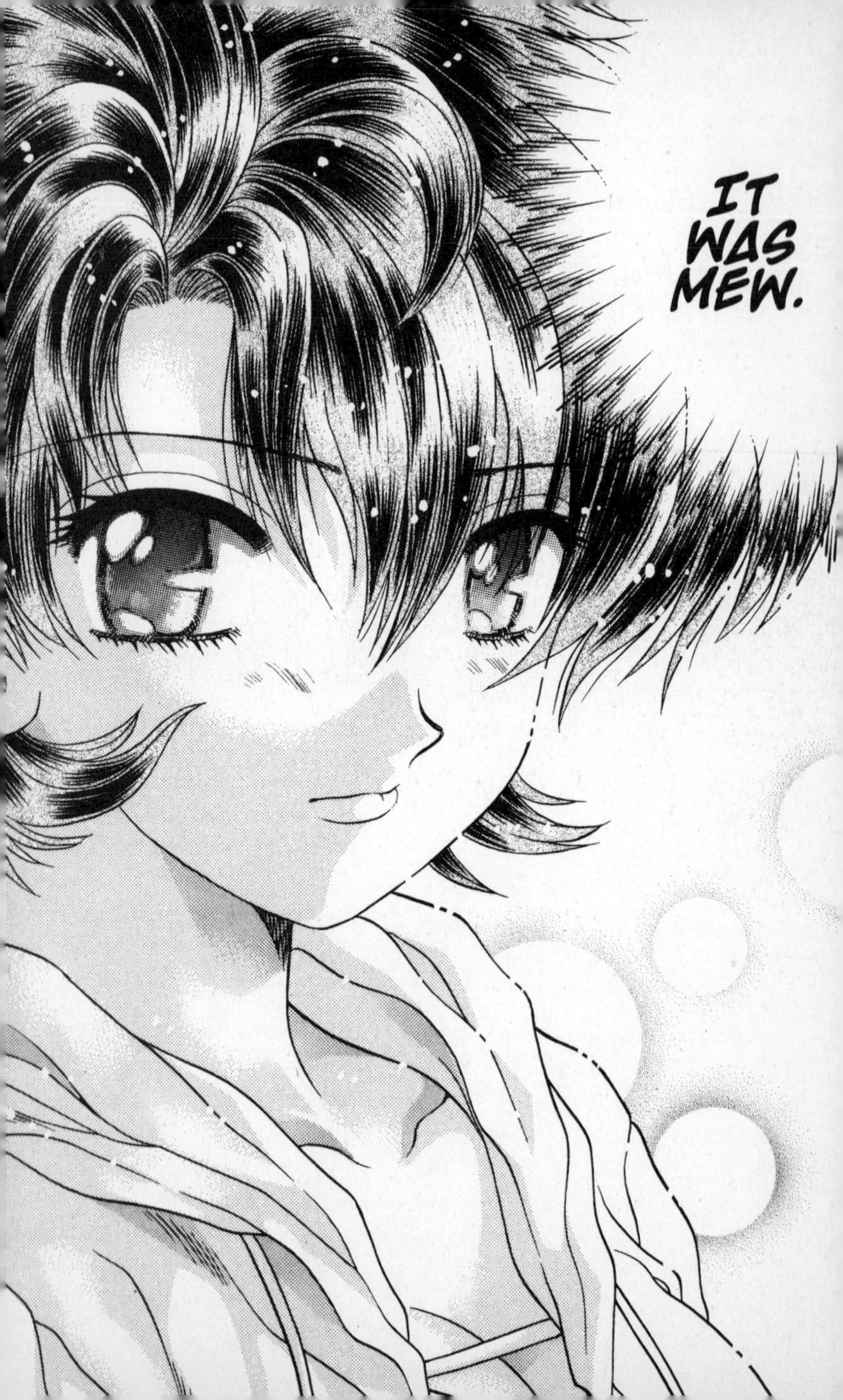
IT WAS MEW.

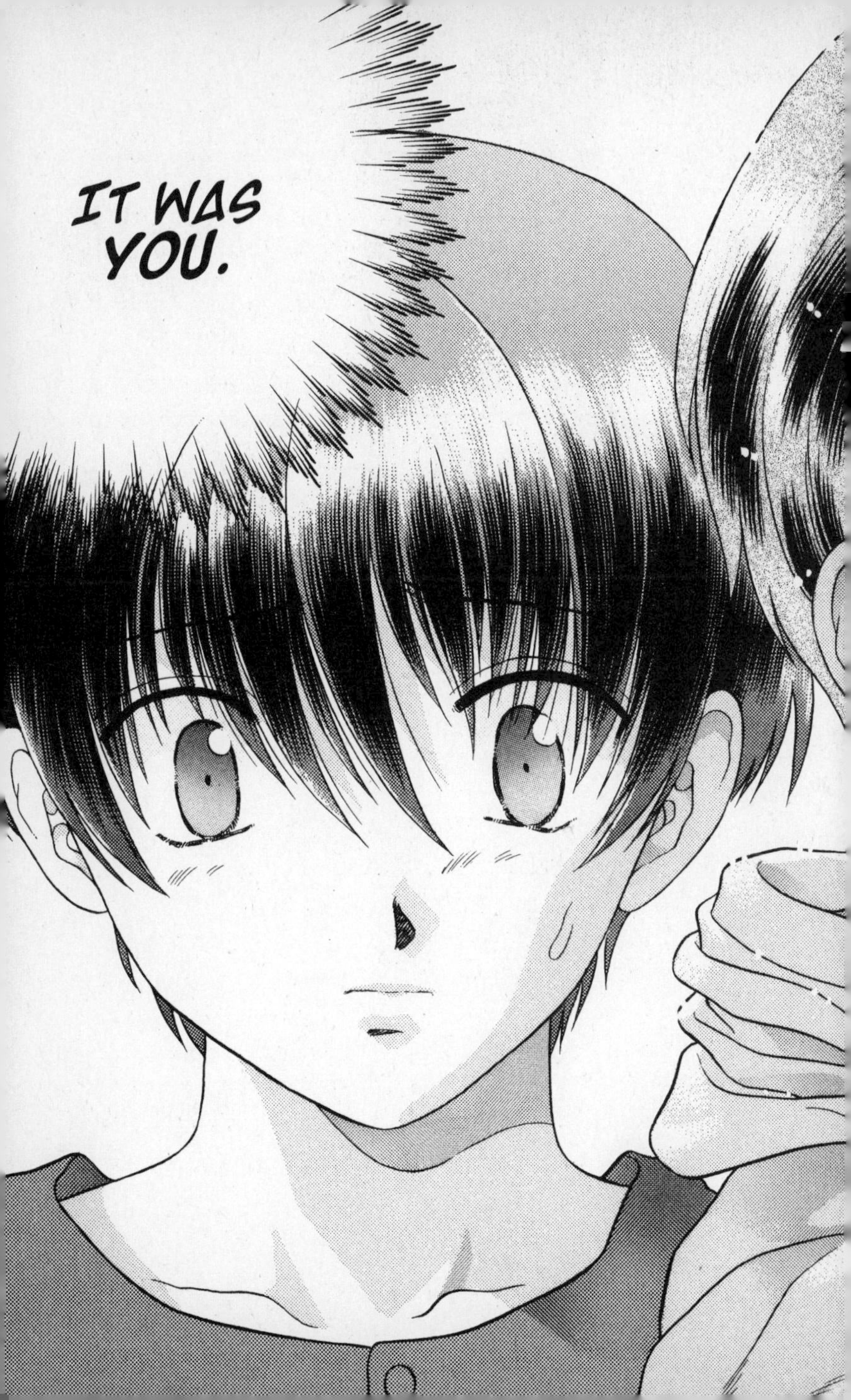
IT WAS YOU.

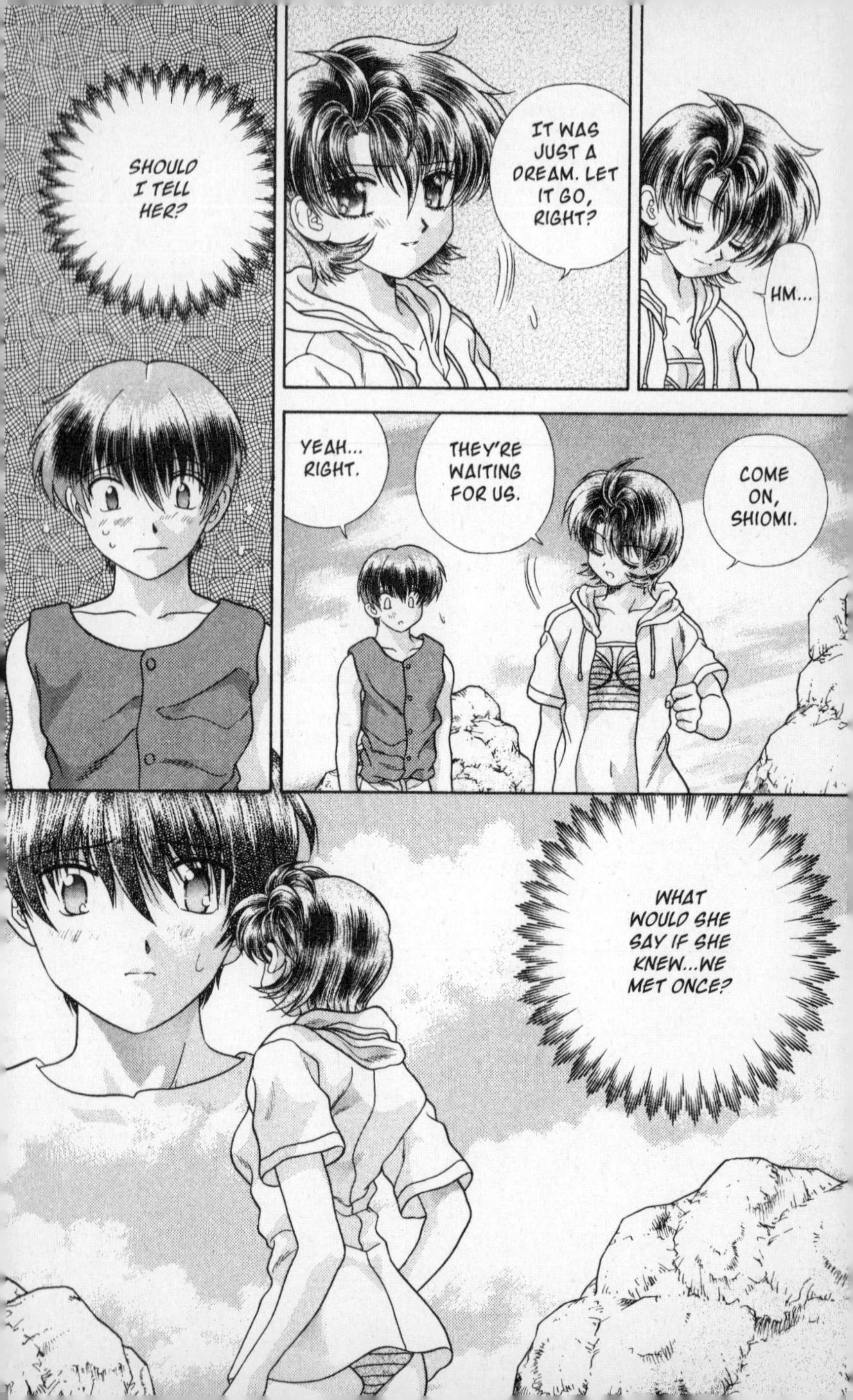
HM...
IT WAS JUST A DREAM. LET IT GO, RIGHT?
COME ON, SHIOMI.
THEY'RE WAITING FOR US.
YEAH... RIGHT.
SHOULD I TELL HER?
WHAT WOULD SHE SAY IF SHE KNEW...WE MET ONCE?

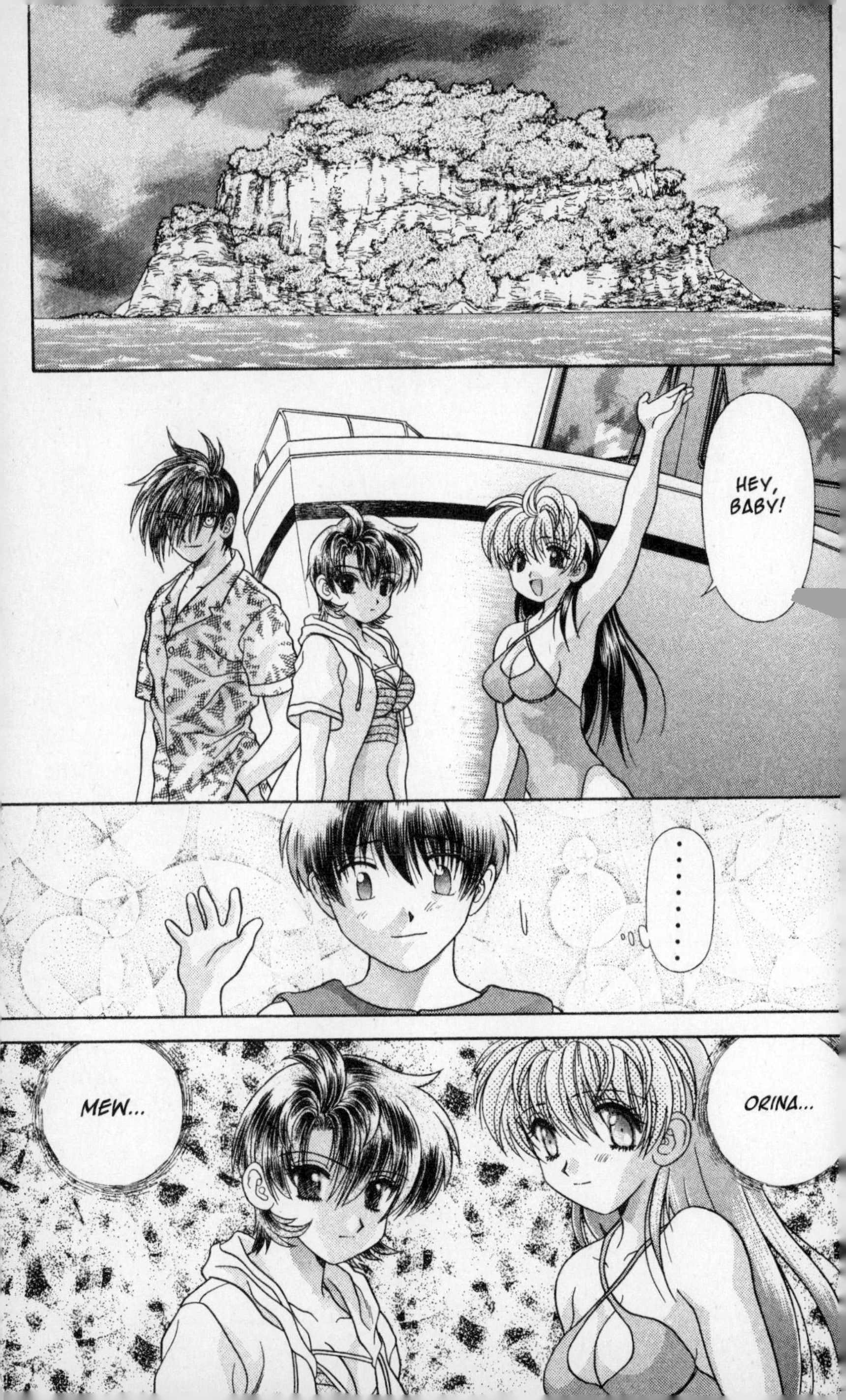
HEY, BABY!
......
ORINA...
MEW...

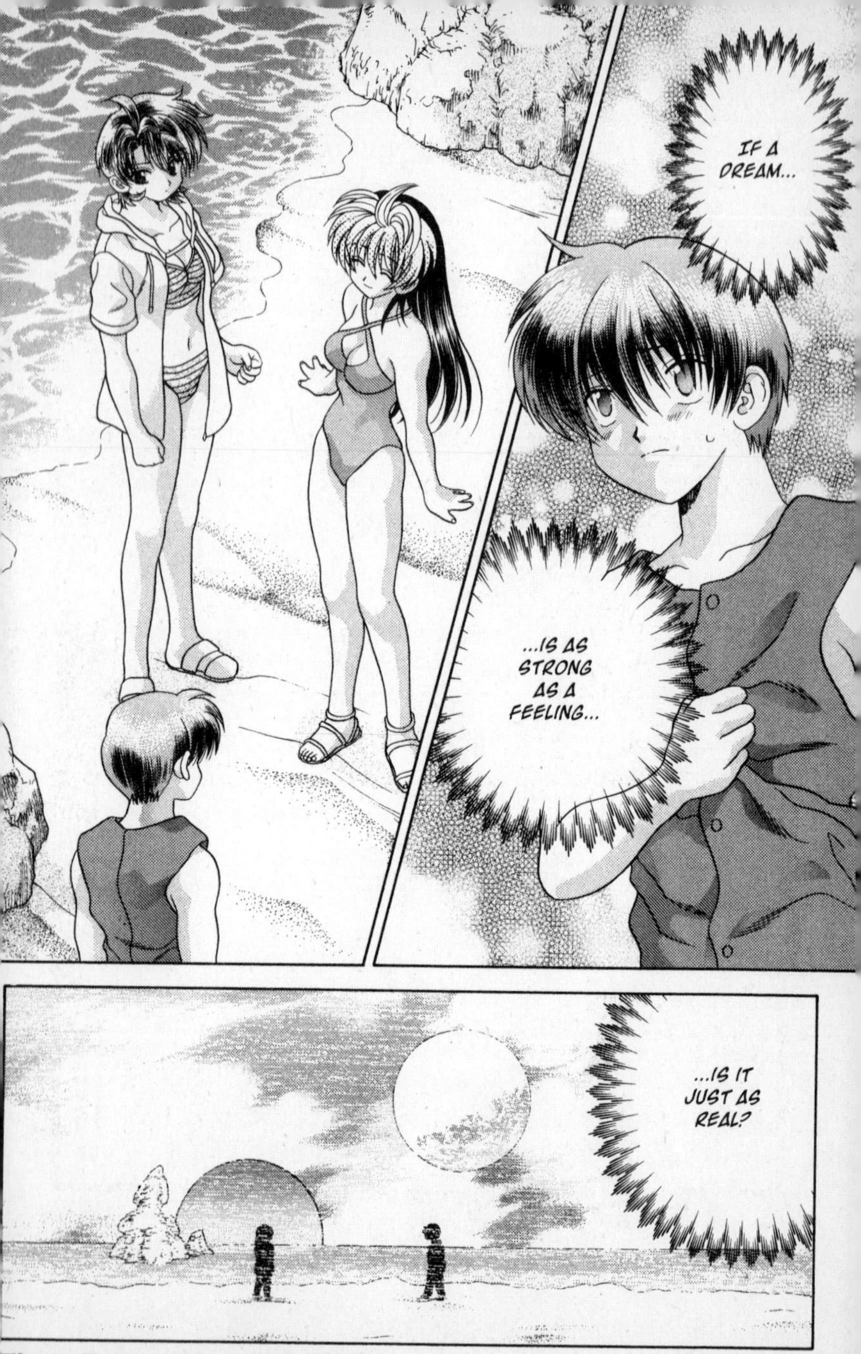
IF A DREAM...
...IS AS STRONG AS A FEELING...
...IS IT JUST AS REAL?

That Damn Beach END

Chapter 15: Where the Heart Is

Flag: Dedicated to Summer Festival

Sign on left: ...Taiyaki Sweet...   Back Sign: Real Good Taste...

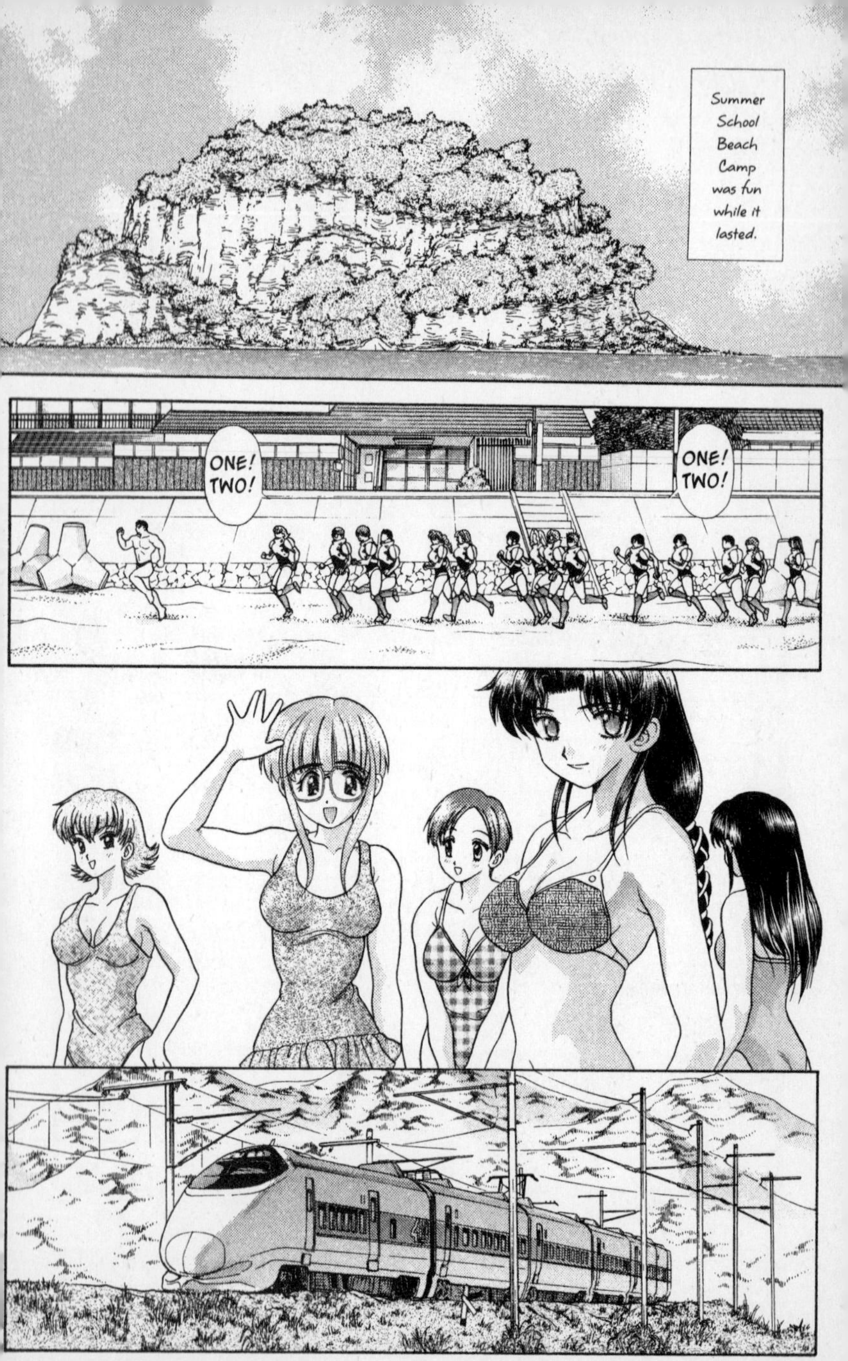

Summer School Beach Camp was fun while it lasted.
ONE! TWO!
ONE! TWO!

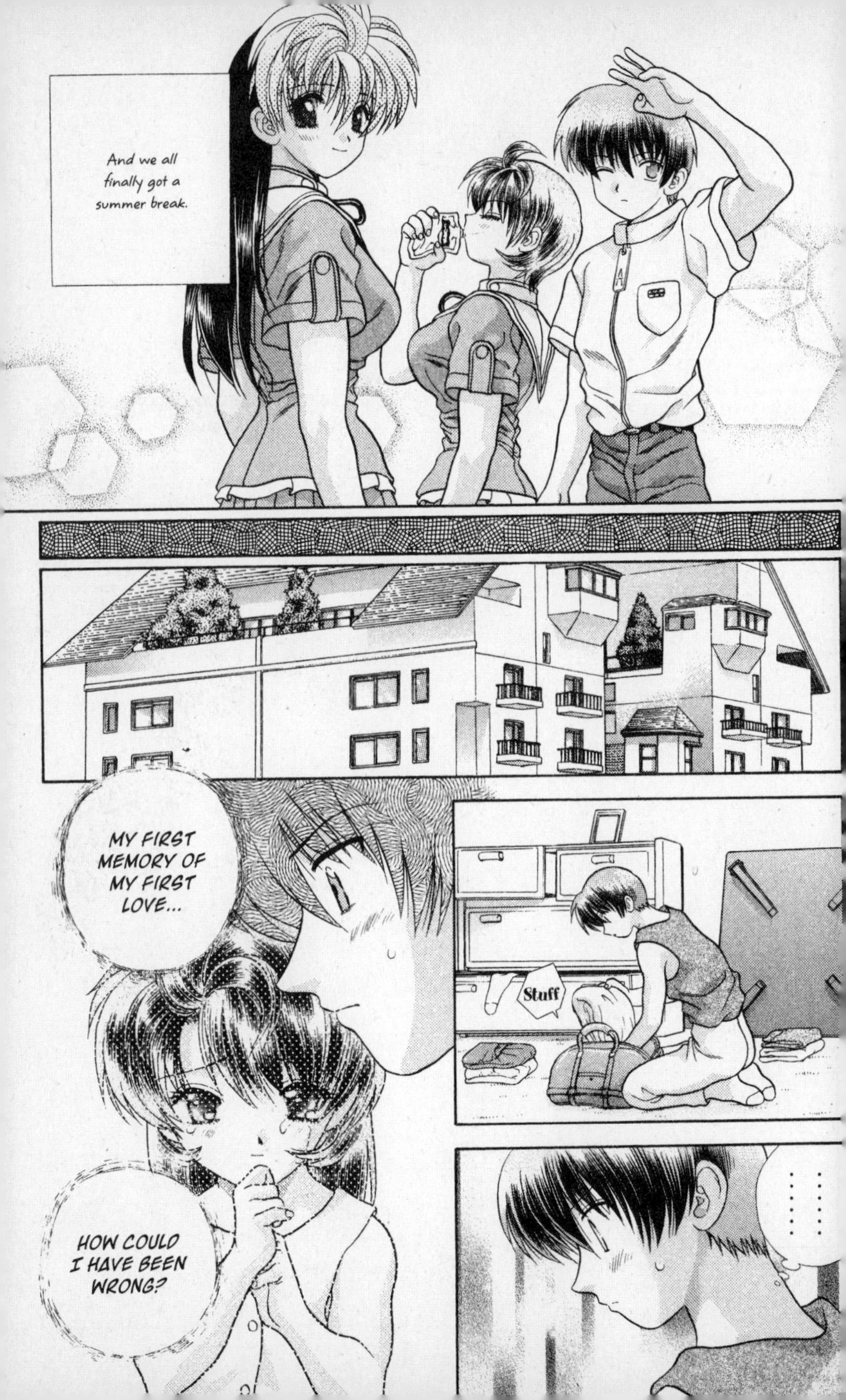
And we all finally got a summer break.
Stuff
......
MY FIRST MEMORY OF MY FIRST LOVE...
HOW COULD I HAVE BEEN WRONG?

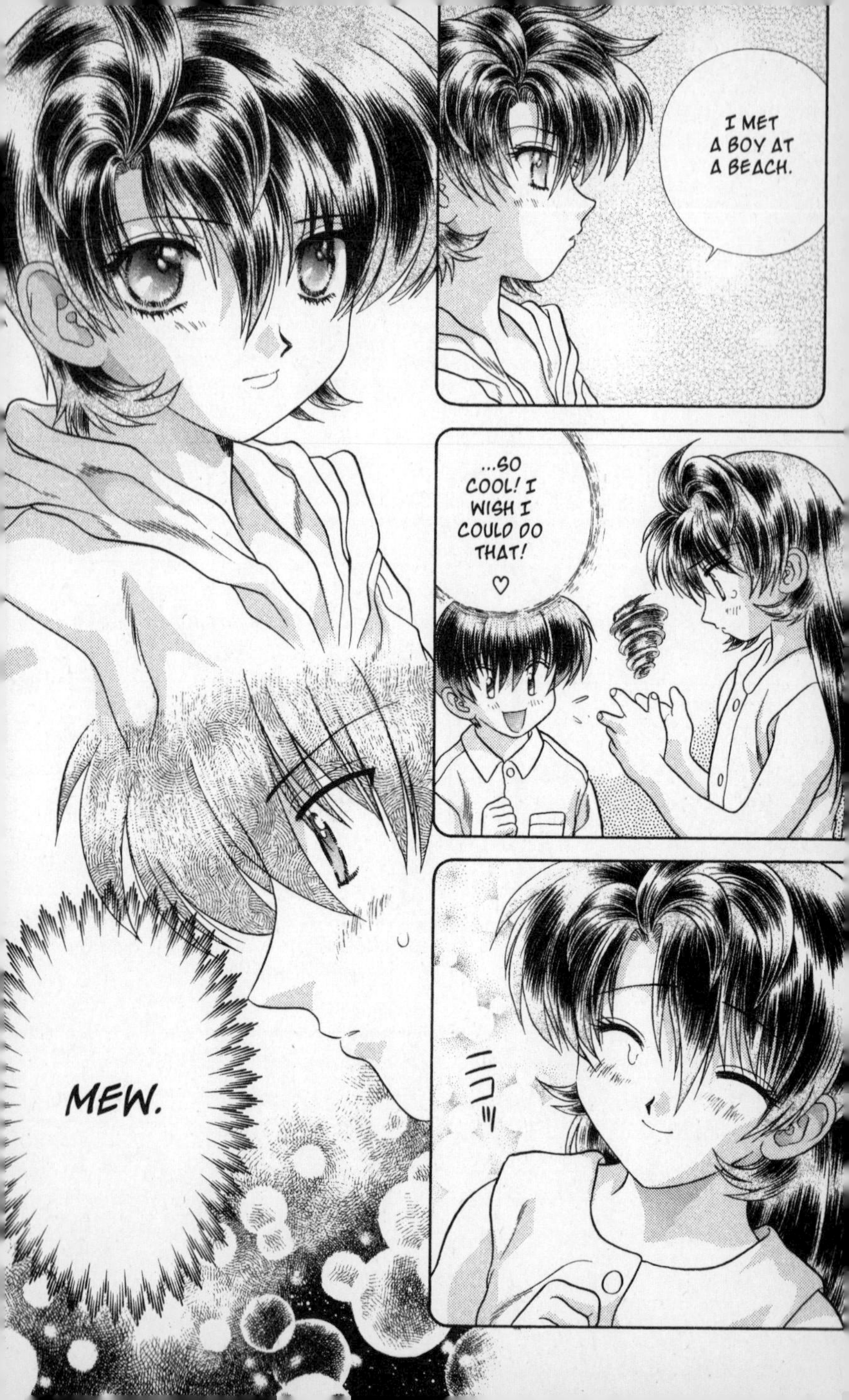
I MET A BOY AT A BEACH.
...SO COOL! I WISH I COULD DO THAT! ♡
ニコッ
MEW.

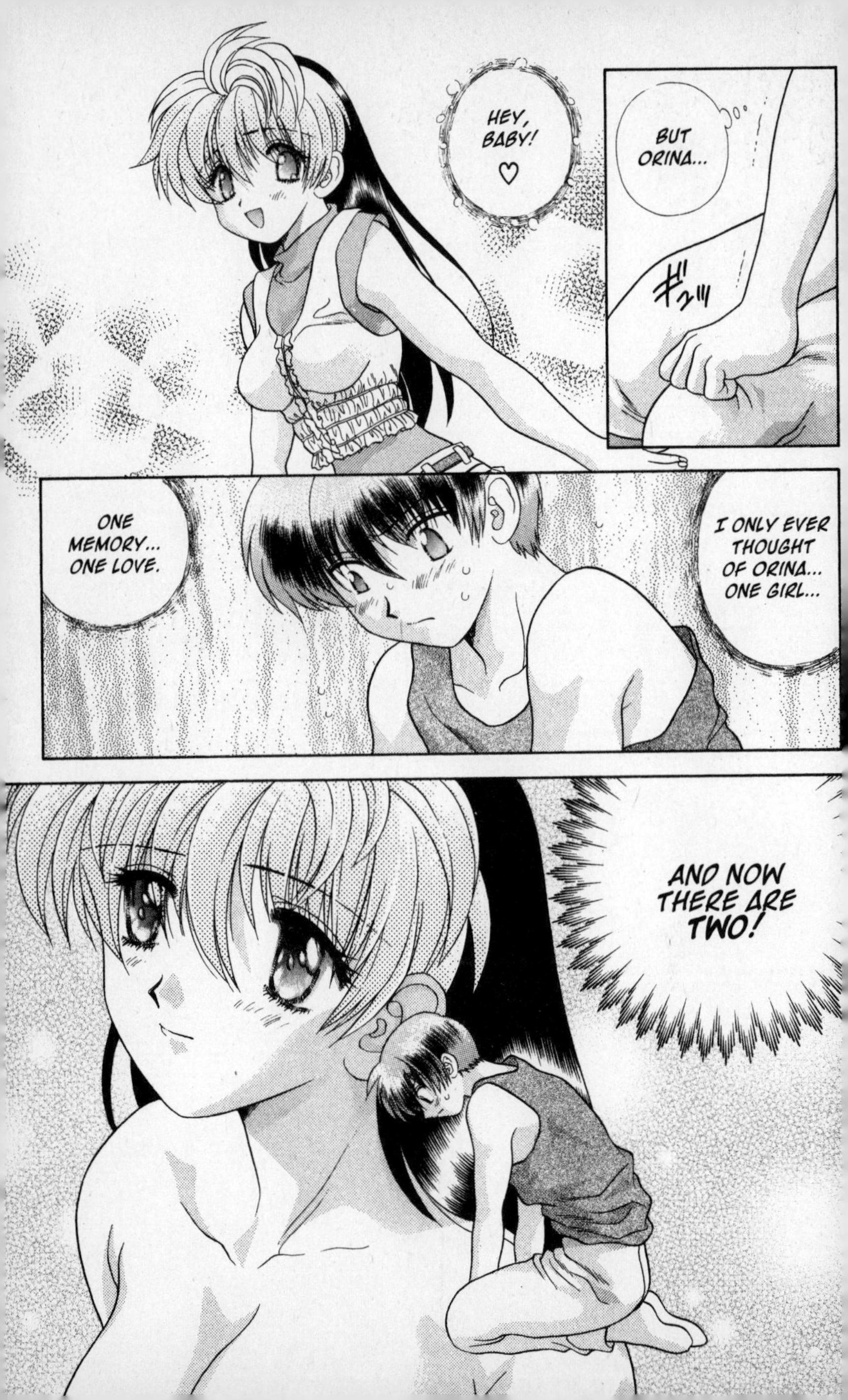

BUT ORINA...
ギュッ
HEY, BABY! ♡
I ONLY EVER THOUGHT OF ORINA... ONE GIRL...
ONE MEMORY... ONE LOVE.
AND NOW THERE ARE TWO!

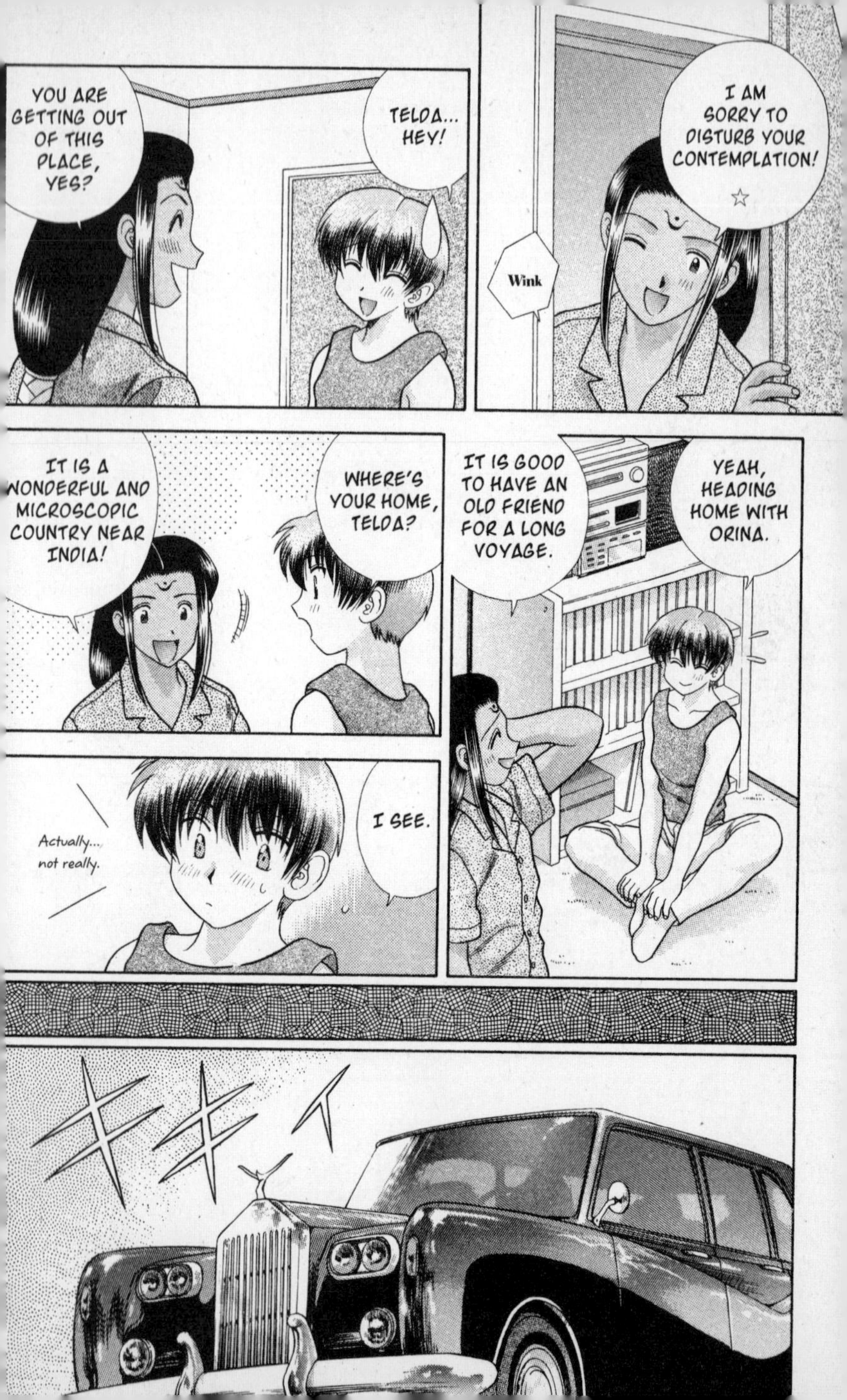
I AM SORRY TO DISTURB YOUR CONTEMPLATION! ☆
Wink
TELDA... HEY!
YOU ARE GETTING OUT OF THIS PLACE, YES?
YEAH, HEADING HOME WITH ORINA.
IT IS GOOD TO HAVE AN OLD FRIEND FOR A LONG VOYAGE.
WHERE'S YOUR HOME, TELDA?
IT IS A WONDERFUL AND MICROSCOPIC COUNTRY NEAR INDIA!
I SEE.
Actually... not really.

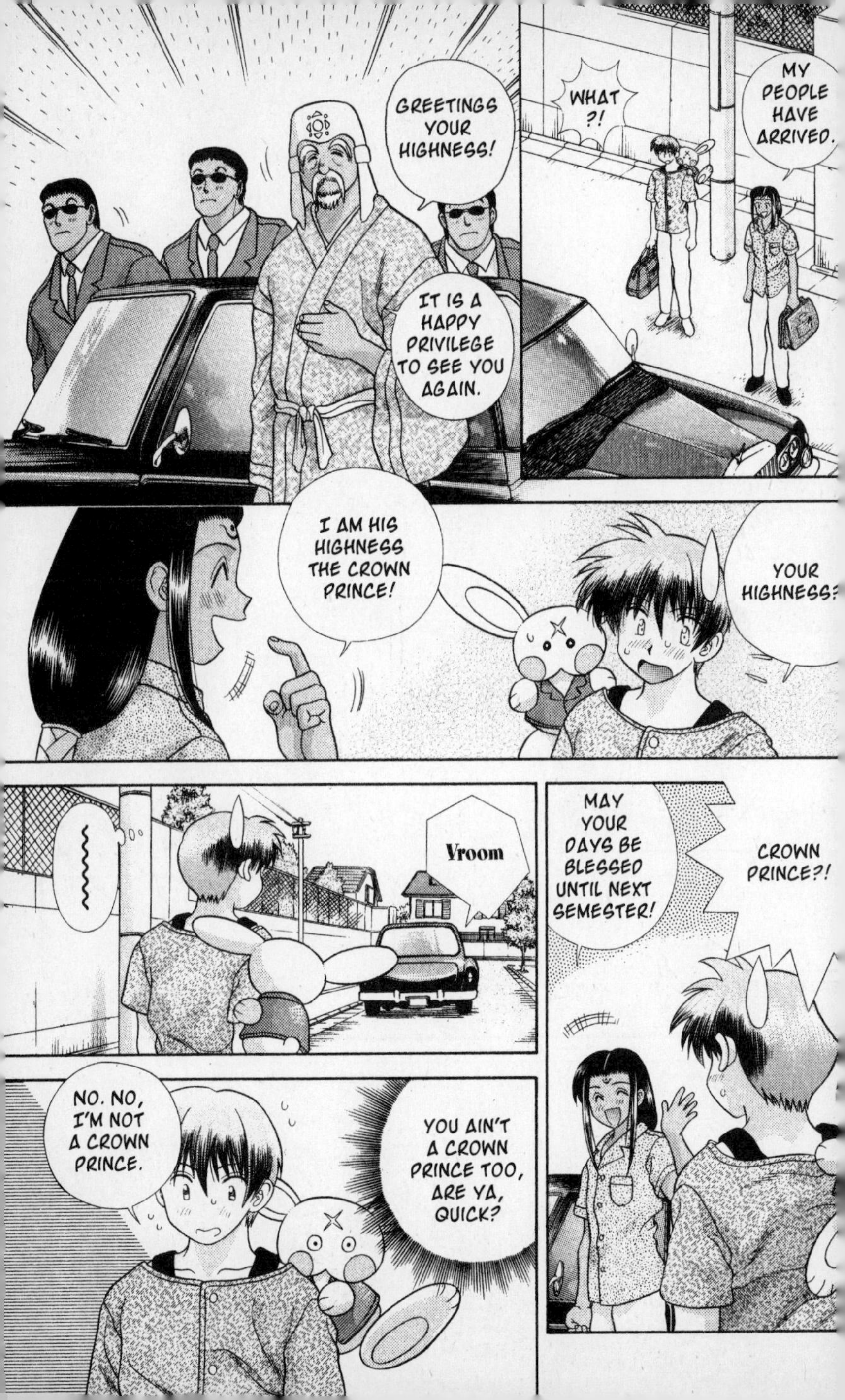
MY PEOPLE HAVE ARRIVED.
WHAT ?!
GREETINGS YOUR HIGHNESS!
IT IS A HAPPY PRIVILEGE TO SEE YOU AGAIN.
YOUR HIGHNESS?
I AM HIS HIGHNESS THE CROWN PRINCE!
CROWN PRINCE?!
MAY YOUR DAYS BE BLESSED UNTIL NEXT SEMESTER!
Vroom
YOU AIN'T A CROWN PRINCE TOO, ARE YA, QUICK?
NO. NO, I'M NOT A CROWN PRINCE.

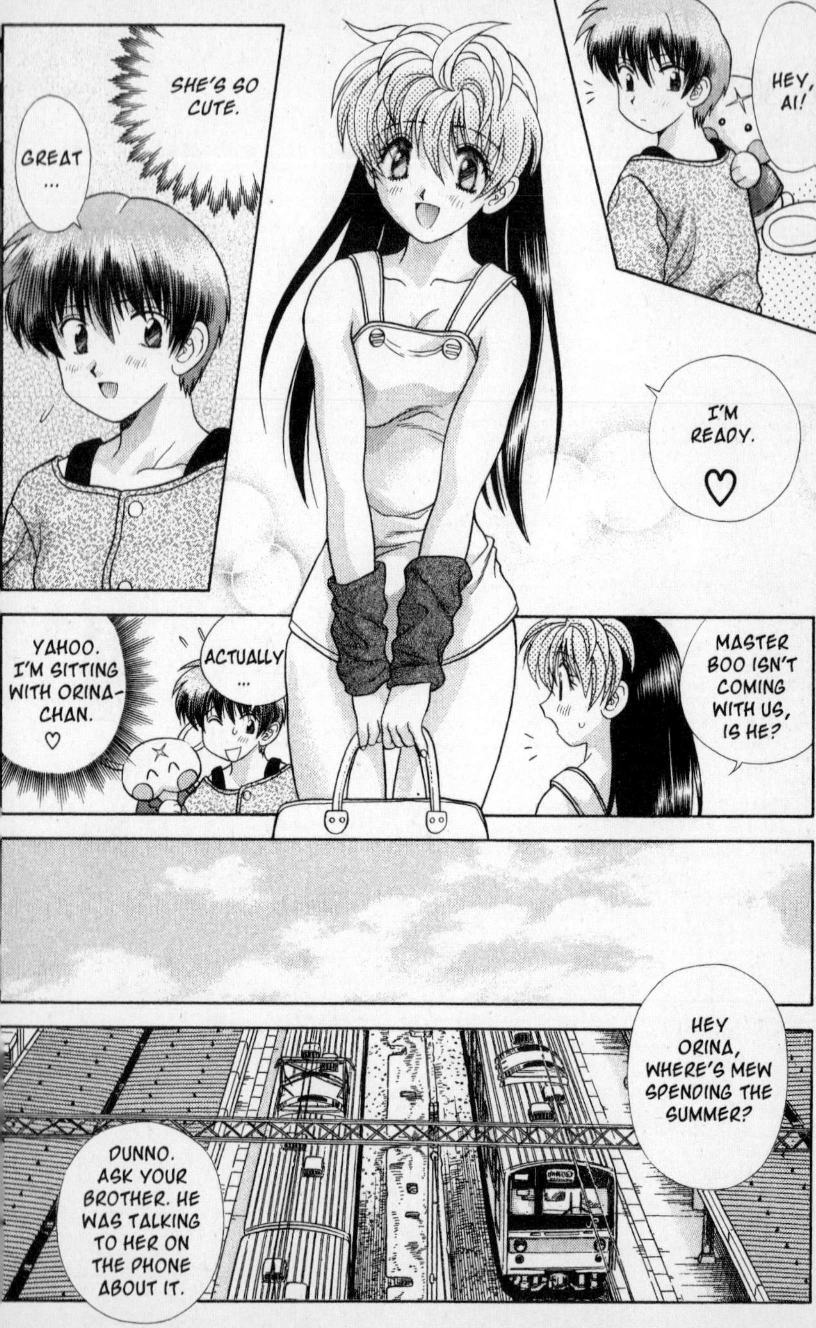
HEY, AI!
I'M READY. ♡
SHE'S SO CUTE.
GREAT ...
MASTER BOO ISN'T COMING WITH US, IS HE?
ACTUALLY ...
YAHOO. I'M SITTING WITH ORINA-CHAN. ♡
HEY ORINA, WHERE'S MEW SPENDING THE SUMMER?
DUNNO. ASK YOUR BROTHER. HE WAS TALKING TO HER ON THE PHONE ABOUT IT.

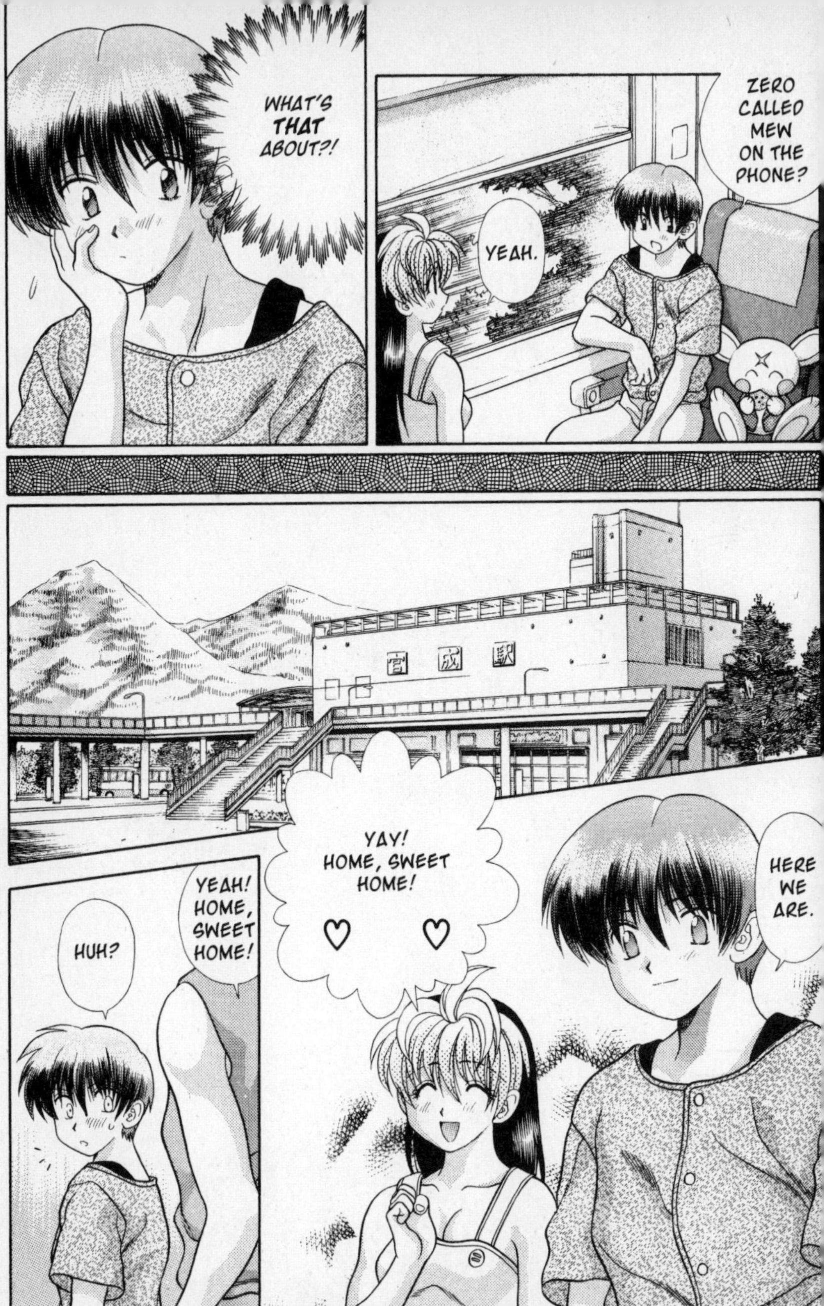
ZERO CALLED MEW ON THE PHONE?
YEAH.
WHAT'S THAT ABOUT?!
HERE WE ARE.
YAY! HOME, SWEET HOME! ♡ ♡
YEAH! HOME, SWEET HOME!
HUH?

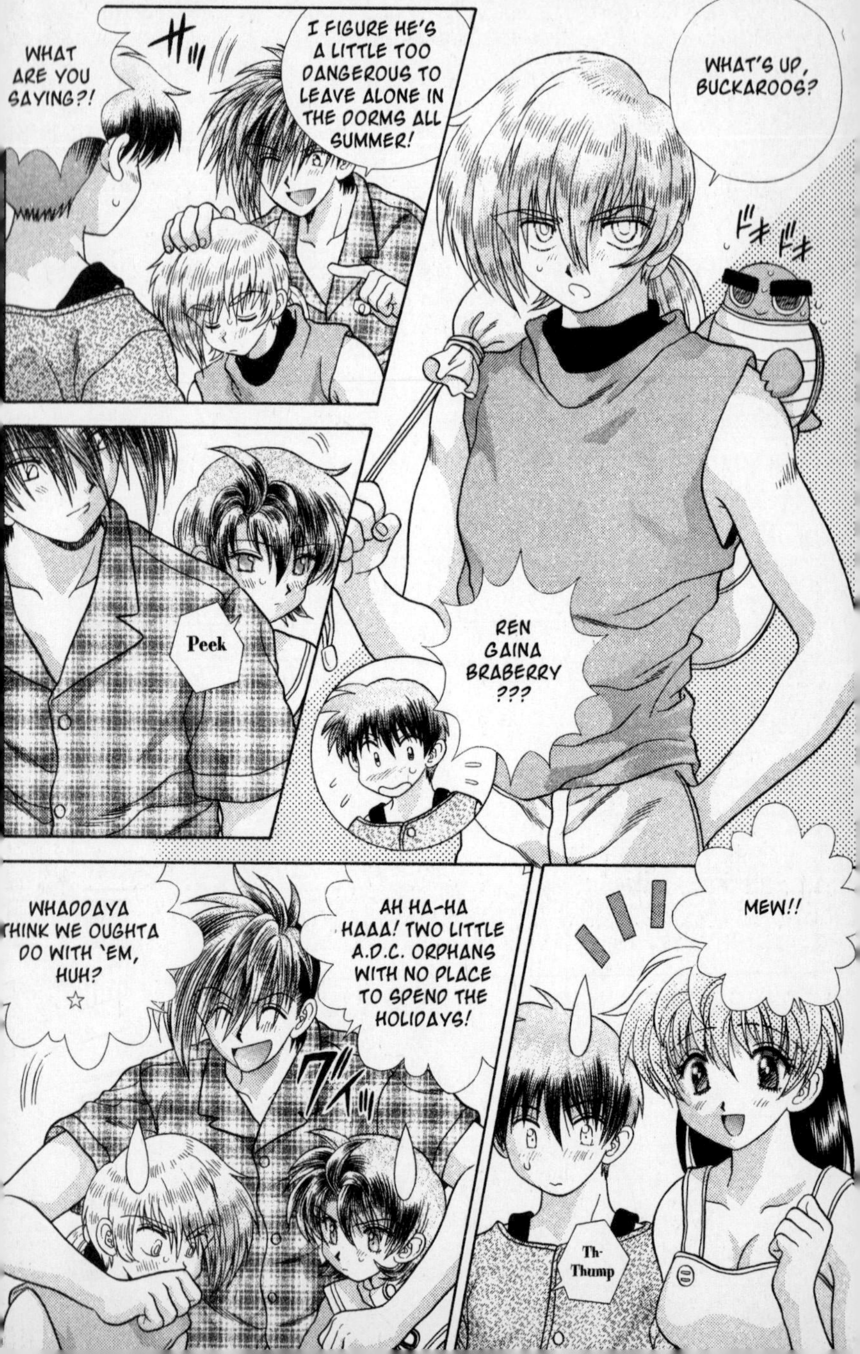
WHAT'S UP, BUCKAROOS?
ドキドキ
REN GAINA BRABERRY ???
I FIGURE HE'S A LITTLE TOO DANGEROUS TO LEAVE ALONE IN THE DORMS ALL SUMMER!
WHAT ARE YOU SAYING?!
Peek
MEW!!
Th-Thump
AH HA-HA HAAA! TWO LITTLE A.D.C. ORPHANS WITH NO PLACE TO SPEND THE HOLIDAYS!
WHADDAYA THINK WE OUGHTA DO WITH 'EM, HUH? ☆

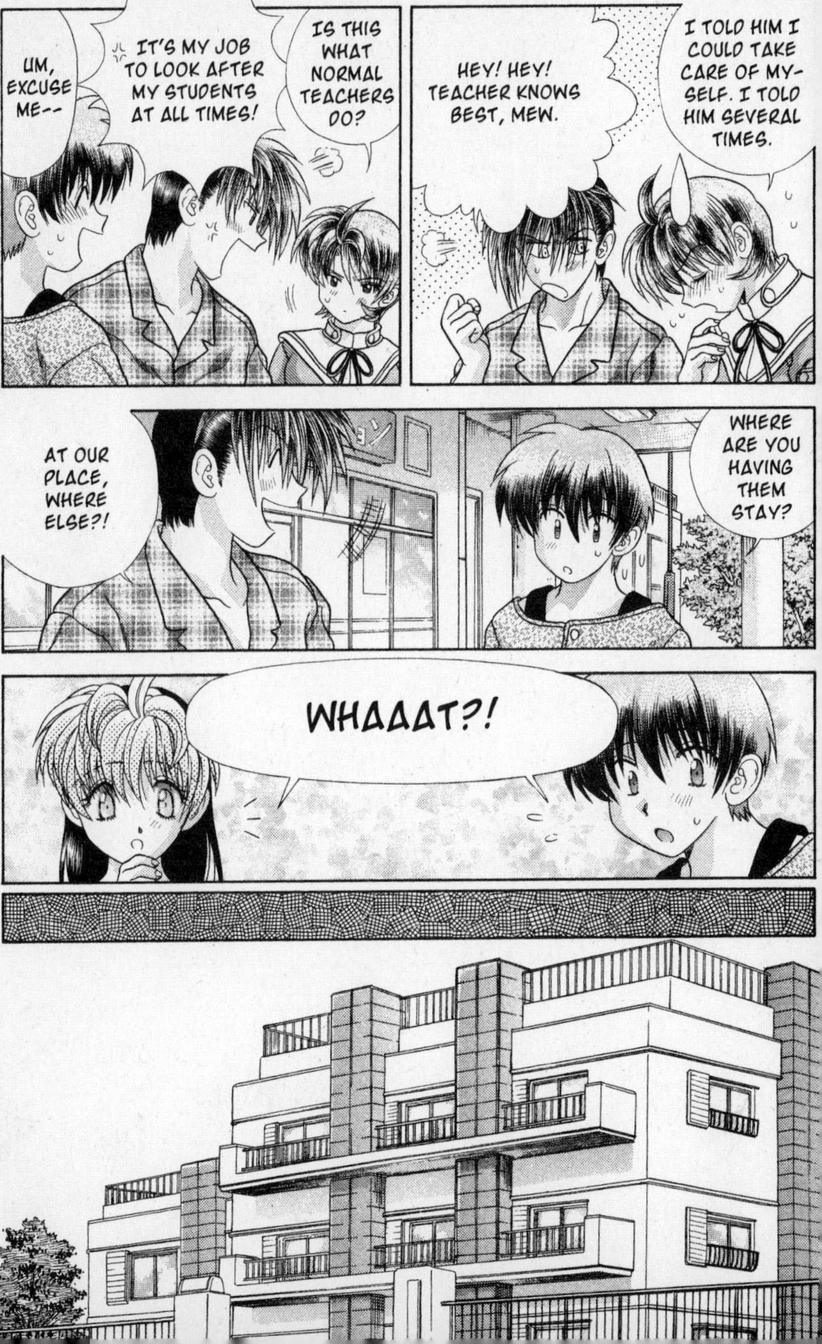
I TOLD HIM I COULD TAKE CARE OF MY-SELF. I TOLD HIM SEVERAL TIMES.
HEY! HEY! TEACHER KNOWS BEST, MEW.
IS THIS WHAT NORMAL TEACHERS DO?
IT'S MY JOB TO LOOK AFTER MY STUDENTS AT ALL TIMES!
UM, EXCUSE ME--
WHERE ARE YOU HAVING THEM STAY?
AT OUR PLACE, WHERE ELSE?!
WHAAAT?!

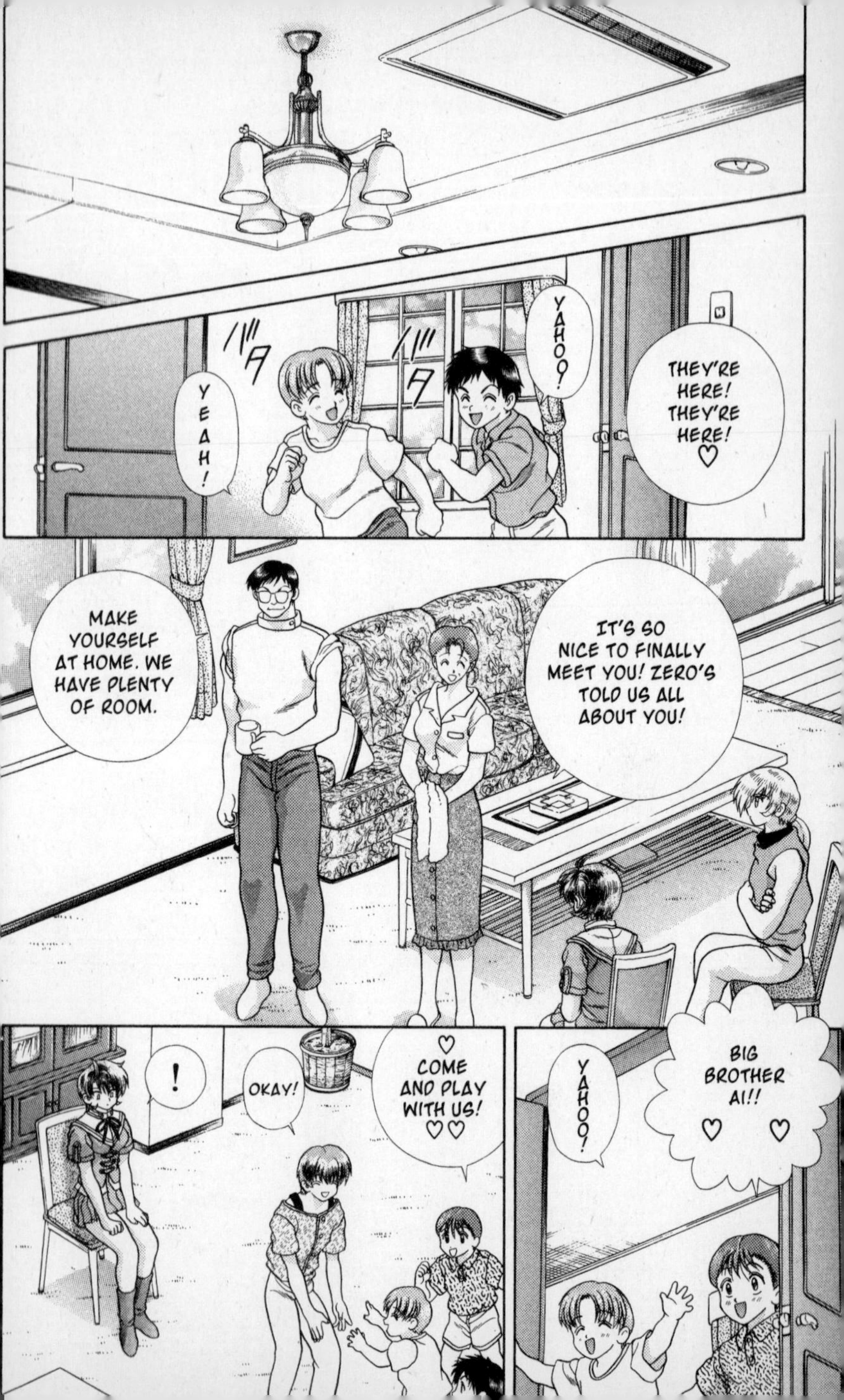
THEY'RE HERE! THEY'RE HERE! ♡
YAHOO!
バタ
YEAH!
バタ
IT'S SO NICE TO FINALLY MEET YOU! ZERO'S TOLD US ALL ABOUT YOU!
MAKE YOURSELF AT HOME. WE HAVE PLENTY OF ROOM.
BIG BROTHER AI!! ♡ ♡
YAHOO!
♡ COME AND PLAY WITH US! ♡♡
OKAY!
!

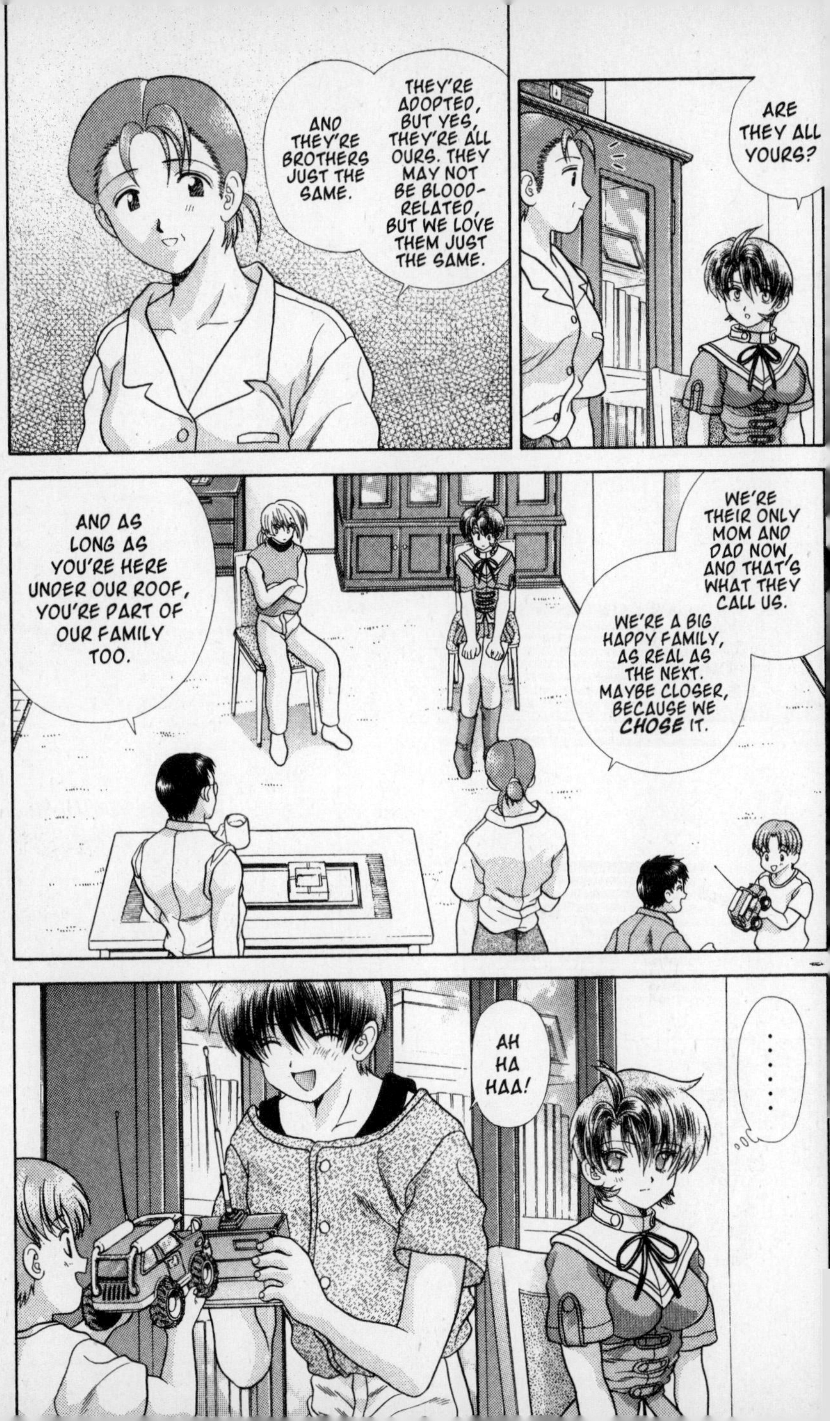
ARE THEY ALL YOURS?
THEY'RE ADOPTED, BUT YES, THEY'RE ALL OURS. THEY MAY NOT BE BLOOD-RELATED, BUT WE LOVE THEM JUST THE SAME.
AND THEY'RE BROTHERS JUST THE SAME.
WE'RE THEIR ONLY MOM AND DAD NOW, AND THAT'S WHAT THEY CALL US.
WE'RE A BIG HAPPY FAMILY, AS REAL AS THE NEXT. MAYBE CLOSER, BECAUSE WE *CHOSE* IT.
AND AS LONG AS YOU'RE HERE UNDER OUR ROOF, YOU'RE PART OF OUR FAMILY TOO.
......
AH HA HAA!

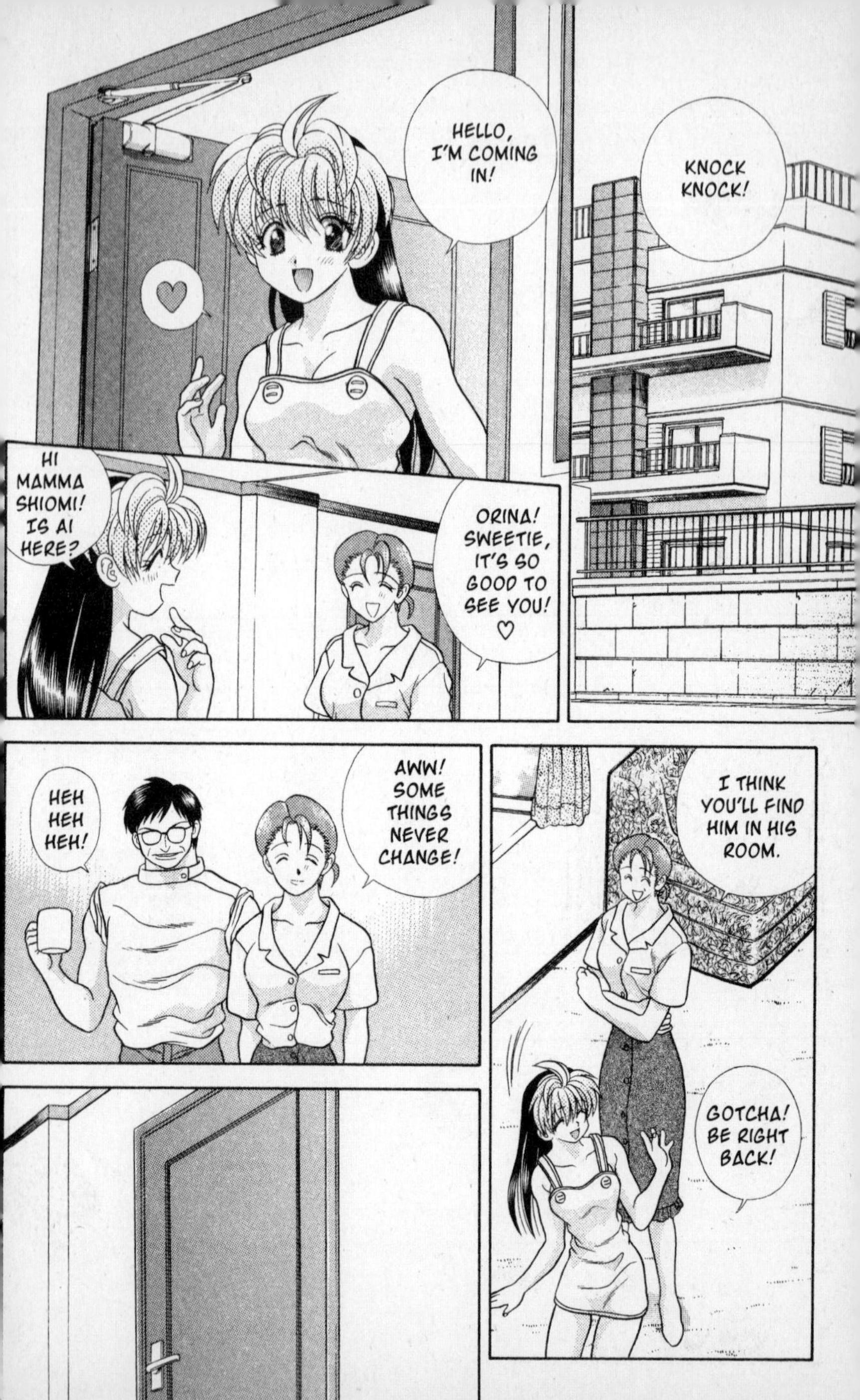
KNOCK KNOCK!
HELLO, I'M COMING IN!
♡
ORINA! SWEETIE, IT'S SO GOOD TO SEE YOU! ♡
HI MAMMA SHIOMI! IS AI HERE?
I THINK YOU'LL FIND HIM IN HIS ROOM.
GOTCHA! BE RIGHT BACK!
AWW! SOME THINGS NEVER CHANGE!
HEH HEH HEH!

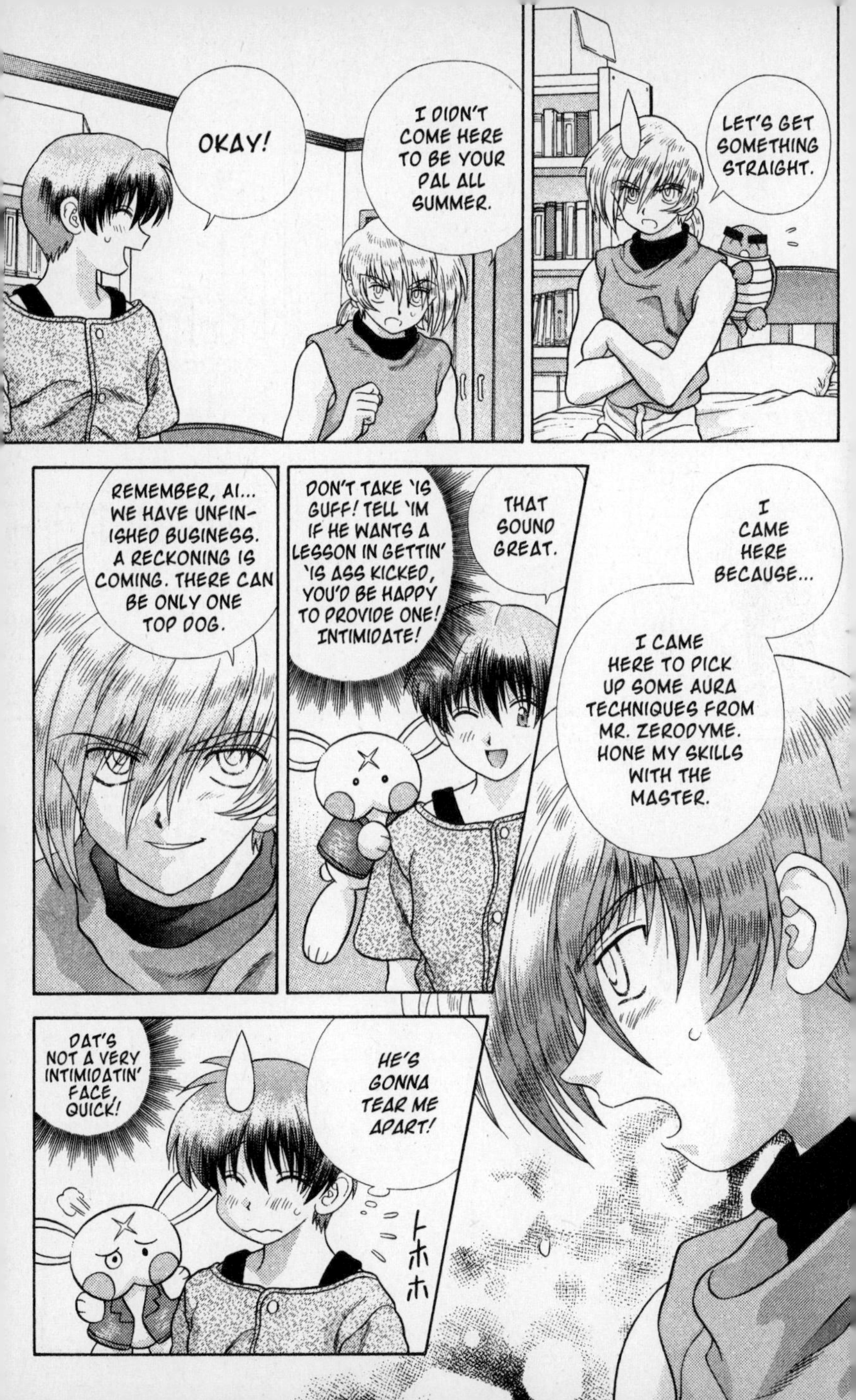

LET'S GET SOMETHING STRAIGHT.
I DIDN'T COME HERE TO BE YOUR PAL ALL SUMMER.
OKAY!
I CAME HERE BECAUSE...
I CAME HERE TO PICK UP SOME AURA TECHNIQUES FROM MR. ZERODYME. HONE MY SKILLS WITH THE MASTER.
THAT SOUND GREAT.
DON'T TAKE 'IS GUFF! TELL 'IM IF HE WANTS A LESSON IN GETTIN' 'IS ASS KICKED, YOU'D BE HAPPY TO PROVIDE ONE! INTIMIDATE!
REMEMBER, AI... WE HAVE UNFIN-ISHED BUSINESS. A RECKONING IS COMING. THERE CAN BE ONLY ONE TOP DOG.
HE'S GONNA TEAR ME APART!
DAT'S NOT A VERY INTIMIDATIN' FACE. QUICK!
トホホ

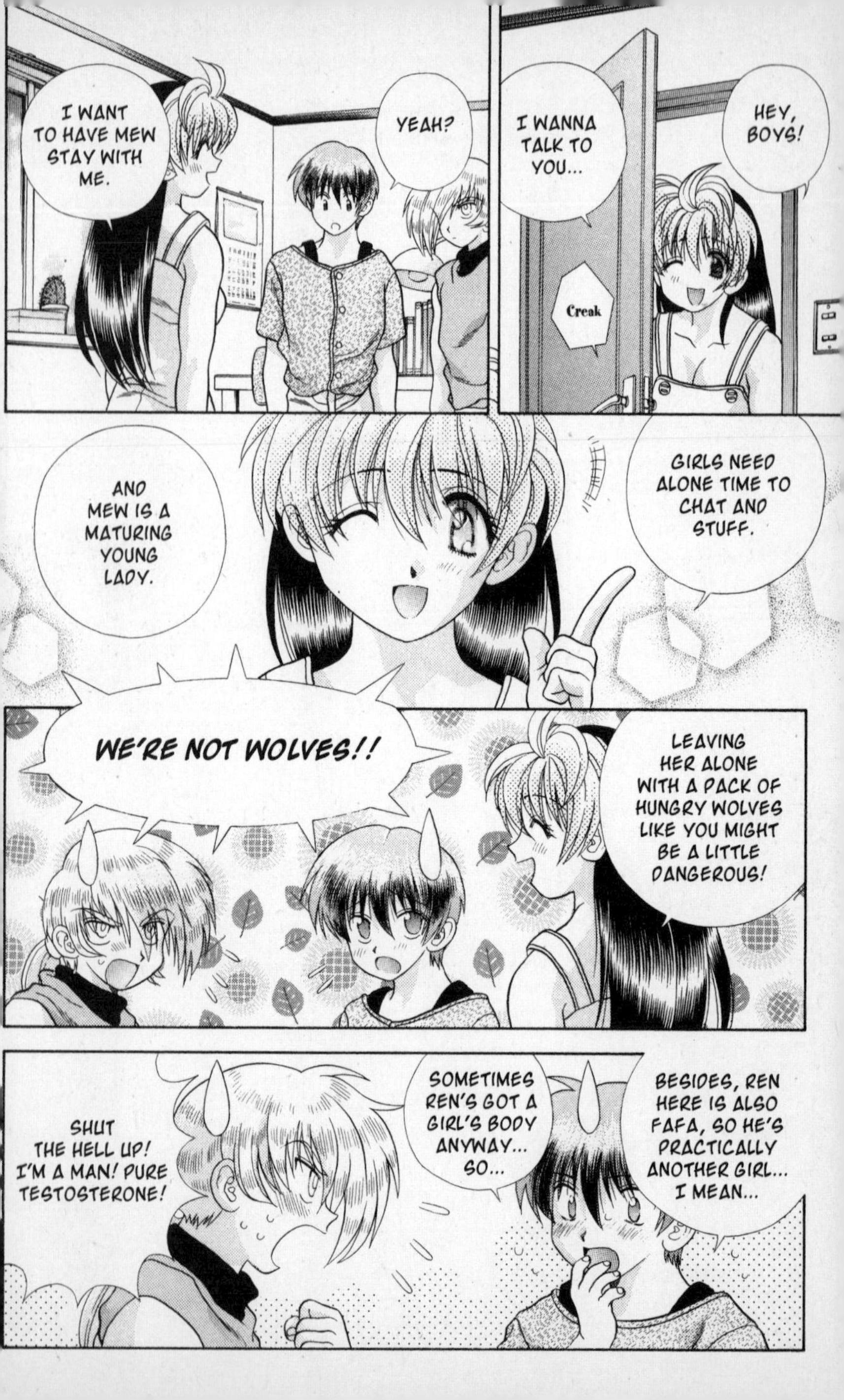
HEY, BOYS!
I WANNA TALK TO YOU...
Creak
YEAH?
I WANT TO HAVE MEW STAY WITH ME.
GIRLS NEED ALONE TIME TO CHAT AND STUFF.
AND MEW IS A MATURING YOUNG LADY.
LEAVING HER ALONE WITH A PACK OF HUNGRY WOLVES LIKE YOU MIGHT BE A LITTLE DANGEROUS!
WE'RE NOT WOLVES!!
BESIDES, REN HERE IS ALSO FAFA, SO HE'S PRACTICALLY ANOTHER GIRL... I MEAN...
SOMETIMES REN'S GOT A GIRL'S BODY ANYWAY... SO...
SHUT THE HELL UP! I'M A MAN! PURE TESTOSTERONE!

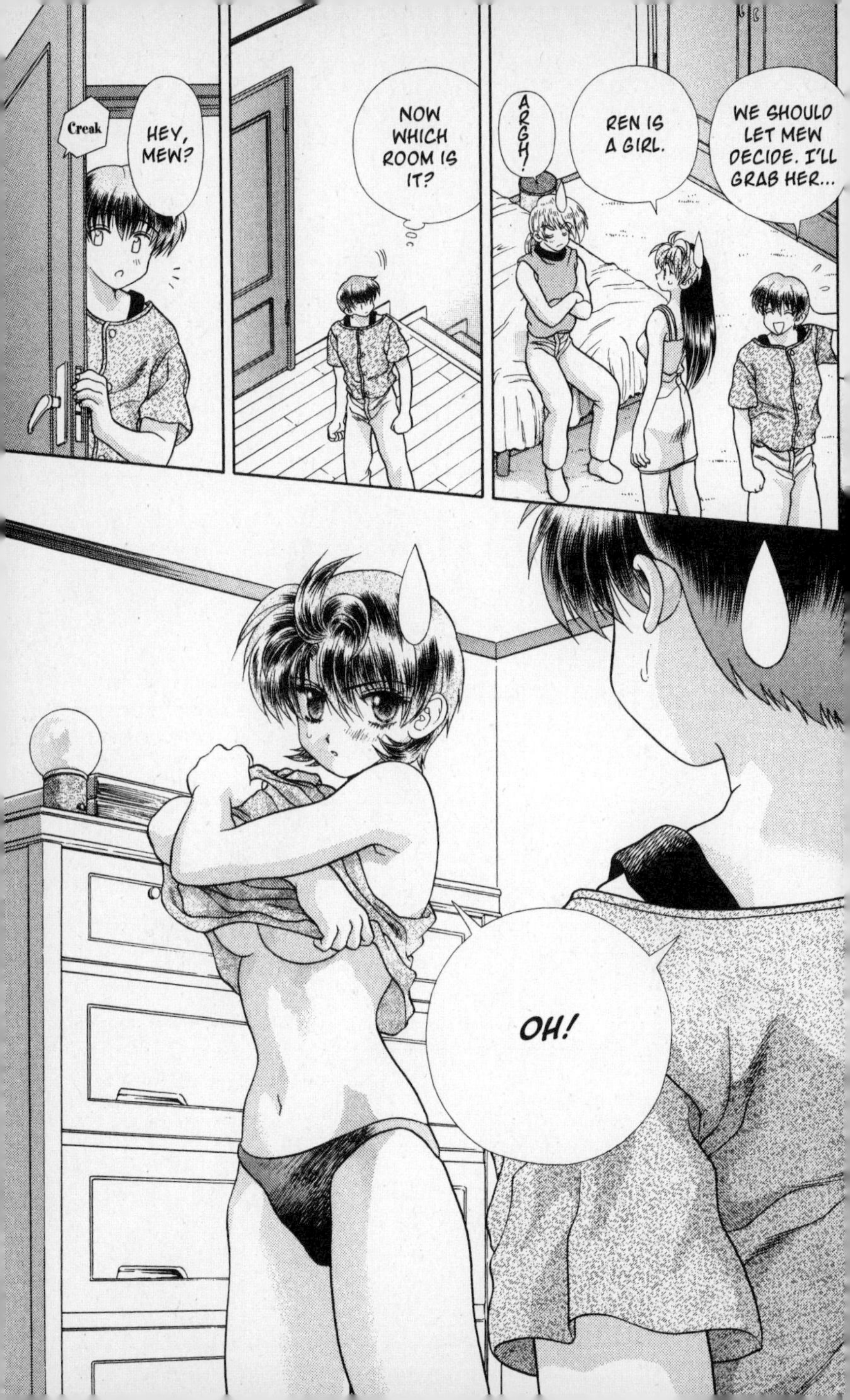
WE SHOULD LET MEW DECIDE. I'LL GRAB HER...
REN IS A GIRL.
ARGH!
NOW WHICH ROOM IS IT?
Creak
HEY, MEW?
OH!

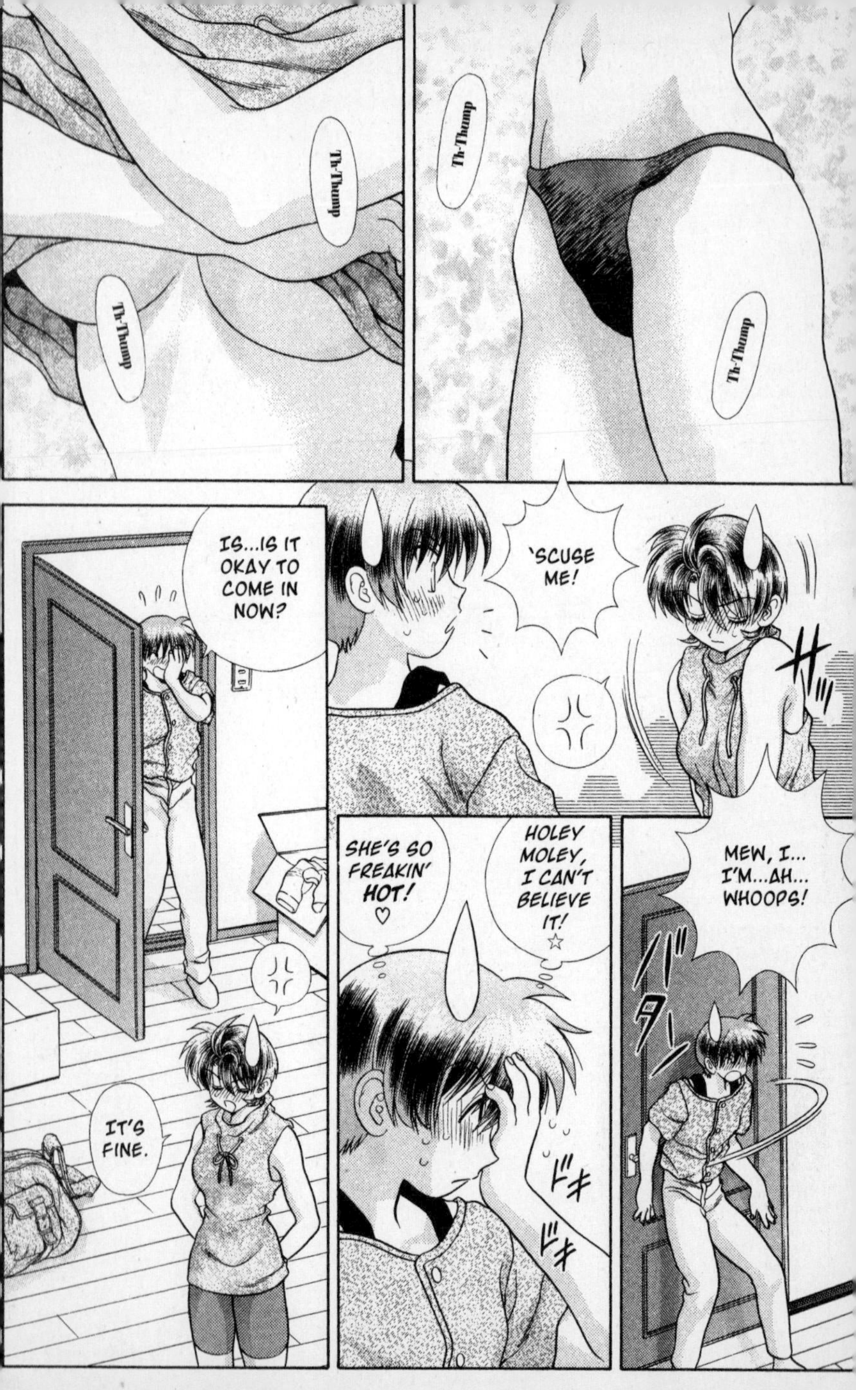
Th-Thump
Th-Thump
Th-Thump
Th-Thump
'SCUSE ME!
MEW, I... I'M...AH... WHOOPS!
バタン
HOLEY MOLEY, I CAN'T BELIEVE IT! ☆
SHE'S SO FREAKIN' HOT! ♡
ドキ
ドキ
IS...IS IT OKAY TO COME IN NOW?
IT'S FINE.

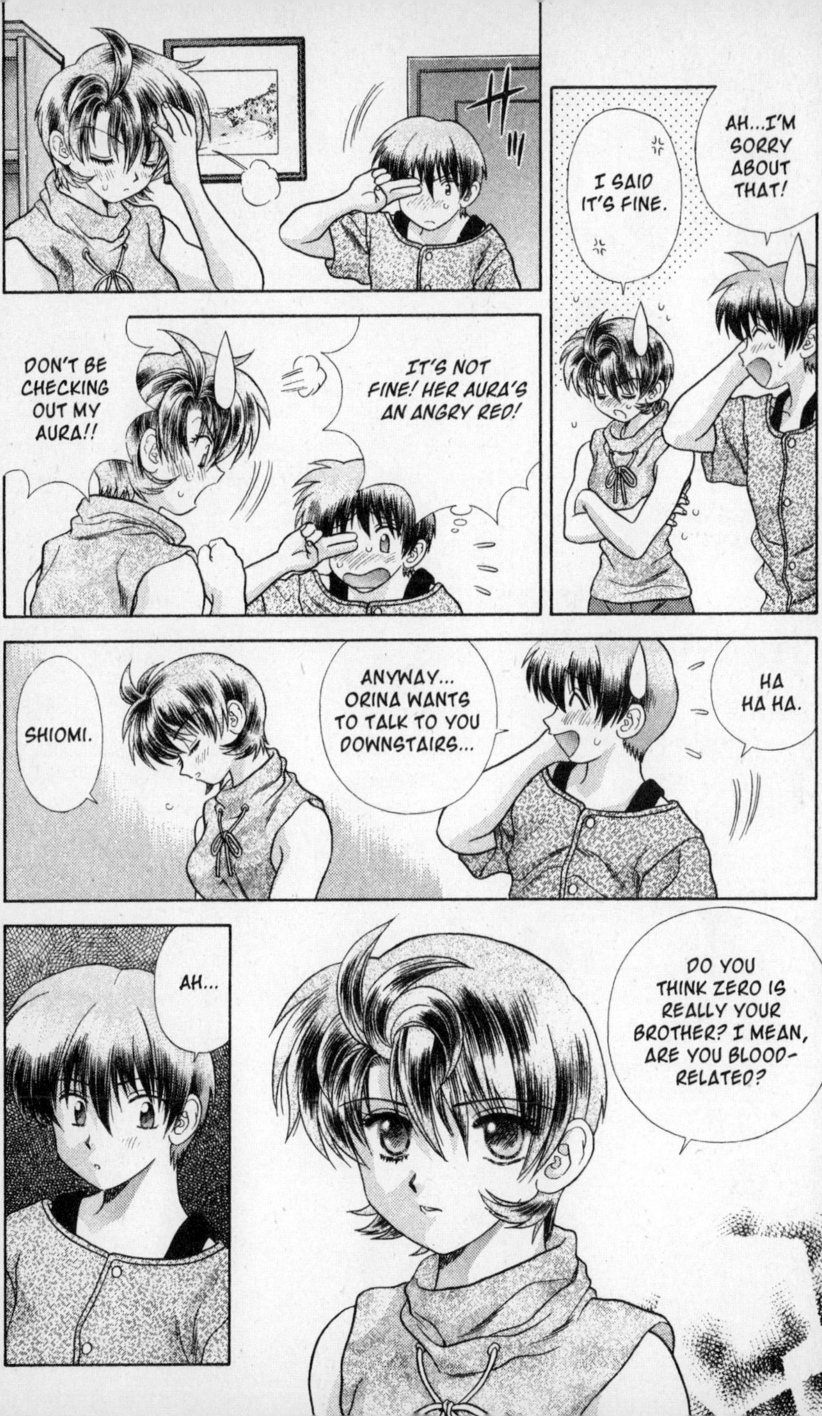
AH...I'M SORRY ABOUT THAT!
I SAID IT'S FINE.
IT'S NOT FINE! HER AURA'S AN ANGRY RED!
DON'T BE CHECKING OUT MY AURA!!
HA HA HA.
ANYWAY... ORINA WANTS TO TALK TO YOU DOWNSTAIRS...
SHIOMI.
DO YOU THINK ZERO IS REALLY YOUR BROTHER? I MEAN, ARE YOU BLOOD-RELATED?
AH...

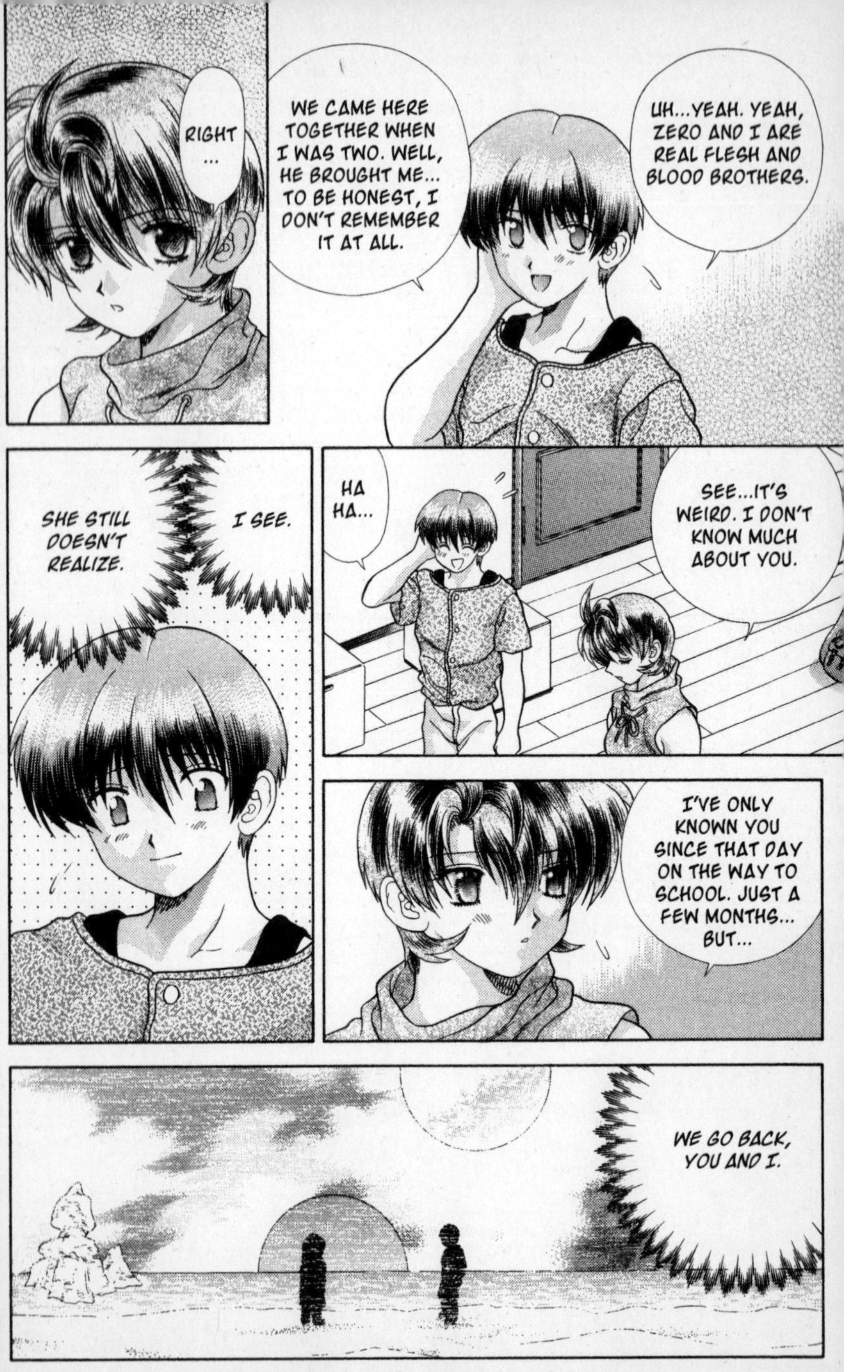
UH...YEAH. YEAH, ZERO AND I ARE REAL FLESH AND BLOOD BROTHERS.
WE CAME HERE TOGETHER WHEN I WAS TWO. WELL, HE BROUGHT ME... TO BE HONEST, I DON'T REMEMBER IT AT ALL.
RIGHT ...
SEE...IT'S WEIRD. I DON'T KNOW MUCH ABOUT YOU.
HA HA...
I'VE ONLY KNOWN YOU SINCE THAT DAY ON THE WAY TO SCHOOL. JUST A FEW MONTHS... BUT...
I SEE.
SHE STILL DOESN'T REALIZE.
WE GO BACK, YOU AND I.

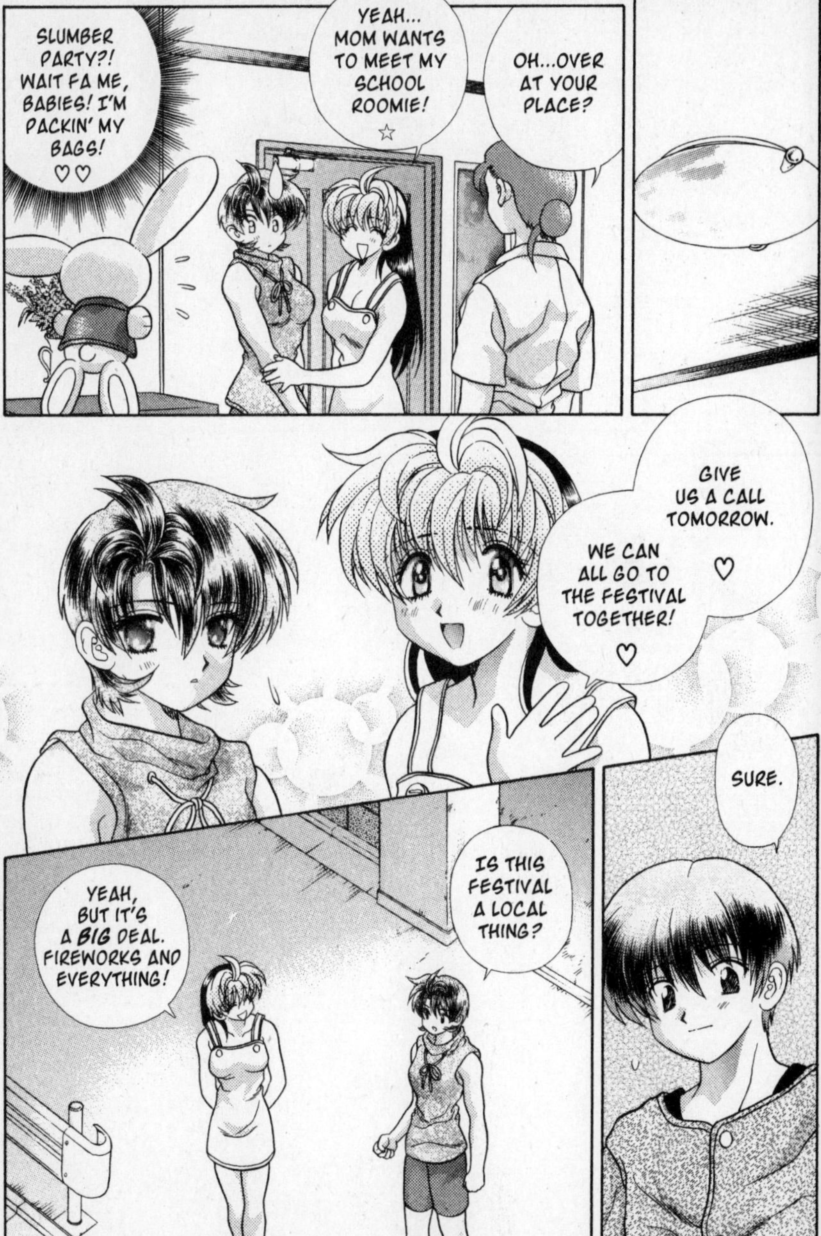
OH...OVER AT YOUR PLACE?
YEAH... MOM WANTS TO MEET MY SCHOOL ROOMIE! ☆
SLUMBER PARTY?! WAIT FA ME, BABIES! I'M PACKIN' MY BAGS! ♡♡
GIVE US A CALL TOMORROW. ♡
WE CAN ALL GO TO THE FESTIVAL TOGETHER! ♡
SURE.
IS THIS FESTIVAL A LOCAL THING?
YEAH, BUT IT'S A *BIG* DEAL. FIREWORKS AND EVERYTHING!

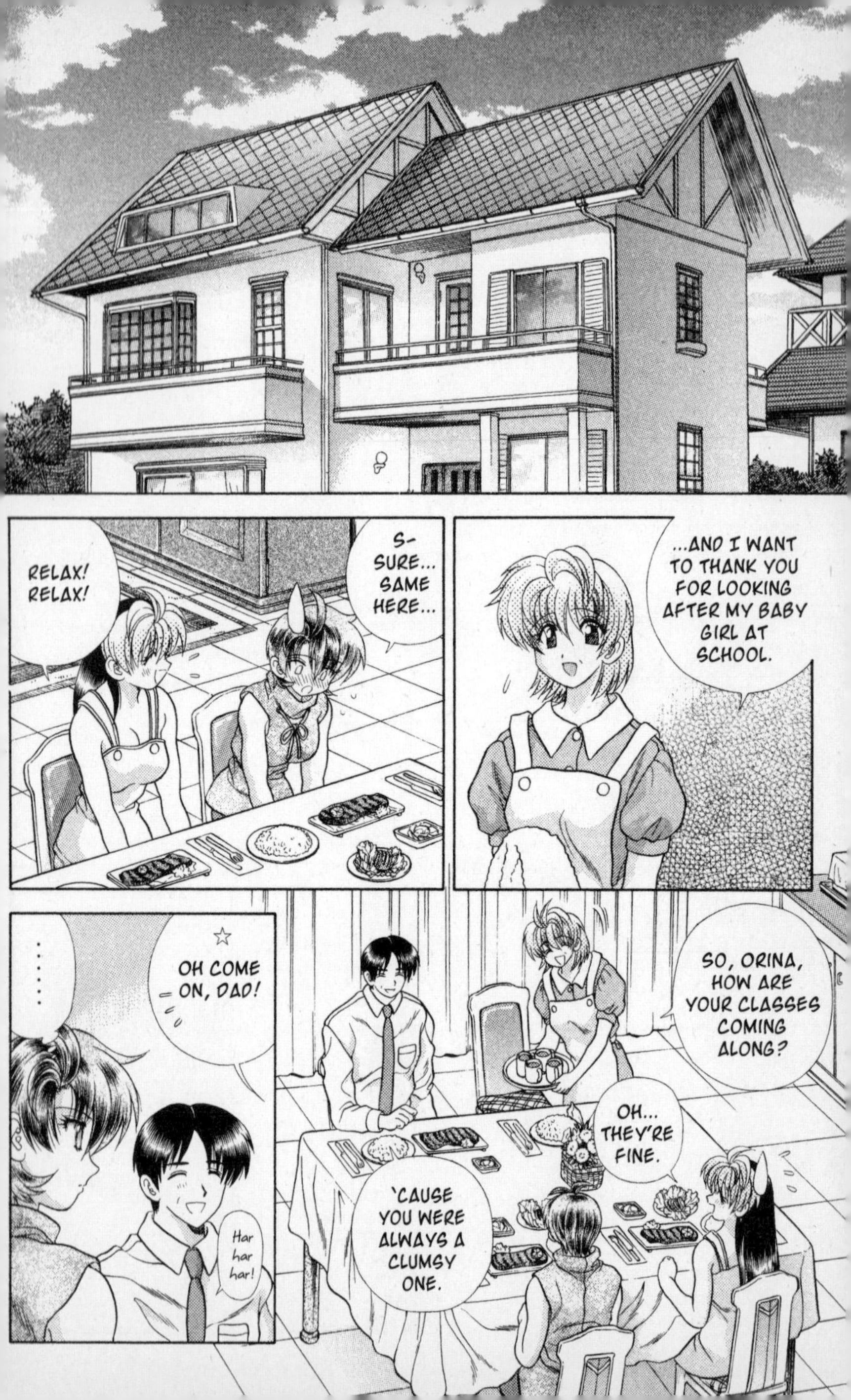
...AND I WANT TO THANK YOU FOR LOOKING AFTER MY BABY GIRL AT SCHOOL.
S-SURE... SAME HERE...
RELAX! RELAX!
SO, ORINA, HOW ARE YOUR CLASSES COMING ALONG?
OH... THEY'RE FINE.
'CAUSE YOU WERE ALWAYS A CLUMSY ONE.
OH COME ON, DAD!
......
Har har har!

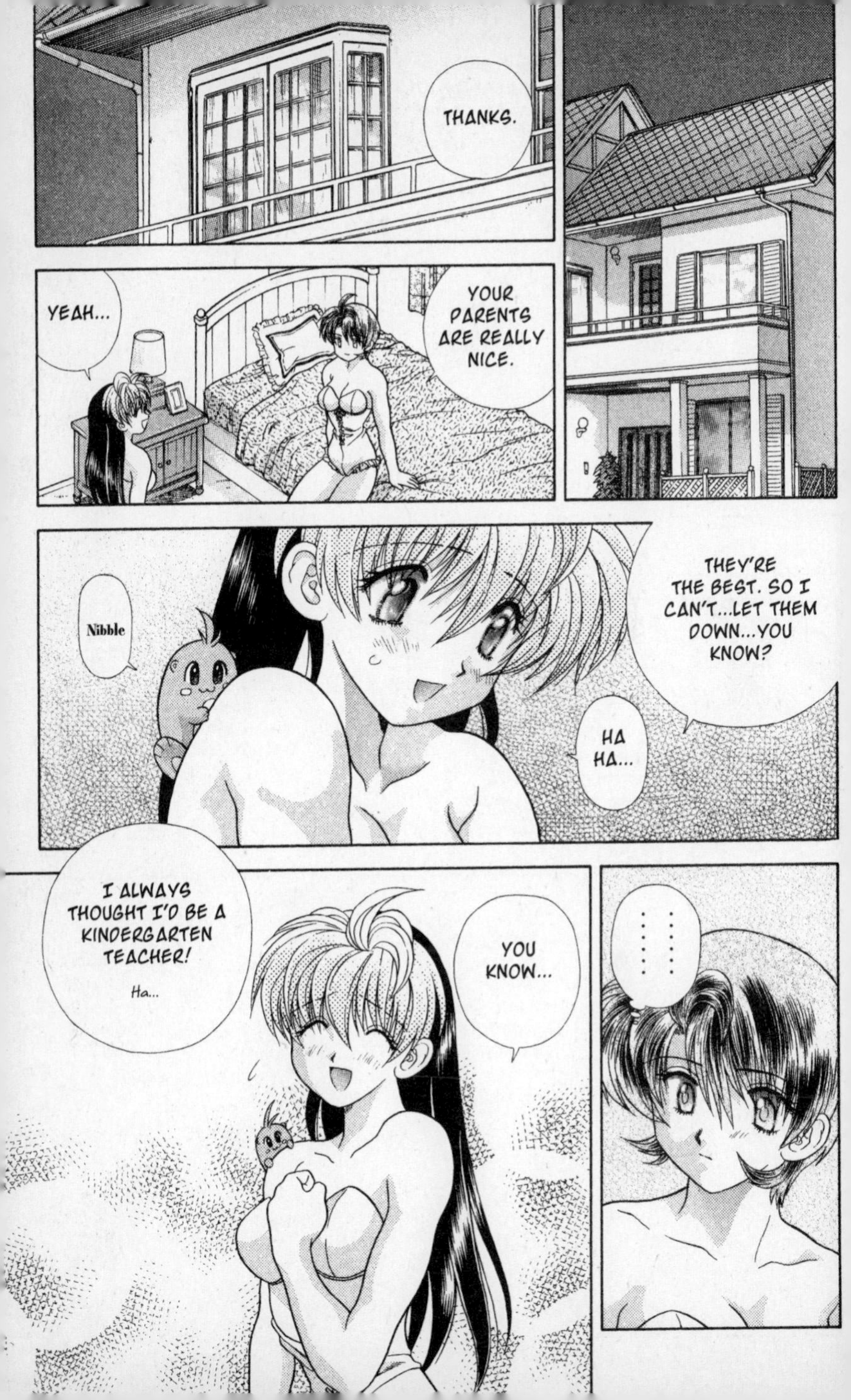
THANKS.
YOUR PARENTS ARE REALLY NICE.
YEAH...
THEY'RE THE BEST. SO I CAN'T...LET THEM DOWN...YOU KNOW?
HA HA...
Nibble
......
YOU KNOW...
I ALWAYS THOUGHT I'D BE A KINDERGARTEN TEACHER!
Ha...

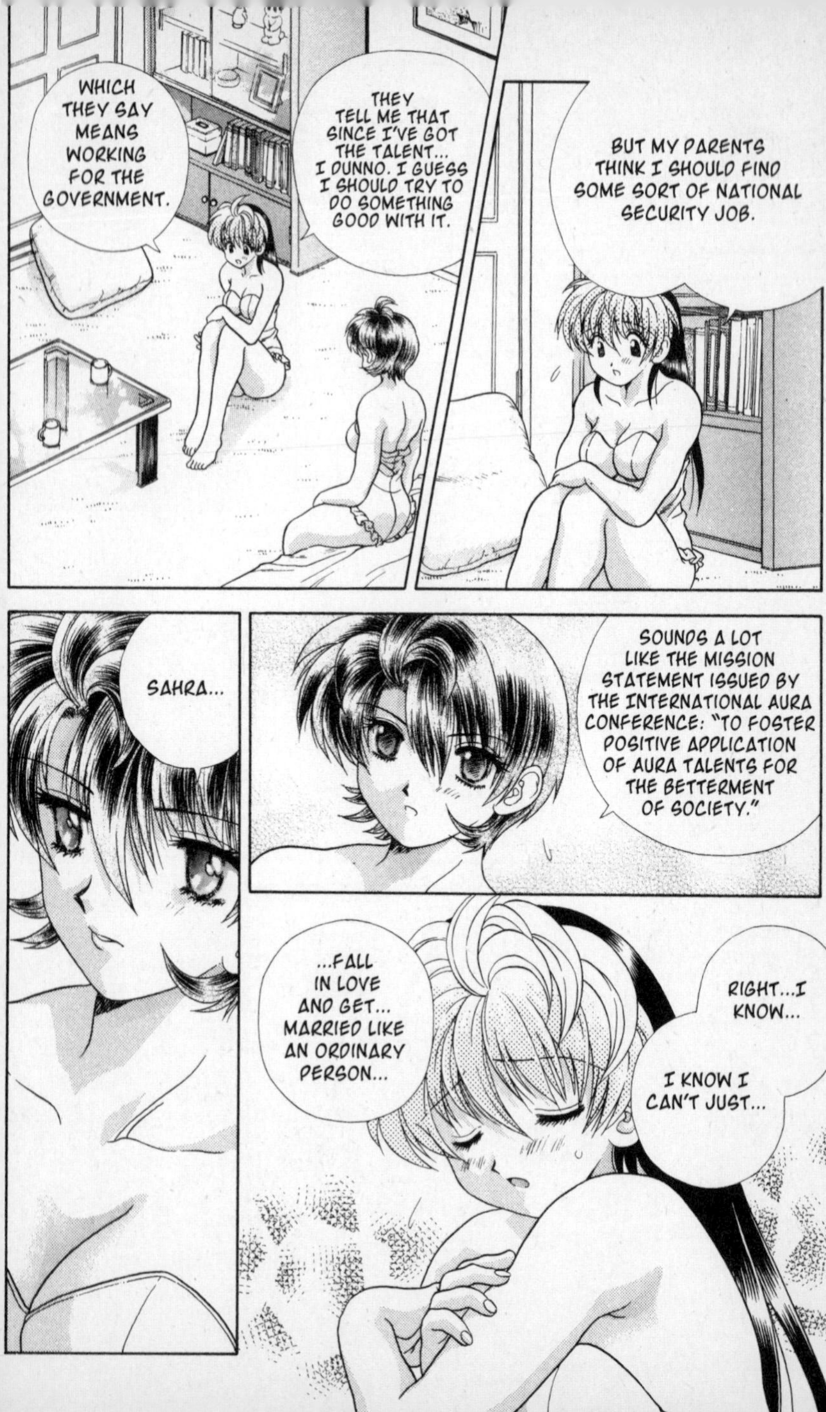
BUT MY PARENTS THINK I SHOULD FIND SOME SORT OF NATIONAL SECURITY JOB.
THEY TELL ME THAT SINCE I'VE GOT THE TALENT... I DUNNO. I GUESS I SHOULD TRY TO DO SOMETHING GOOD WITH IT.
WHICH THEY SAY MEANS WORKING FOR THE GOVERNMENT.
SOUNDS A LOT LIKE THE MISSION STATEMENT ISSUED BY THE INTERNATIONAL AURA CONFERENCE: "TO FOSTER POSITIVE APPLICATION OF AURA TALENTS FOR THE BETTERMENT OF SOCIETY."
RIGHT...I KNOW...
I KNOW I CAN'T JUST...
...FALL IN LOVE AND GET... MARRIED LIKE AN ORDINARY PERSON...
SAHRA...

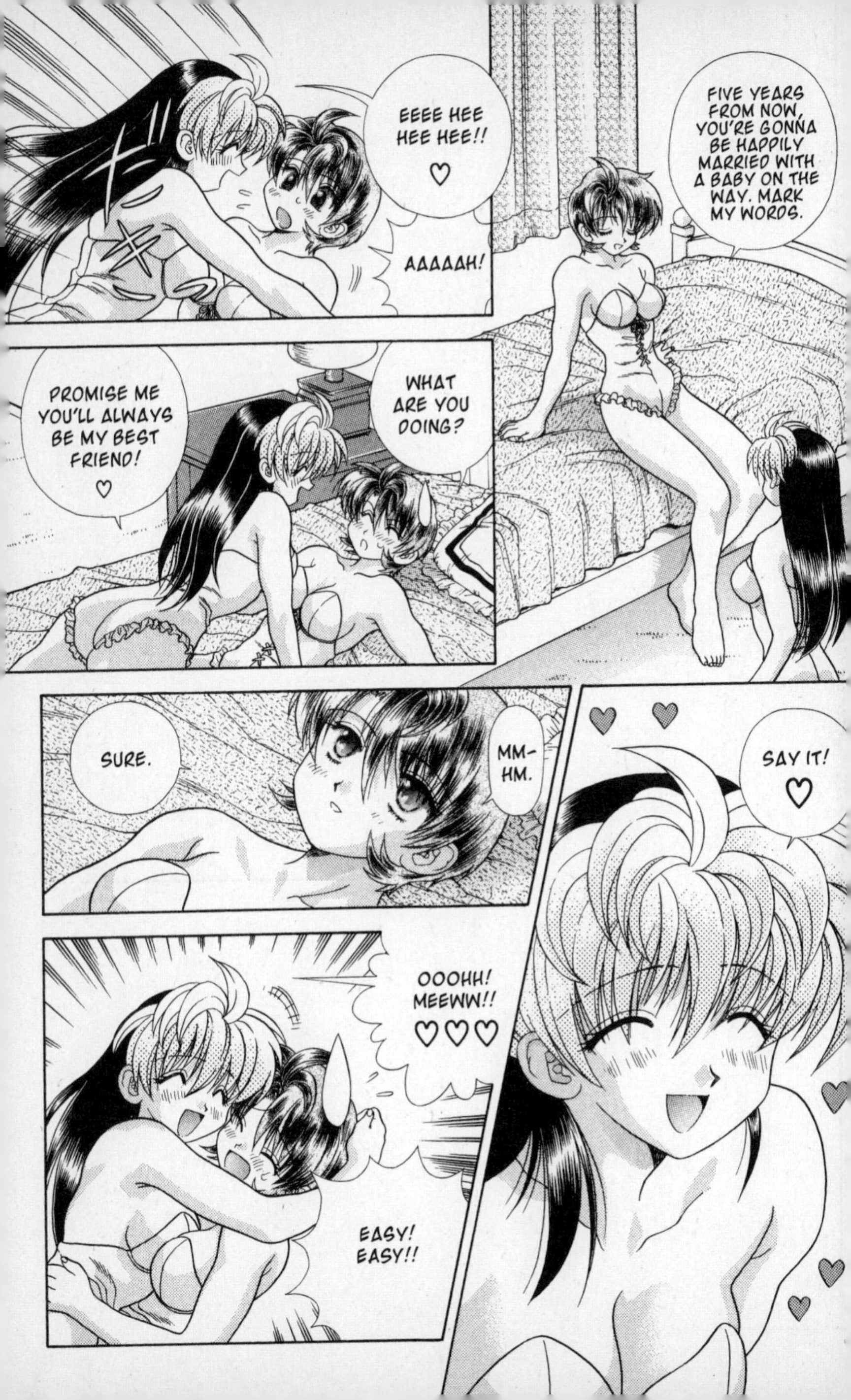
FIVE YEARS FROM NOW, YOU'RE GONNA BE HAPPILY MARRIED WITH A BABY ON THE WAY. MARK MY WORDS.
EEEE HEE HEE HEE!! ♡
AAAAAH!
WHAT ARE YOU DOING?
PROMISE ME YOU'LL ALWAYS BE MY BEST FRIEND! ♡
SAY IT! ♡
MM-HM.
SURE.
OOOHH! MEEWW!! ♡♡♡
EASY! EASY!!

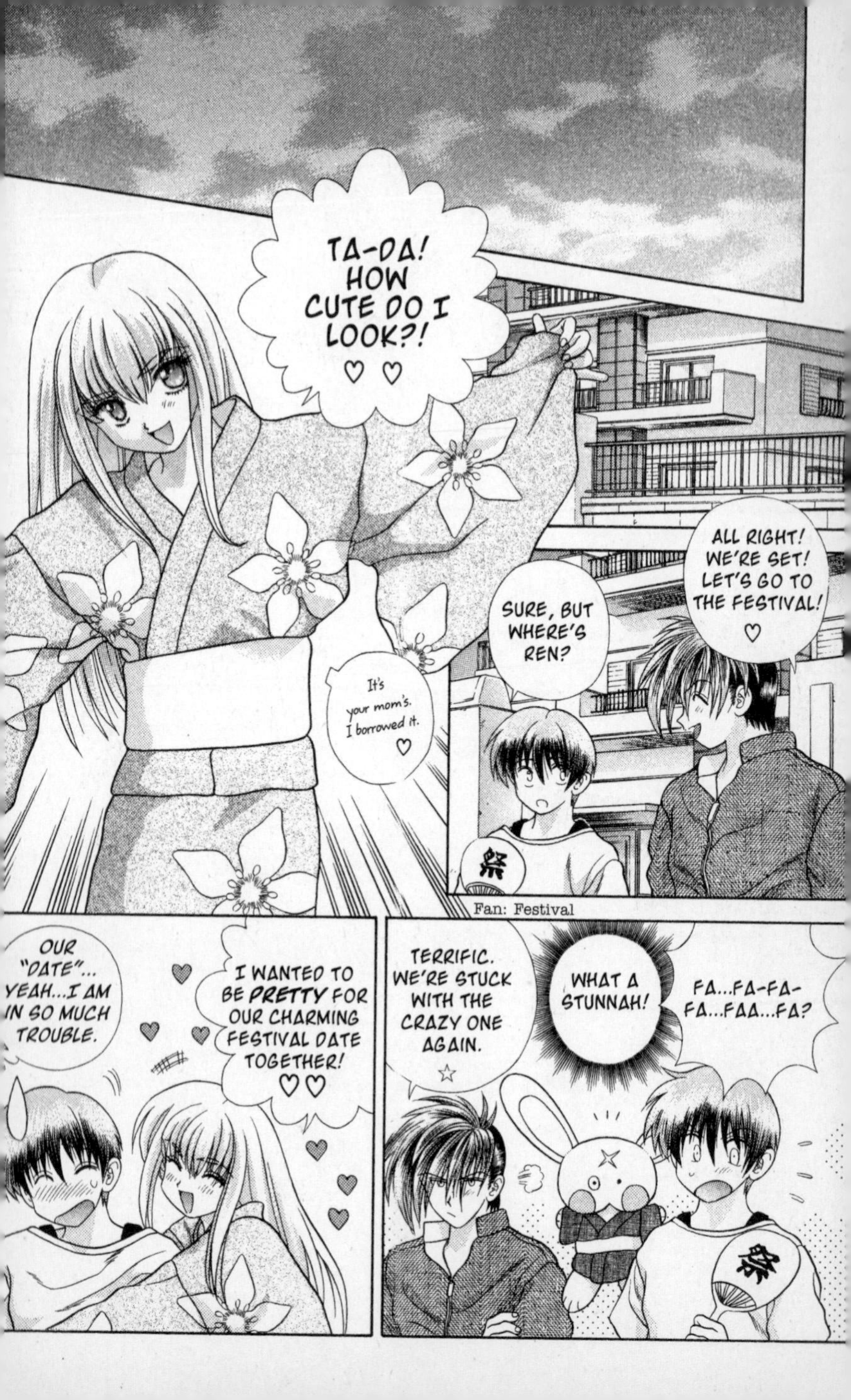
ALL RIGHT! WE'RE SET! LET'S GO TO THE FESTIVAL! ♡
SURE, BUT WHERE'S REN?
TA-DA! HOW CUTE DO I LOOK?! ♡ ♡
It's your mom's. I borrowed it. ♡
FA...FA-FA-FA...FAA...FA?
WHAT A STUNNAH!
TERRIFIC. WE'RE STUCK WITH THE CRAZY ONE AGAIN. ☆
I WANTED TO BE **PRETTY** FOR OUR CHARMING FESTIVAL DATE TOGETHER! ♡♡
OUR "DATE"... YEAH...I AM IN SO MUCH TROUBLE.
Fan: Festival

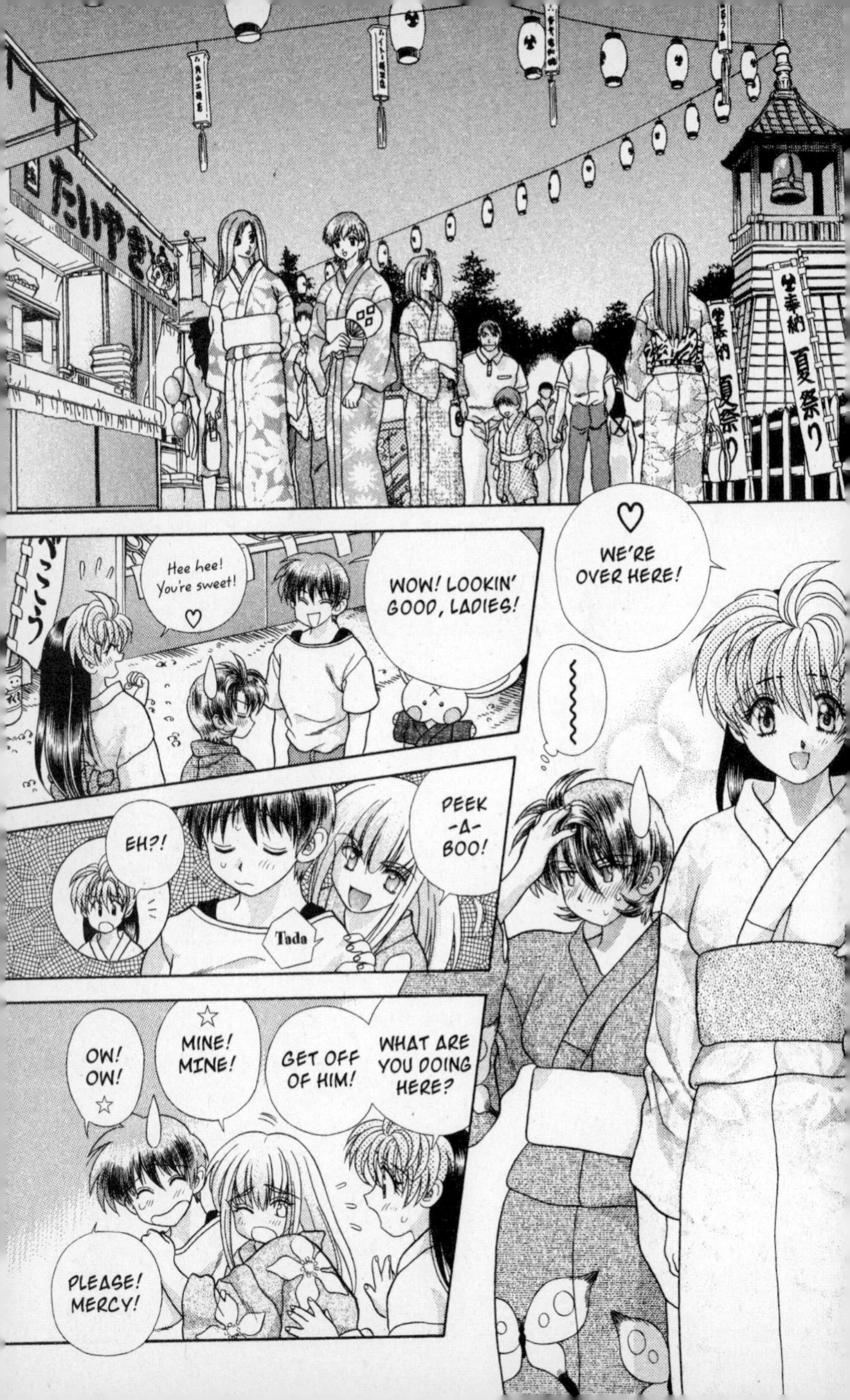

たいやき
WE'RE OVER HERE!
WOW! LOOKIN' GOOD, LADIES!
Hee hee! You're sweet!
PEEK -A- BOO!
Tada
EH?!
WHAT ARE YOU DOING HERE?
GET OFF OF HIM!
MINE! MINE!
OW! OW!
PLEASE! MERCY!

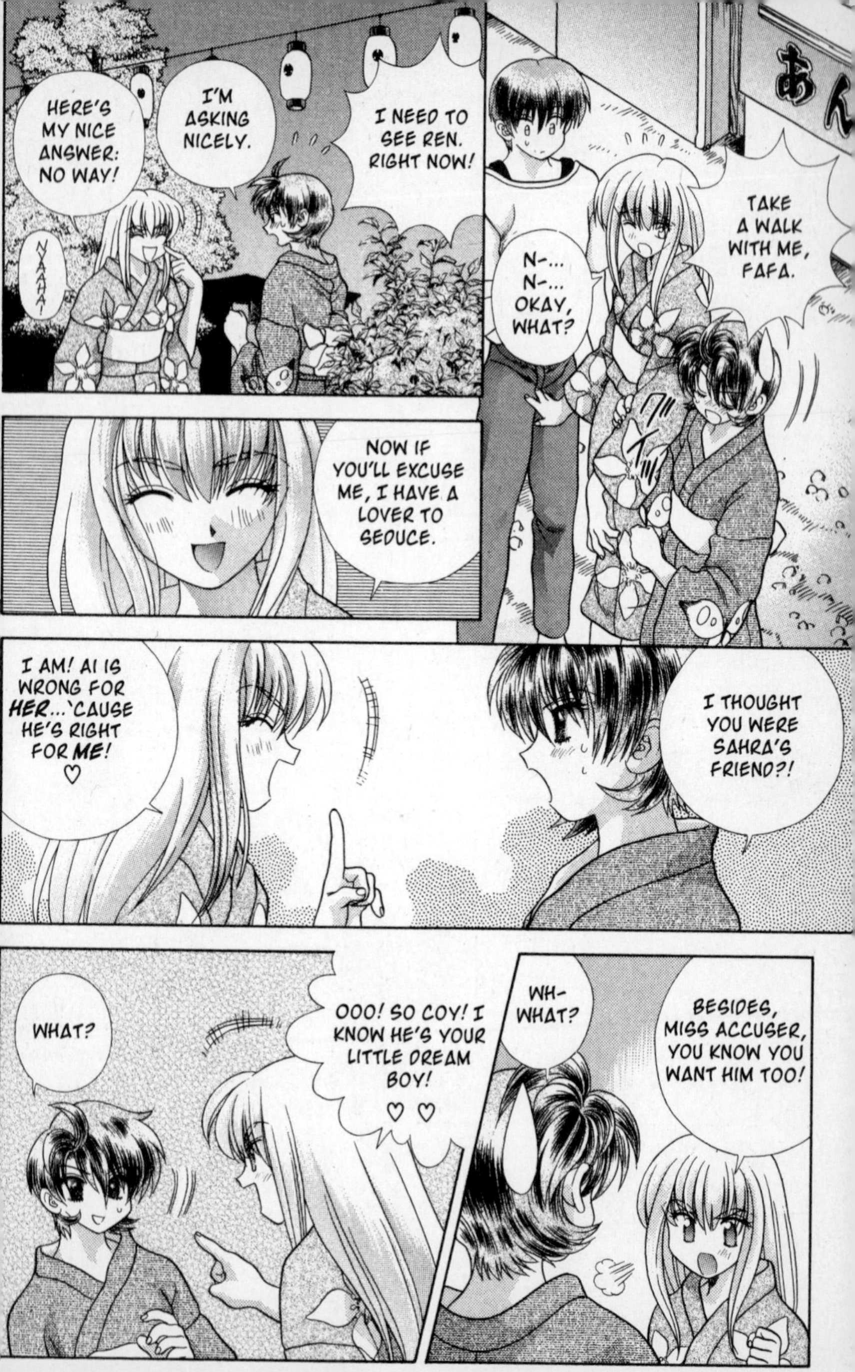
TAKE A WALK WITH ME, FAFA.
N-... N-... OKAY, WHAT?
I NEED TO SEE REN. RIGHT NOW!
I'M ASKING NICELY.
HERE'S MY NICE ANSWER: NO WAY!
NYAAHA!
NOW IF YOU'LL EXCUSE ME, I HAVE A LOVER TO SEDUCE.
I THOUGHT YOU WERE SAHRA'S FRIEND?!
I AM! AI IS WRONG FOR **HER**...'CAUSE HE'S RIGHT FOR **ME**! ♡
BESIDES, MISS ACCUSER, YOU KNOW YOU WANT HIM TOO!
WH-WHAT?
OOO! SO COY! I KNOW HE'S YOUR LITTLE DREAM BOY! ♡ ♡
WHAT?

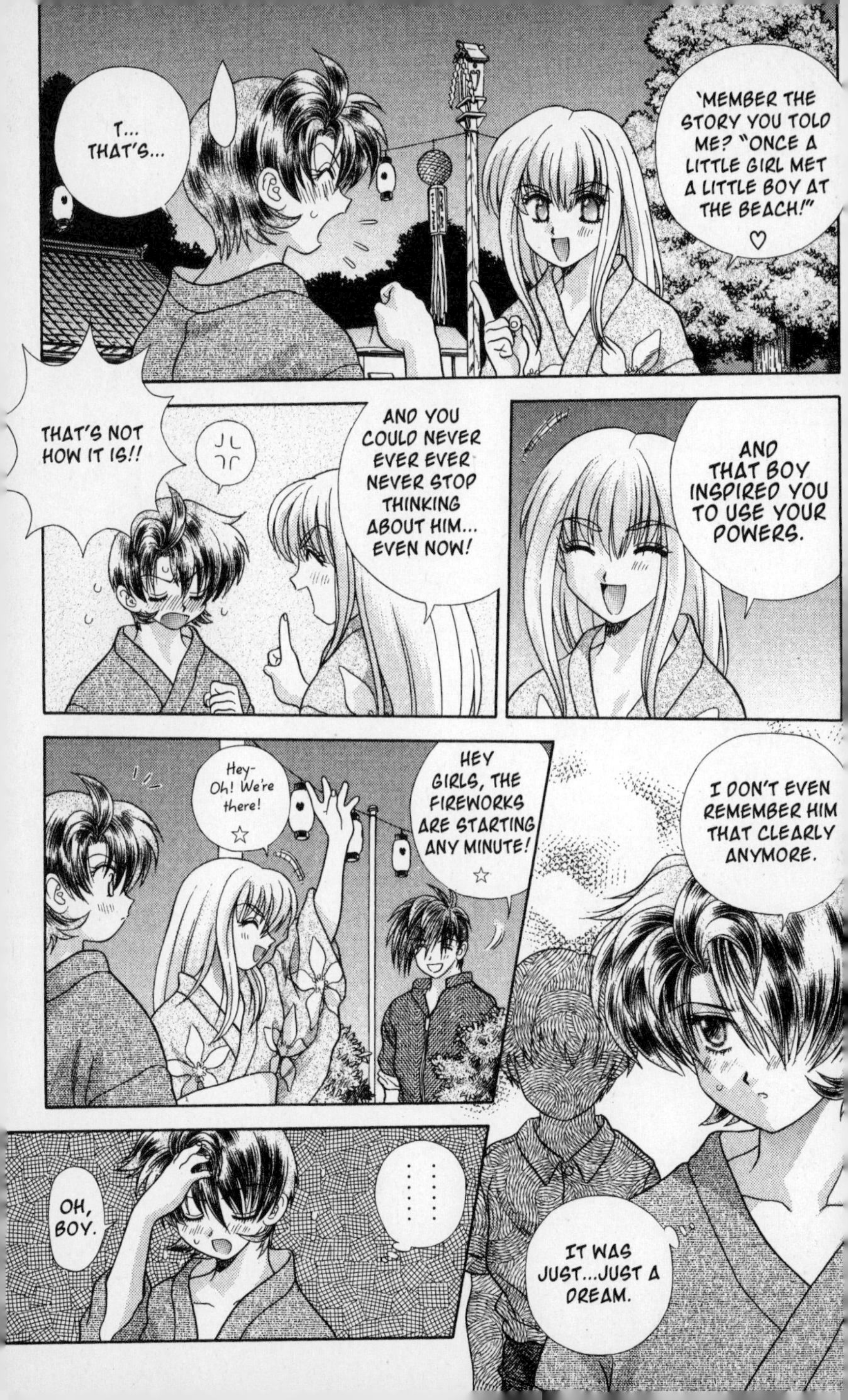
'MEMBER THE STORY YOU TOLD ME? "ONCE A LITTLE GIRL MET A LITTLE BOY AT THE BEACH!" ♡
T... THAT'S...
AND THAT BOY INSPIRED YOU TO USE YOUR POWERS.
AND YOU COULD NEVER EVER EVER NEVER STOP THINKING ABOUT HIM... EVEN NOW!
THAT'S NOT HOW IT IS!!
I DON'T EVEN REMEMBER HIM THAT CLEARLY ANYMORE.
IT WAS JUST...JUST A DREAM.
HEY GIRLS, THE FIREWORKS ARE STARTING ANY MINUTE! ☆
Hey- Oh! We're there! ☆
......
OH, BOY.

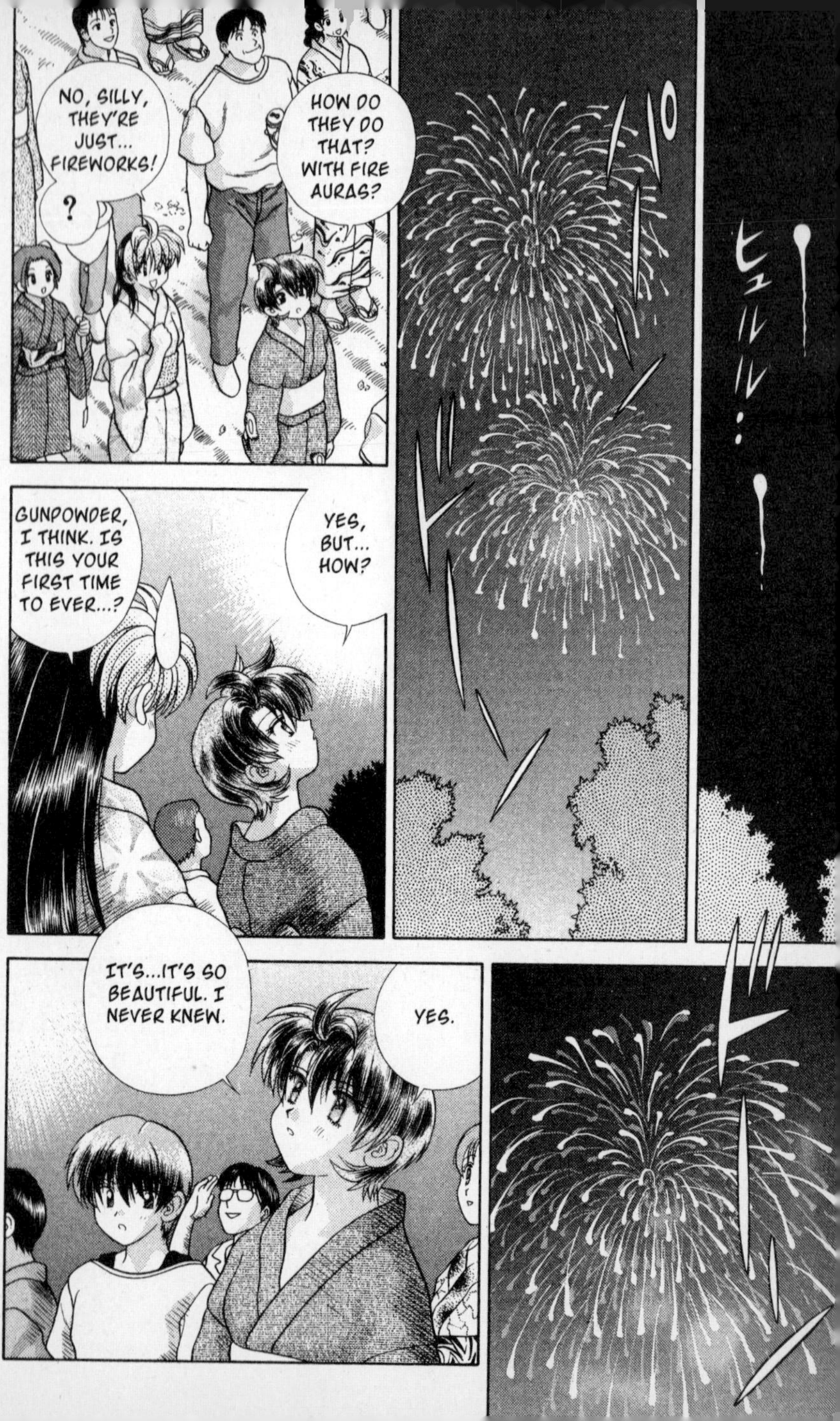
ヒュルル…
パ
HOW DO THEY DO THAT? WITH FIRE AURAS?
NO, SILLY, THEY'RE JUST... FIREWORKS!
?
YES, BUT... HOW?
GUNPOWDER, I THINK. IS THIS YOUR FIRST TIME TO EVER...?
YES.
IT'S...IT'S SO BEAUTIFUL. I NEVER KNEW.

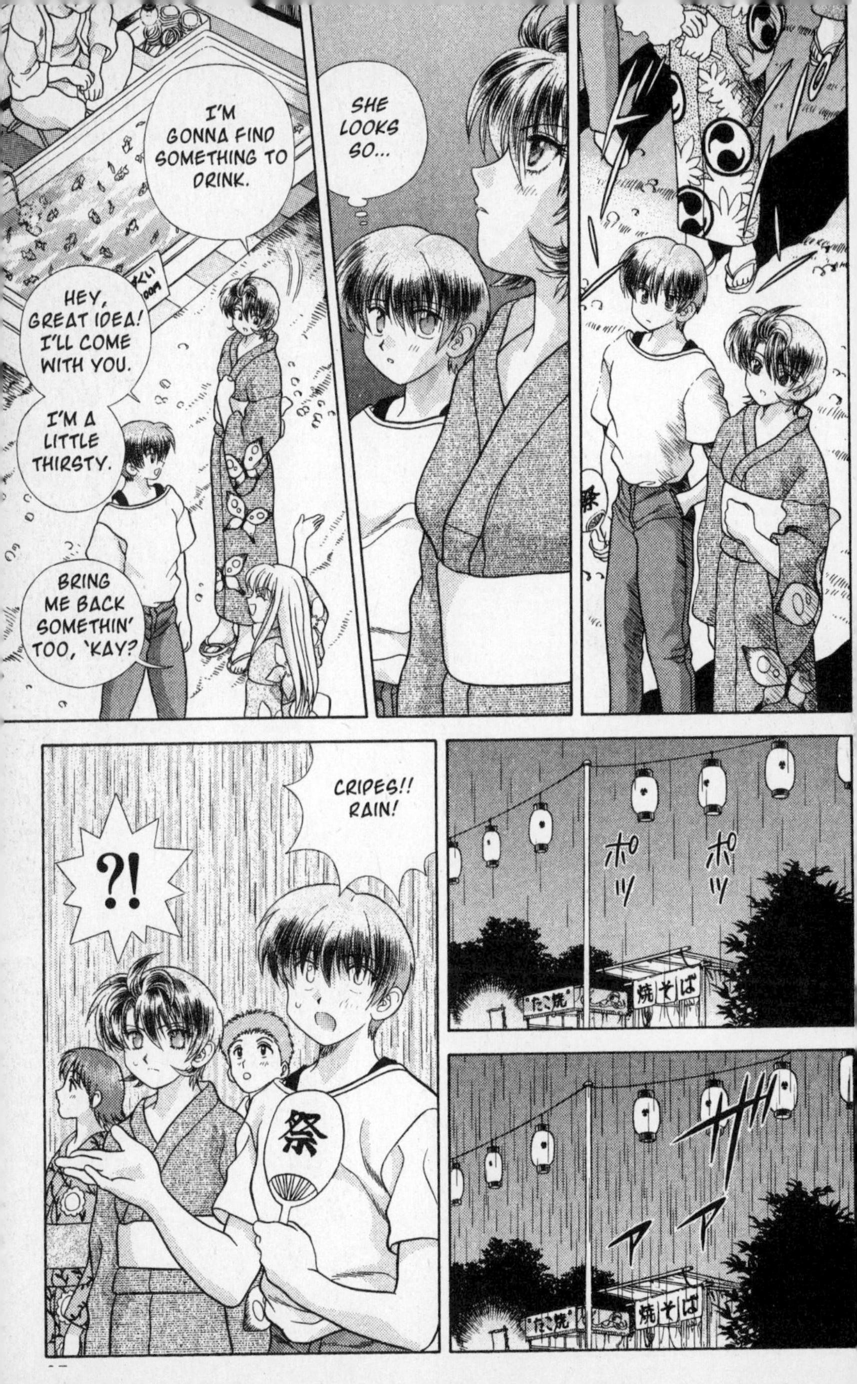
SHE LOOKS SO...
I'M GONNA FIND SOMETHING TO DRINK.
HEY, GREAT IDEA! I'LL COME WITH YOU.
I'M A LITTLE THIRSTY.
BRING ME BACK SOMETHIN' TOO, 'KAY?
祭
ポツ
ポツ
焼そば
"たこ焼"
焼そば
"たこ焼"
CRIPES!! RAIN!
?!
祭

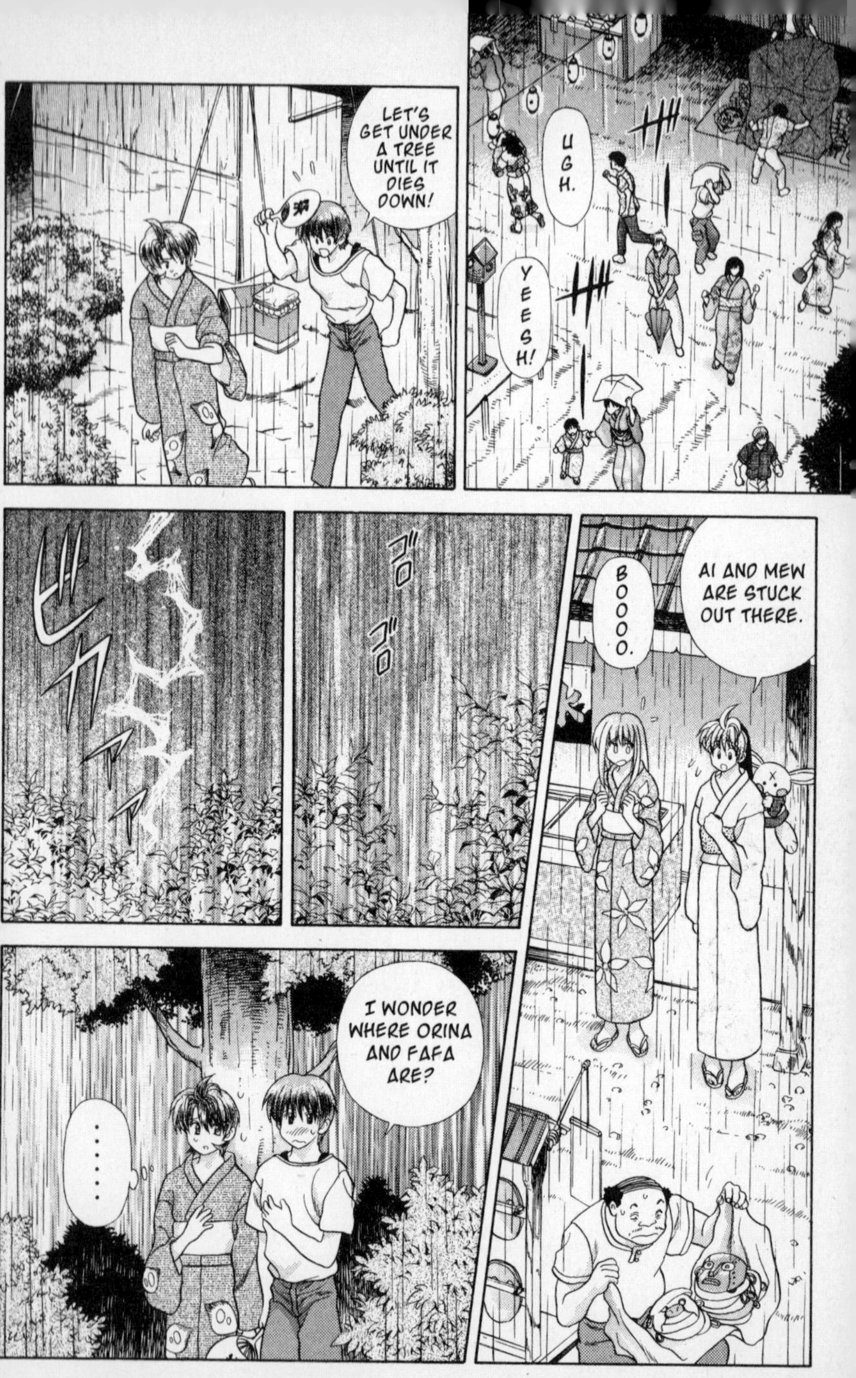
UGH.
YEESH!
LET'S GET UNDER A TREE UNTIL IT DIES DOWN!
AI AND MEW ARE STUCK OUT THERE.
BOOOO.
ゴロゴロ
ピカァァァ
I WONDER WHERE ORINA AND FAFA ARE?
......

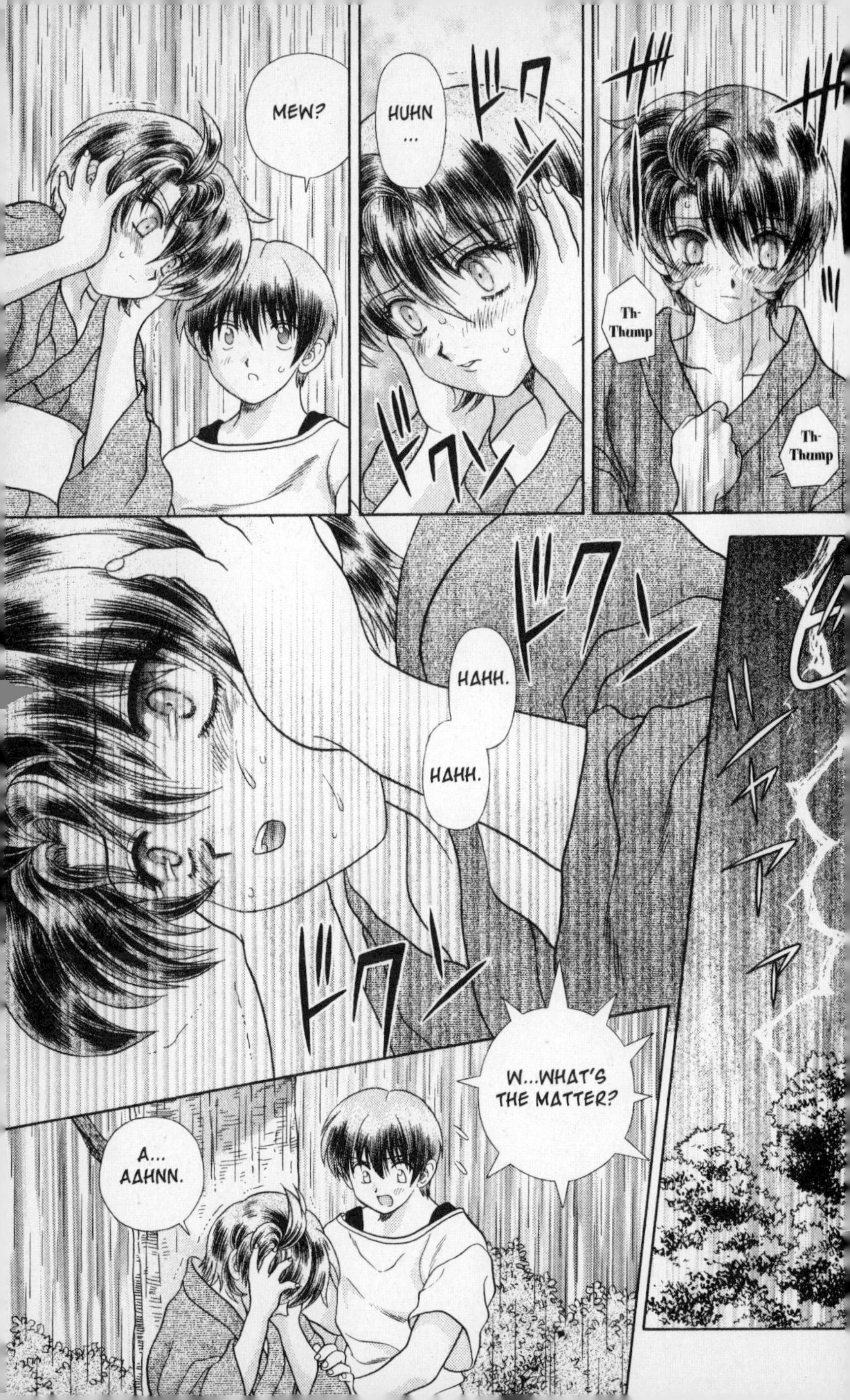
ザ
ザ
Th-Thump
Th-Thump
ドクン
HUHN ...
ドクン
MEW?
ドクン
HAHH.
HAHH.
ドクン
W...WHAT'S THE MATTER?
A... AAHNN.

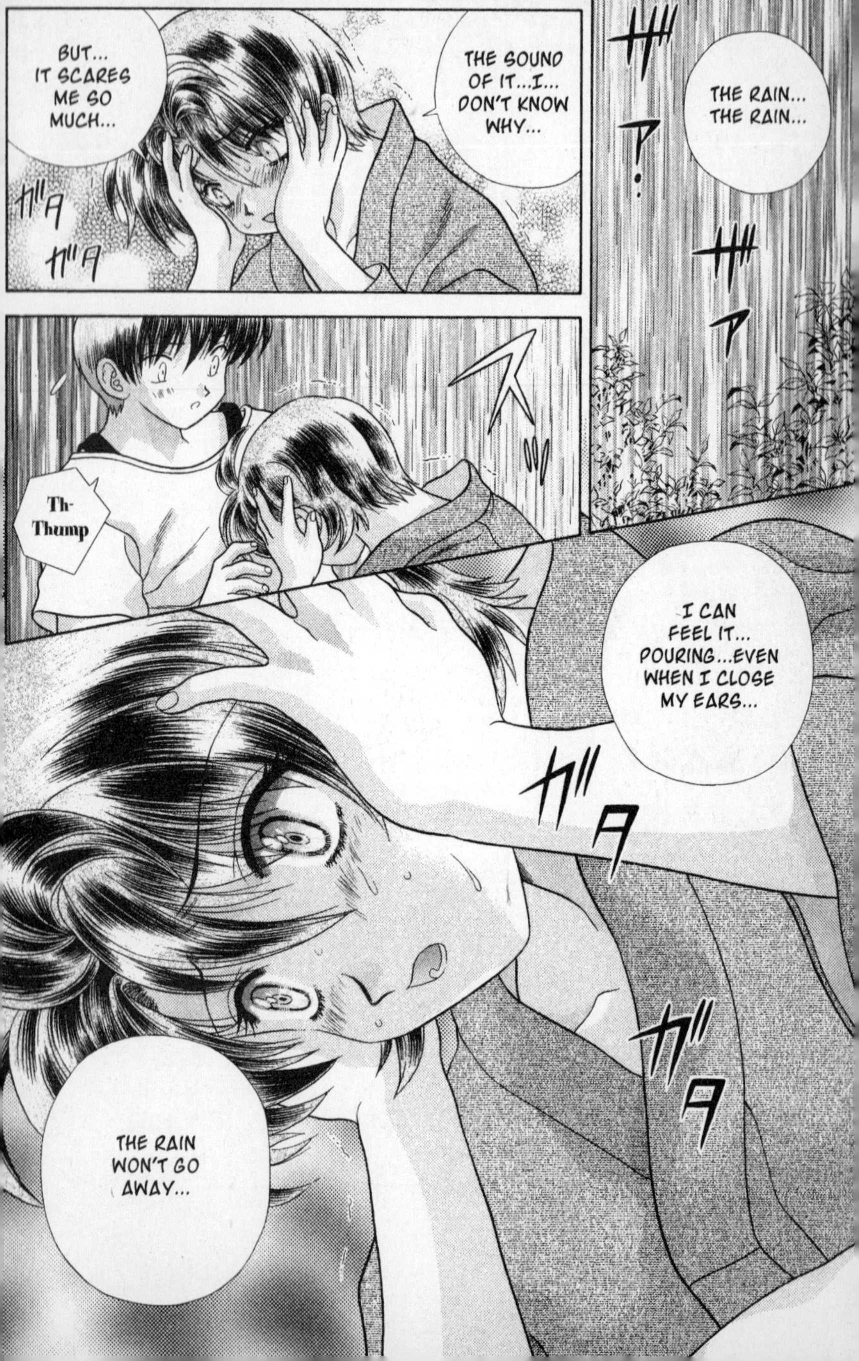

ザァ
THE RAIN... THE RAIN...
ザァ
THE SOUND OF IT...I... DON'T KNOW WHY...
BUT... IT SCARES ME SO MUCH...
ガタ
ガタ
ス
Th-Thump
I CAN FEEL IT... POURING...EVEN WHEN I CLOSE MY EARS...
ガタ
ガタ
THE RAIN WON'T GO AWAY...

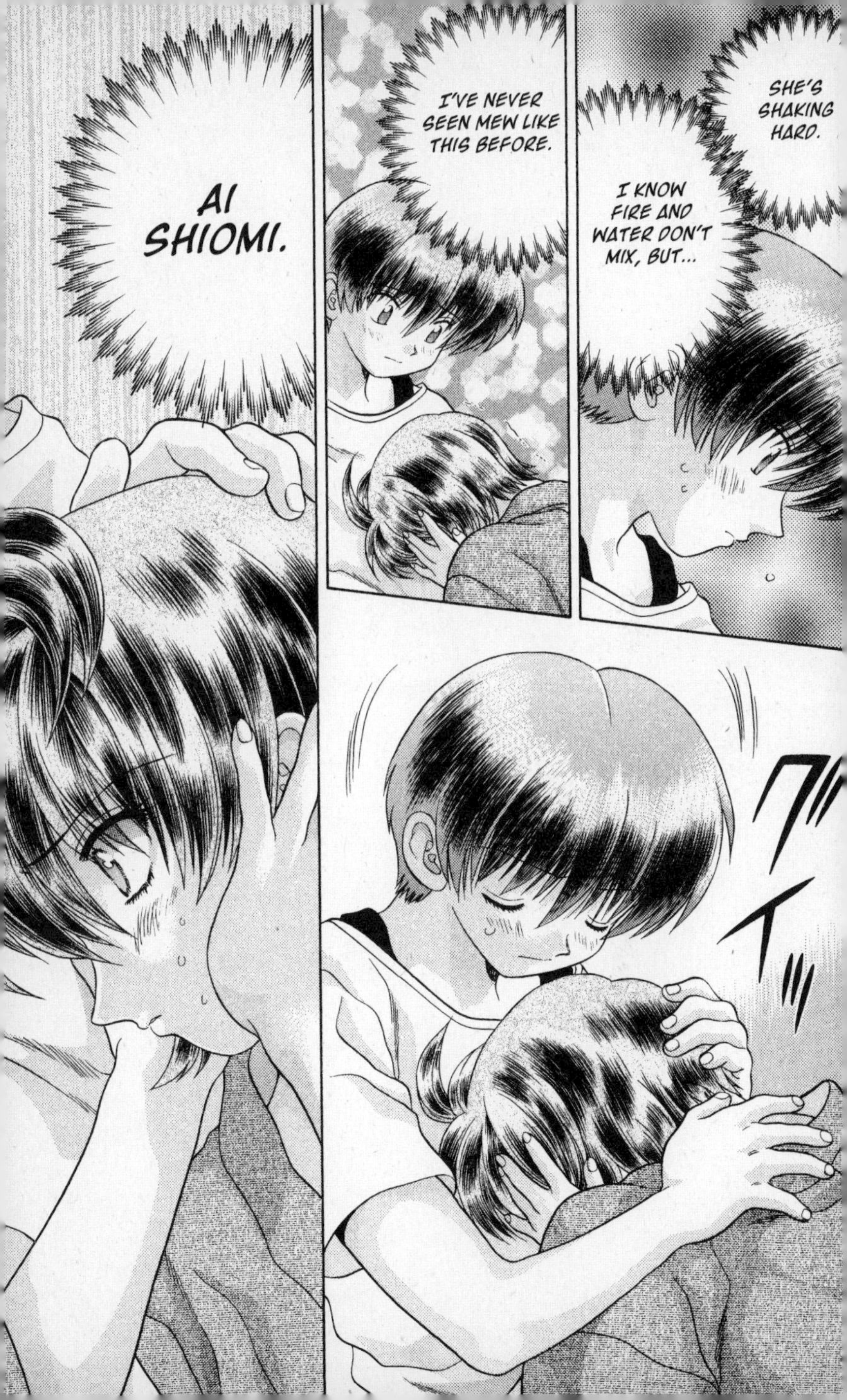
SHE'S SHAKING HARD.
I KNOW FIRE AND WATER DON'T MIX, BUT...
I'VE NEVER SEEN MEW LIKE THIS BEFORE.
AI SHIOMI.

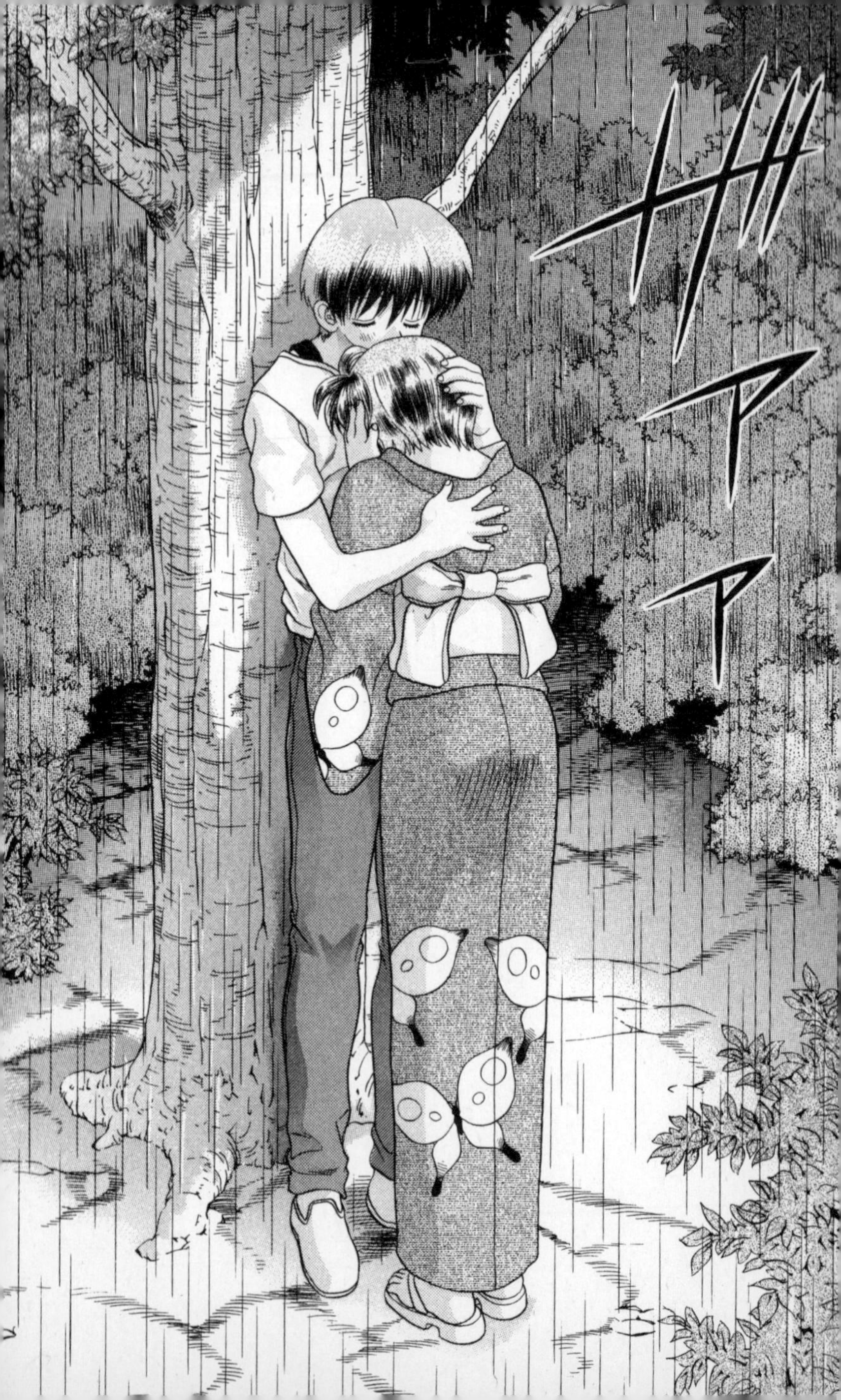
ザァァ

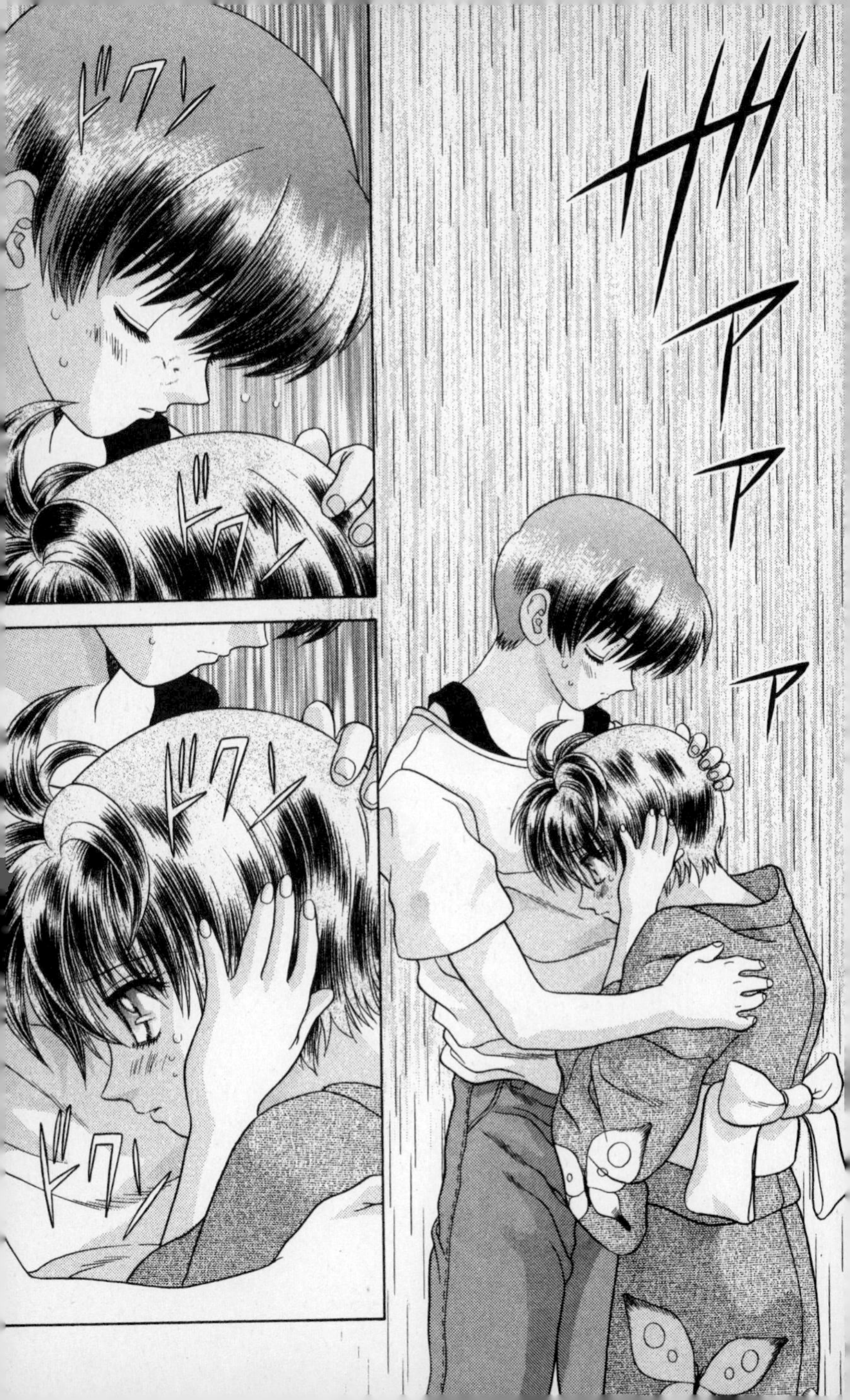
ザアアアア
ドクン
ドクン
ドクン
ドクン

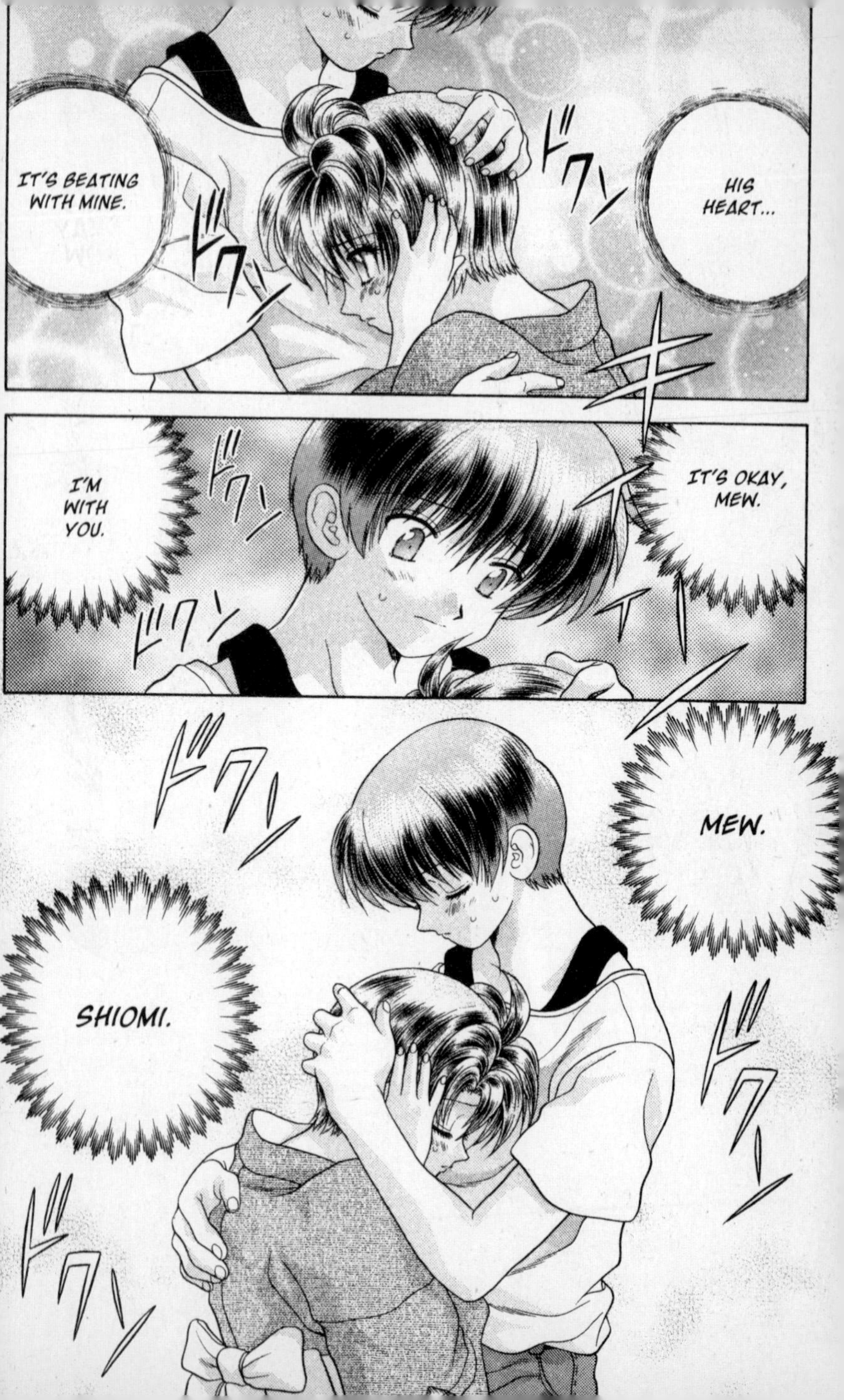
HIS HEART...
ドクン
IT'S BEATING WITH MINE.
ドクン
IT'S OKAY, MEW.
ドクン
I'M WITH YOU.
ドクン
MEW.
ドクン
ドクン
SHIOMI.
ドクン

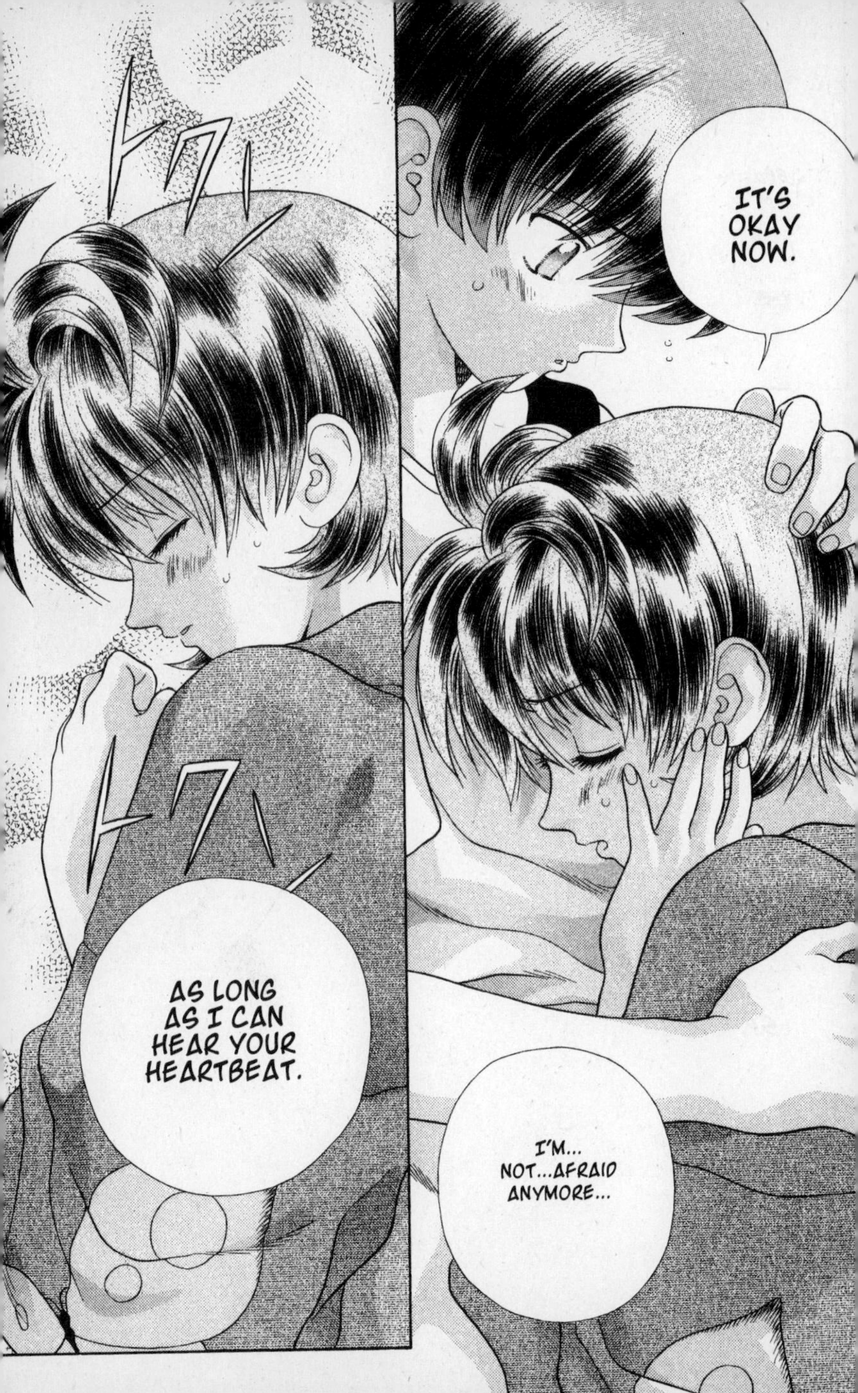
IT'S OKAY NOW.
I'M... NOT...AFRAID ANYMORE...
トクン
トクン
AS LONG AS I CAN HEAR YOUR HEARTBEAT.

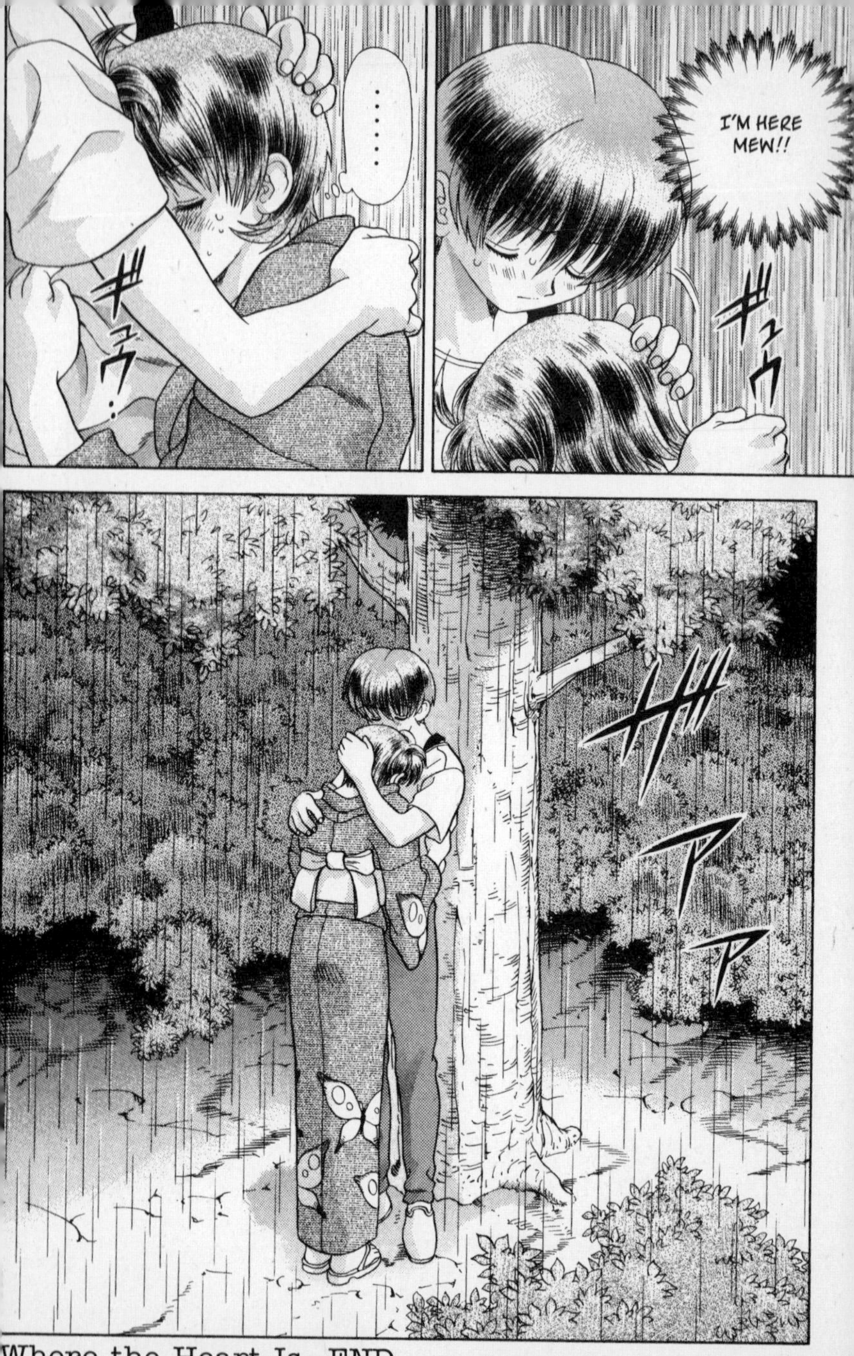
I'M HERE MEW!!
ギュウ
……
ギュウ‥
ザァァ

Where the Heart Is END

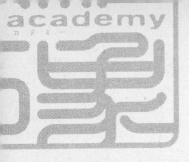

Chapter 16: Every Vow Under the Sun

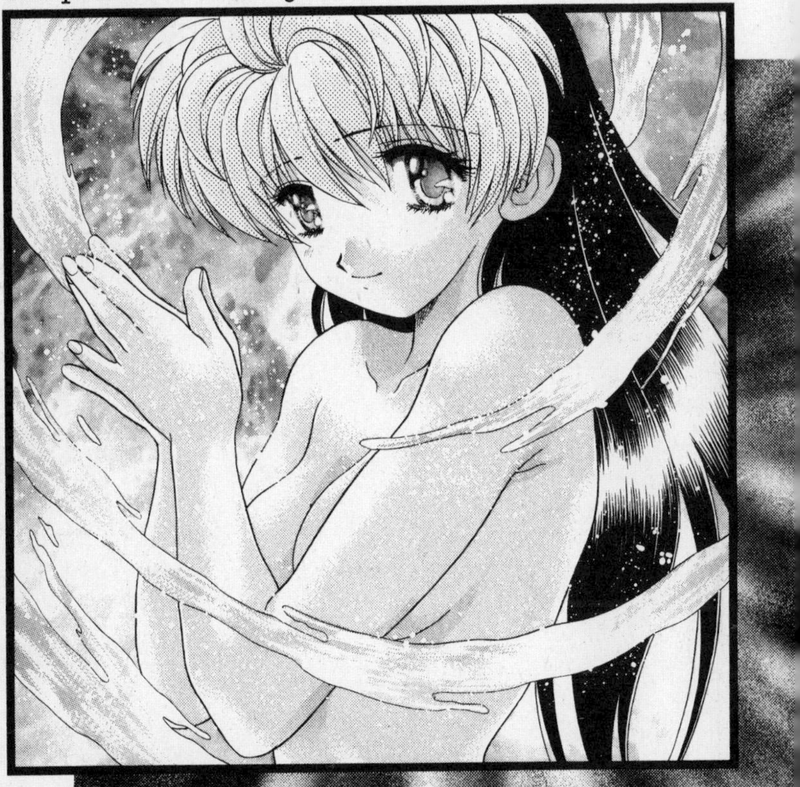

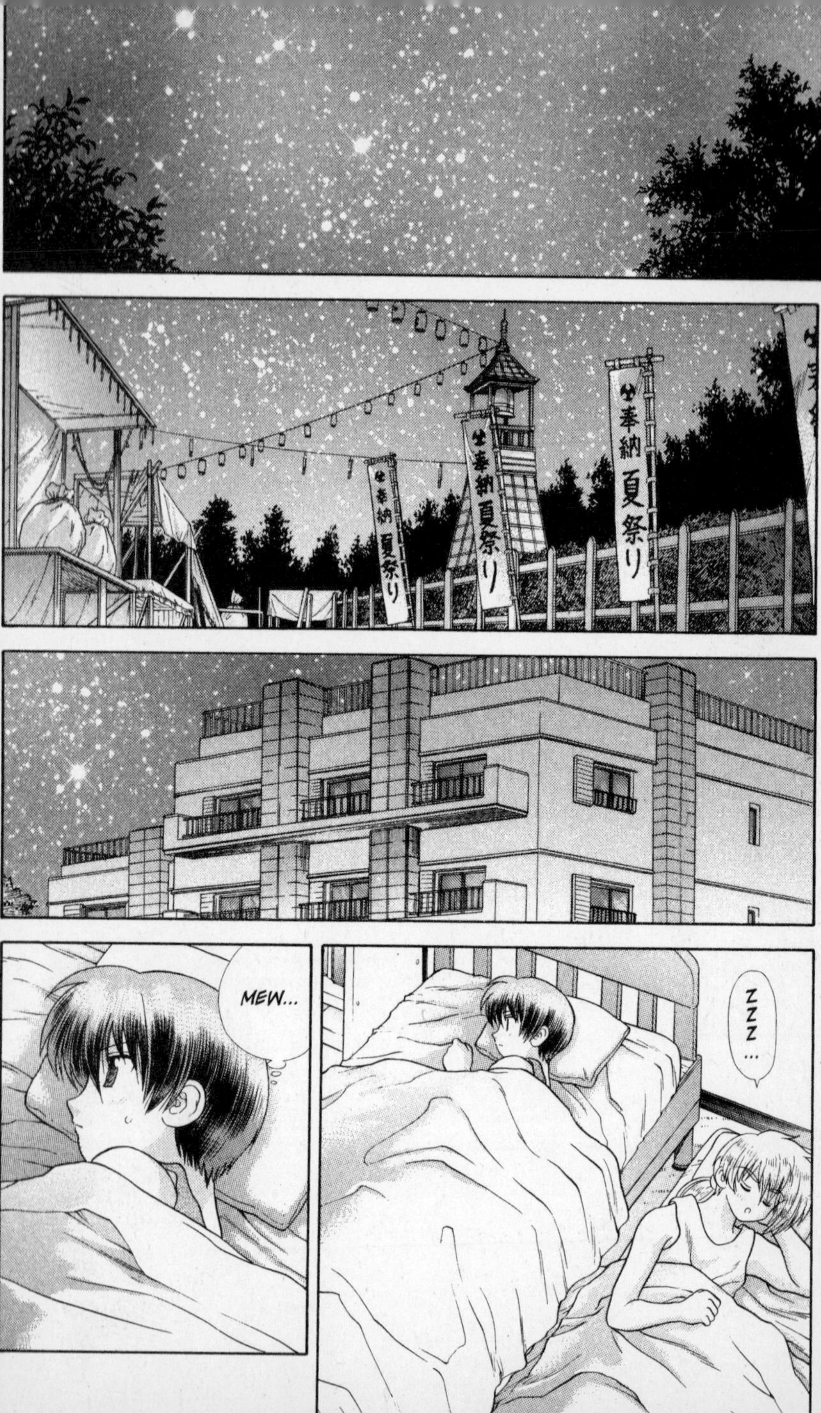
奉納 夏祭り
奉納 夏祭り
奉納 夏祭り
ZZZ ...
MEW...

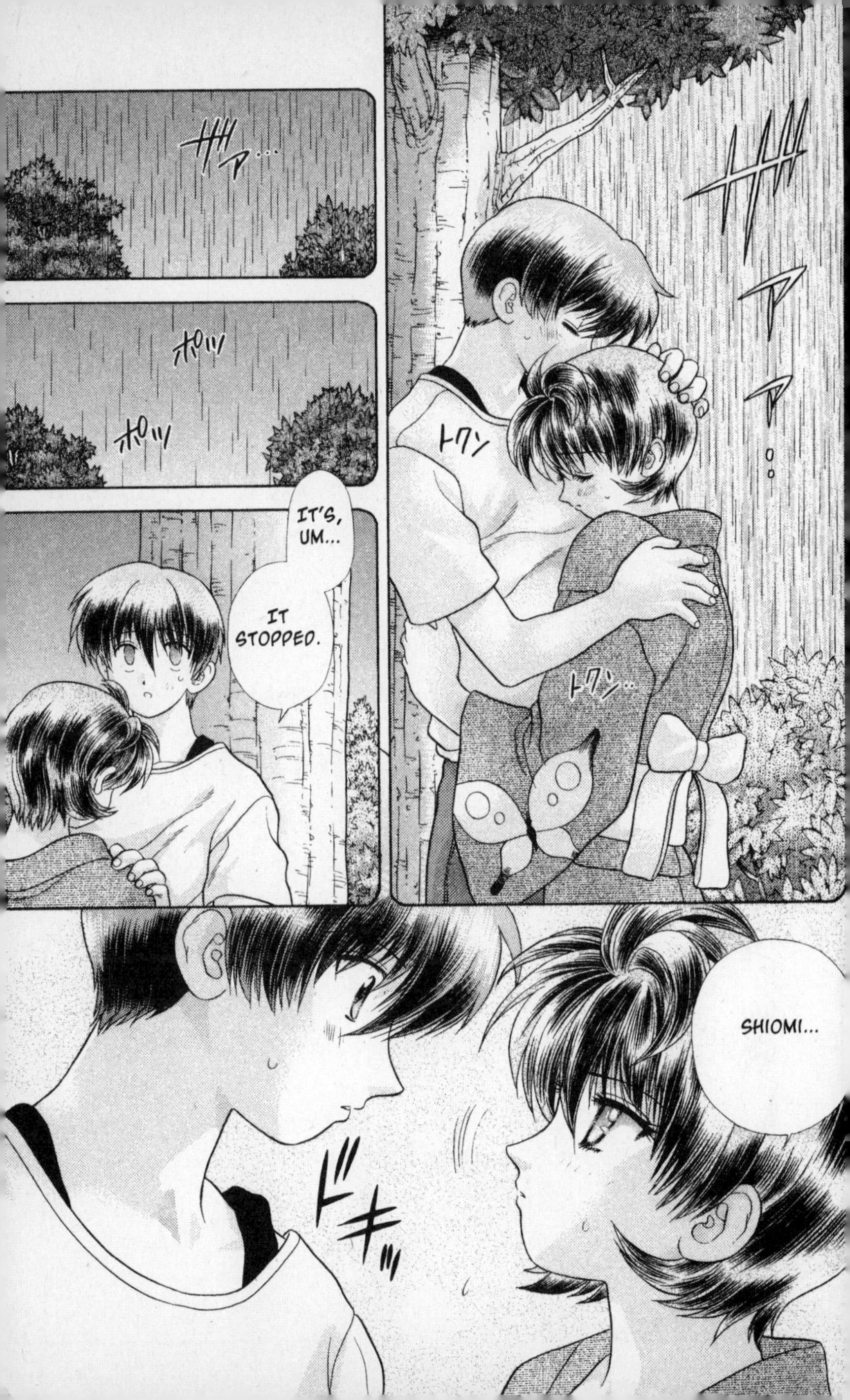
ザァァァ…
トクン
トクン…
ザァ…
ポツ
ポツ
IT'S, UM...
IT STOPPED.
SHIOMI...

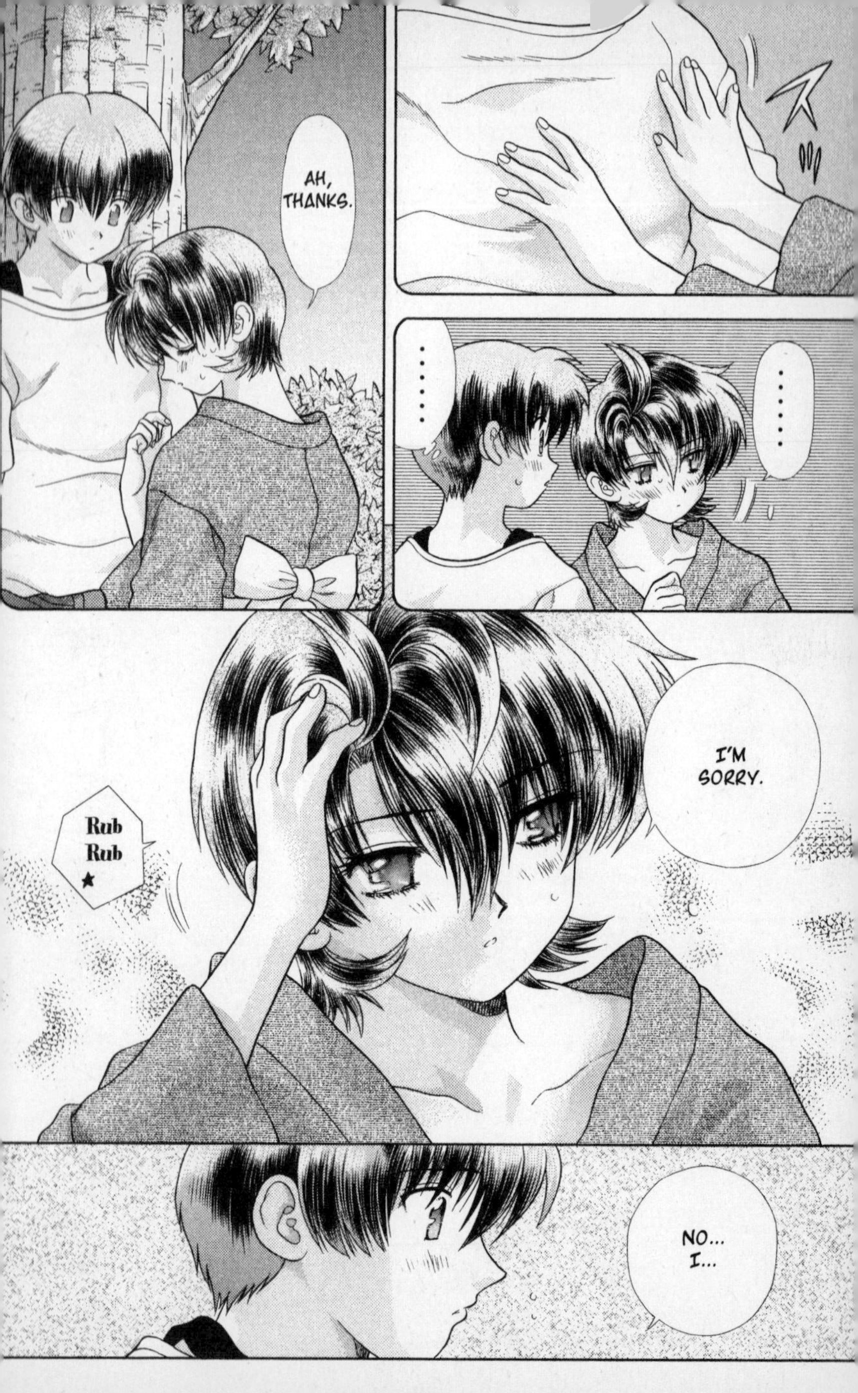
ス
......
......
AH, THANKS.
I'M SORRY.
Rub Rub ★
NO... I...

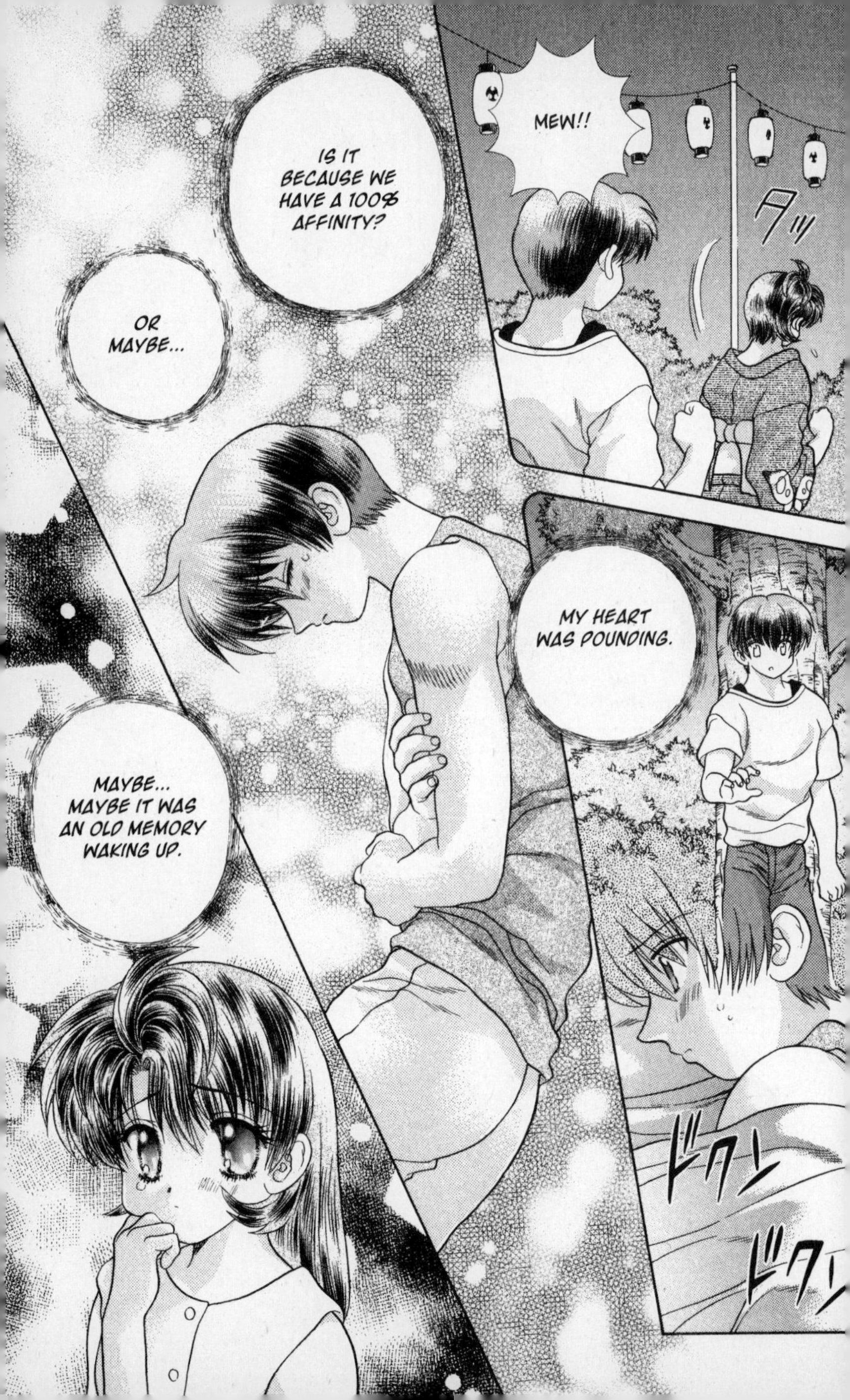
MEW!!
タッ
MY HEART WAS POUNDING.
ドクン
ドクン
IS IT BECAUSE WE HAVE A 100% AFFINITY?
OR MAYBE...
MAYBE... MAYBE IT WAS AN OLD MEMORY WAKING UP.

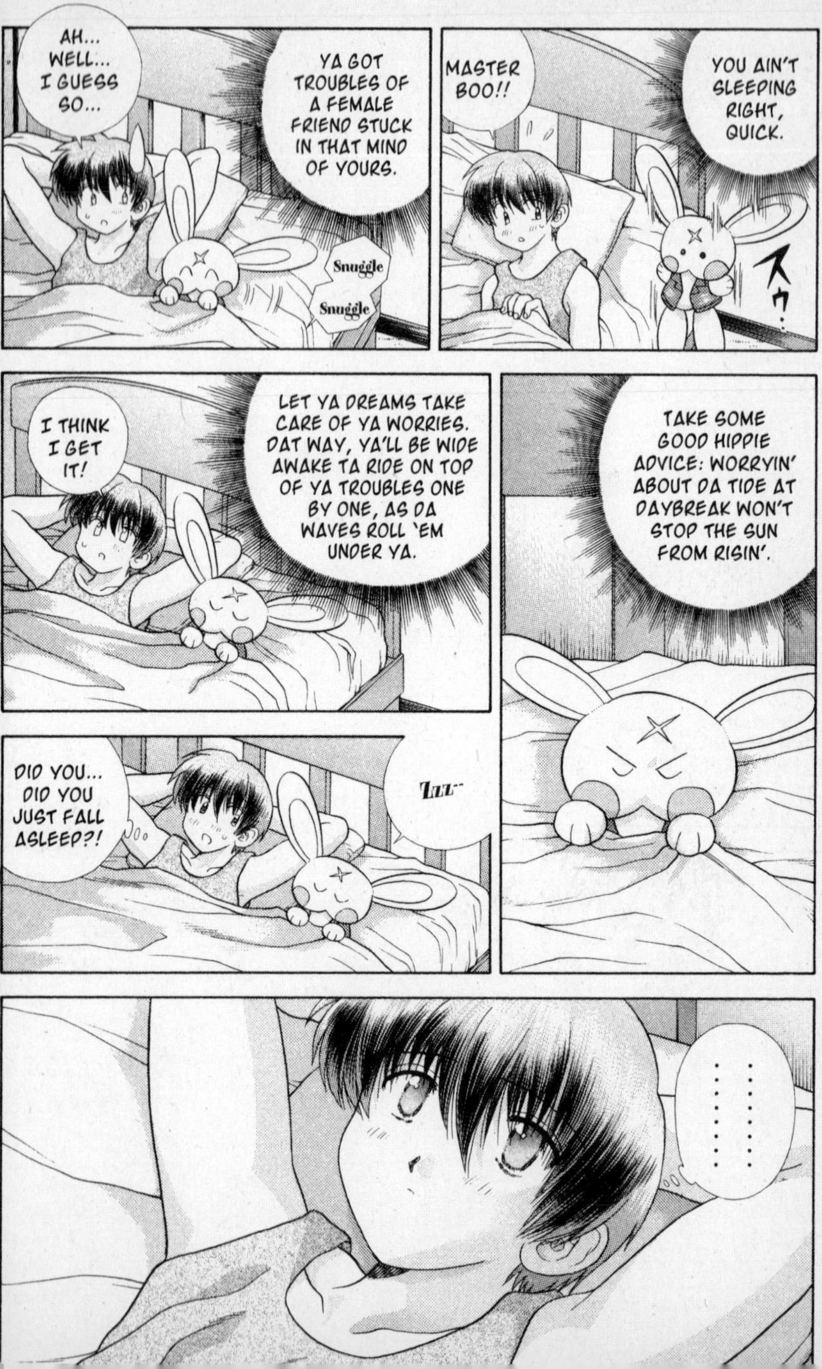
YOU AIN'T SLEEPING RIGHT, QUICK.
MASTER BOO!!
スゥ…
YA GOT TROUBLES OF A FEMALE FRIEND STUCK IN THAT MIND OF YOURS.
AH... WELL... I GUESS SO...
Snuggle
Snuggle
TAKE SOME GOOD HIPPIE ADVICE: WORRYIN' ABOUT DA TIDE AT DAYBREAK WON'T STOP THE SUN FROM RISIN'.
LET YA DREAMS TAKE CARE OF YA WORRIES. DAT WAY, YA'LL BE WIDE AWAKE TA RIDE ON TOP OF YA TROUBLES ONE BY ONE, AS DA WAVES ROLL 'EM UNDER YA.
I THINK I GET IT!
Zzz--
DID YOU... DID YOU JUST FALL ASLEEP?!
......

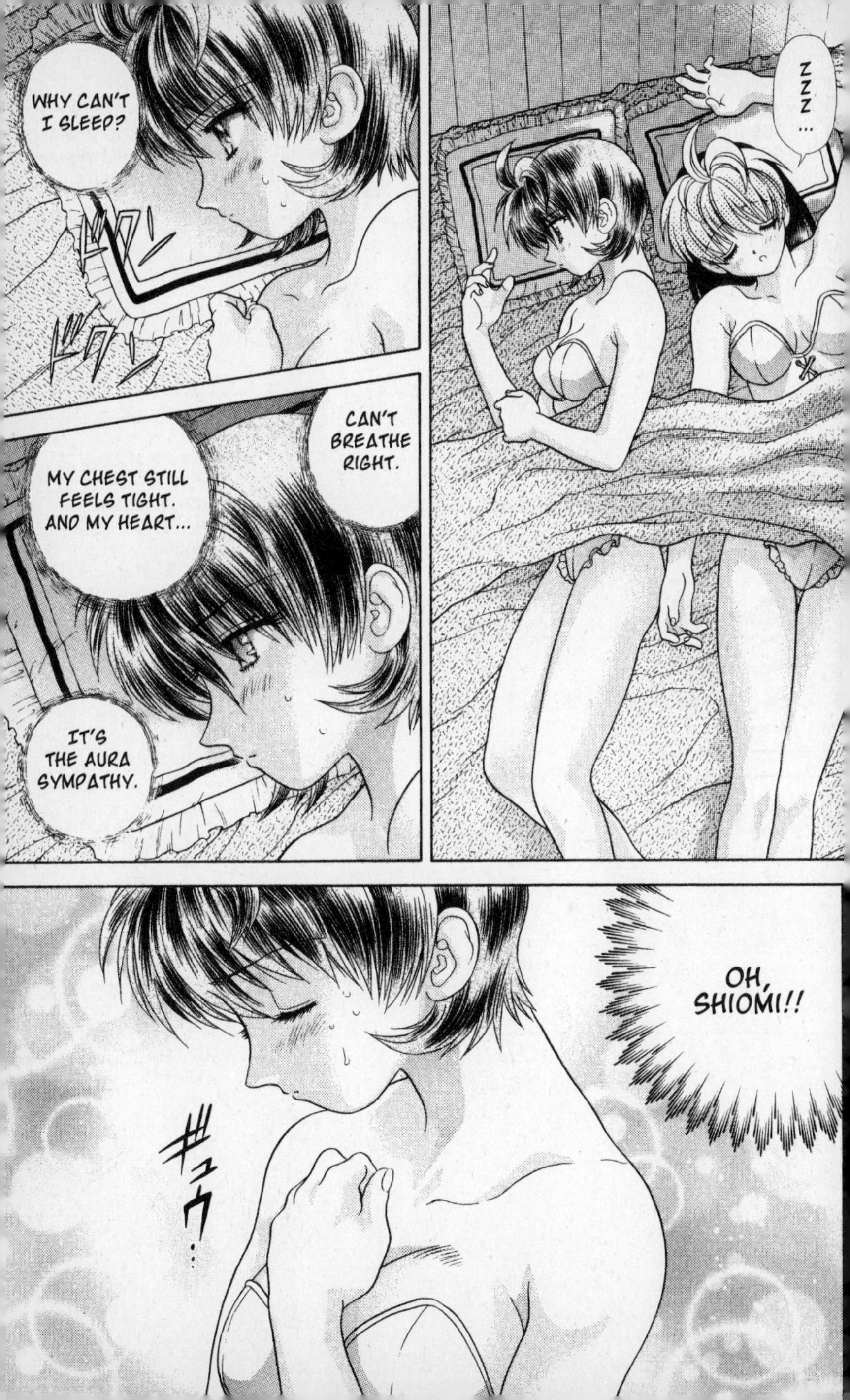
ZZZ ...
WHY CAN'T I SLEEP?
ドクン
ドクン
CAN'T BREATHE RIGHT.
MY CHEST STILL FEELS TIGHT. AND MY HEART...
IT'S THE AURA SYMPATHY.
OH, SHIOMI!!
ギュウ...

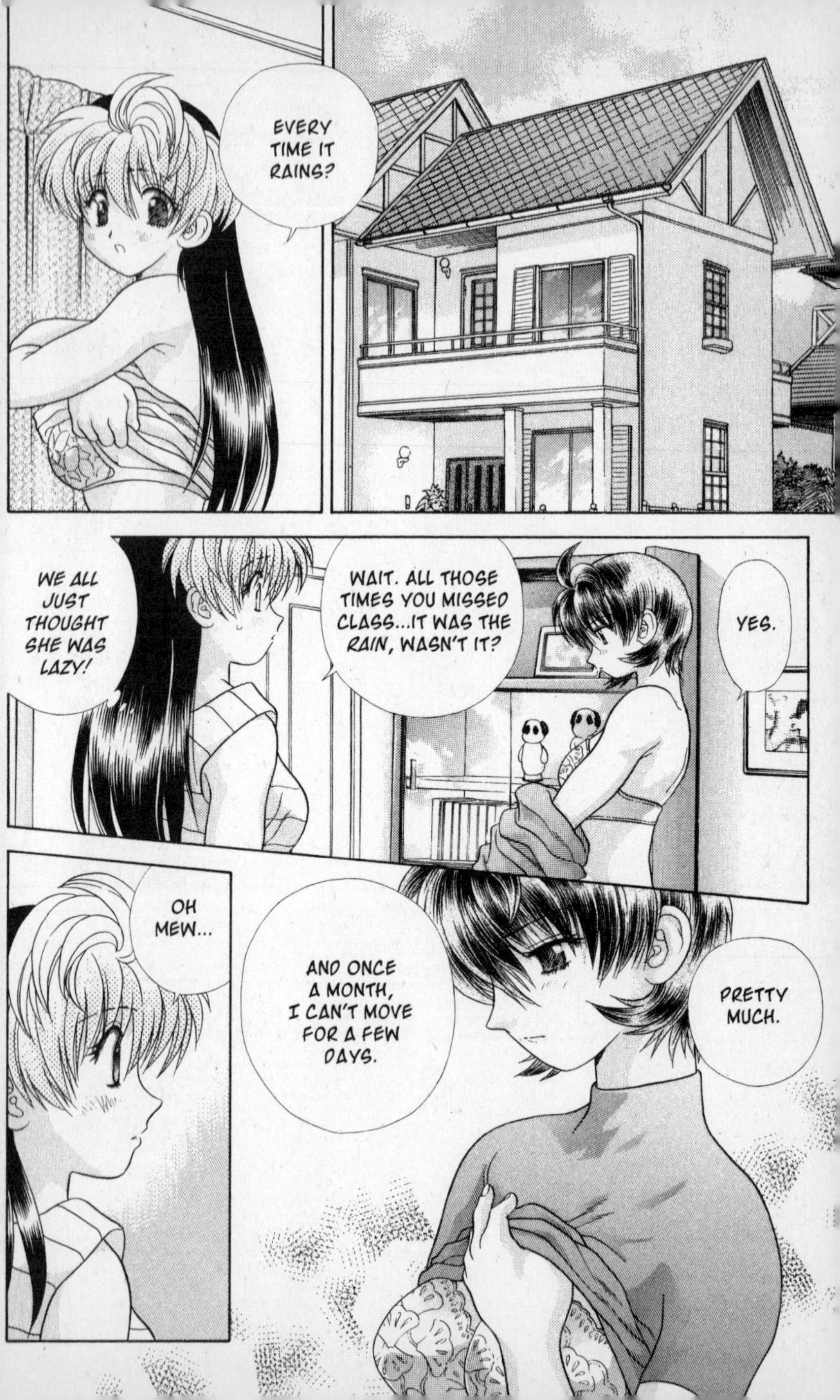
EVERY TIME IT RAINS?
WE ALL JUST THOUGHT SHE WAS LAZY!
WAIT. ALL THOSE TIMES YOU MISSED CLASS...IT WAS THE RAIN, WASN'T IT?
YES.
OH MEW...
AND ONCE A MONTH, I CAN'T MOVE FOR A FEW DAYS.
PRETTY MUCH.

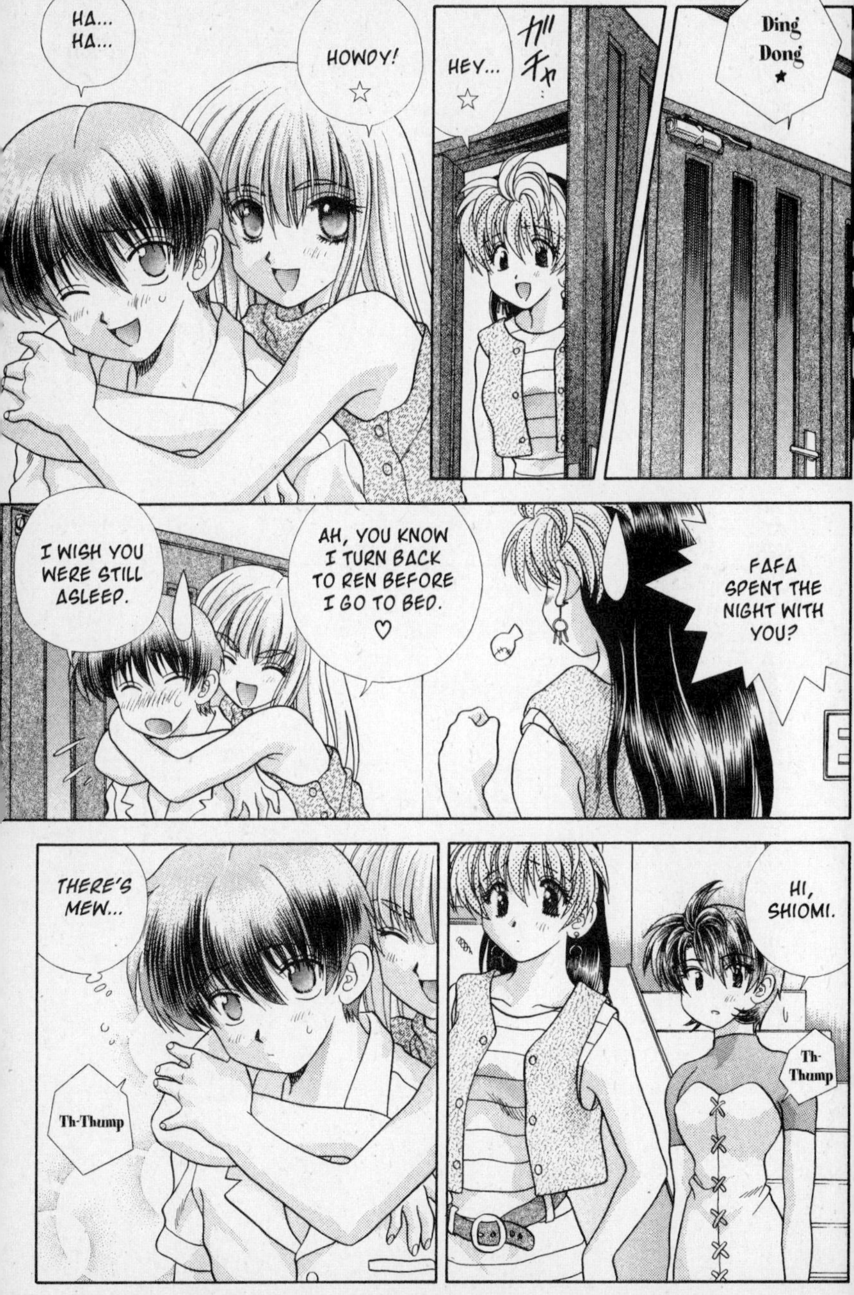

Ding Dong ★
ガチャ
HEY... ☆
HOWDY! ☆
HA... HA...
FAFA SPENT THE NIGHT WITH YOU?
AH, YOU KNOW I TURN BACK TO REN BEFORE I GO TO BED. ♡
I WISH YOU WERE STILL ASLEEP.
HI, SHIOMI.
Th-Thump
THERE'S MEW...
Th-Thump

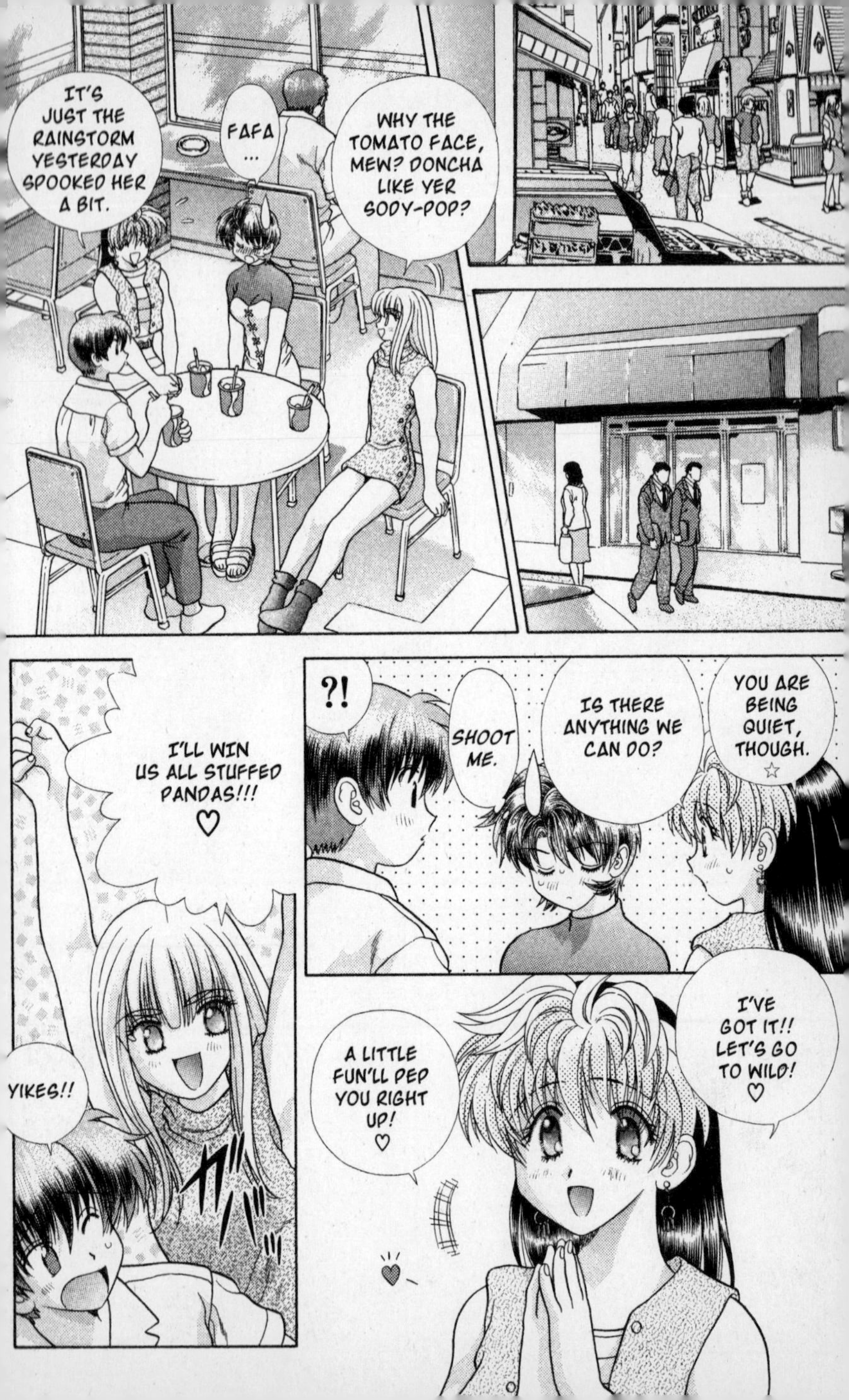
WHY THE TOMATO FACE, MEW? DONCHA LIKE YER SODY-POP?
FAFA ...
IT'S JUST THE RAINSTORM YESTERDAY SPOOKED HER A BIT.
YOU ARE BEING QUIET, THOUGH. ☆
IS THERE ANYTHING WE CAN DO?
SHOOT ME.
?!
I'VE GOT IT!! LET'S GO TO WILD! ♡
A LITTLE FUN'LL PEP YOU RIGHT UP! ♡
I'LL WIN US ALL STUFFED PANDAS!!! ♡
YIKES!!

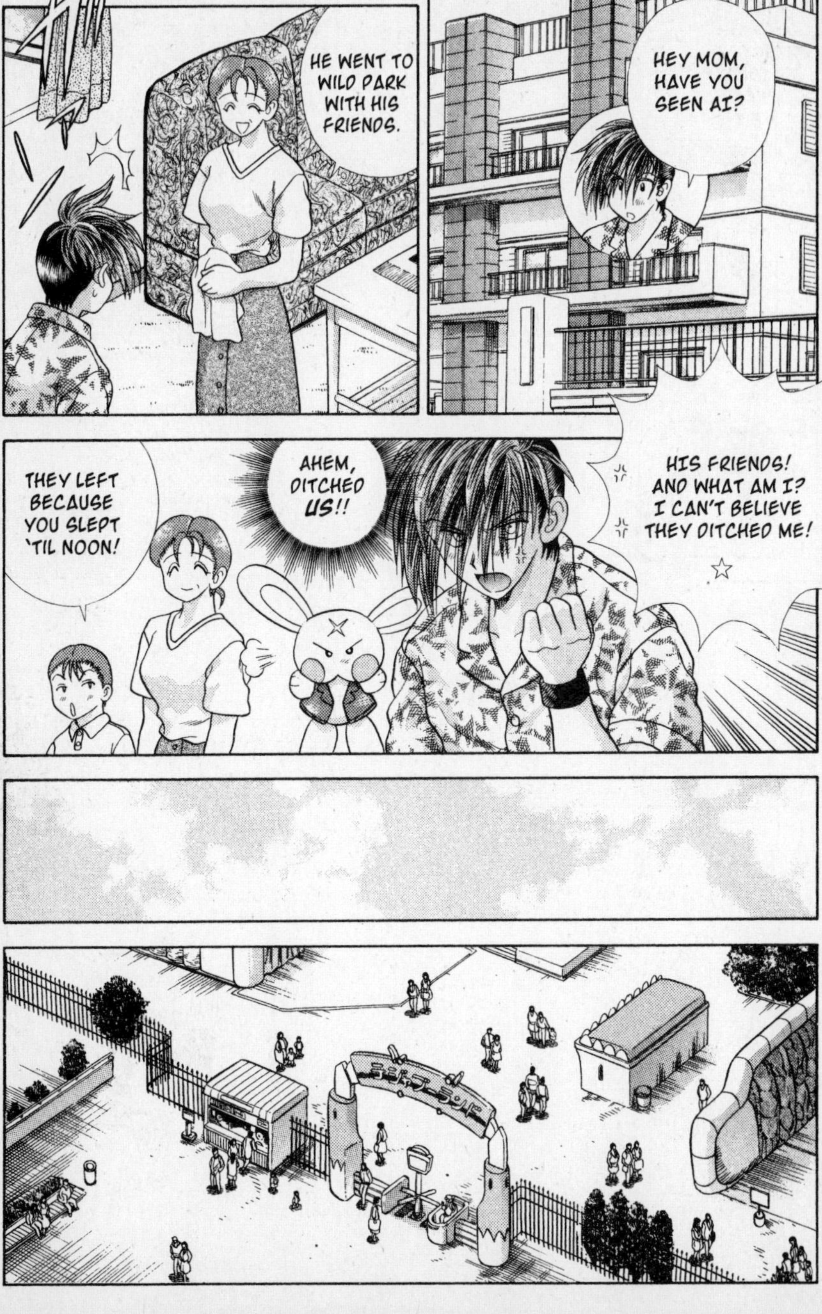
HEY MOM, HAVE YOU SEEN AI?
HE WENT TO WILD PARK WITH HIS FRIENDS.
HIS FRIENDS! AND WHAT AM I? I CAN'T BELIEVE THEY DITCHED ME!
AHEM, DITCHED US!!
THEY LEFT BECAUSE YOU SLEPT 'TIL NOON!

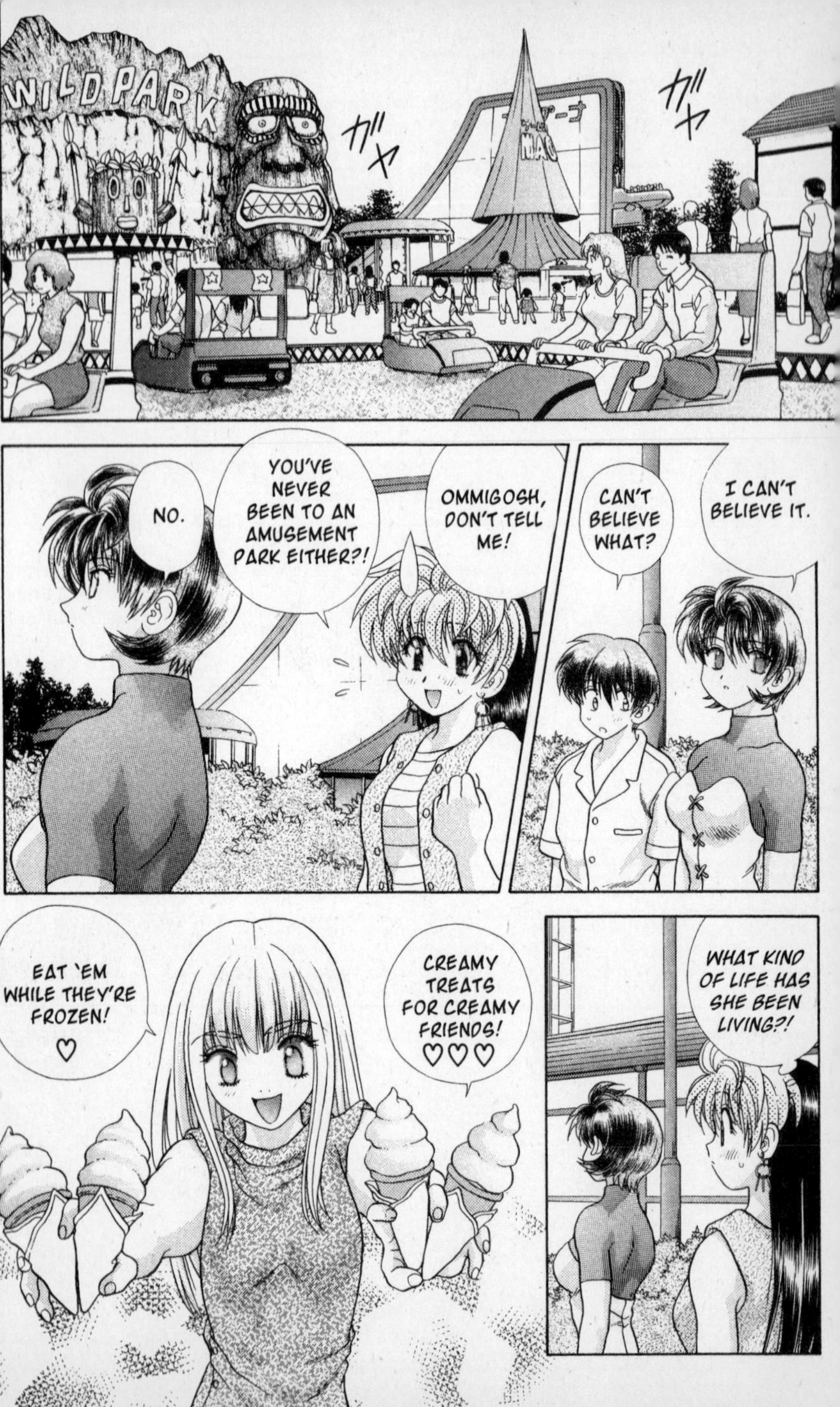
ガヤ
ガヤ
WILD PARK
I CAN'T BELIEVE IT.
CAN'T BELIEVE WHAT?
OMMIGOSH, DON'T TELL ME!
YOU'VE NEVER BEEN TO AN AMUSEMENT PARK EITHER?!
NO.
WHAT KIND OF LIFE HAS SHE BEEN LIVING?!
CREAMY TREATS FOR CREAMY FRIENDS! ♡♡♡
EAT 'EM WHILE THEY'RE FROZEN! ♡

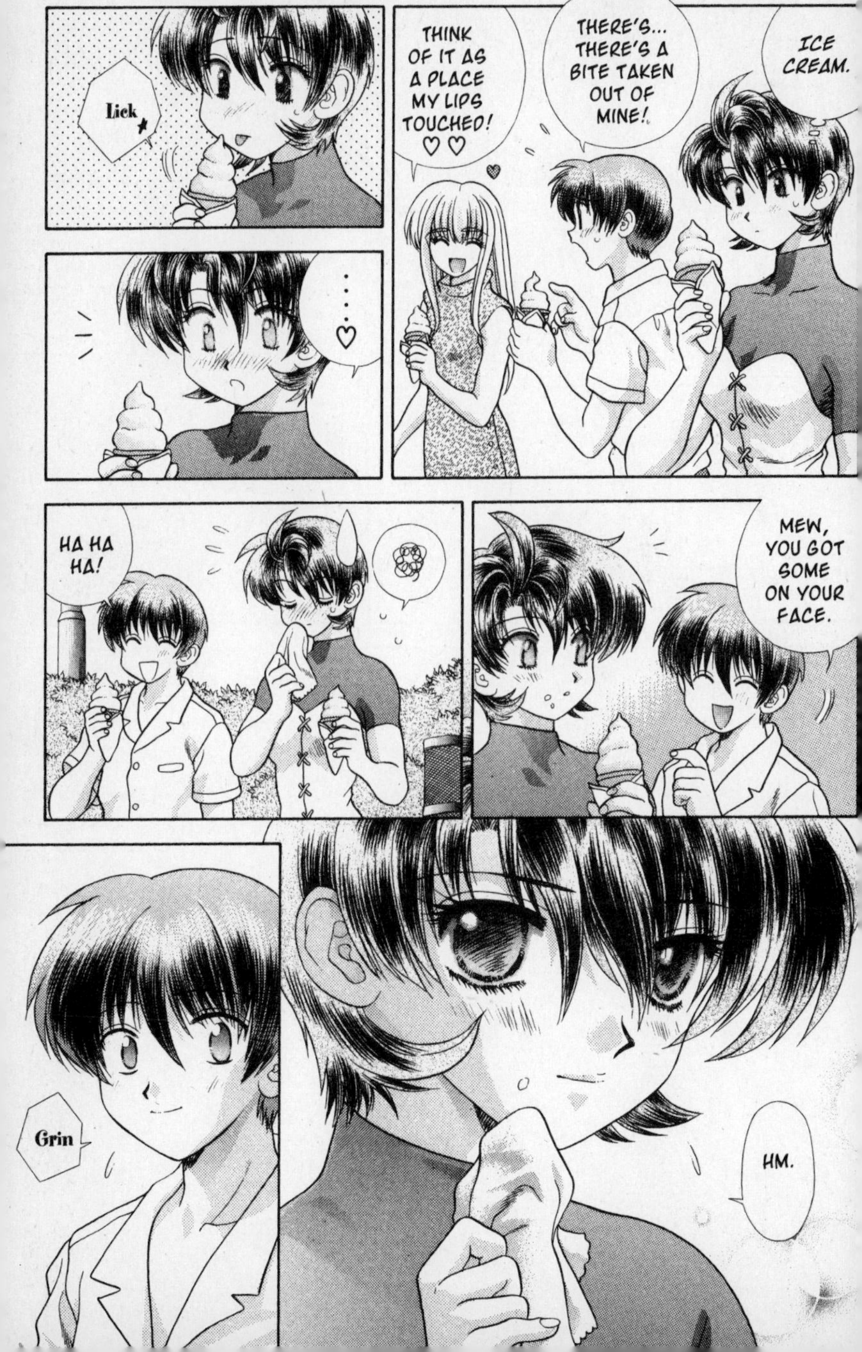
ICE CREAM.
THERE'S... THERE'S A BITE TAKEN OUT OF MINE!
THINK OF IT AS A PLACE MY LIPS TOUCHED! ♡ ♡
Lick
...♡
MEW, YOU GOT SOME ON YOUR FACE.
HA HA HA!
HM.
Grin

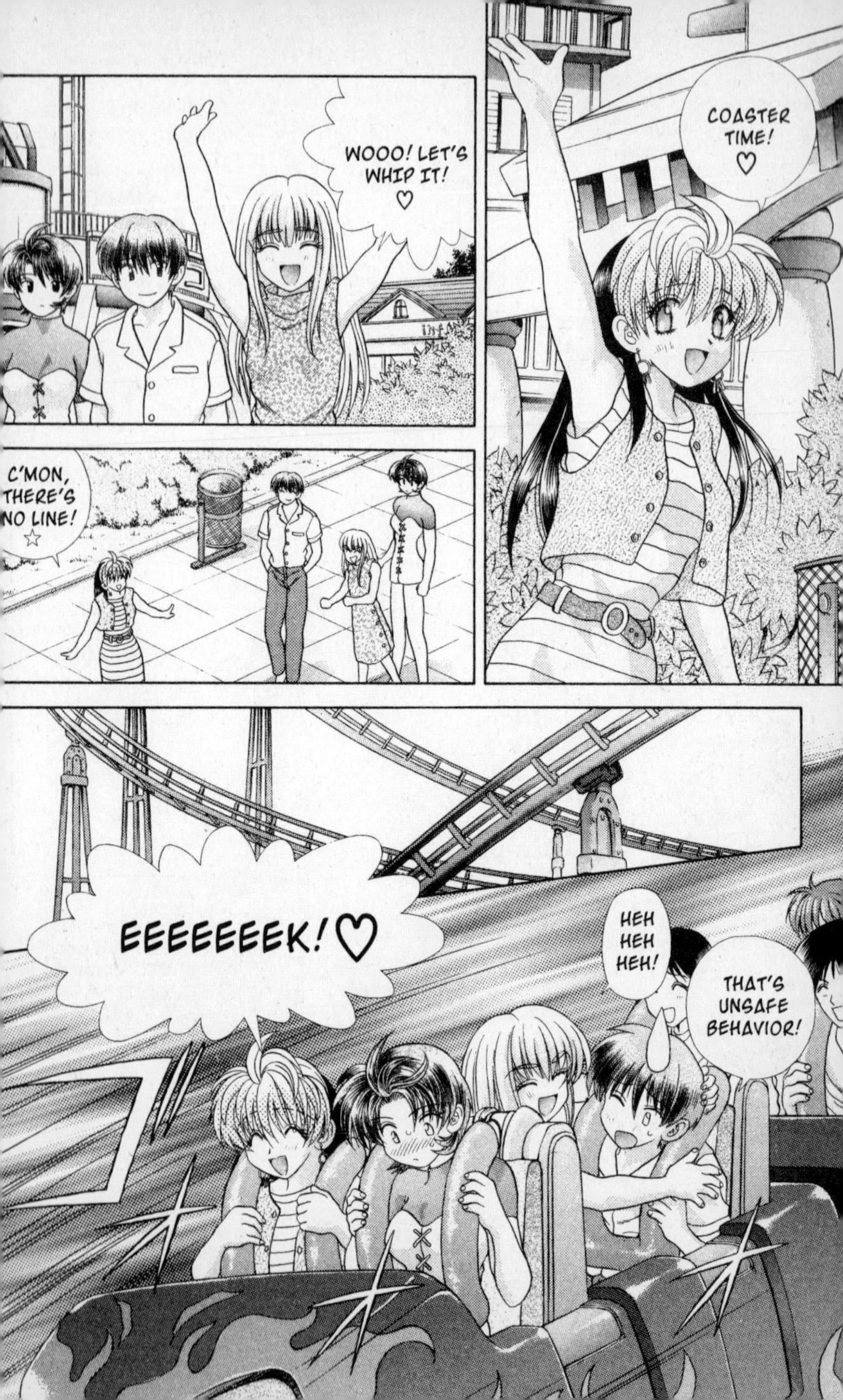
COASTER TIME! ♡
WOOO! LET'S WHIP IT! ♡
C'MON, THERE'S NO LINE! ☆
EEEEEEEK! ♡
HEH HEH HEH!
THAT'S UNSAFE BEHAVIOR!

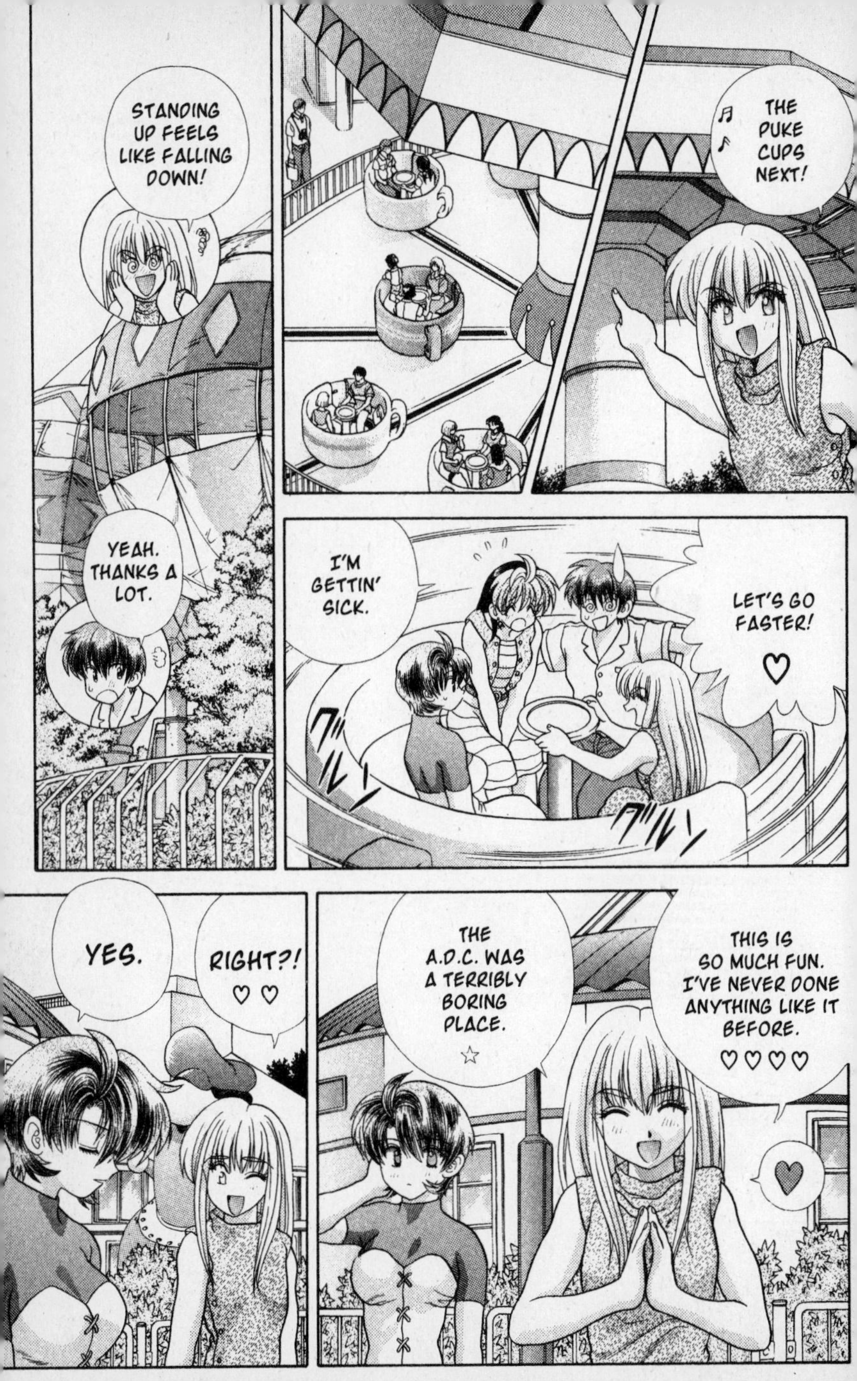
THE PUKE CUPS NEXT!
LET'S GO FASTER! ♡
I'M GETTIN' SICK.
STANDING UP FEELS LIKE FALLING DOWN!
YEAH. THANKS A LOT.
THIS IS SO MUCH FUN. I'VE NEVER DONE ANYTHING LIKE IT BEFORE. ♡♡♡♡
THE A.D.C. WAS A TERRIBLY BORING PLACE. ☆
RIGHT?! ♡ ♡
YES.

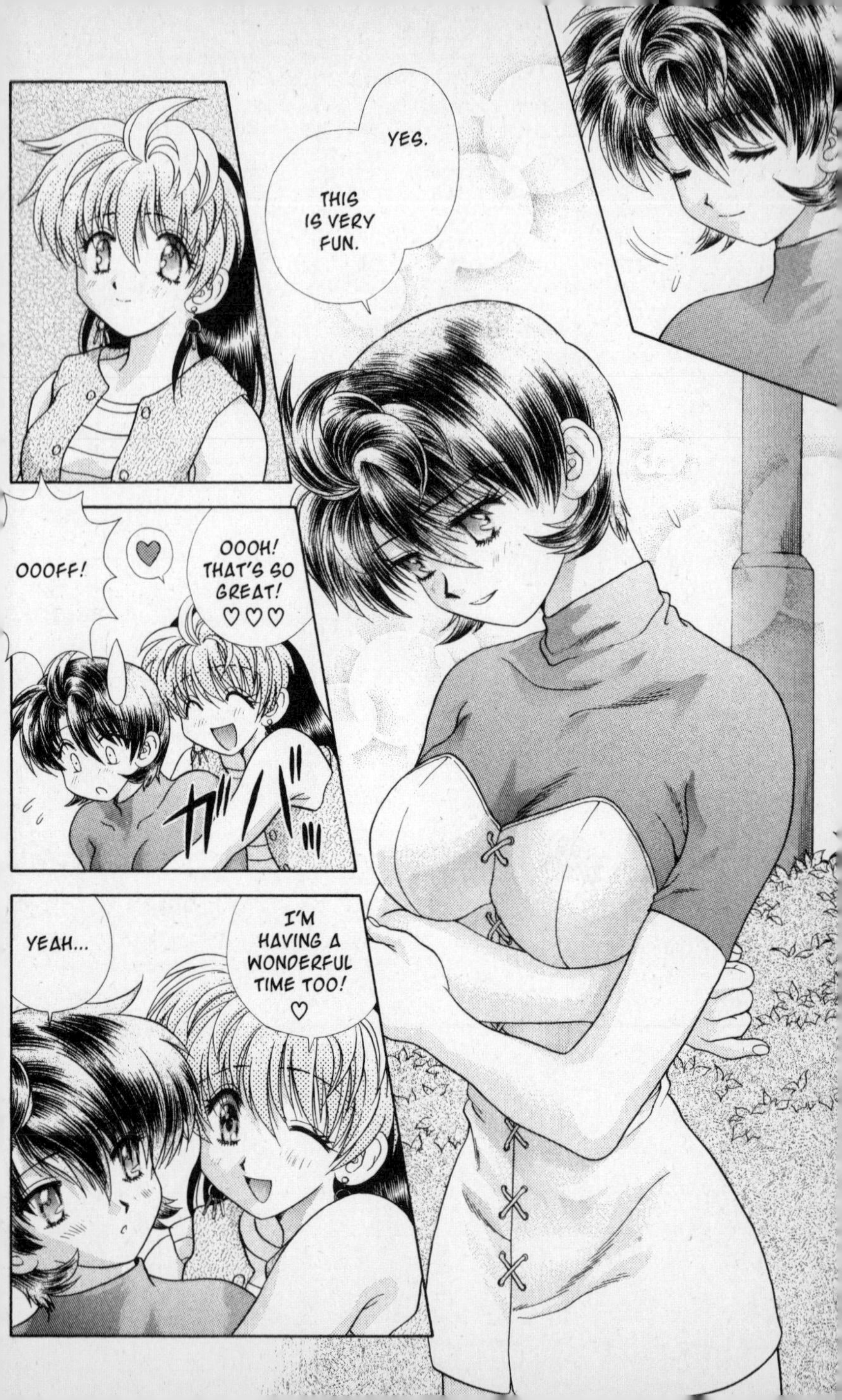
YES.
THIS IS VERY FUN.
OOOH! THAT'S SO GREAT! ♡♡♡
♥
OOOFF!
I'M HAVING A WONDERFUL TIME TOO! ♡
YEAH...

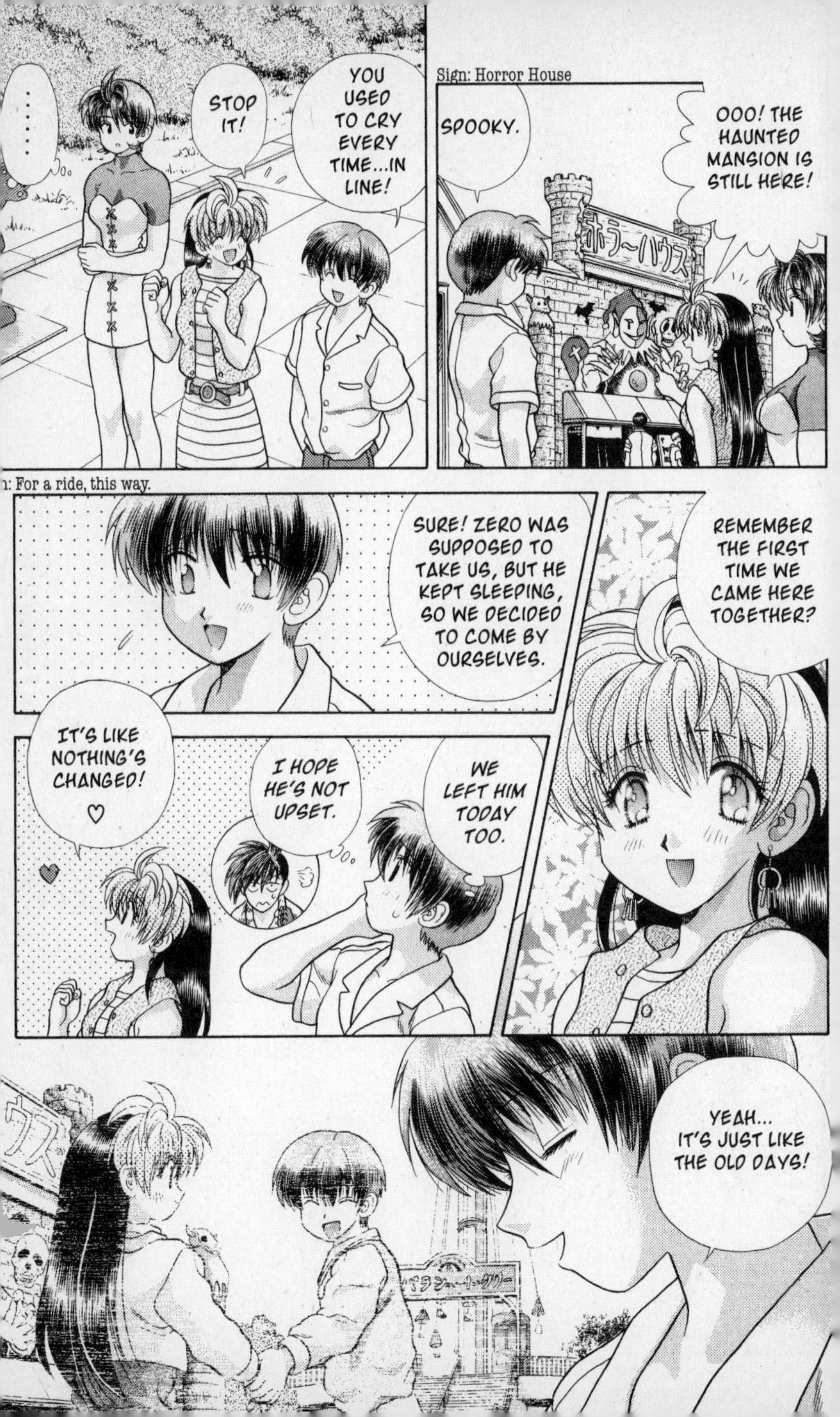
Sign: Horror House
OOO! THE HAUNTED MANSION IS STILL HERE!
SPOOKY.
YOU USED TO CRY EVERY TIME...IN LINE!
STOP IT!
......
REMEMBER THE FIRST TIME WE CAME HERE TOGETHER?
For a ride, this way.
SURE! ZERO WAS SUPPOSED TO TAKE US, BUT HE KEPT SLEEPING, SO WE DECIDED TO COME BY OURSELVES.
WE LEFT HIM TODAY TOO.
I HOPE HE'S NOT UPSET.
IT'S LIKE NOTHING'S CHANGED! ♡
YEAH... IT'S JUST LIKE THE OLD DAYS!

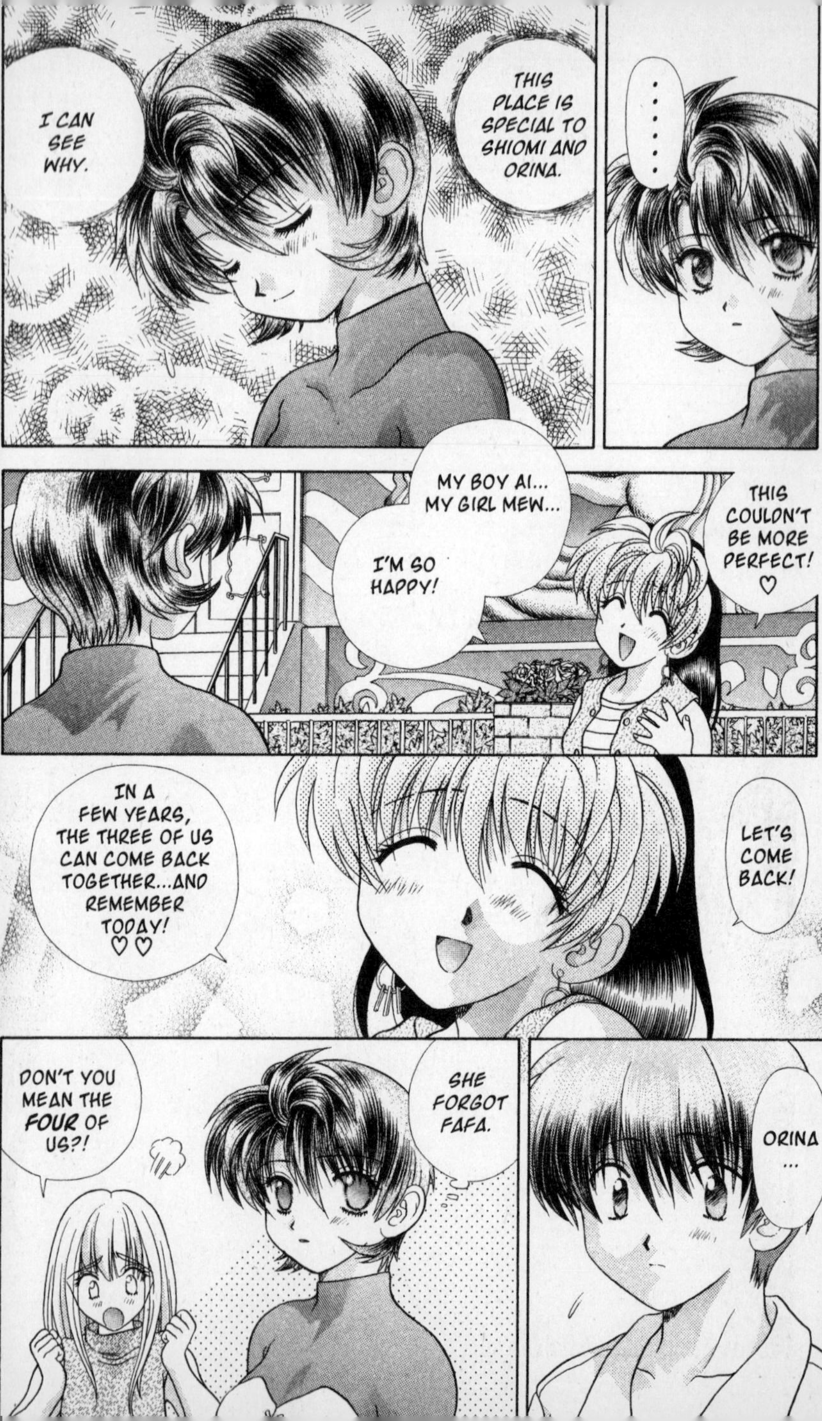
......
THIS PLACE IS SPECIAL TO SHIOMI AND ORINA.
I CAN SEE WHY.
THIS COULDN'T BE MORE PERFECT! ♡
MY BOY AI... MY GIRL MEW...
I'M SO HAPPY!
LET'S COME BACK!
IN A FEW YEARS, THE THREE OF US CAN COME BACK TOGETHER...AND REMEMBER TODAY! ♡♡
ORINA ...
SHE FORGOT FAFA.
DON'T YOU MEAN THE *FOUR* OF US?!

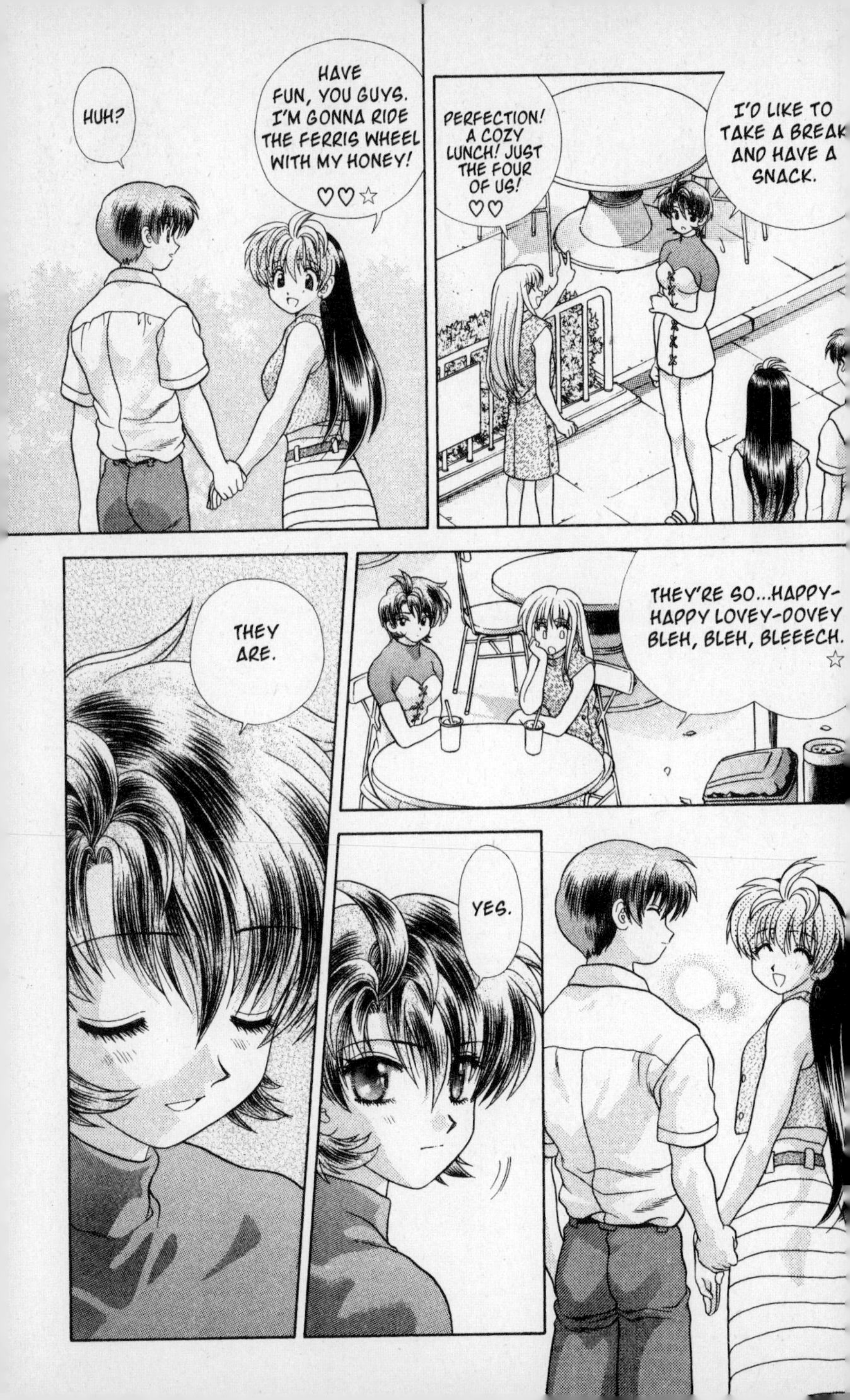
I'D LIKE TO TAKE A BREAK AND HAVE A SNACK.
PERFECTION! A COZY LUNCH! JUST THE FOUR OF US! ♡♡
HAVE FUN, YOU GUYS. I'M GONNA RIDE THE FERRIS WHEEL WITH MY HONEY! ♡♡☆
HUH?
THEY'RE SO...HAPPY-HAPPY LOVEY-DOVEY BLEH, BLEH, BLEEECH. ☆
YES.
THEY ARE.

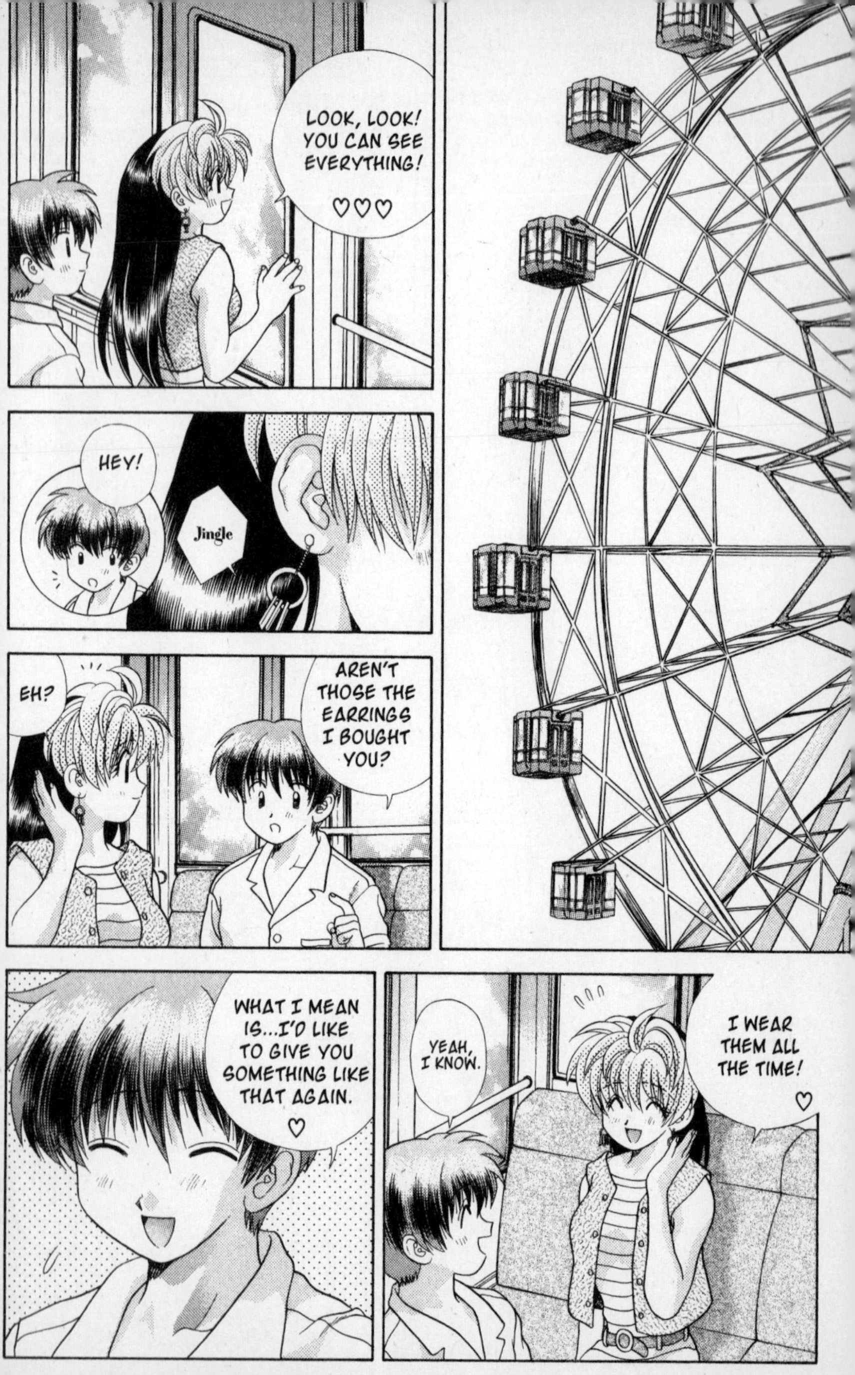
LOOK, LOOK! YOU CAN SEE EVERYTHING! ♡♡♡
HEY!
Jingle
AREN'T THOSE THE EARRINGS I BOUGHT YOU?
EH?
I WEAR THEM ALL THE TIME! ♡
YEAH, I KNOW.
WHAT I MEAN IS...I'D LIKE TO GIVE YOU SOMETHING LIKE THAT AGAIN. ♡

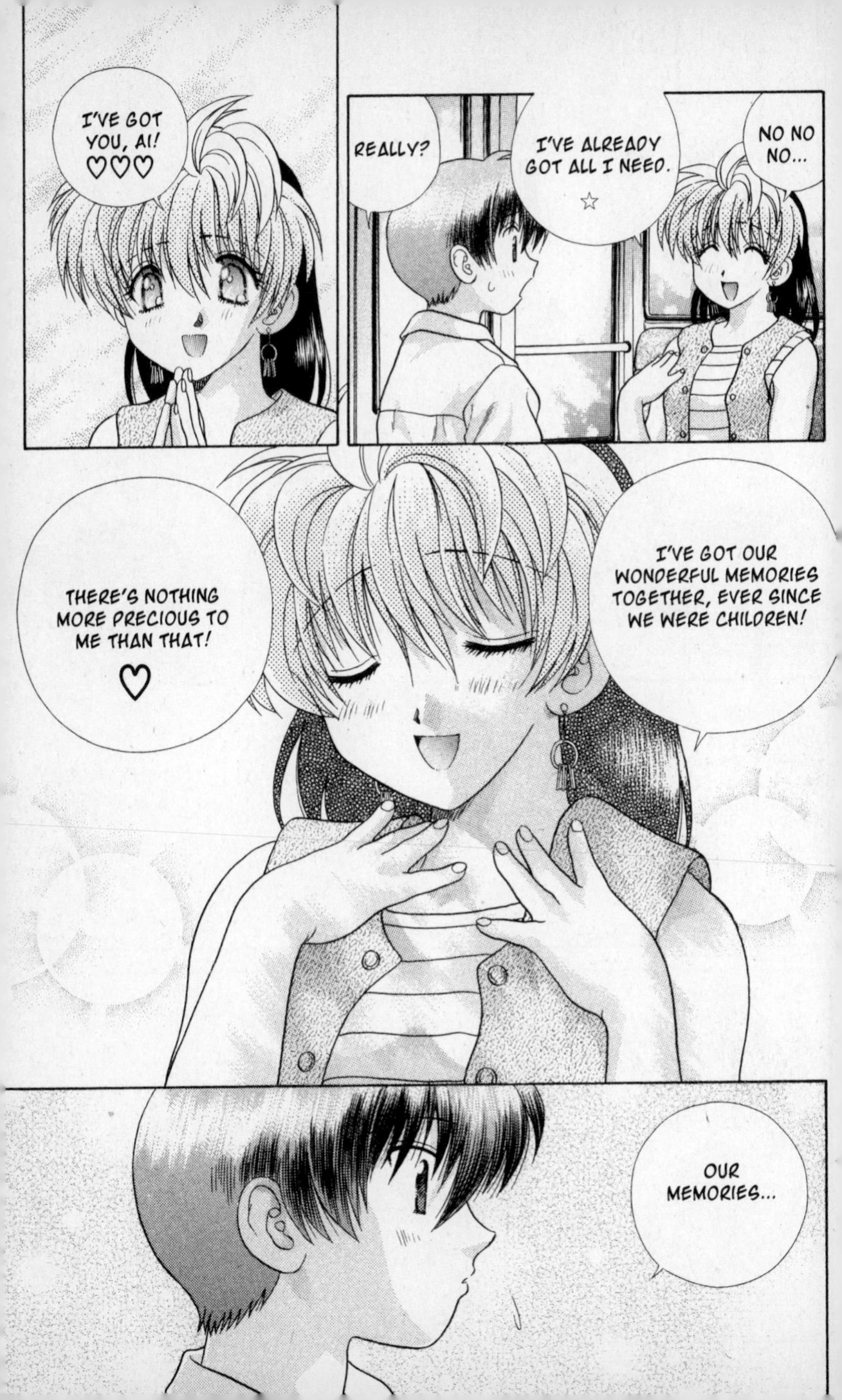
NO NO NO...
I'VE ALREADY GOT ALL I NEED. ☆
REALLY?
I'VE GOT YOU, AI! ♡♡♡
I'VE GOT OUR WONDERFUL MEMORIES TOGETHER, EVER SINCE WE WERE CHILDREN!
THERE'S NOTHING MORE PRECIOUS TO ME THAN THAT! ♡
OUR MEMORIES...

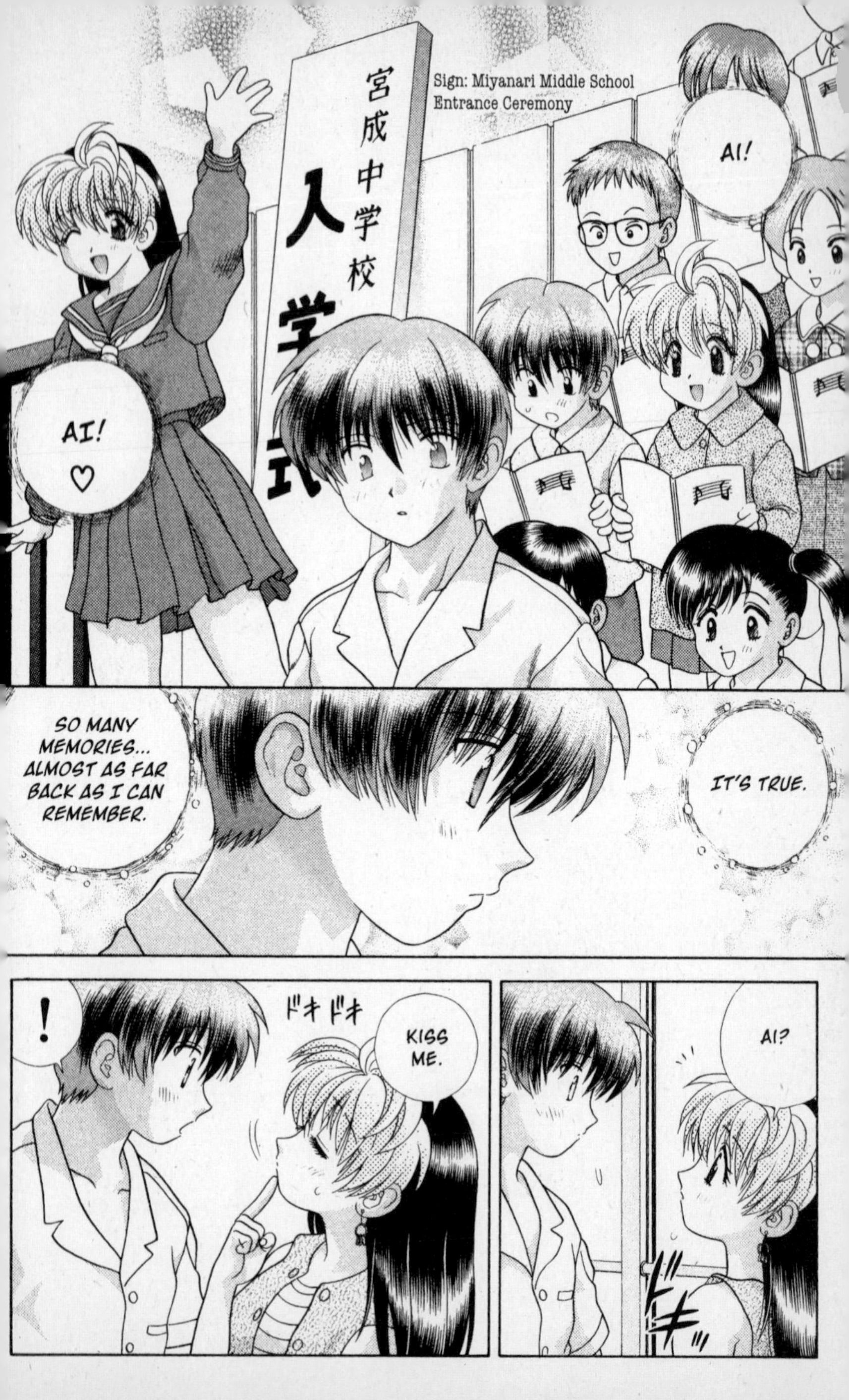

AI!
Sign: Miyanari Middle School Entrance Ceremony
宮成中学校
入学式
AI! ♡
IT'S TRUE.
SO MANY MEMORIES... ALMOST AS FAR BACK AS I CAN REMEMBER.
AI?
ドキ ドキ
KISS ME.
ドキドキ
!

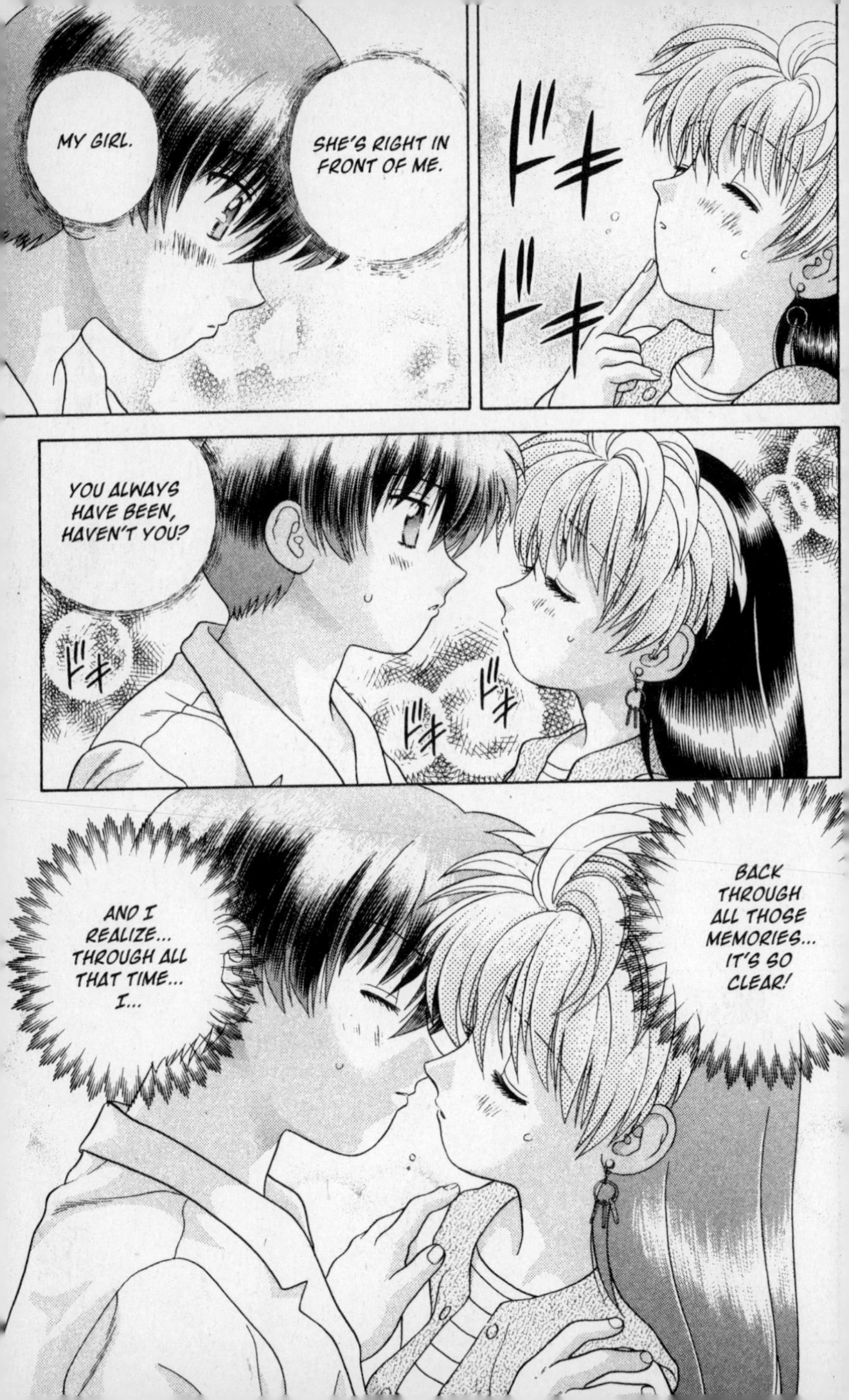
ドキ
ドキ
SHE'S RIGHT IN FRONT OF ME.
MY GIRL.
ドキ
ドキ
YOU ALWAYS HAVE BEEN, HAVEN'T YOU?
ドキ
BACK THROUGH ALL THOSE MEMORIES... IT'S SO CLEAR!
AND I REALIZE... THROUGH ALL THAT TIME... I...

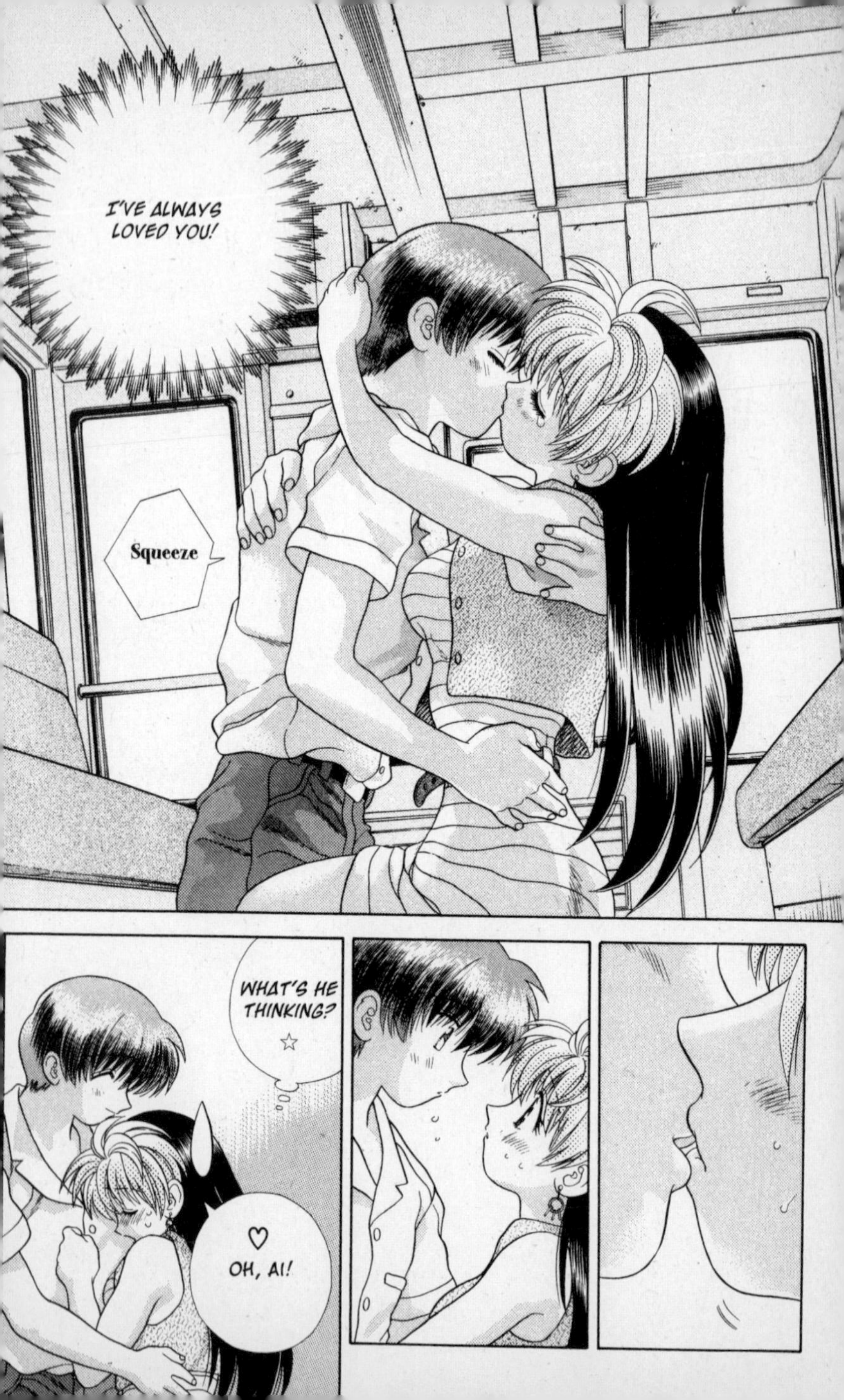
I'VE ALWAYS LOVED YOU!
Squeeze
WHAT'S HE THINKING? ☆
♡ OH, AI!

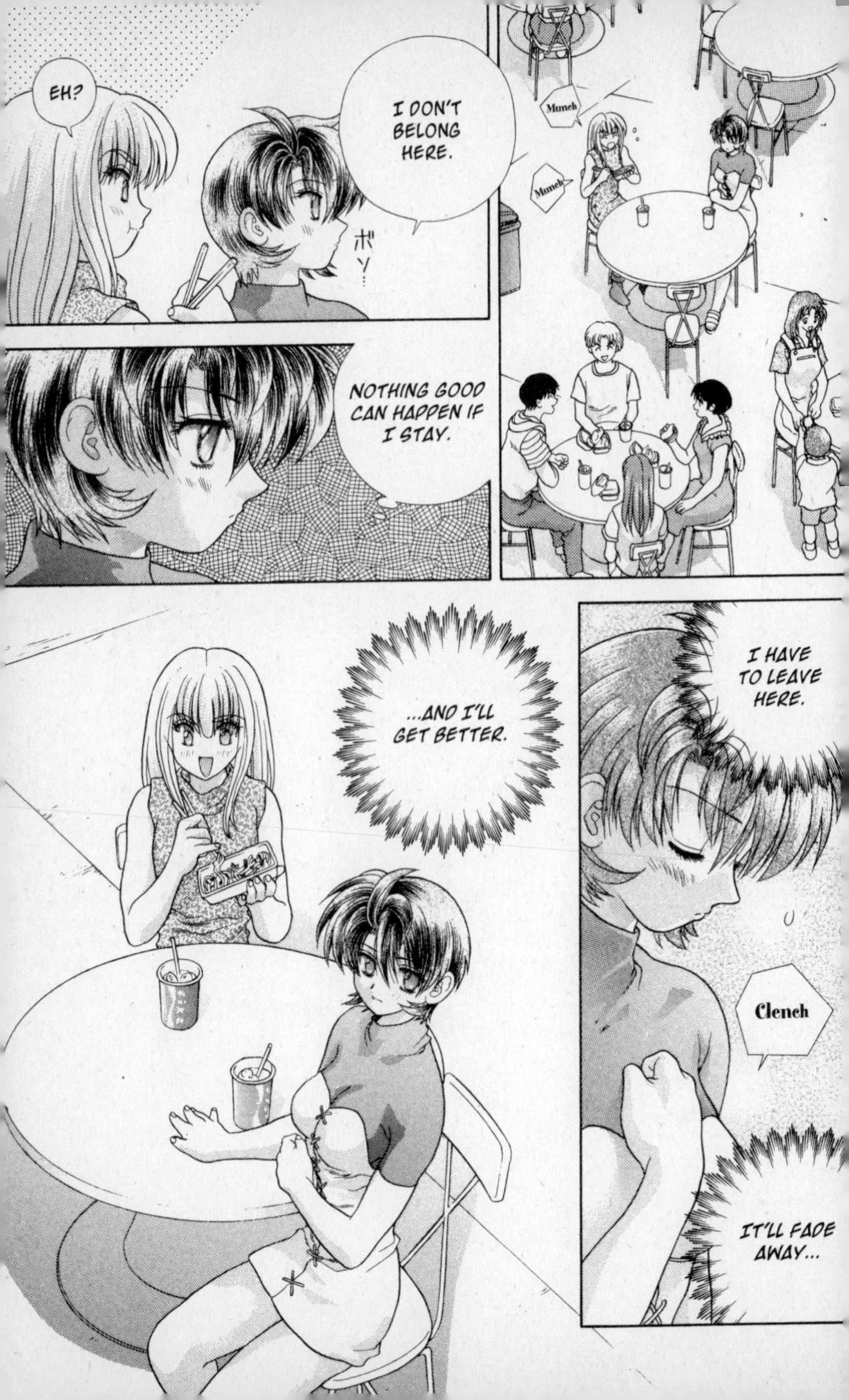
Munch
Munch
I DON'T BELONG HERE.
ボソ…
EH?
NOTHING GOOD CAN HAPPEN IF I STAY.
I HAVE TO LEAVE HERE.
Clench
IT'LL FADE AWAY...
...AND I'LL GET BETTER.

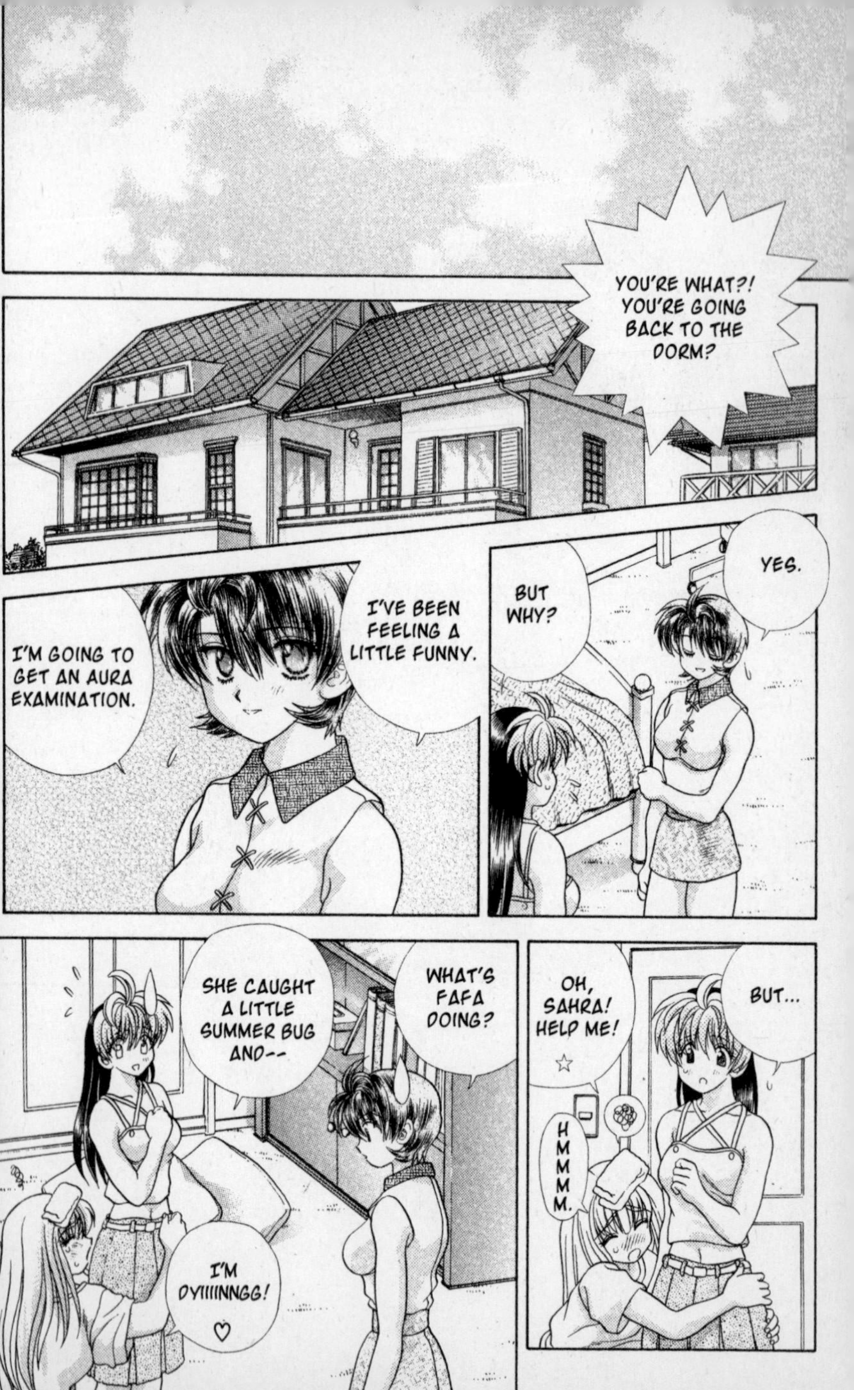
YOU'RE WHAT?! YOU'RE GOING BACK TO THE DORM?
YES.
BUT WHY?
I'VE BEEN FEELING A LITTLE FUNNY.
I'M GOING TO GET AN AURA EXAMINATION.
BUT...
OH, SAHRA! HELP ME! ☆
HMMMM.
WHAT'S FAFA DOING?
SHE CAUGHT A LITTLE SUMMER BUG AND--
I'M DYIIIINNGG! ♡

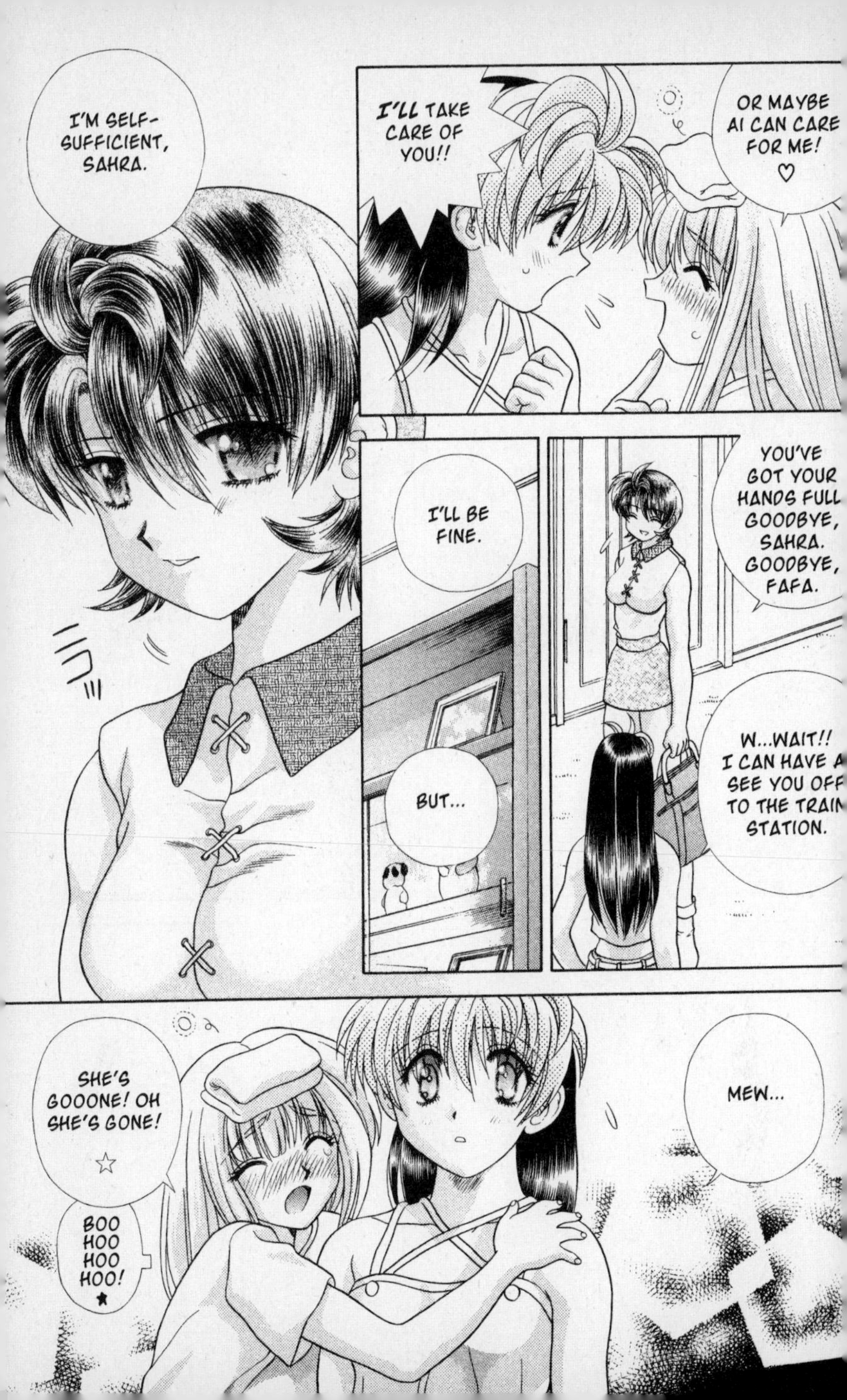
OR MAYBE AI CAN CARE FOR ME! ♡
I'LL TAKE CARE OF YOU!!
YOU'VE GOT YOUR HANDS FULL GOODBYE, SAHRA. GOODBYE, FAFA.
W...WAIT!! I CAN HAVE A SEE YOU OFF TO THE TRAIN STATION.
I'LL BE FINE.
BUT...
I'M SELF-SUFFICIENT, SAHRA.
MEW...
SHE'S GOOONE! OH SHE'S GONE! ☆
BOO HOO HOO HOO! ★

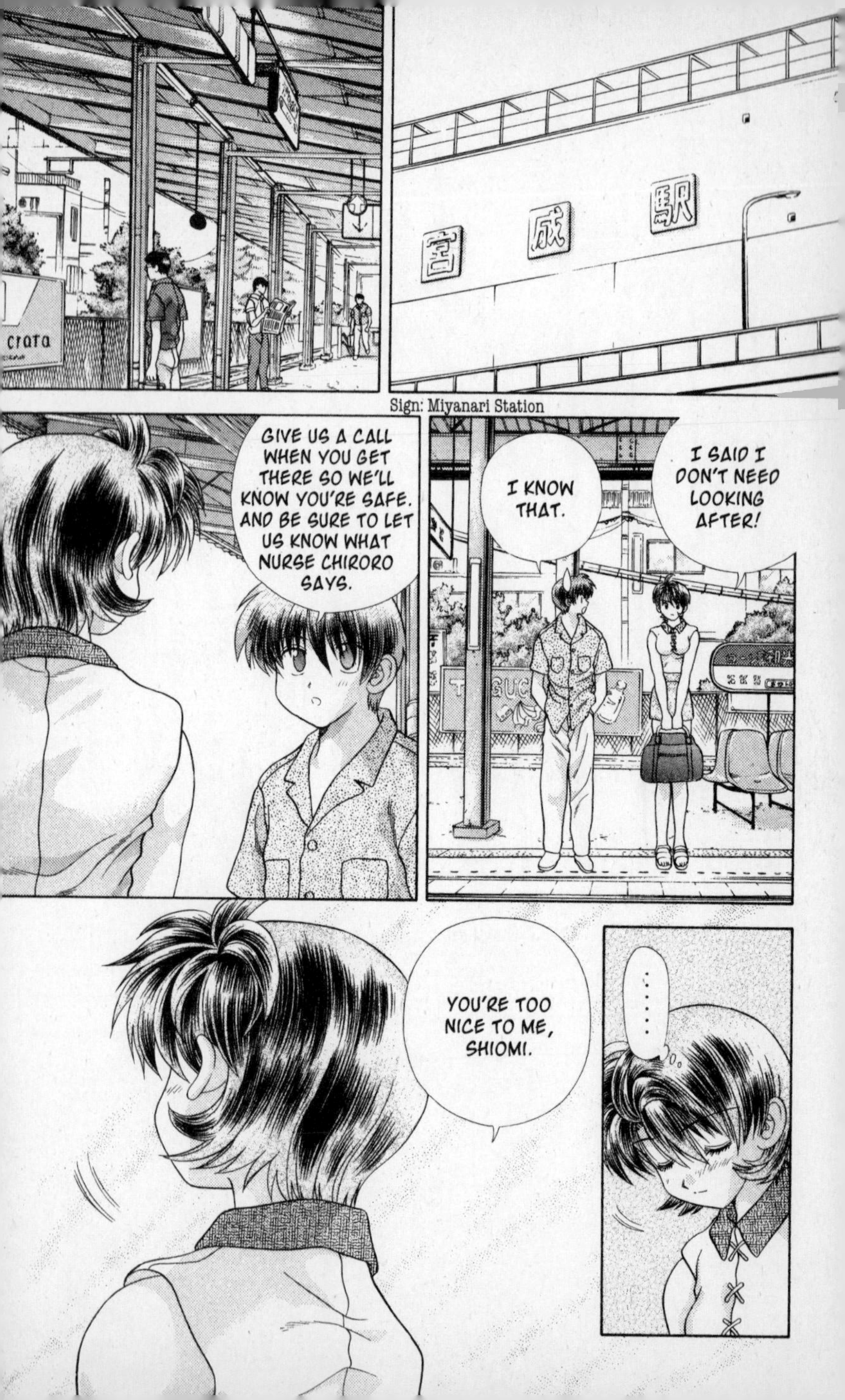
宮成駅
crata
Sign: Miyanari Station
I SAID I DON'T NEED LOOKING AFTER!
I KNOW THAT.
GIVE US A CALL WHEN YOU GET THERE SO WE'LL KNOW YOU'RE SAFE. AND BE SURE TO LET US KNOW WHAT NURSE CHIRORO SAYS.
......
YOU'RE TOO NICE TO ME, SHIOMI.

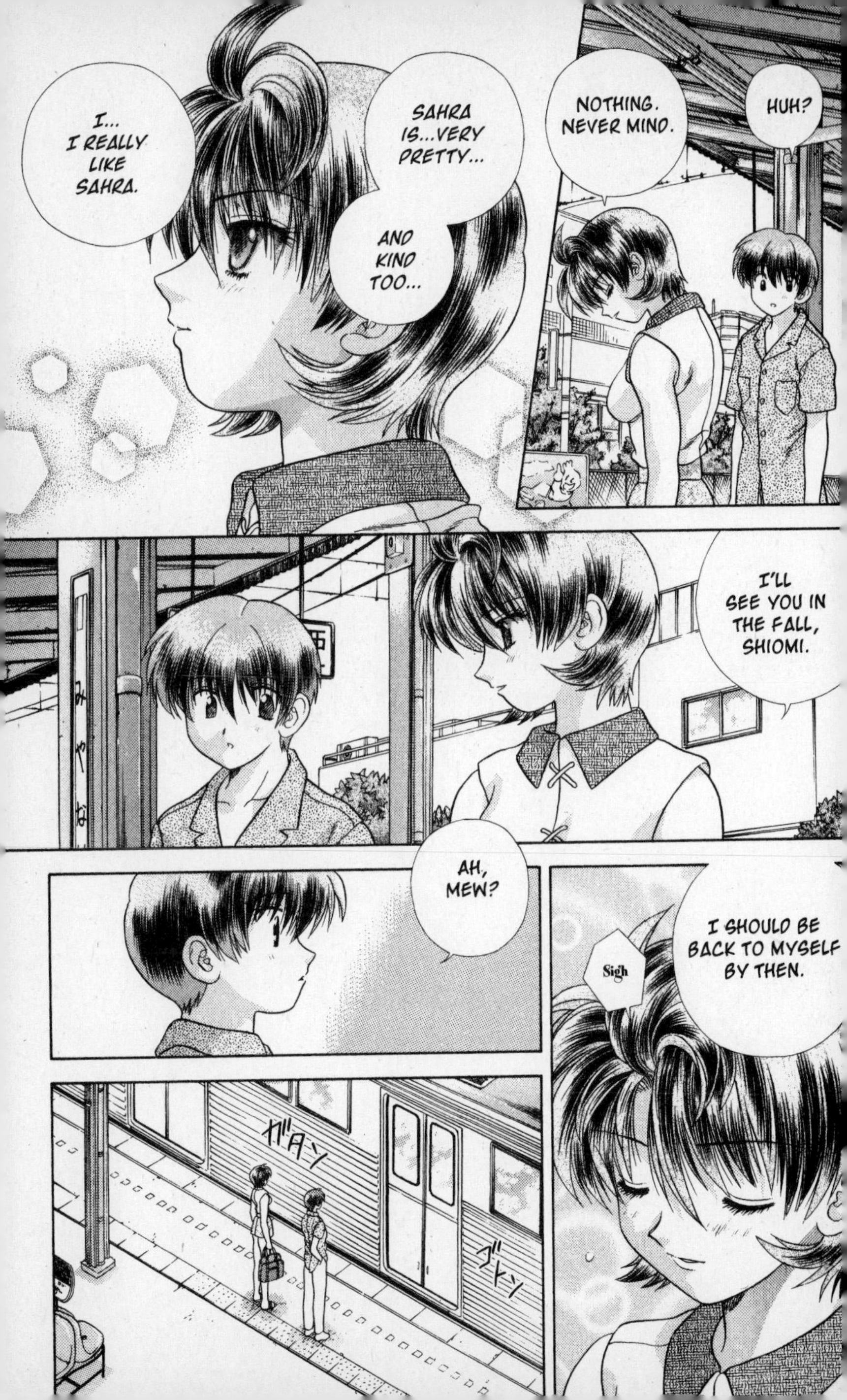
HUH?
NOTHING. NEVER MIND.
SAHRA IS...VERY PRETTY...
AND KIND TOO...
I... I REALLY LIKE SAHRA.
I'LL SEE YOU IN THE FALL, SHIOMI.
I SHOULD BE BACK TO MYSELF BY THEN.
Sigh
AH, MEW?
ガタン
ゴトン

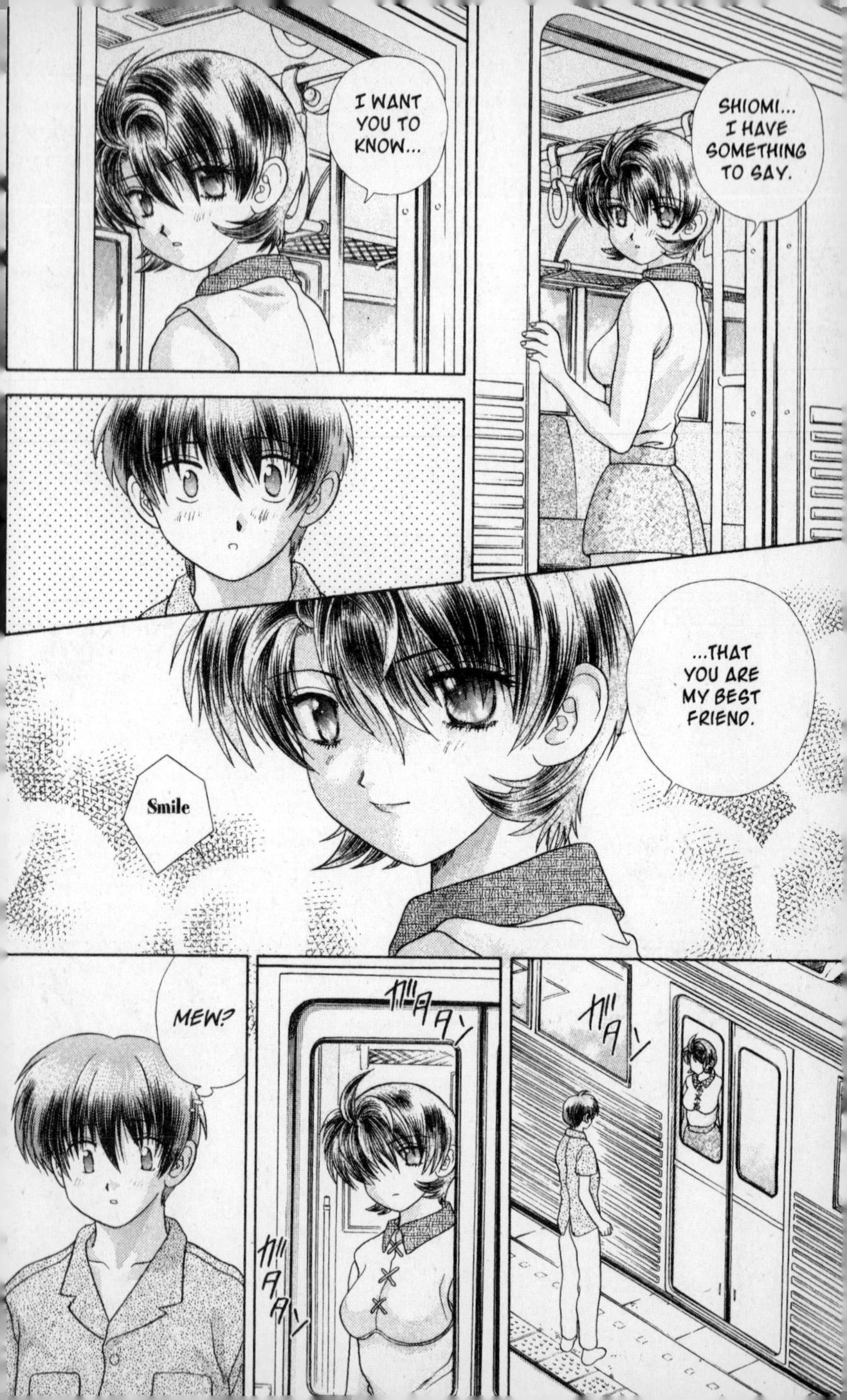
SHIOMI... I HAVE SOMETHING TO SAY.
I WANT YOU TO KNOW...
...THAT YOU ARE MY BEST FRIEND.
Smile
ガタン
ガタン
ガタン
MEW?

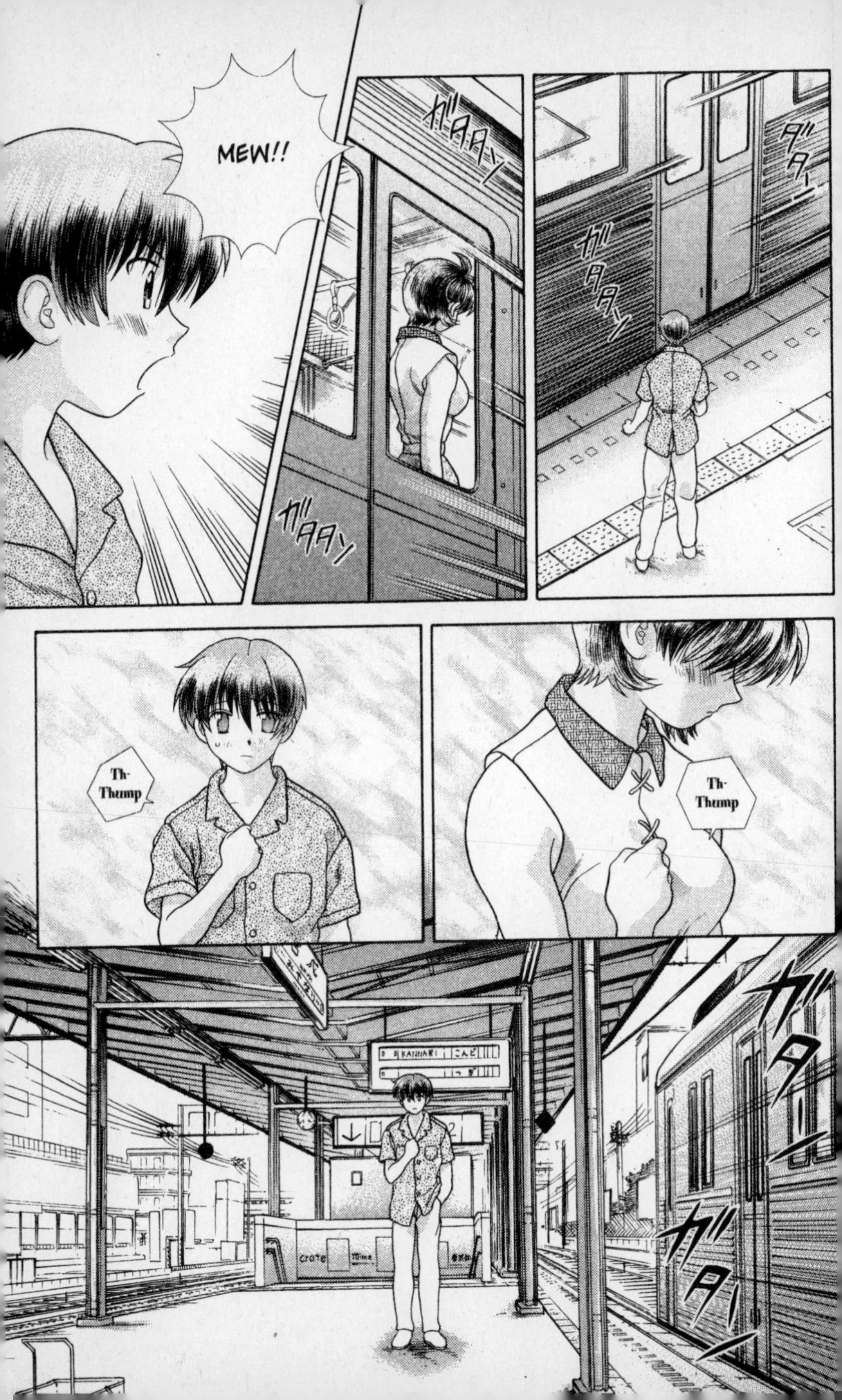
ダダー
ガタタン
ガタタン
ガタタン
MEW!!
Th-Thump
Th-Thump
KANNARI
こんど
つぎ

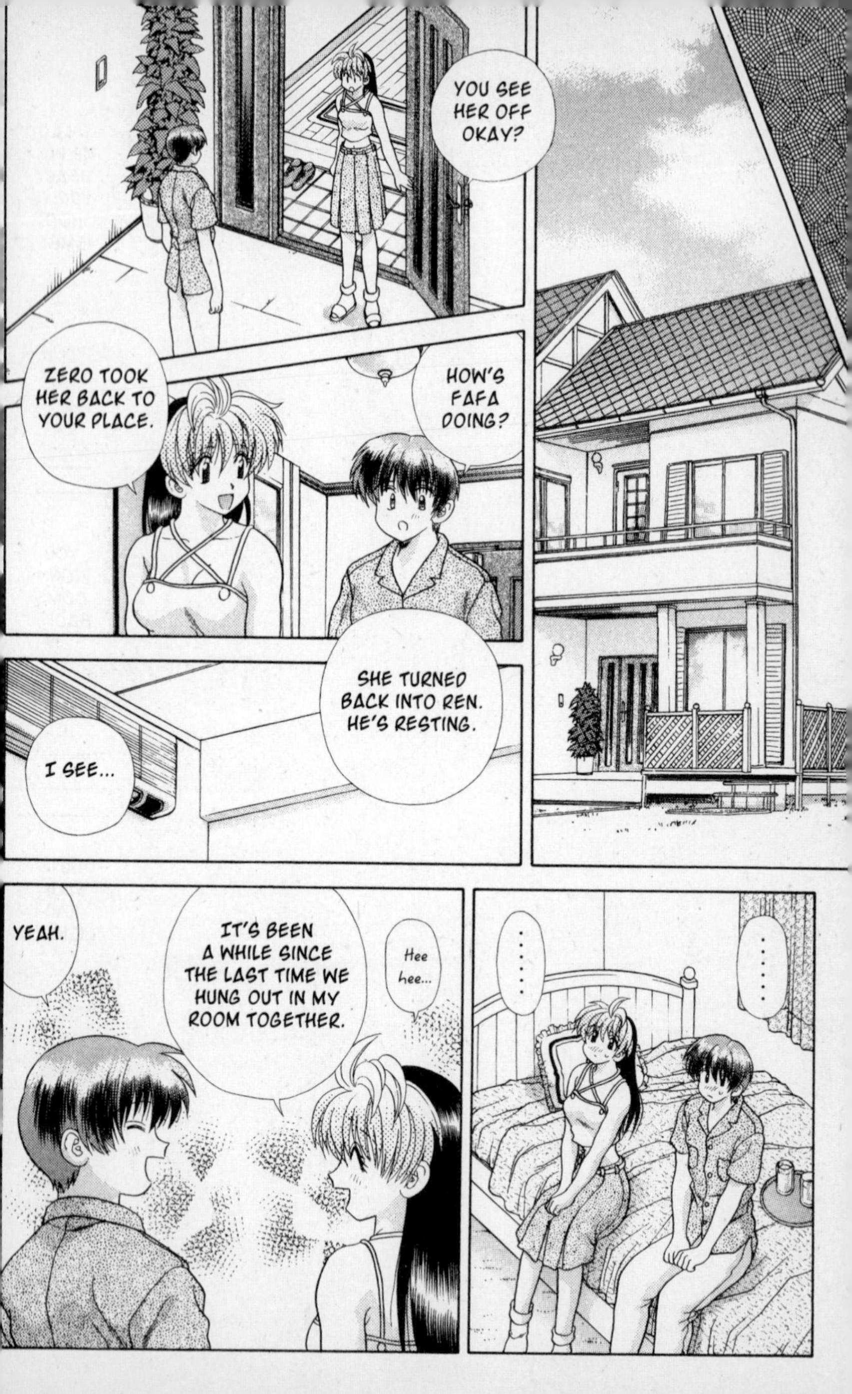
YOU SEE HER OFF OKAY?
HOW'S FAFA DOING?
ZERO TOOK HER BACK TO YOUR PLACE.
SHE TURNED BACK INTO REN. HE'S RESTING.
I SEE...
......
......
Hee hee...
IT'S BEEN A WHILE SINCE THE LAST TIME WE HUNG OUT IN MY ROOM TOGETHER.
YEAH.

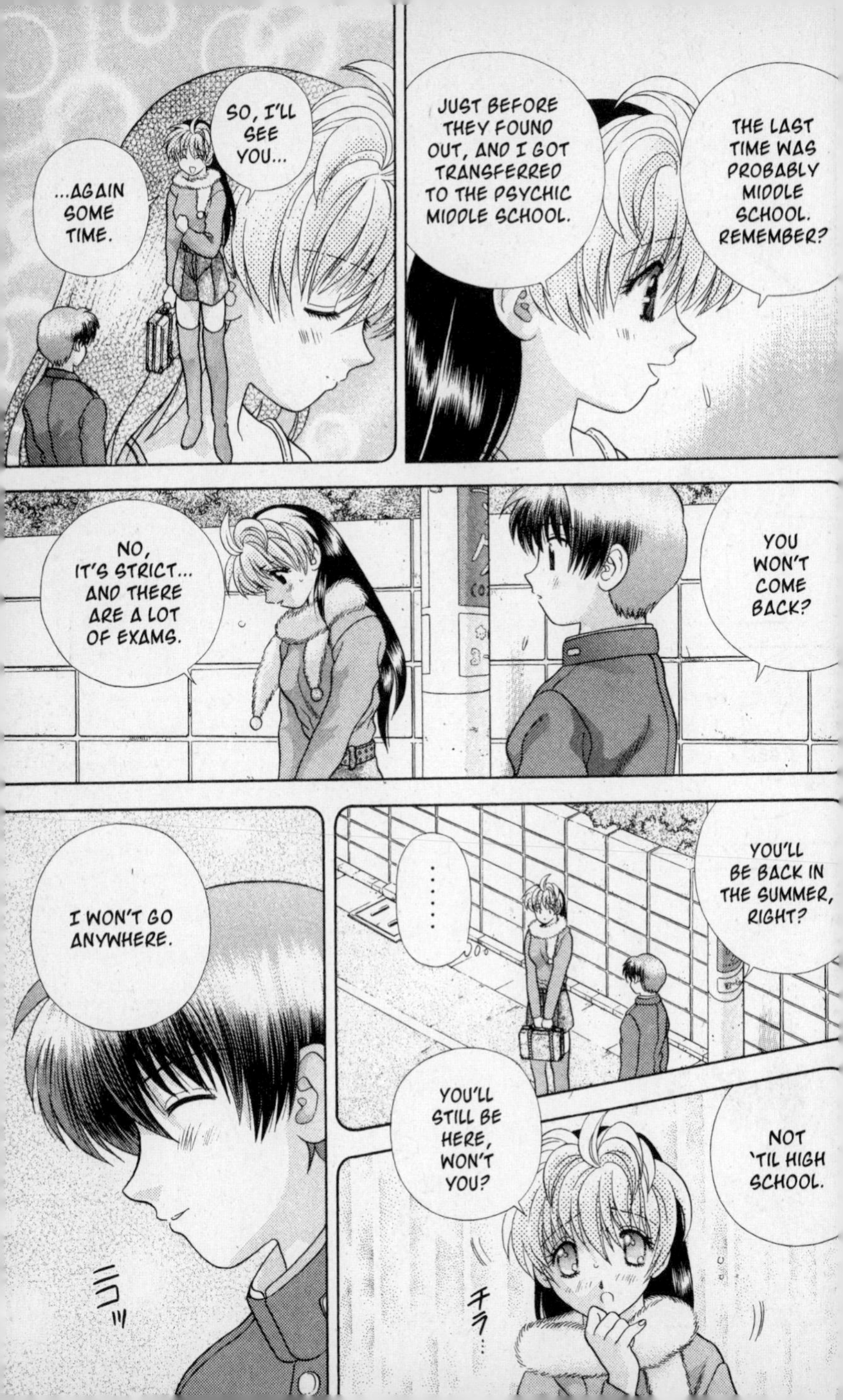
THE LAST TIME WAS PROBABLY MIDDLE SCHOOL. REMEMBER?
JUST BEFORE THEY FOUND OUT, AND I GOT TRANSFERRED TO THE PSYCHIC MIDDLE SCHOOL.
SO, I'LL SEE YOU...
...AGAIN SOME TIME.
YOU WON'T COME BACK?
NO, IT'S STRICT... AND THERE ARE A LOT OF EXAMS.
YOU'LL BE BACK IN THE SUMMER, RIGHT?
......
NOT 'TIL HIGH SCHOOL.
YOU'LL STILL BE HERE, WON'T YOU?
チラ…
I WON'T GO ANYWHERE.
ニコッ

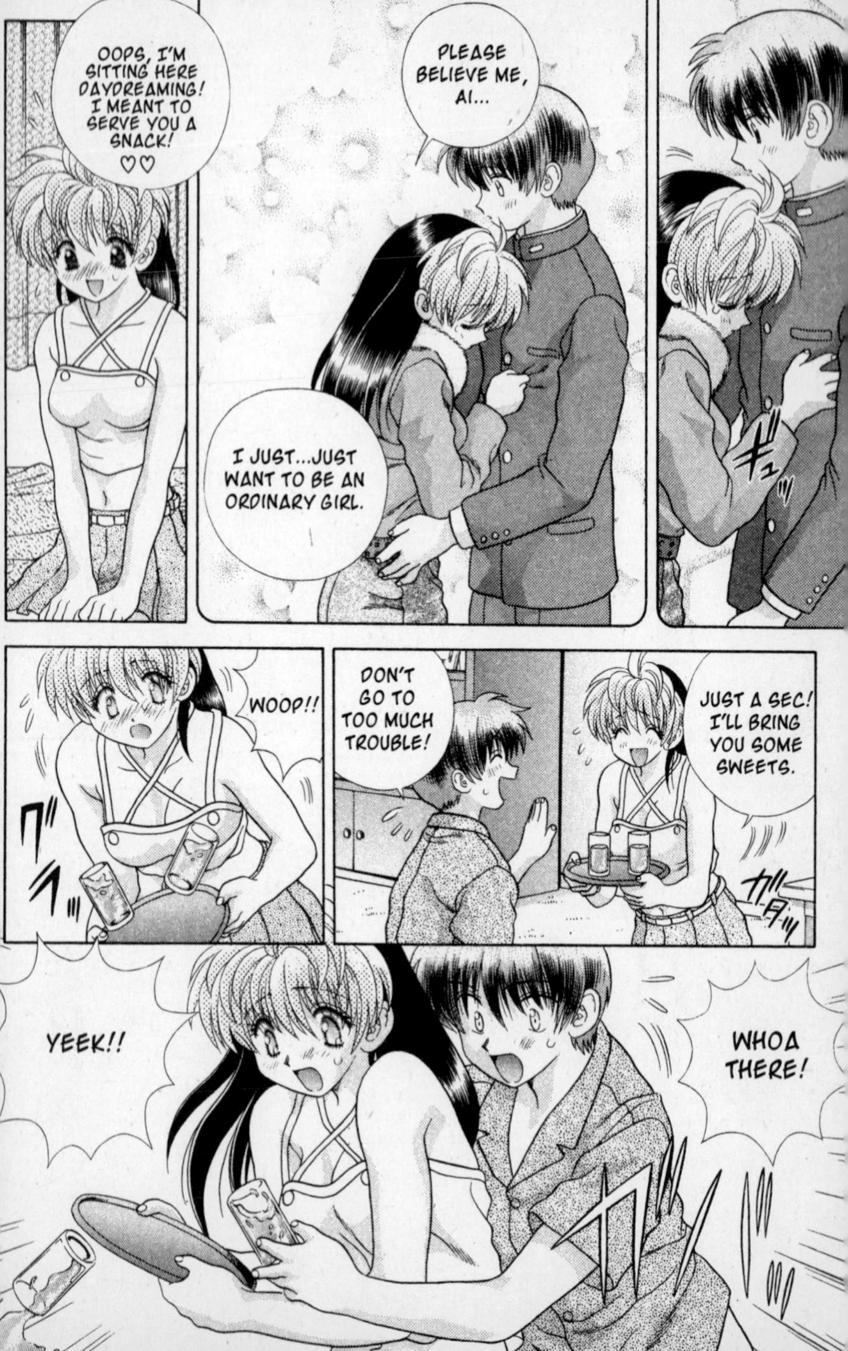
PLEASE BELIEVE ME, AI...
I JUST...JUST WANT TO BE AN ORDINARY GIRL.
OOPS, I'M SITTING HERE DAYDREAMING! I MEANT TO SERVE YOU A SNACK! ♡♡
JUST A SEC! I'LL BRING YOU SOME SWEETS.
DON'T GO TO TOO MUCH TROUBLE!
WOOP!!
WHOA THERE!
YEEK!!

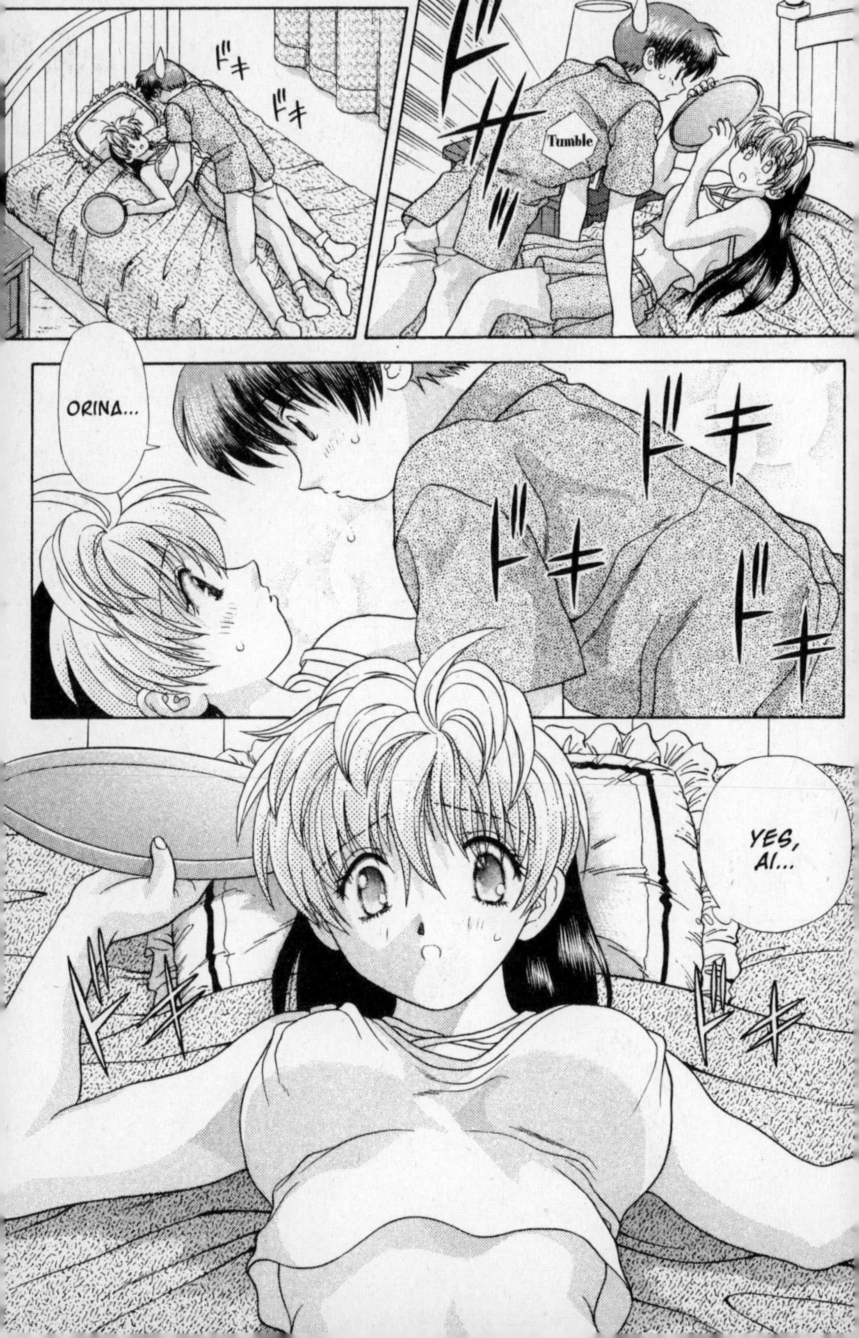

Tumble
ドキ
ドキ
ORINA...
ドキ
ドキ
ドキ
YES, AI...
ドキ
ドキ

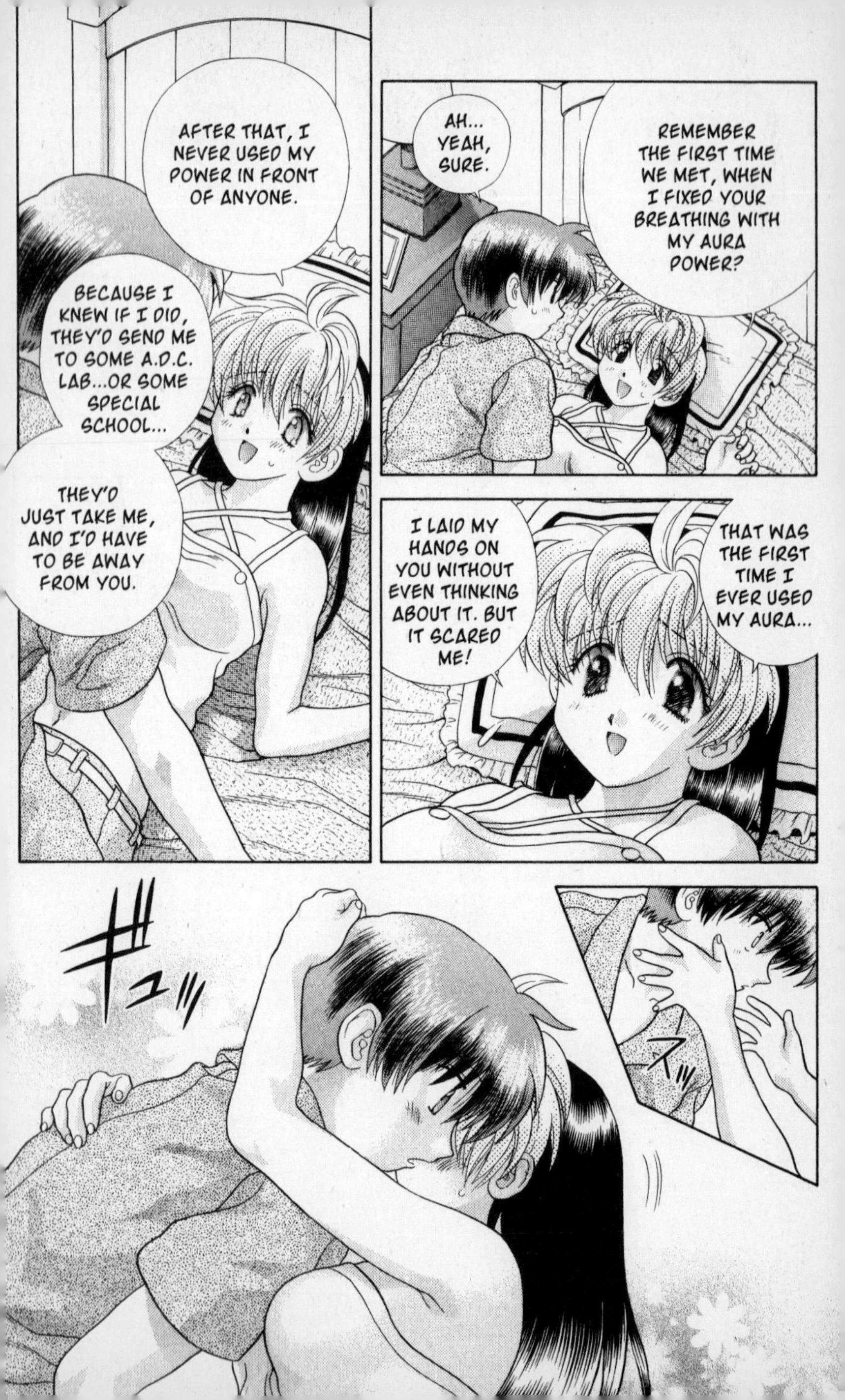
REMEMBER THE FIRST TIME WE MET, WHEN I FIXED YOUR BREATHING WITH MY AURA POWER?
AH... YEAH, SURE.
THAT WAS THE FIRST TIME I EVER USED MY AURA...
I LAID MY HANDS ON YOU WITHOUT EVEN THINKING ABOUT IT. BUT IT SCARED ME!
AFTER THAT, I NEVER USED MY POWER IN FRONT OF ANYONE.
BECAUSE I KNEW IF I DID, THEY'D SEND ME TO SOME A.D.C. LAB...OR SOME SPECIAL SCHOOL...
THEY'D JUST TAKE ME, AND I'D HAVE TO BE AWAY FROM YOU.
ス
ギュ

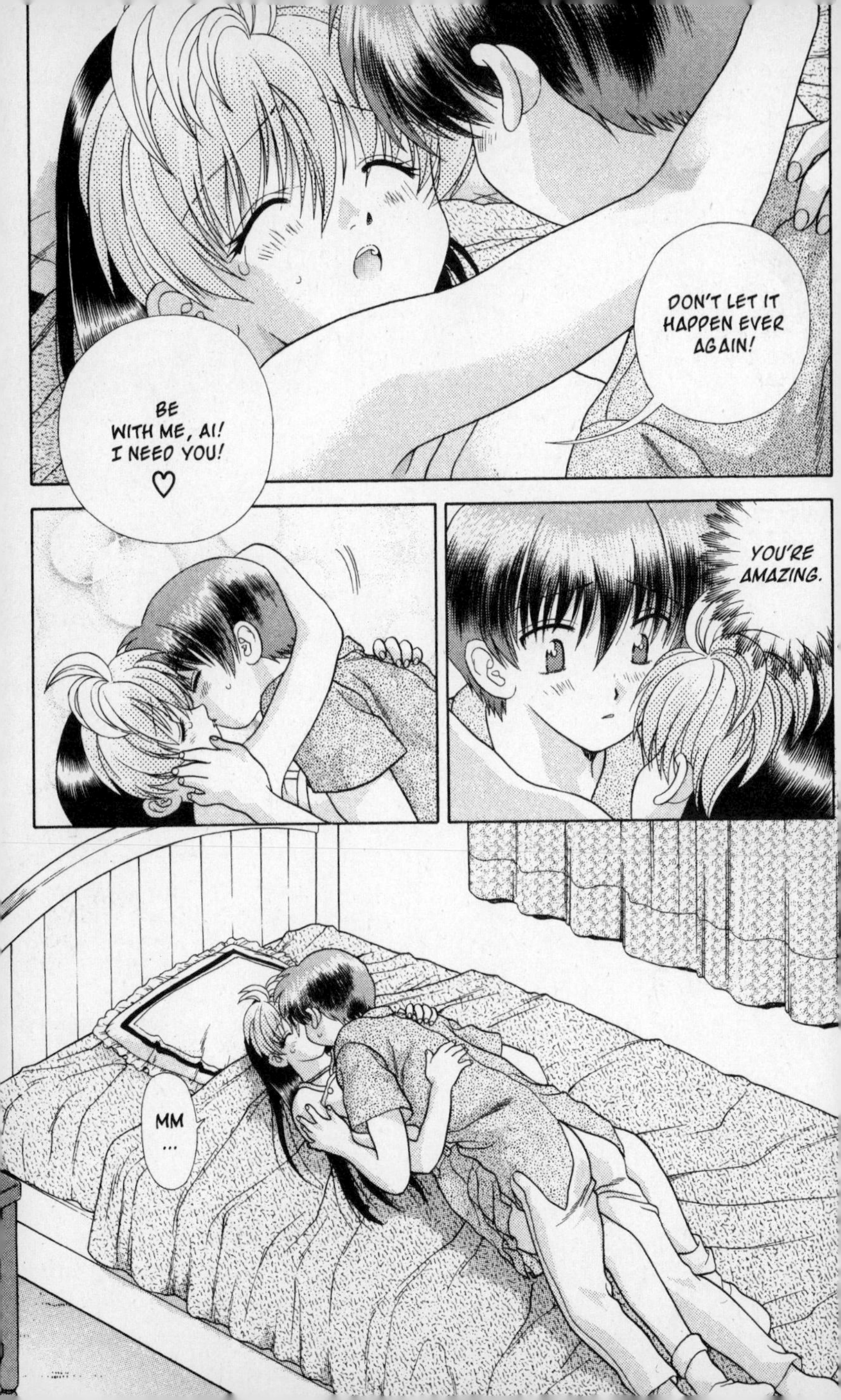
DON'T LET IT HAPPEN EVER AGAIN!
BE WITH ME, AI! I NEED YOU! ♡
YOU'RE AMAZING.
MM ...

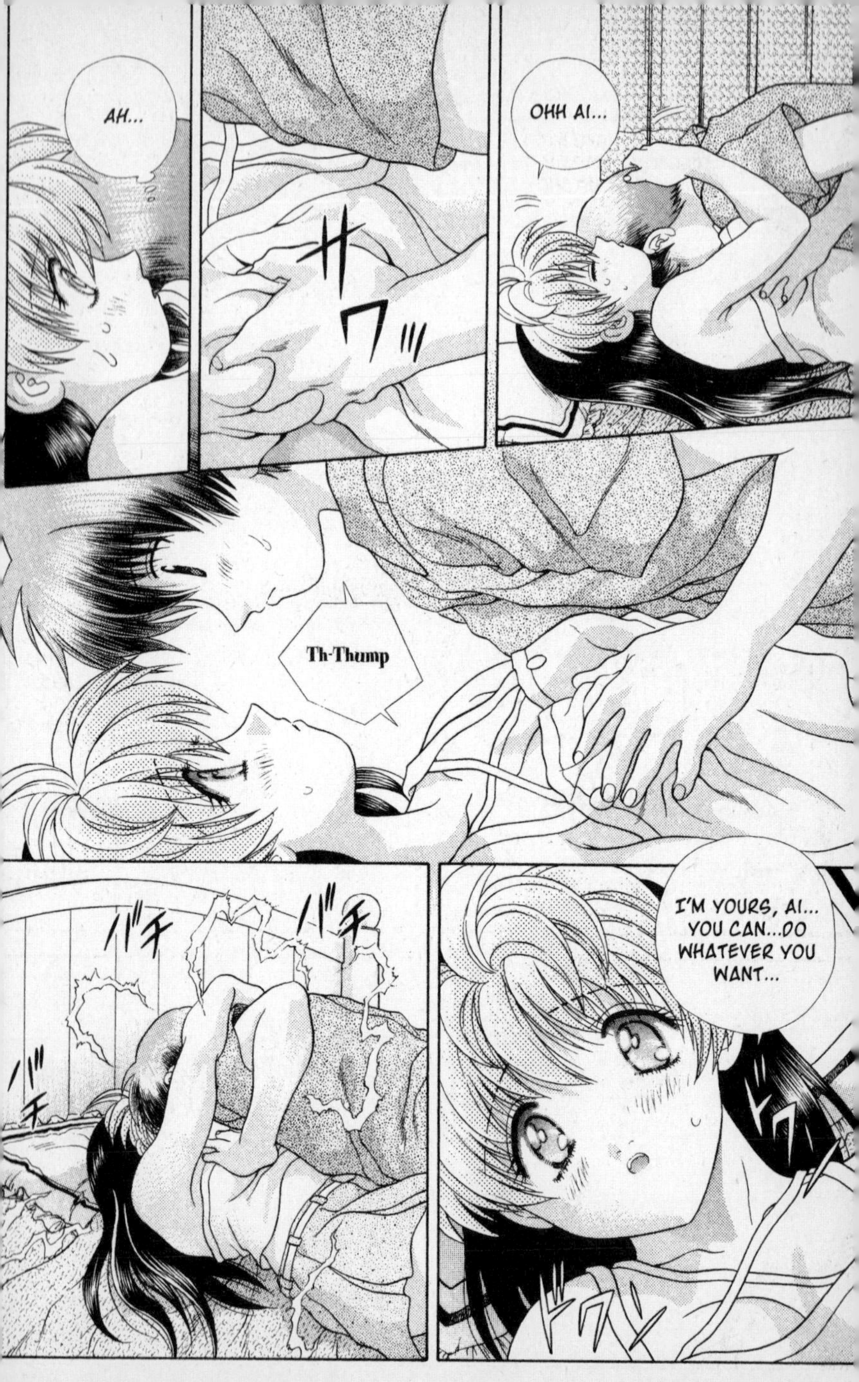
OHH AI...
AH...
Th-Thump
I'M YOURS, AI... YOU CAN...DO WHATEVER YOU WANT...
ドクン
バチ
バチ
バチ

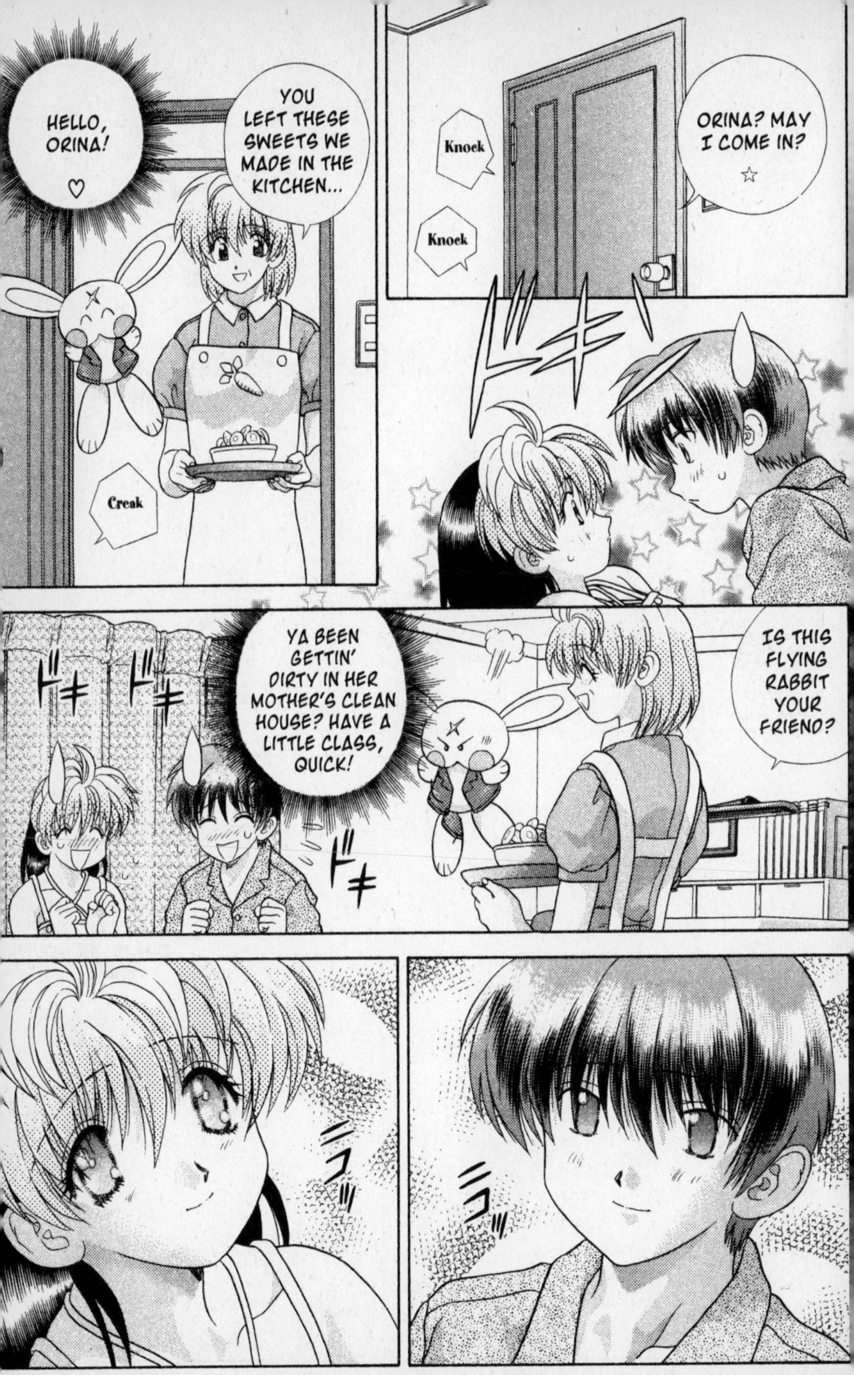
Knock
Knock
ORINA? MAY I COME IN? ☆
ドキッ
HELLO, ORINA! ♡
YOU LEFT THESE SWEETS WE MADE IN THE KITCHEN...
Creak
IS THIS FLYING RABBIT YOUR FRIEND?
ドキ
YA BEEN GETTIN' DIRTY IN HER MOTHER'S CLEAN HOUSE? HAVE A LITTLE CLASS, QUICK!
ドキ
ドキ
ニコッ
ニコッ

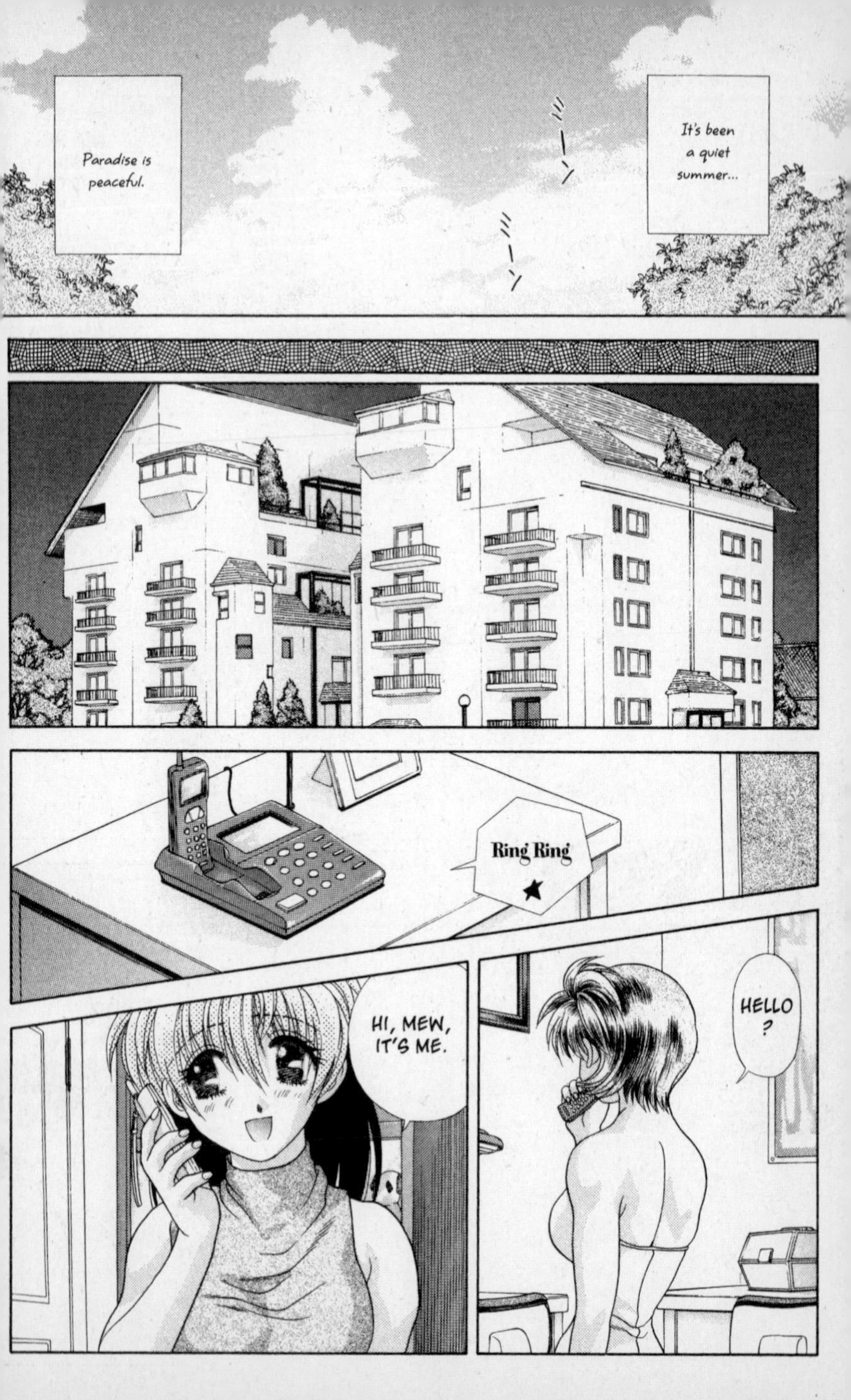
It's been a quiet summer...
ミーン
ミーン
Paradise is peaceful.
Ring Ring ★
HELLO ?
HI, MEW, IT'S ME.

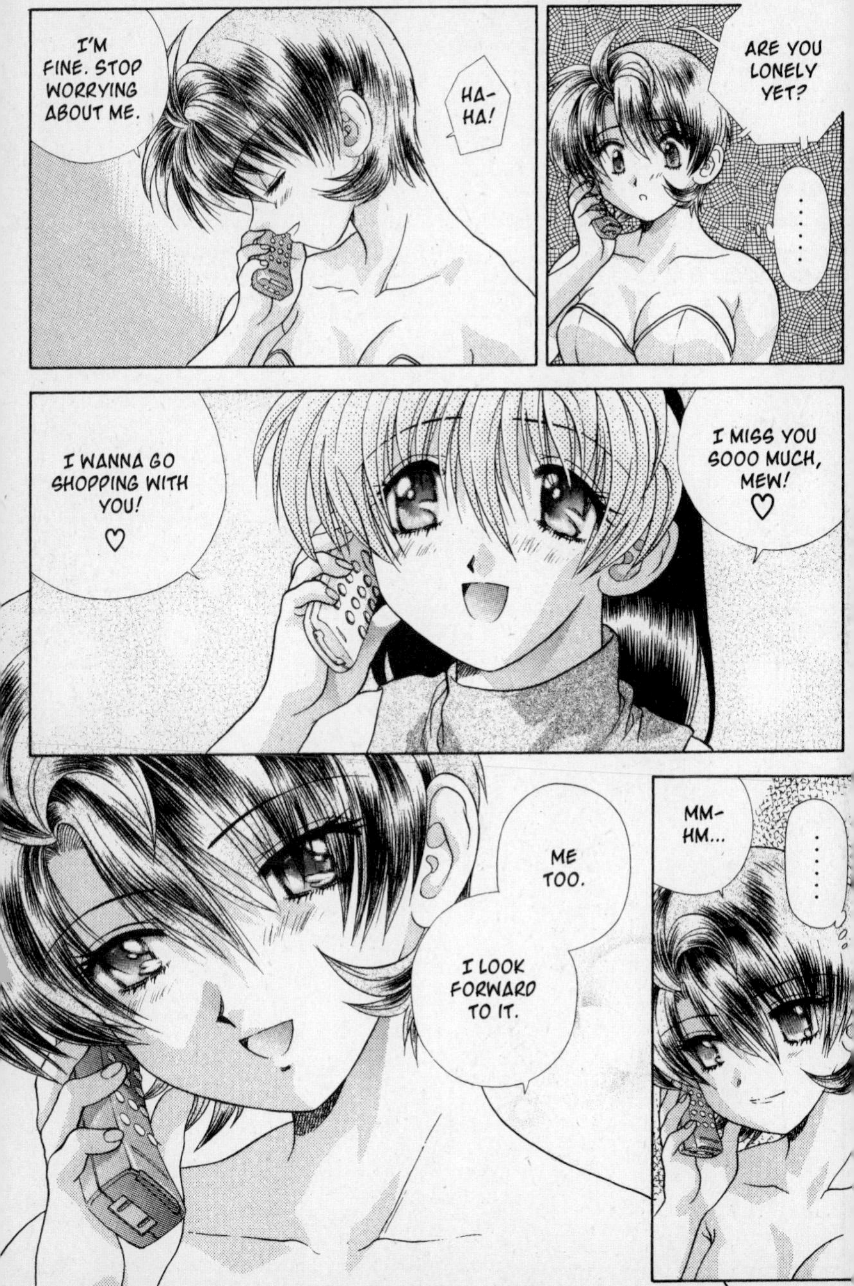
ARE YOU LONELY YET?
......
I'M FINE. STOP WORRYING ABOUT ME.
HA-HA!
I MISS YOU SOOO MUCH, MEW! ♡
I WANNA GO SHOPPING WITH YOU! ♡
......
MM-HM...
ME TOO.
I LOOK FORWARD TO IT.

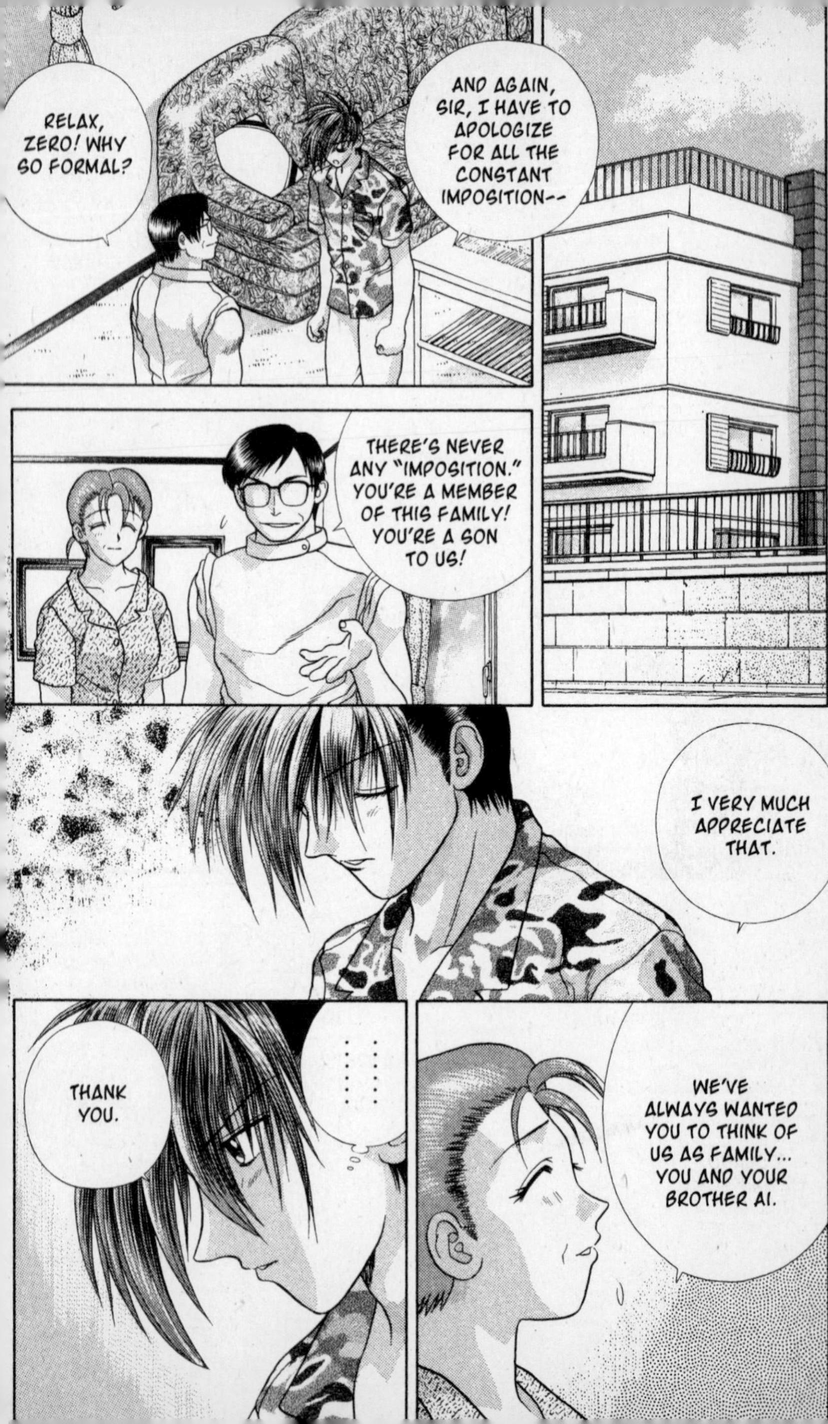
AND AGAIN, SIR, I HAVE TO APOLOGIZE FOR ALL THE CONSTANT IMPOSITION--
RELAX, ZERO! WHY SO FORMAL?
THERE'S NEVER ANY "IMPOSITION." YOU'RE A MEMBER OF THIS FAMILY! YOU'RE A SON TO US!
I VERY MUCH APPRECIATE THAT.
WE'VE ALWAYS WANTED YOU TO THINK OF US AS FAMILY... YOU AND YOUR BROTHER AI.
......
THANK YOU.

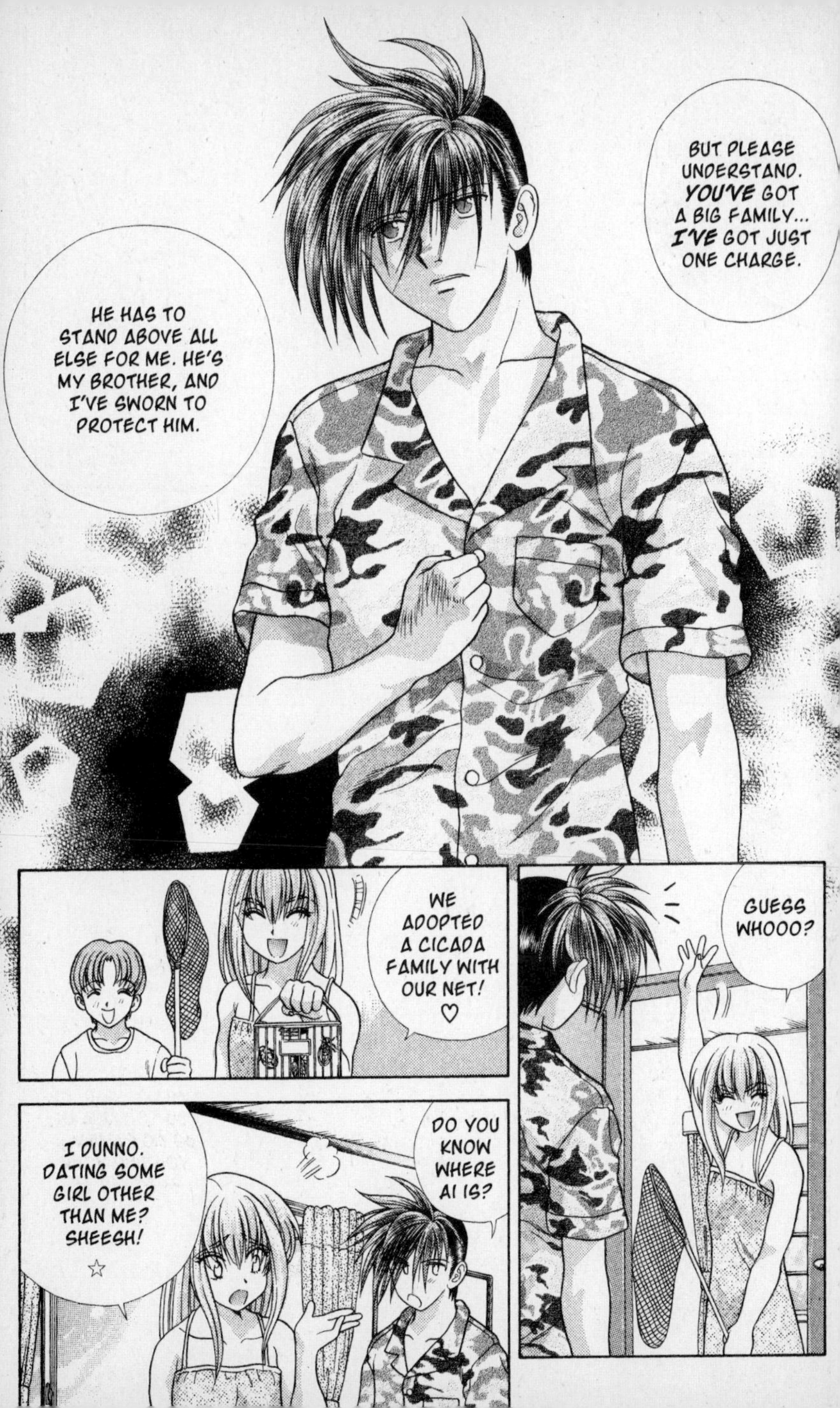
BUT PLEASE UNDERSTAND. *YOU'VE* GOT A BIG FAMILY... *I'VE* GOT JUST ONE CHARGE.
HE HAS TO STAND ABOVE ALL ELSE FOR ME. HE'S MY BROTHER, AND I'VE SWORN TO PROTECT HIM.
GUESS WHOOO?
WE ADOPTED A CICADA FAMILY WITH OUR NET! ♡
DO YOU KNOW WHERE AI IS?
I DUNNO. DATING SOME GIRL OTHER THAN ME? SHEESH! ☆

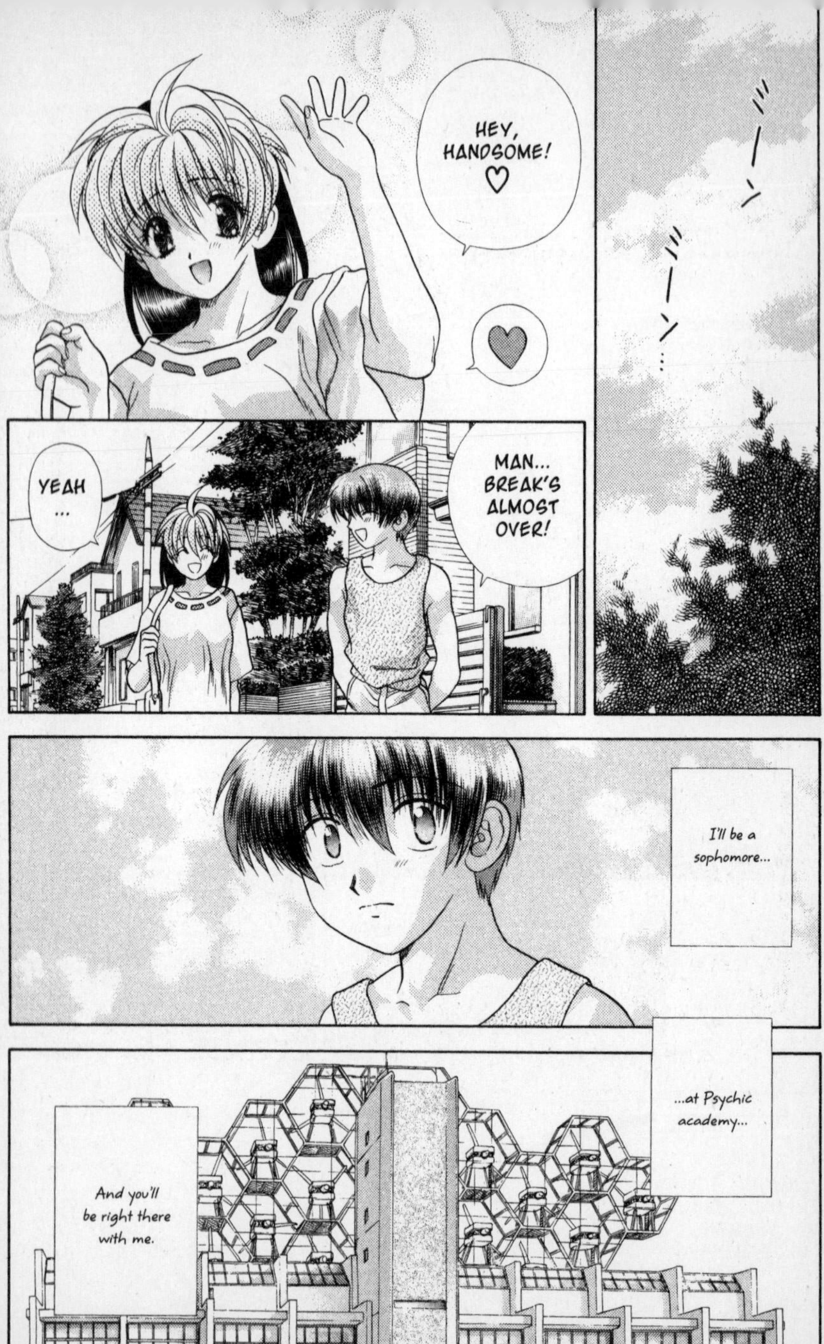
ジーン ジーン…
HEY, HANDSOME! ♡
♡
MAN... BREAK'S ALMOST OVER!
YEAH ...
I'll be a sophomore...
...at Psychic academy...
And you'll be right there with me.

Every Vow Under the Sun END

Chapter 17: The American Agents

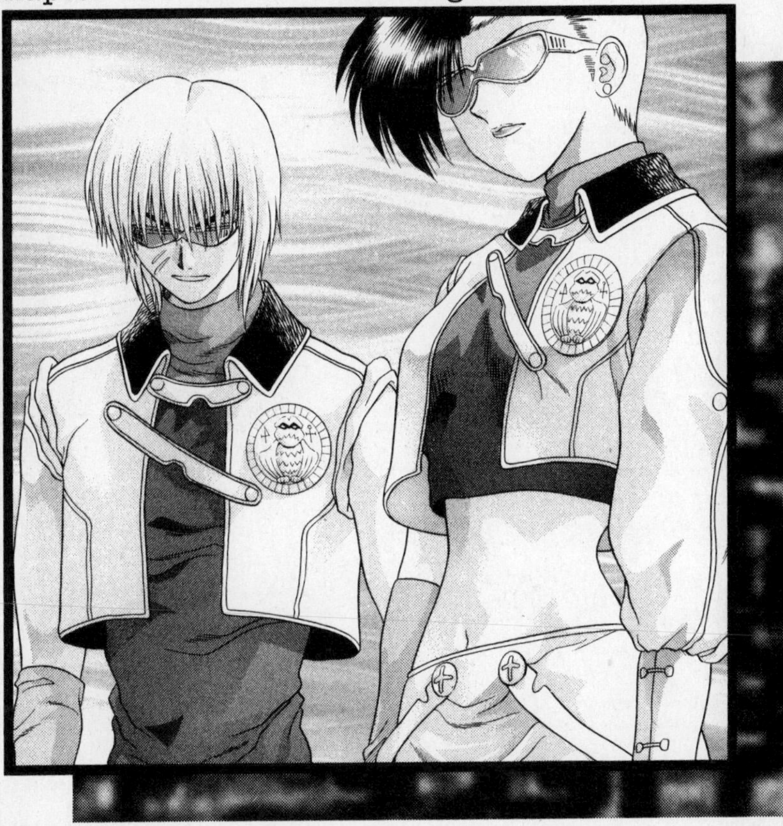

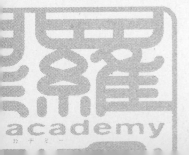

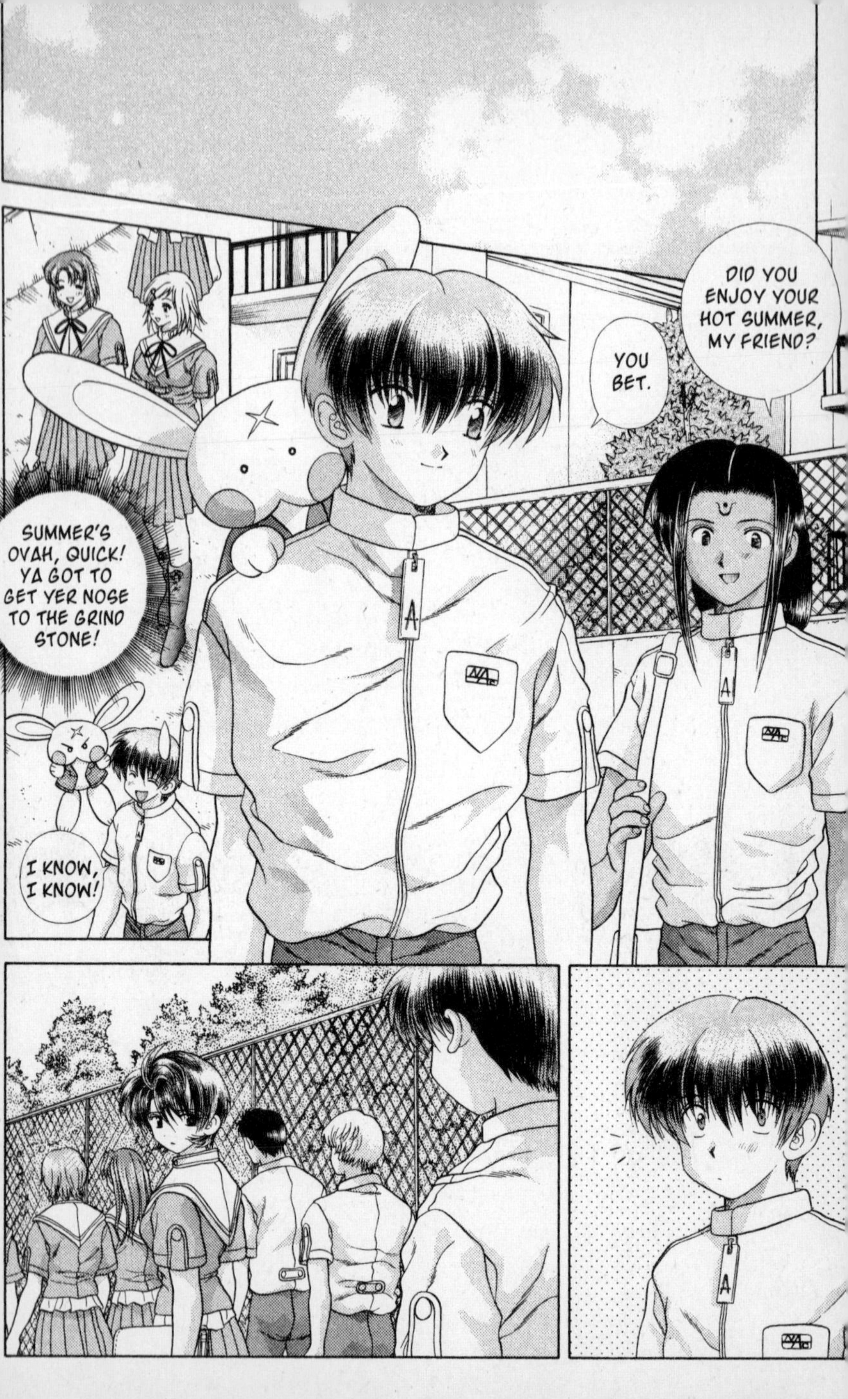
DID YOU ENJOY YOUR HOT SUMMER, MY FRIEND?
YOU BET.
SUMMER'S OVAH, QUICK! YA GOT TO GET YER NOSE TO THE GRIND STONE!
I KNOW, I KNOW!

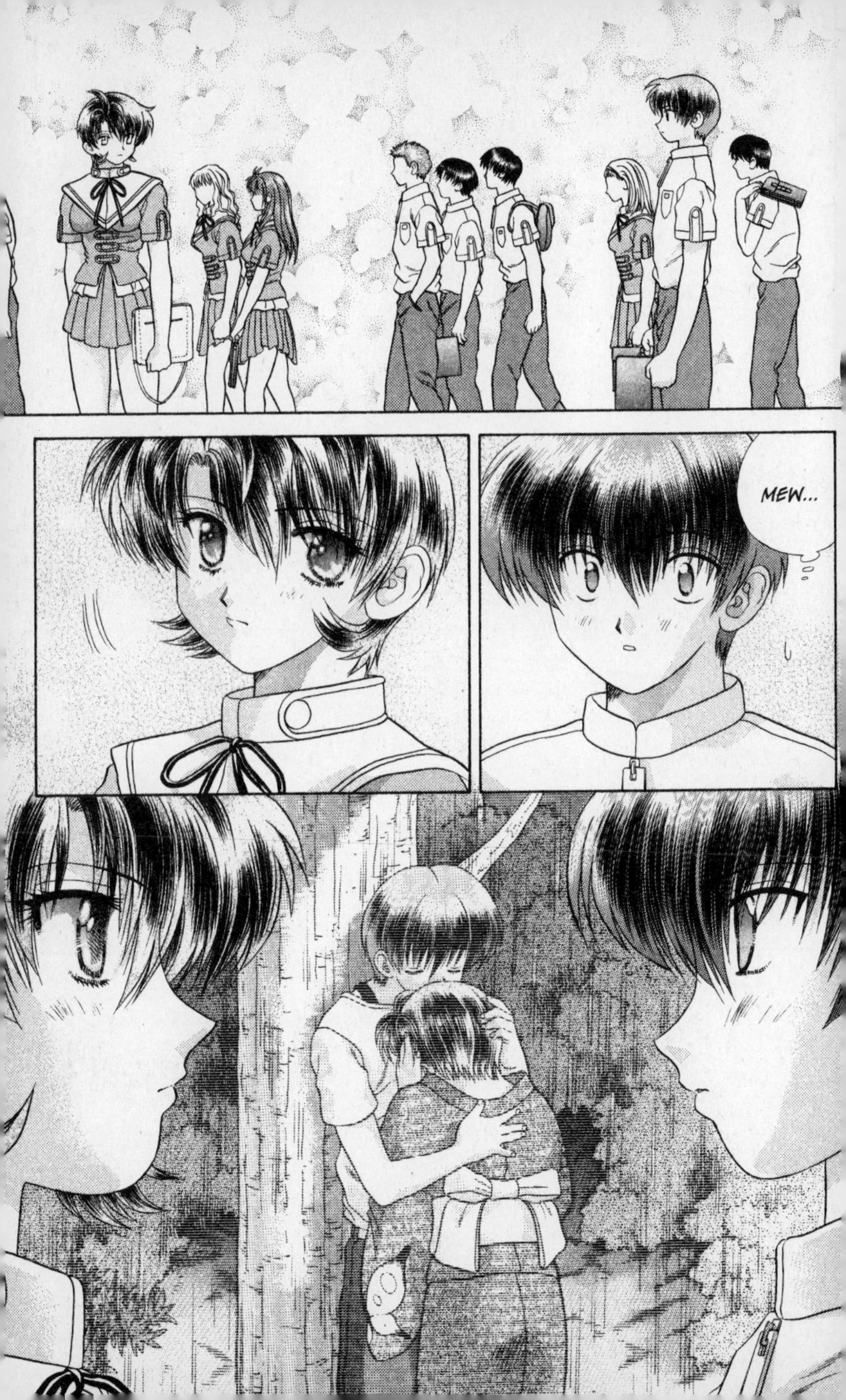
MEW...

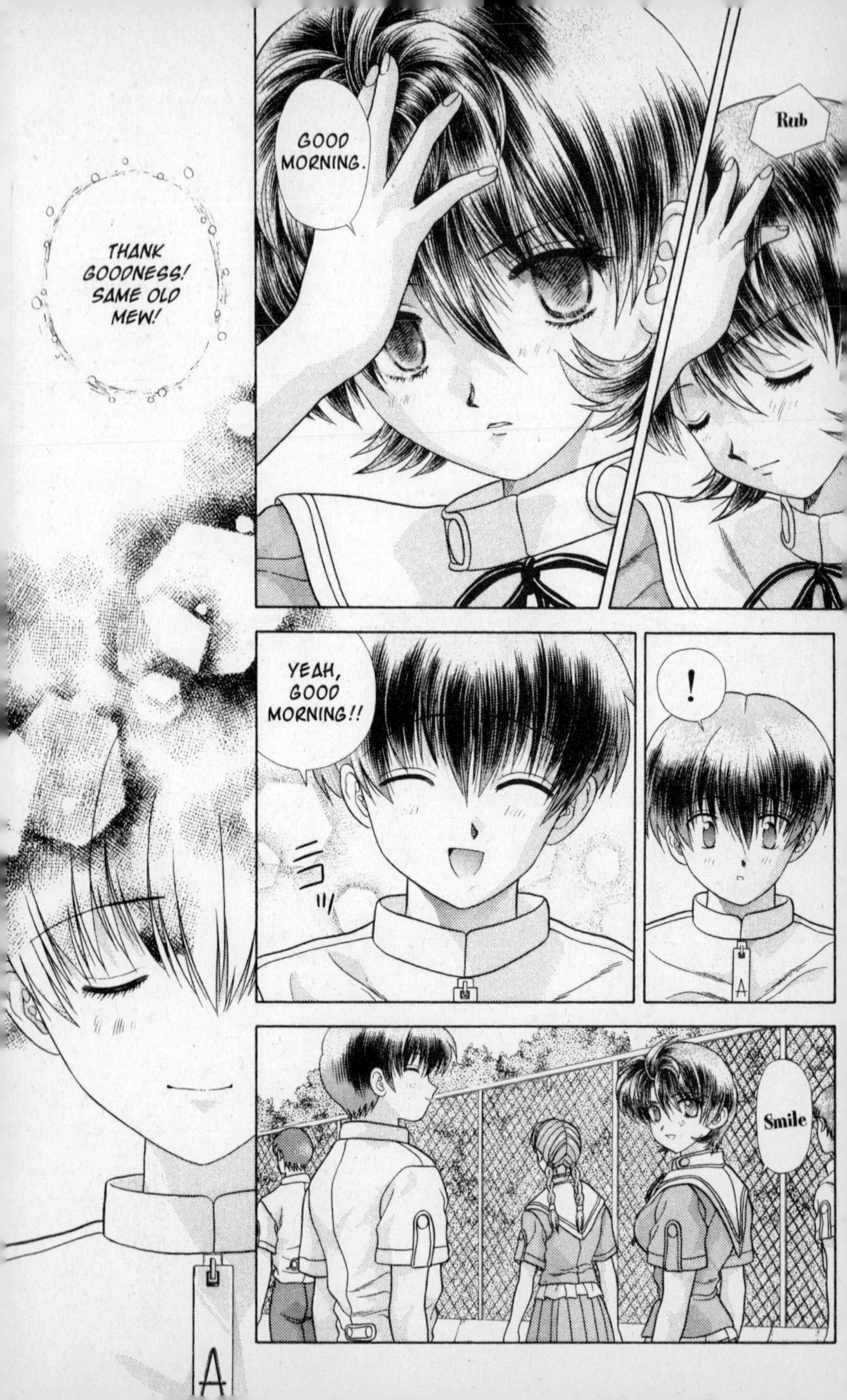
Rub
GOOD MORNING.
!
YEAH, GOOD MORNING!!
Smile
THANK GOODNESS! SAME OLD MEW!

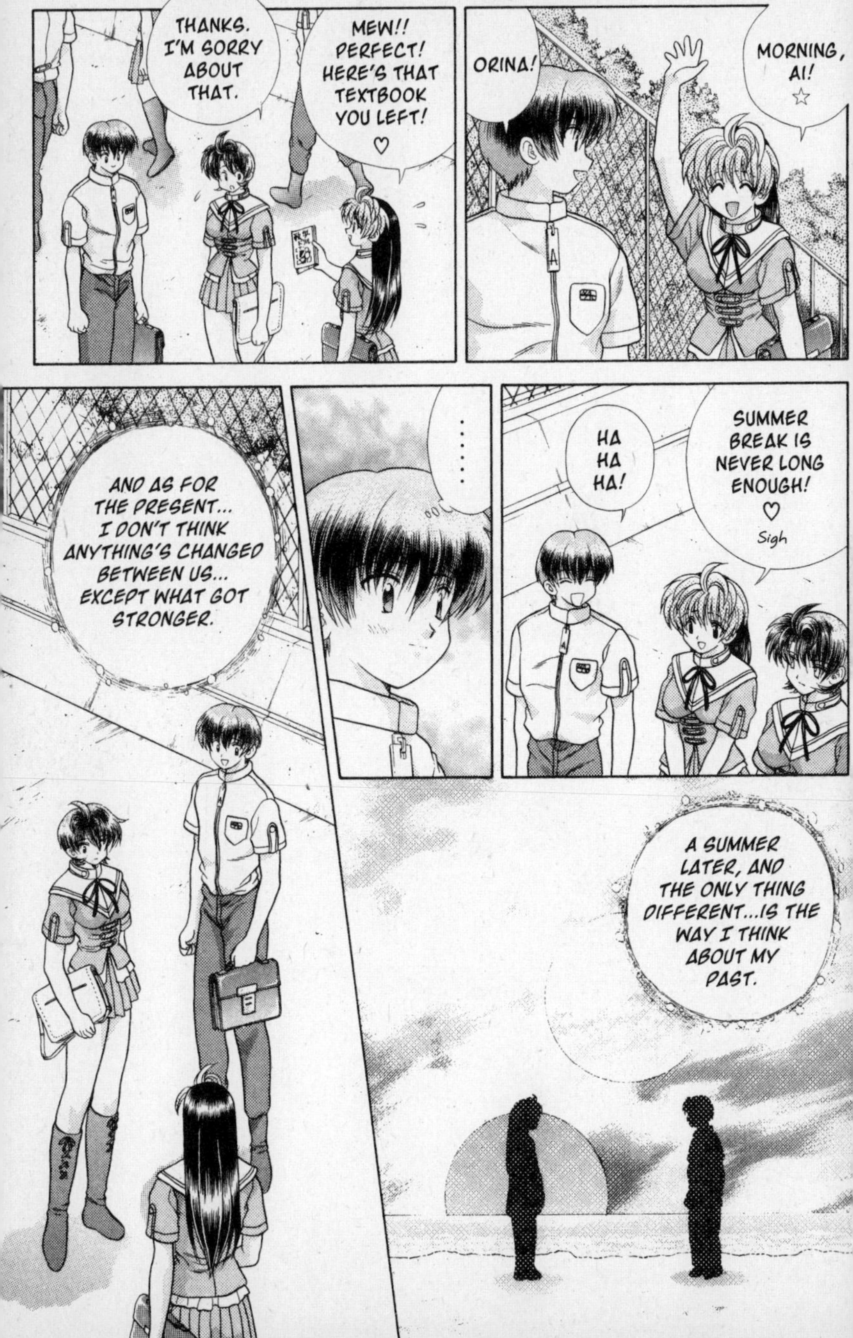
MORNING, AI! ☆
ORINA!
MEW!! PERFECT! HERE'S THAT TEXTBOOK YOU LEFT! ♡
THANKS. I'M SORRY ABOUT THAT.
SUMMER BREAK IS NEVER LONG ENOUGH! ♡
Sigh
HA HA HA!
......
AND AS FOR THE PRESENT... I DON'T THINK ANYTHING'S CHANGED BETWEEN US... EXCEPT WHAT GOT STRONGER.
A SUMMER LATER, AND THE ONLY THING DIFFERENT...IS THE WAY I THINK ABOUT MY PAST.

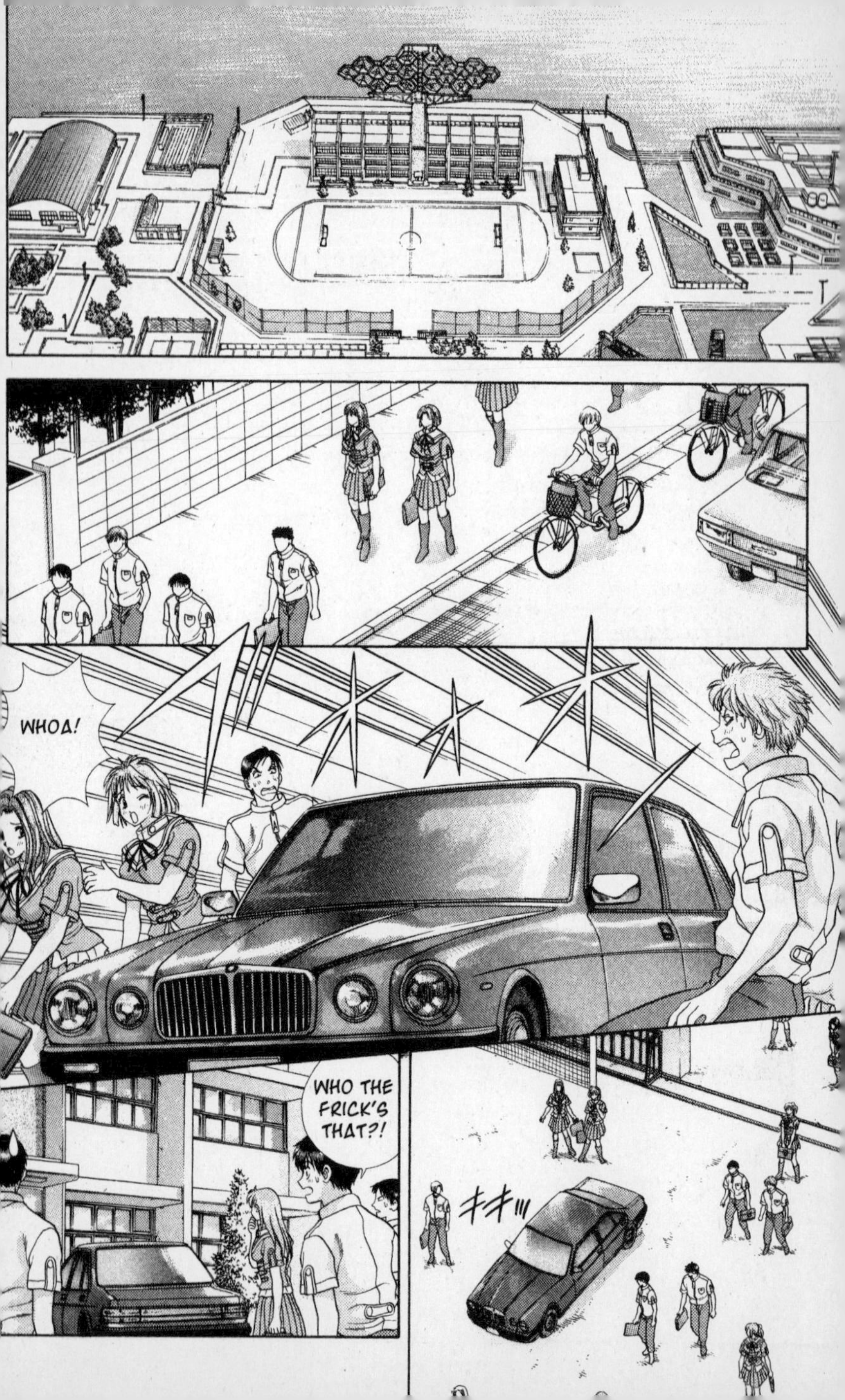
WHOA!
WHO THE FRICK'S THAT?!
キキッ

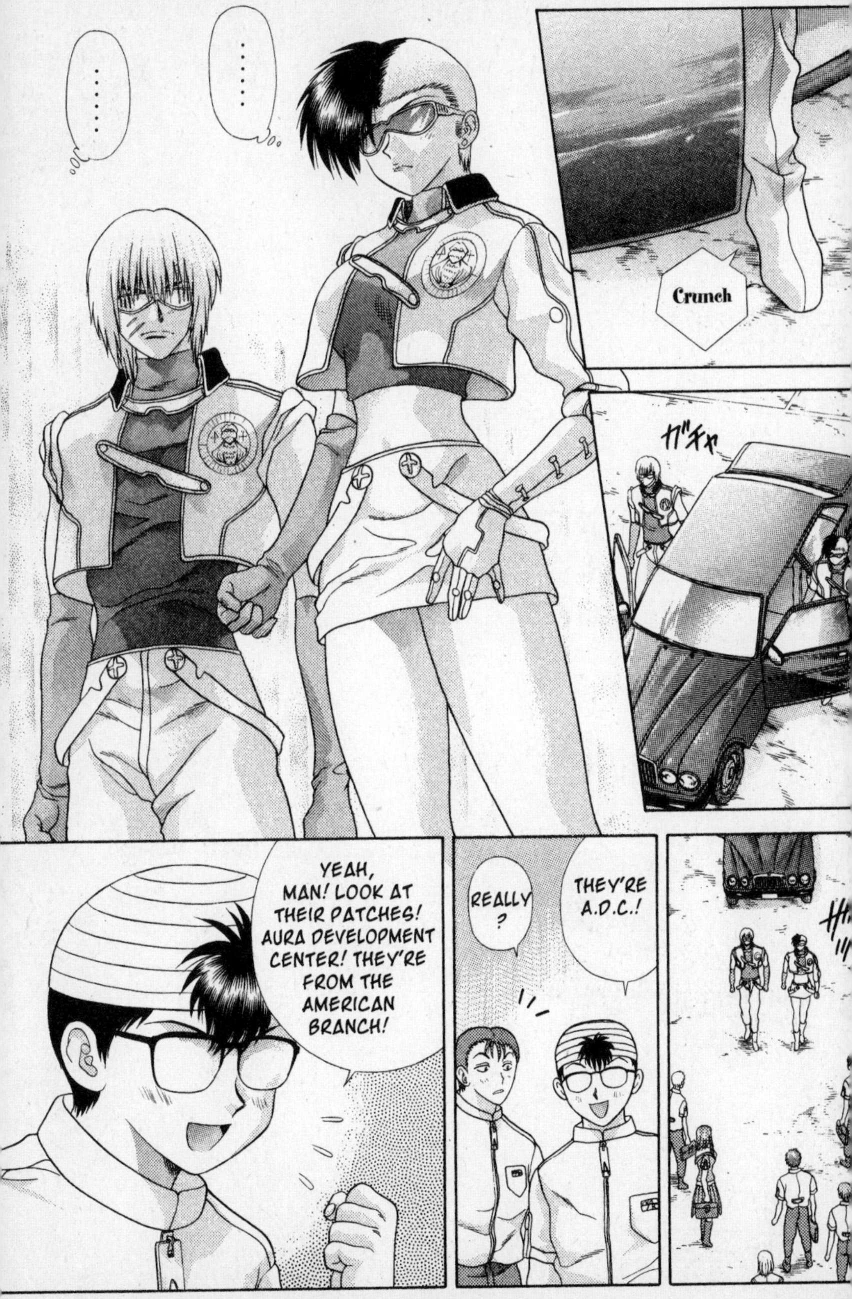
Crunch
ガチャ
……
……
THEY'RE A.D.C.!
REALLY?
YEAH, MAN! LOOK AT THEIR PATCHES! AURA DEVELOPMENT CENTER! THEY'RE FROM THE AMERICAN BRANCH!

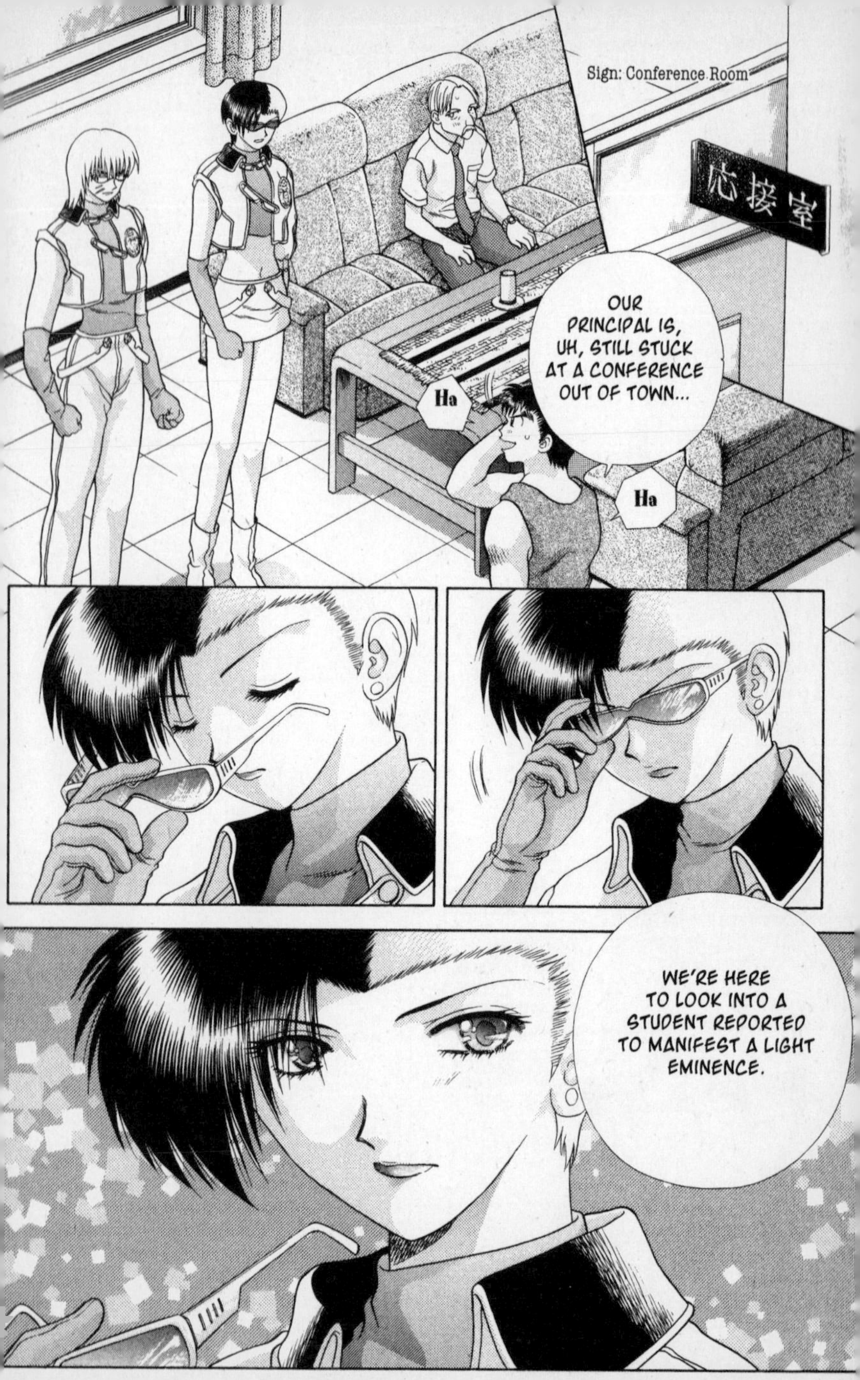
Sign: Conference Room
応接室
OUR PRINCIPAL IS, UH, STILL STUCK AT A CONFERENCE OUT OF TOWN...
Ha
Ha
WE'RE HERE TO LOOK INTO A STUDENT REPORTED TO MANIFEST A LIGHT EMINENCE.

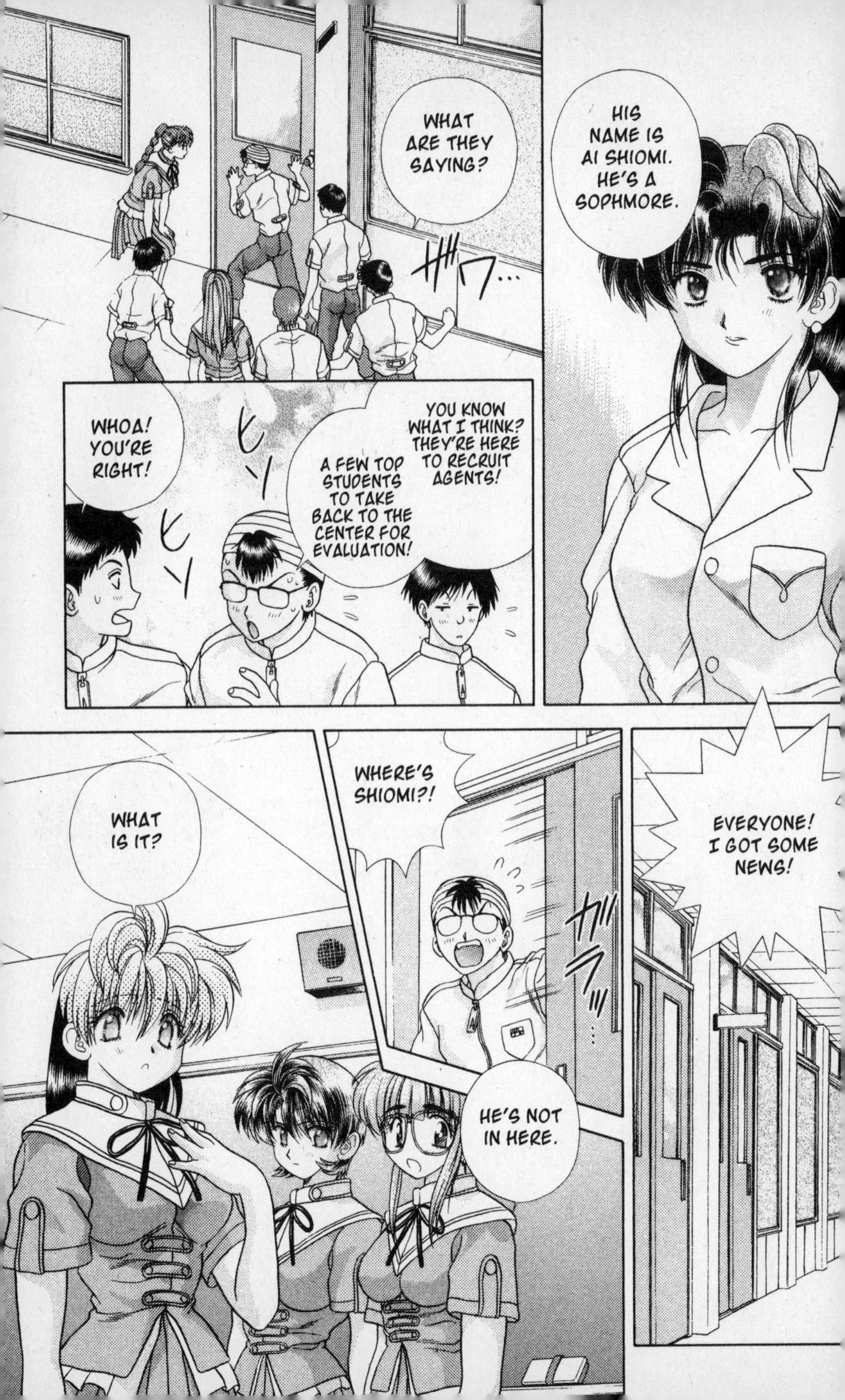
HIS NAME IS AI SHIOMI. HE'S A SOPHMORE.
WHAT ARE THEY SAYING?
YOU KNOW WHAT I THINK? THEY'RE HERE TO RECRUIT AGENTS!
A FEW TOP STUDENTS TO TAKE BACK TO THE CENTER FOR EVALUATION!
WHOA! YOU'RE RIGHT!
EVERYONE! I GOT SOME NEWS!
WHERE'S SHIOMI?!
WHAT IS IT?
HE'S NOT IN HERE.

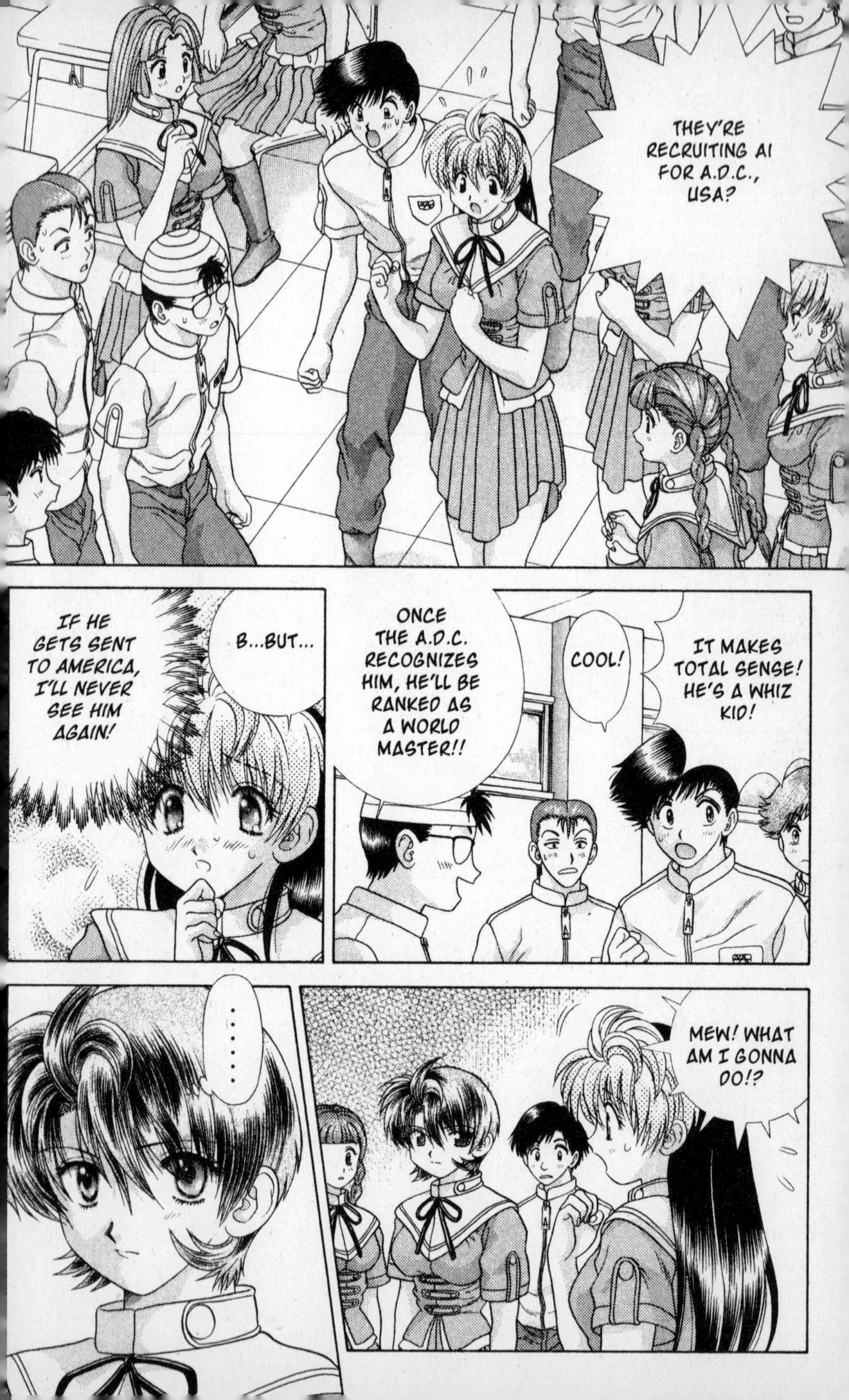
THEY'RE RECRUITING AI FOR A.D.C., USA?
IT MAKES TOTAL SENSE! HE'S A WHIZ KID!
COOL!
ONCE THE A.D.C. RECOGNIZES HIM, HE'LL BE RANKED AS A WORLD MASTER!!
B...BUT...
IF HE GETS SENT TO AMERICA, I'LL NEVER SEE HIM AGAIN!
MEW! WHAT AM I GONNA DO!?
......

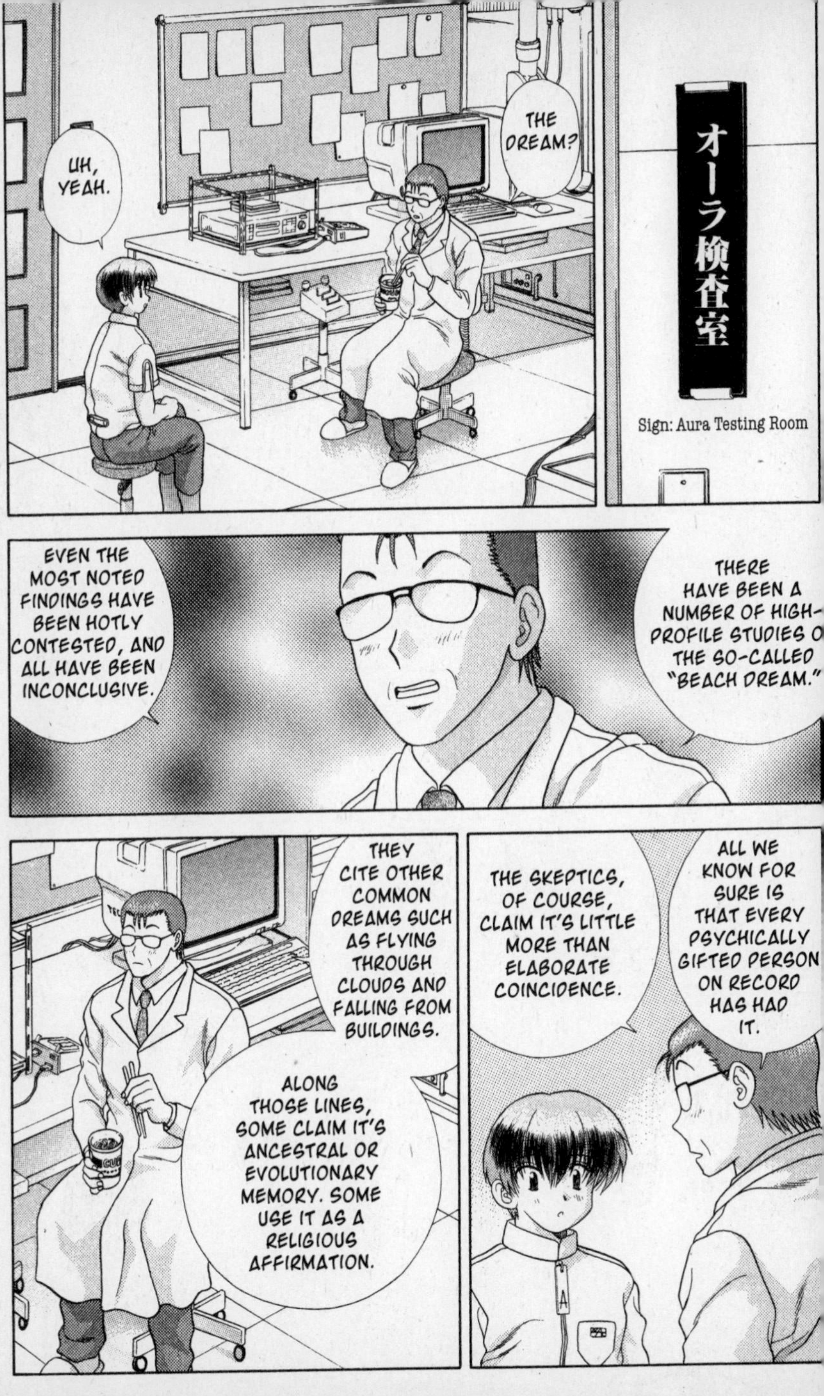
オーラ検査室
Sign: Aura Testing Room
THE DREAM?
UH, YEAH.
THERE HAVE BEEN A NUMBER OF HIGH-PROFILE STUDIES O THE SO-CALLED "BEACH DREAM."
EVEN THE MOST NOTED FINDINGS HAVE BEEN HOTLY CONTESTED, AND ALL HAVE BEEN INCONCLUSIVE.
ALL WE KNOW FOR SURE IS THAT EVERY PSYCHICALLY GIFTED PERSON ON RECORD HAS HAD IT.
THE SKEPTICS, OF COURSE, CLAIM IT'S LITTLE MORE THAN ELABORATE COINCIDENCE.
THEY CITE OTHER COMMON DREAMS SUCH AS FLYING THROUGH CLOUDS AND FALLING FROM BUILDINGS.
ALONG THOSE LINES, SOME CLAIM IT'S ANCESTRAL OR EVOLUTIONARY MEMORY. SOME USE IT AS A RELIGIOUS AFFIRMATION.

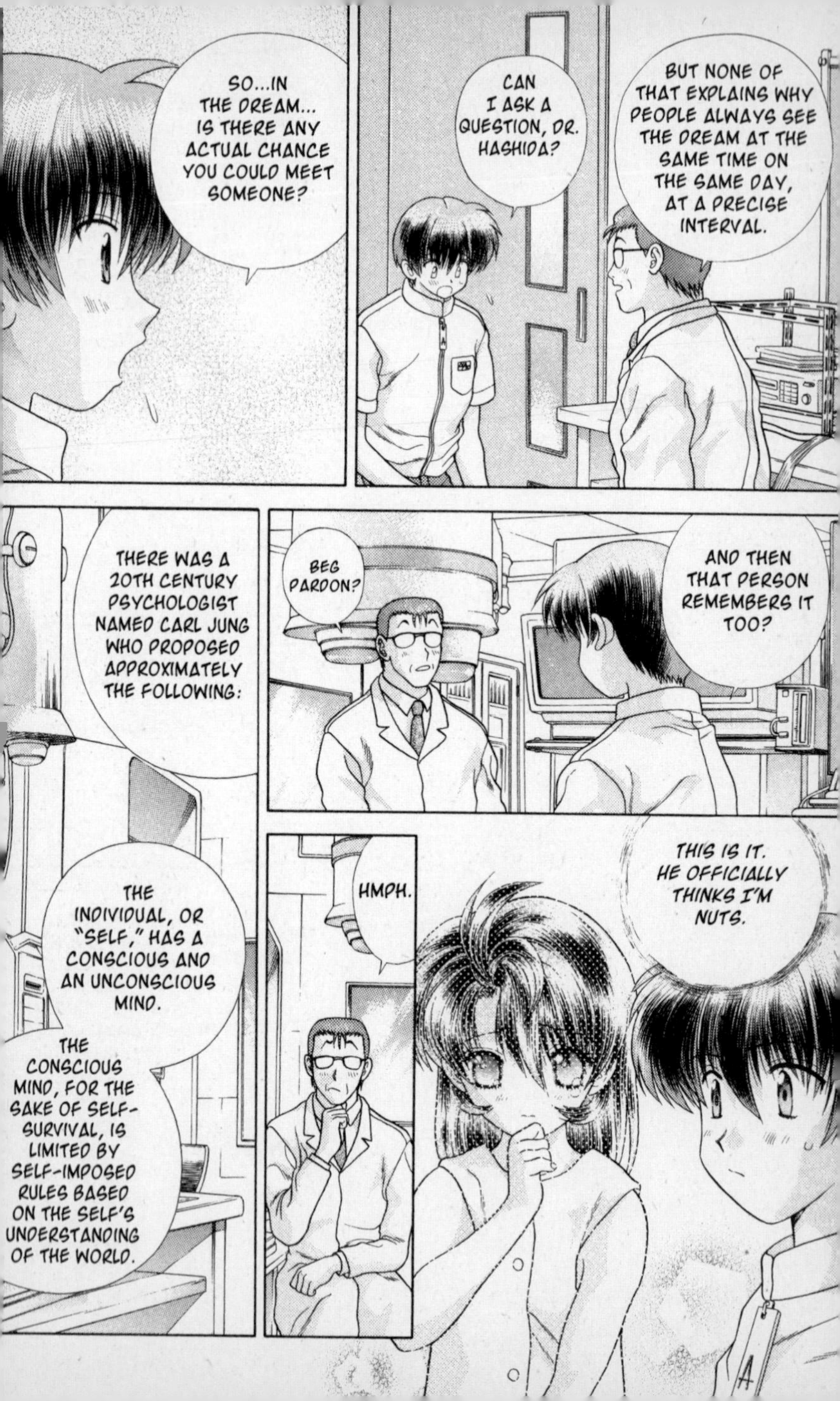
BUT NONE OF THAT EXPLAINS WHY PEOPLE ALWAYS SEE THE DREAM AT THE SAME TIME ON THE SAME DAY, AT A PRECISE INTERVAL.
CAN I ASK A QUESTION, DR. HASHIDA?
SO...IN THE DREAM... IS THERE ANY ACTUAL CHANCE YOU COULD MEET SOMEONE?
AND THEN THAT PERSON REMEMBERS IT TOO?
BEG PARDON?
THIS IS IT. HE OFFICIALLY THINKS I'M NUTS.
HMPH.
THERE WAS A 20TH CENTURY PSYCHOLOGIST NAMED CARL JUNG WHO PROPOSED APPROXIMATELY THE FOLLOWING:
THE INDIVIDUAL, OR "SELF," HAS A CONSCIOUS AND AN UNCONSCIOUS MIND.
THE CONSCIOUS MIND, FOR THE SAKE OF SELF-SURVIVAL, IS LIMITED BY SELF-IMPOSED RULES BASED ON THE SELF'S UNDERSTANDING OF THE WORLD.

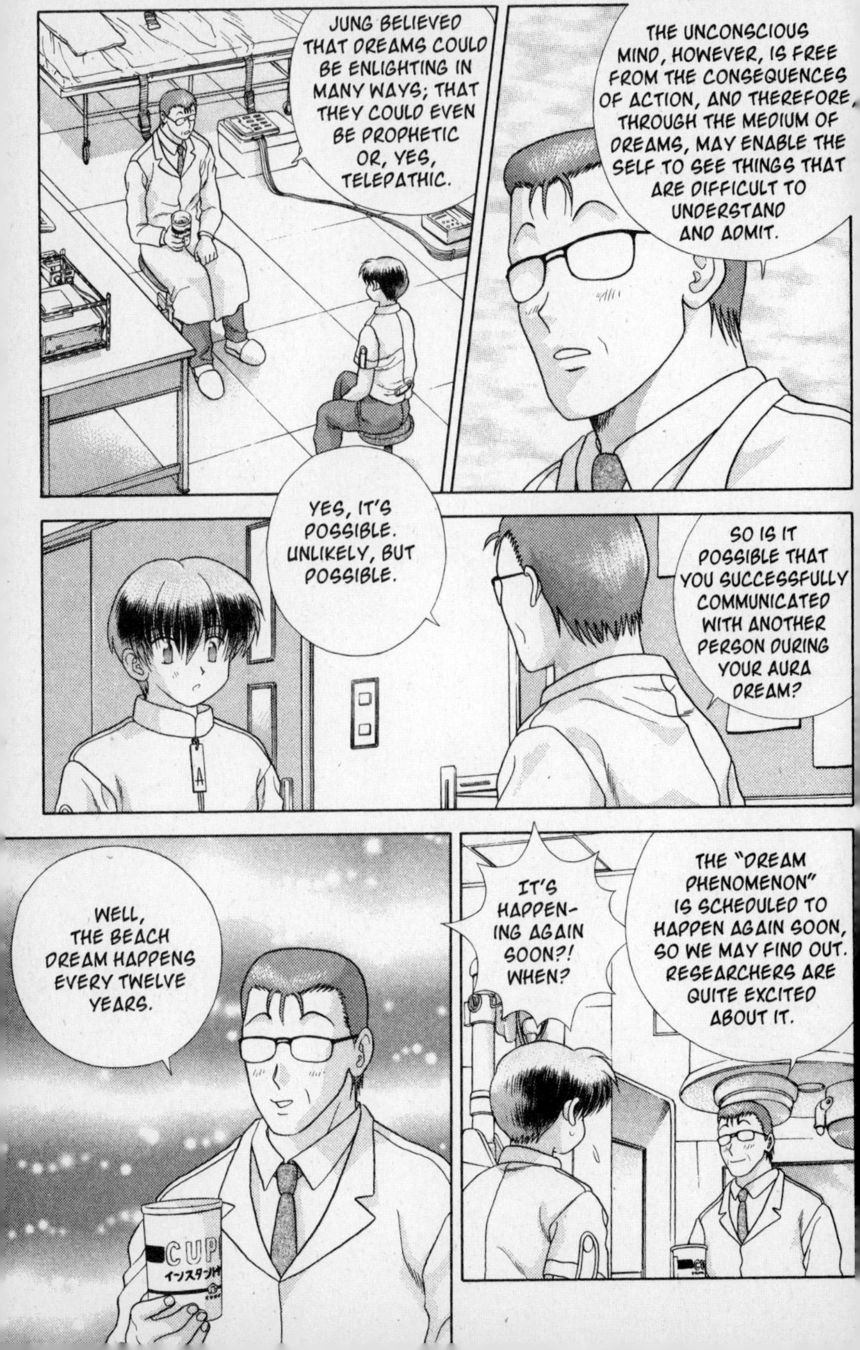
THE UNCONSCIOUS MIND, HOWEVER, IS FREE FROM THE CONSEQUENCES OF ACTION, AND THEREFORE, THROUGH THE MEDIUM OF DREAMS, MAY ENABLE THE SELF TO SEE THINGS THAT ARE DIFFICULT TO UNDERSTAND AND ADMIT.
JUNG BELIEVED THAT DREAMS COULD BE ENLIGHTING IN MANY WAYS; THAT THEY COULD EVEN BE PROPHETIC OR, YES, TELEPATHIC.
SO IS IT POSSIBLE THAT YOU SUCCESSFULLY COMMUNICATED WITH ANOTHER PERSON DURING YOUR AURA DREAM?
YES, IT'S POSSIBLE. UNLIKELY, BUT POSSIBLE.
THE "DREAM PHENOMENON" IS SCHEDULED TO HAPPEN AGAIN SOON, SO WE MAY FIND OUT. RESEARCHERS ARE QUITE EXCITED ABOUT IT.
IT'S HAPPEN-ING AGAIN SOON?! WHEN?
WELL, THE BEACH DREAM HAPPENS EVERY TWELVE YEARS.

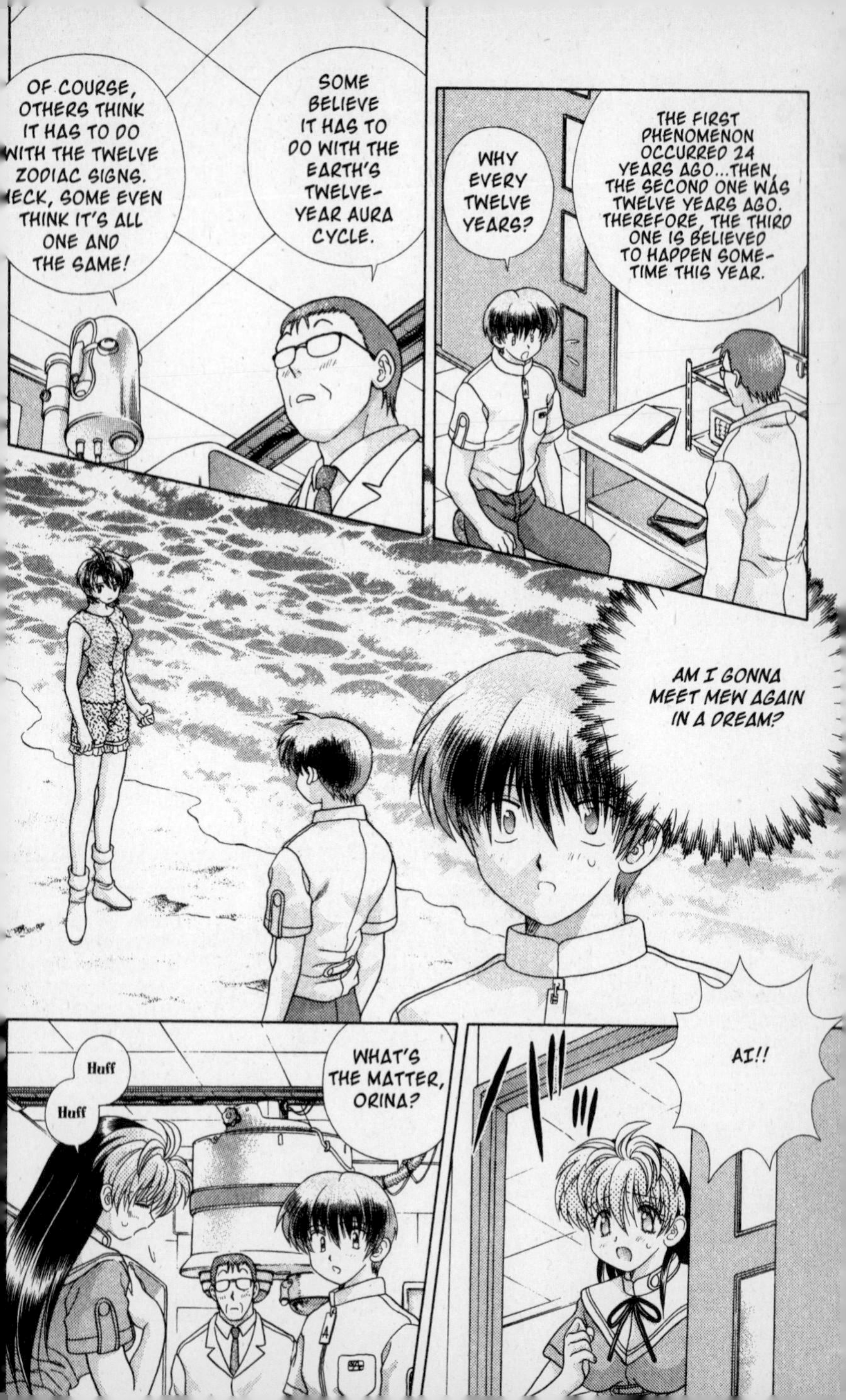
THE FIRST PHENOMENON OCCURRED 24 YEARS AGO...THEN, THE SECOND ONE WAS TWELVE YEARS AGO. THEREFORE, THE THIRD ONE IS BELIEVED TO HAPPEN SOME-TIME THIS YEAR.
WHY EVERY TWELVE YEARS?
SOME BELIEVE IT HAS TO DO WITH THE EARTH'S TWELVE-YEAR AURA CYCLE.
OF COURSE, OTHERS THINK IT HAS TO DO WITH THE TWELVE ZODIAC SIGNS. HECK, SOME EVEN THINK IT'S ALL ONE AND THE SAME!
AM I GONNA MEET MEW AGAIN IN A DREAM?
AI!!
WHAT'S THE MATTER, ORINA?
Huff
Huff

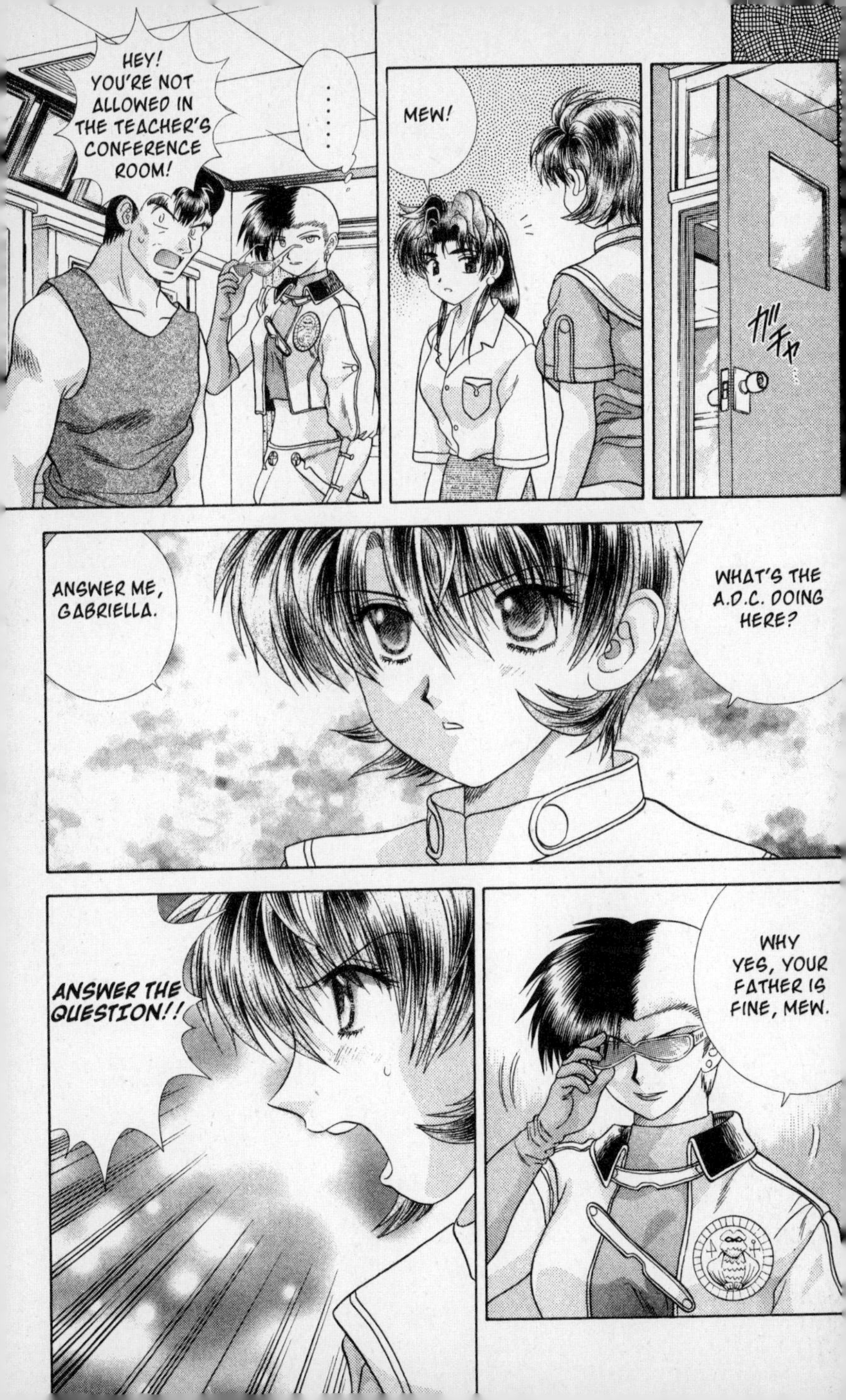
ガチャ…
MEW!
......
HEY! YOU'RE NOT ALLOWED IN THE TEACHER'S CONFERENCE ROOM!
WHAT'S THE A.D.C. DOING HERE?
ANSWER ME, GABRIELLA.
WHY YES, YOUR FATHER IS FINE, MEW.
ANSWER THE QUESTION!!

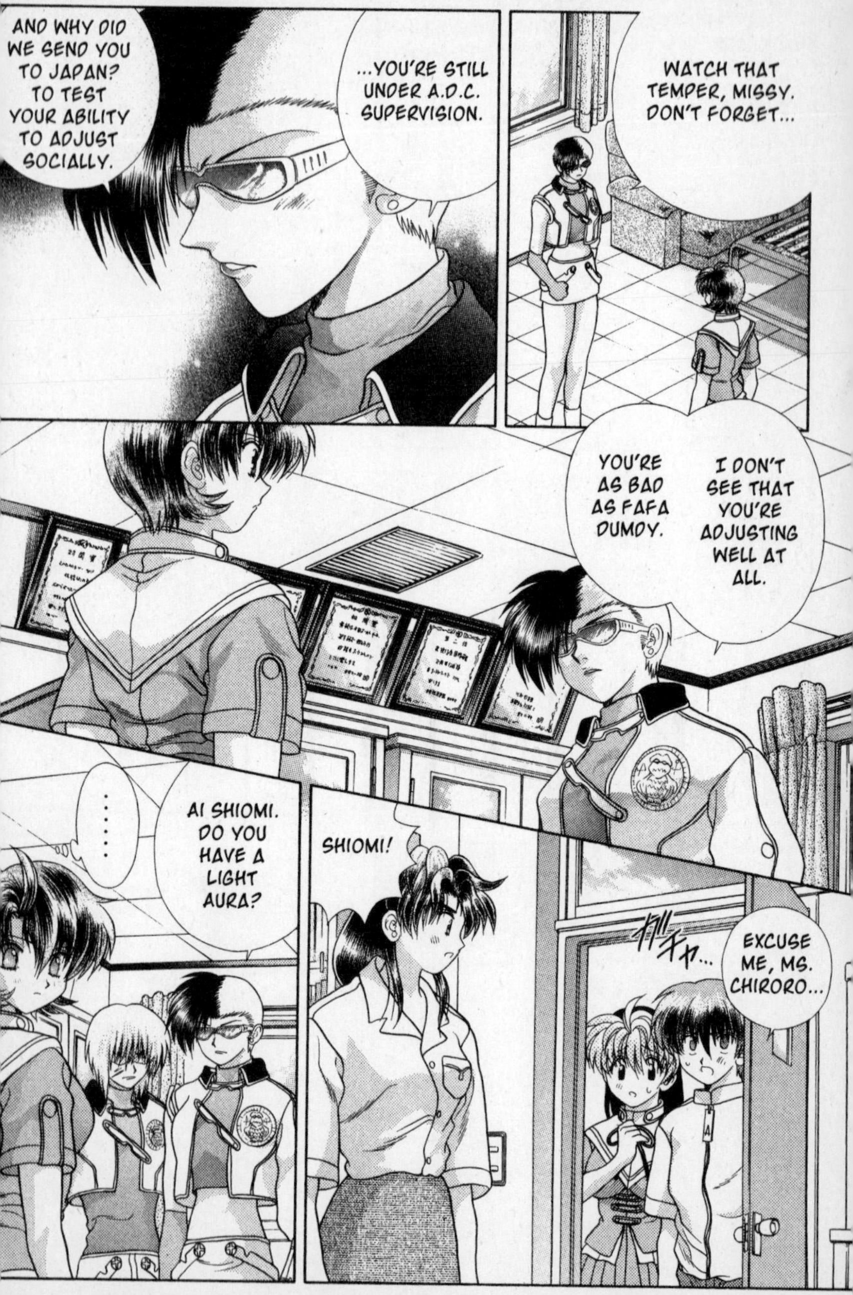
WATCH THAT TEMPER, MISSY. DON'T FORGET...
...YOU'RE STILL UNDER A.D.C. SUPERVISION.
AND WHY DID WE SEND YOU TO JAPAN? TO TEST YOUR ABILITY TO ADJUST SOCIALLY.
I DON'T SEE THAT YOU'RE ADJUSTING WELL AT ALL.
YOU'RE AS BAD AS FAFA DUMDY.
EXCUSE ME, MS. CHIRORO...
ガチャ...
SHIOMI!
AI SHIOMI. DO YOU HAVE A LIGHT AURA?
......

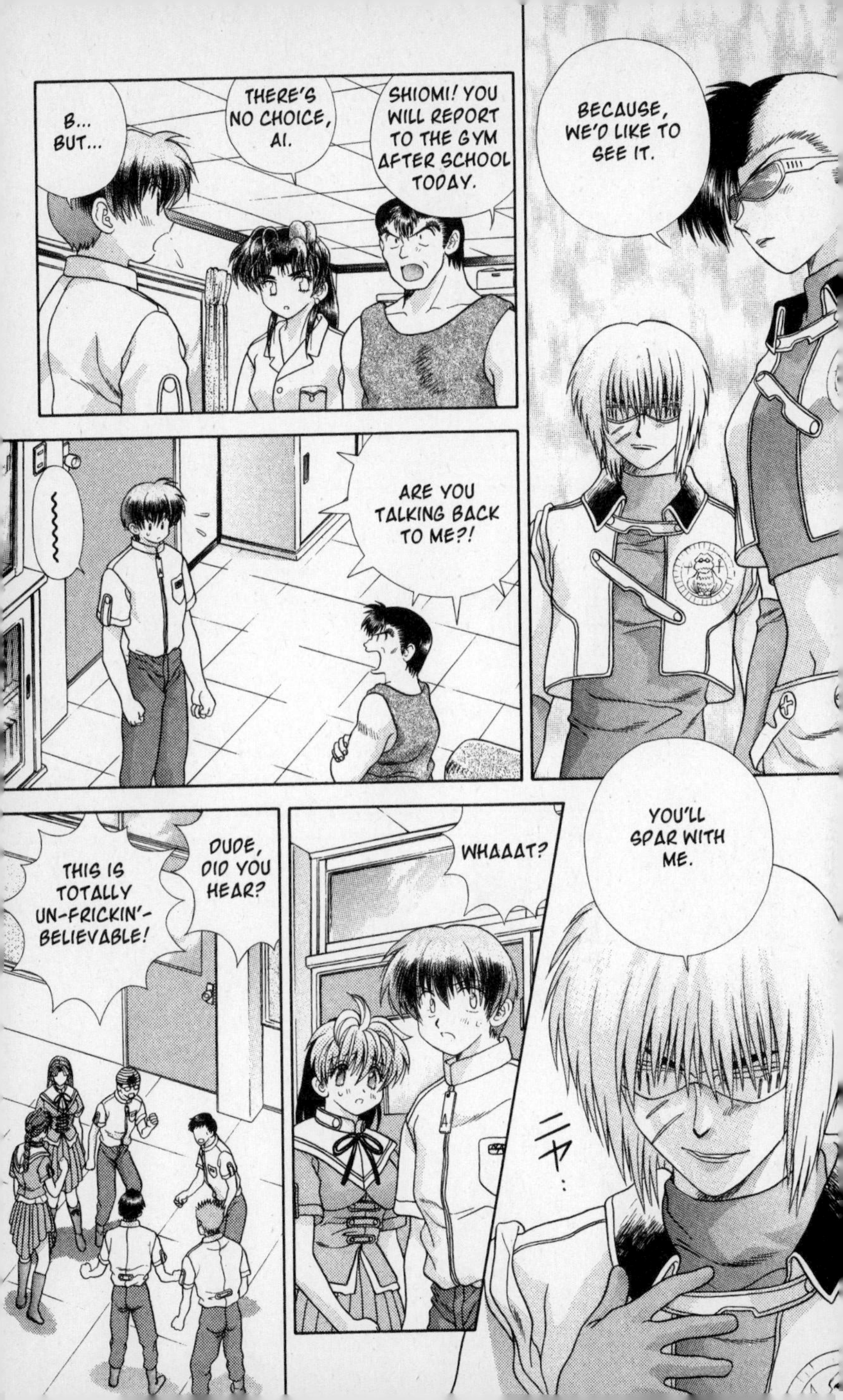
BECAUSE, WE'D LIKE TO SEE IT.
SHIOMI! YOU WILL REPORT TO THE GYM AFTER SCHOOL TODAY.
THERE'S NO CHOICE, AI.
B... BUT...
ARE YOU TALKING BACK TO ME?!
YOU'LL SPAR WITH ME.
ニヤ…
WHAAAT?
DUDE, DID YOU HEAR?
THIS IS TOTALLY UN-FRICKIN'-BELIEVABLE!

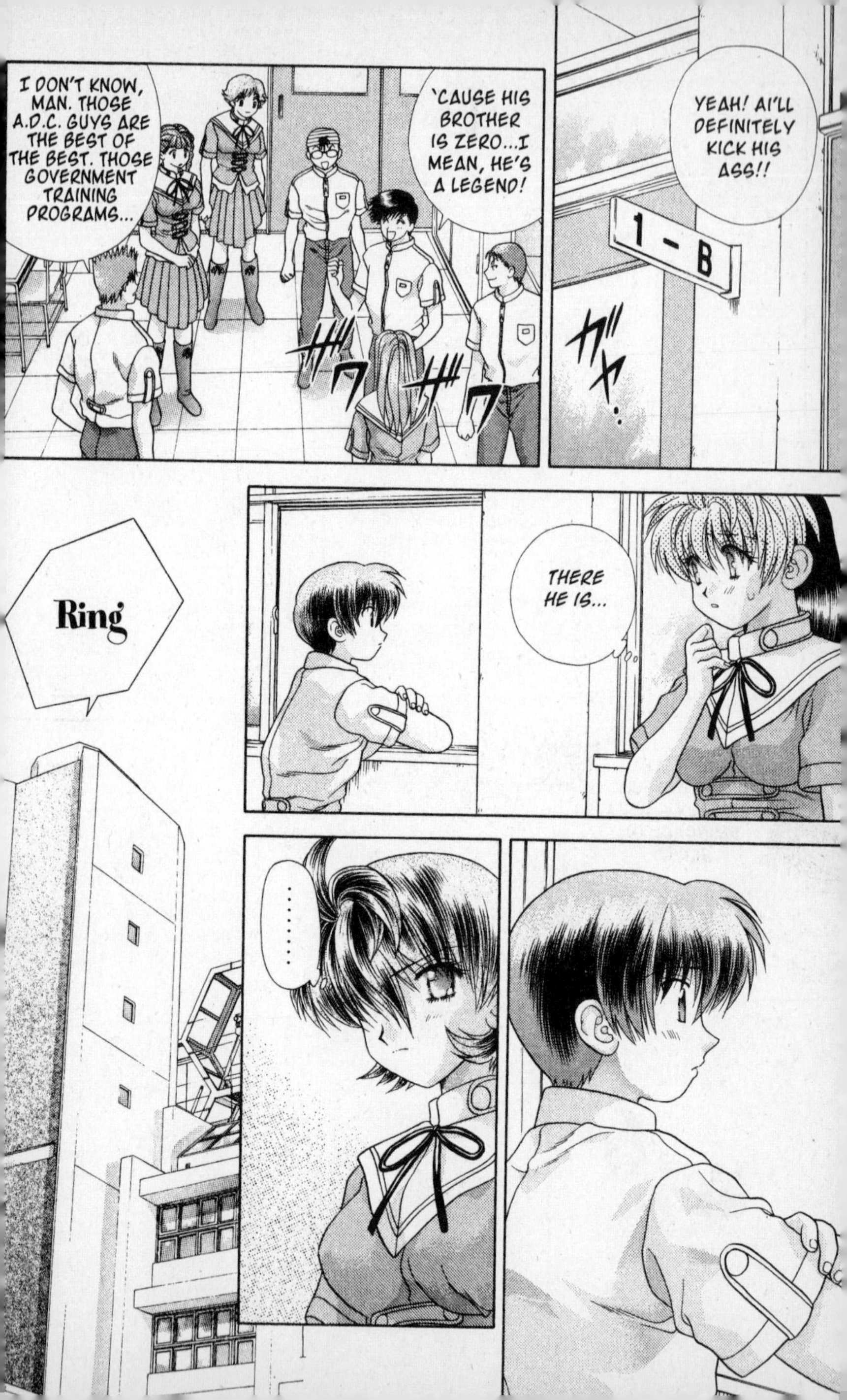
1 - B
YEAH! AI'LL DEFINITELY KICK HIS ASS!!
ガヤ...
`CAUSE HIS BROTHER IS ZERO...I MEAN, HE'S A LEGEND!
I DON'T KNOW, MAN. THOSE A.D.C. GUYS ARE THE BEST OF THE BEST. THOSE GOVERNMENT TRAINING PROGRAMS...
ザワ ザワ
THERE HE IS...
......
Ring

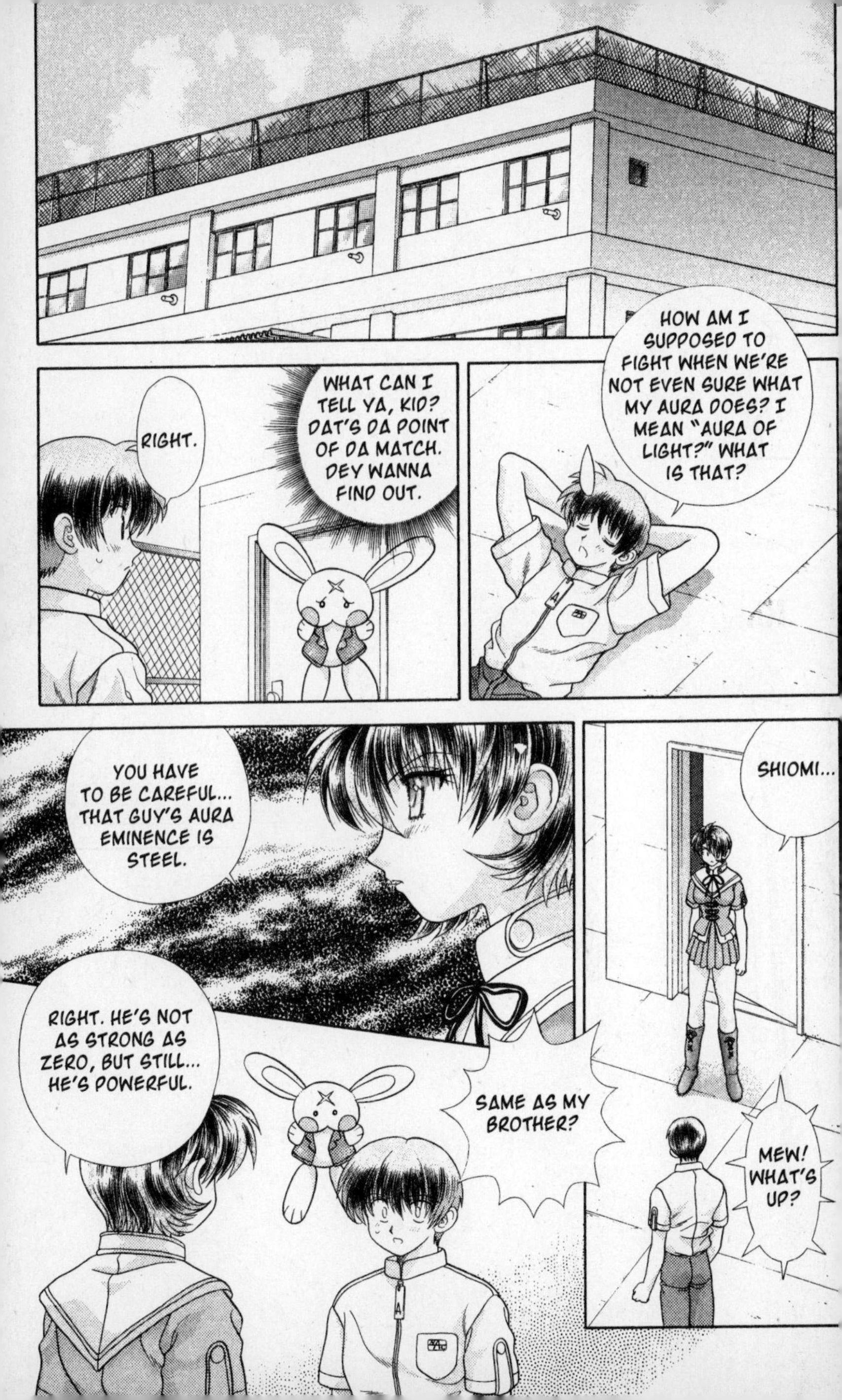
HOW AM I SUPPOSED TO FIGHT WHEN WE'RE NOT EVEN SURE WHAT MY AURA DOES? I MEAN "AURA OF LIGHT?" WHAT IS THAT?
WHAT CAN I TELL YA, KID? DAT'S DA POINT OF DA MATCH. DEY WANNA FIND OUT.
RIGHT.
SHIOMI...
MEW! WHAT'S UP?
YOU HAVE TO BE CAREFUL... THAT GUY'S AURA EMINENCE IS STEEL.
SAME AS MY BROTHER?
RIGHT. HE'S NOT AS STRONG AS ZERO, BUT STILL... HE'S POWERFUL.

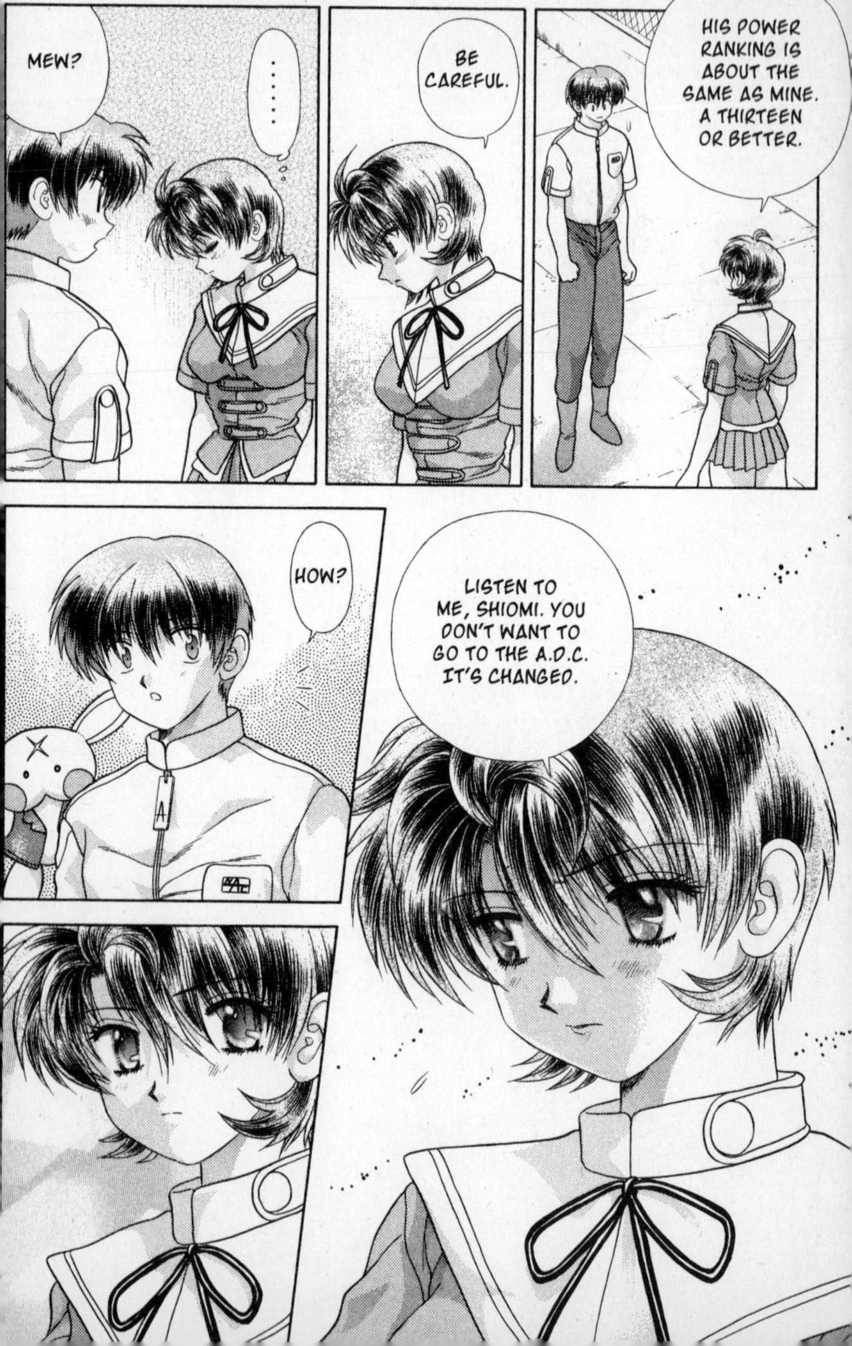
HIS POWER RANKING IS ABOUT THE SAME AS MINE. A THIRTEEN OR BETTER.
BE CAREFUL.
......
MEW?
LISTEN TO ME, SHIOMI. YOU DON'T WANT TO GO TO THE A.D.C. IT'S CHANGED.
HOW?

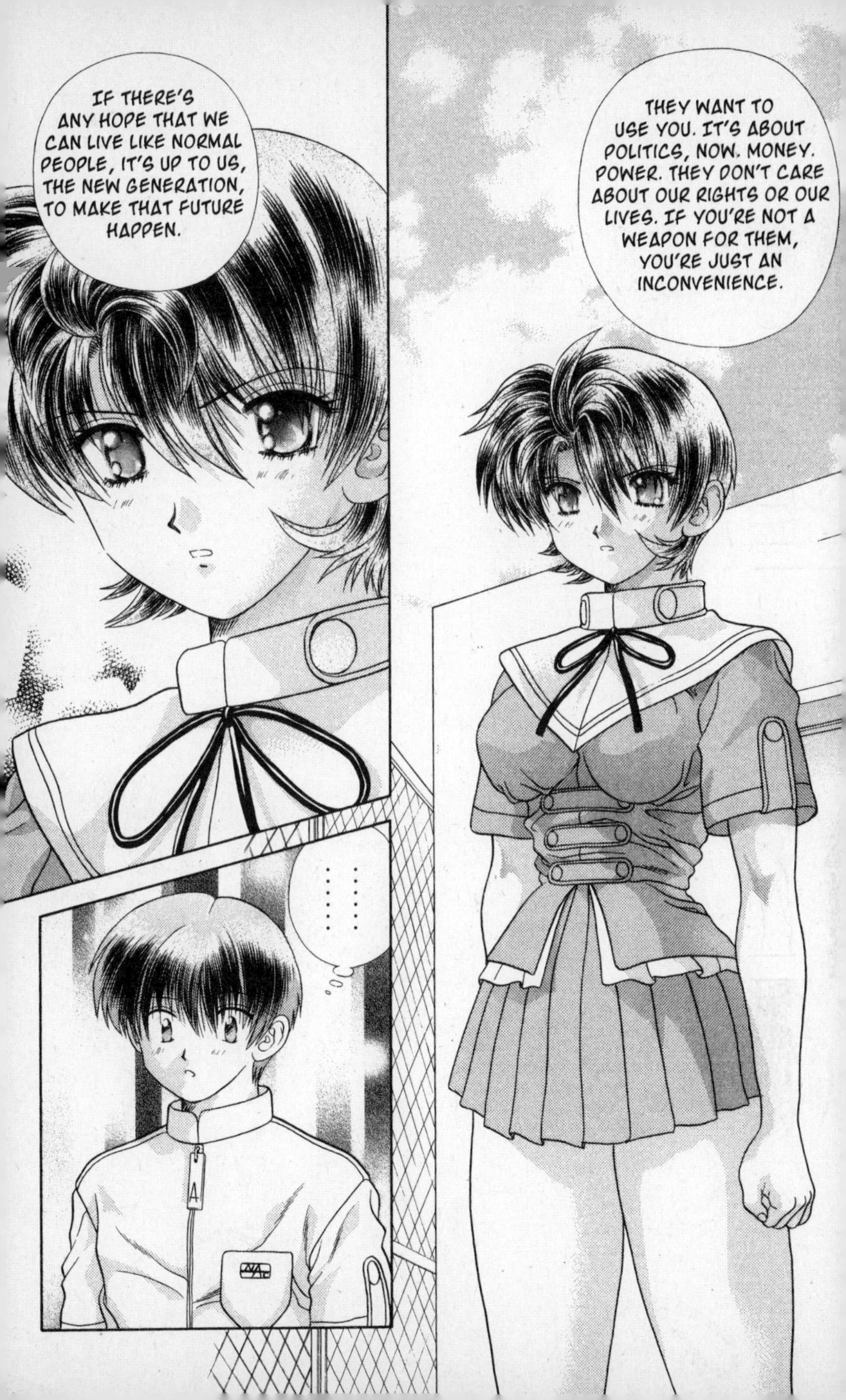
THEY WANT TO USE YOU. IT'S ABOUT POLITICS, NOW. MONEY. POWER. THEY DON'T CARE ABOUT OUR RIGHTS OR OUR LIVES. IF YOU'RE NOT A WEAPON FOR THEM, YOU'RE JUST AN INCONVENIENCE.
IF THERE'S ANY HOPE THAT WE CAN LIVE LIKE NORMAL PEOPLE, IT'S UP TO US, THE NEW GENERATION, TO MAKE THAT FUTURE HAPPEN.
......

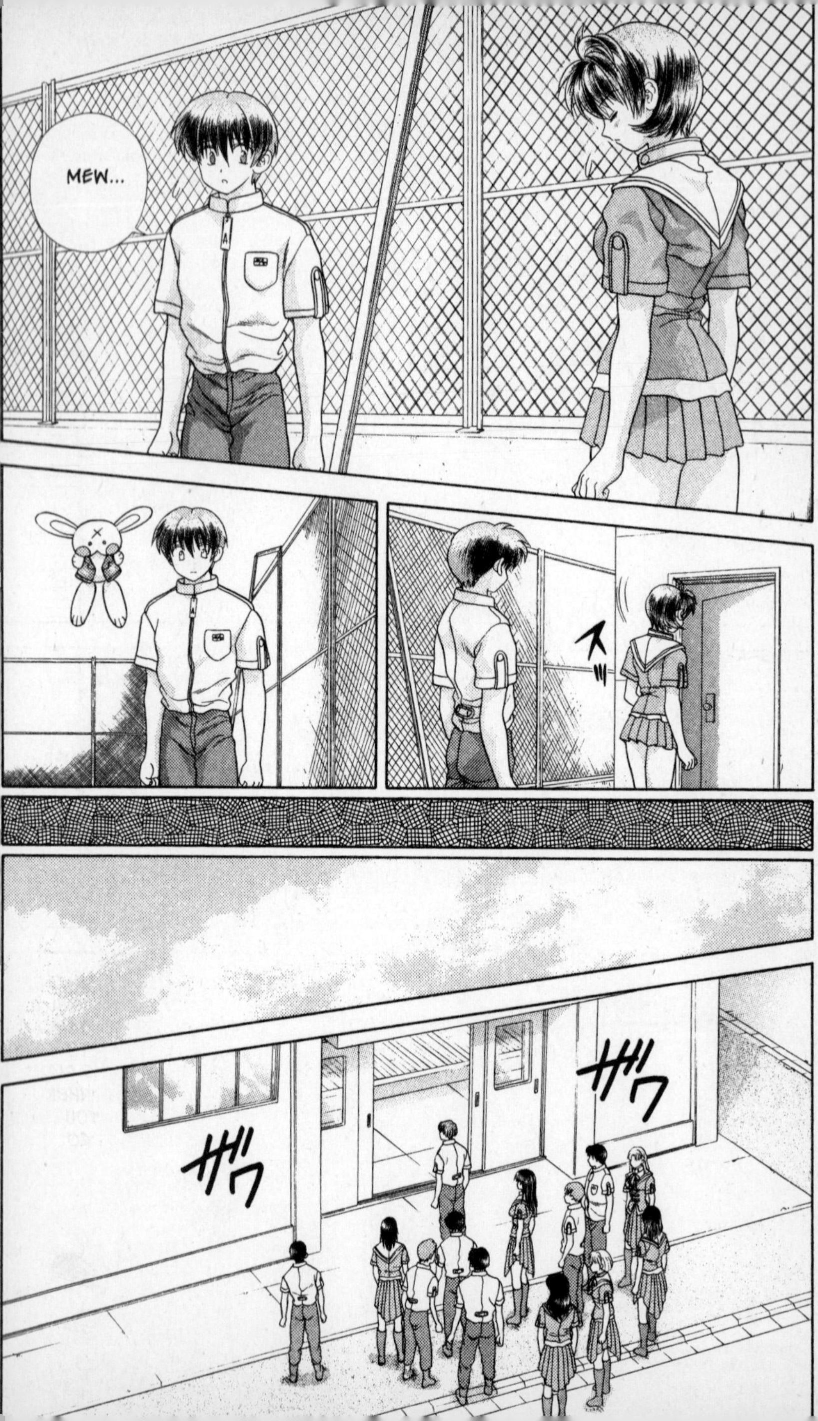
MEW...
スッ
ザワ
ザワ

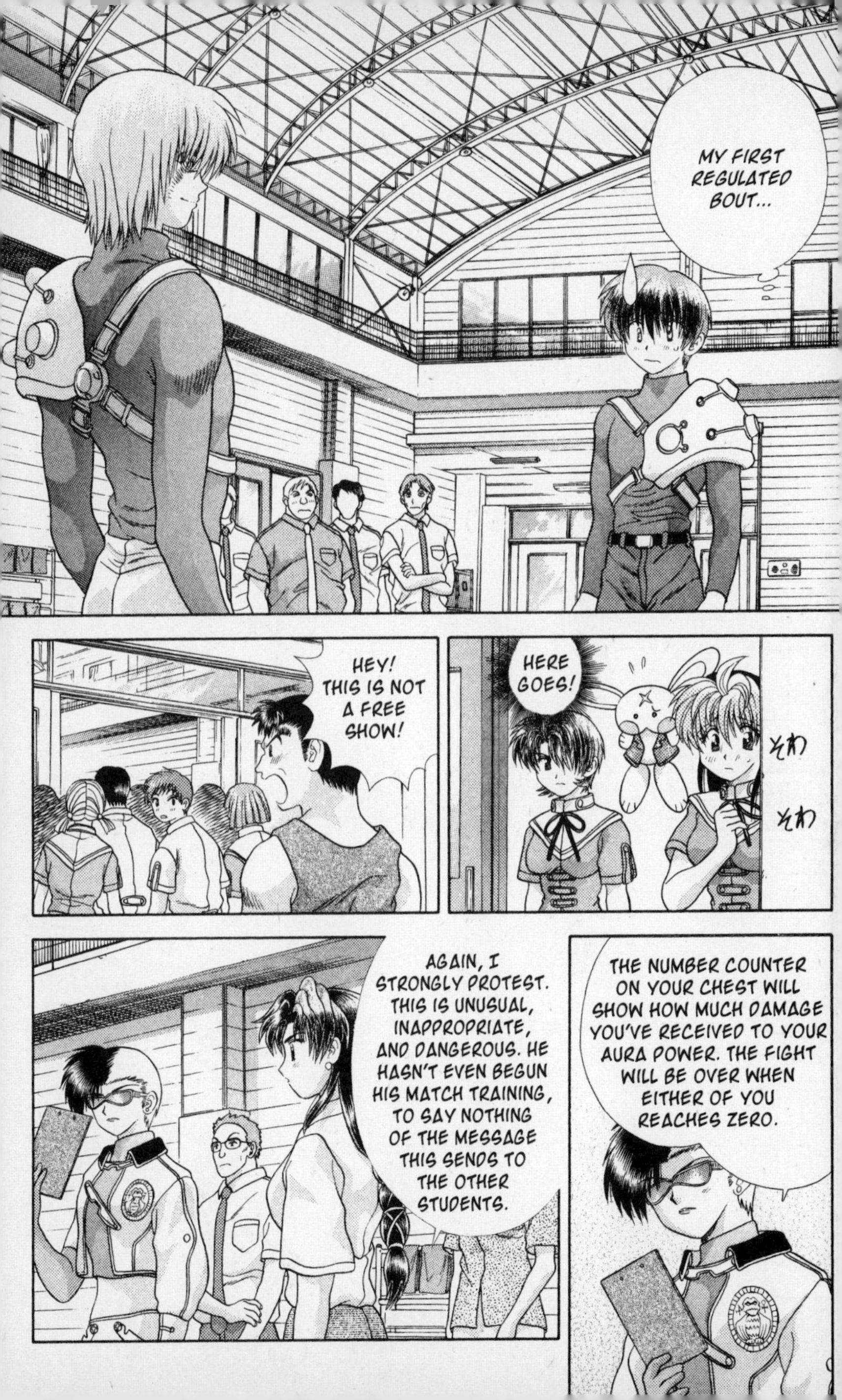
MY FIRST REGULATED BOUT...
HERE GOES!
そわ
そわ
HEY! THIS IS NOT A FREE SHOW!
THE NUMBER COUNTER ON YOUR CHEST WILL SHOW HOW MUCH DAMAGE YOU'VE RECEIVED TO YOUR AURA POWER. THE FIGHT WILL BE OVER WHEN EITHER OF YOU REACHES ZERO.
AGAIN, I STRONGLY PROTEST. THIS IS UNUSUAL, INAPPROPRIATE, AND DANGEROUS. HE HASN'T EVEN BEGUN HIS MATCH TRAINING, TO SAY NOTHING OF THE MESSAGE THIS SENDS TO THE OTHER STUDENTS.

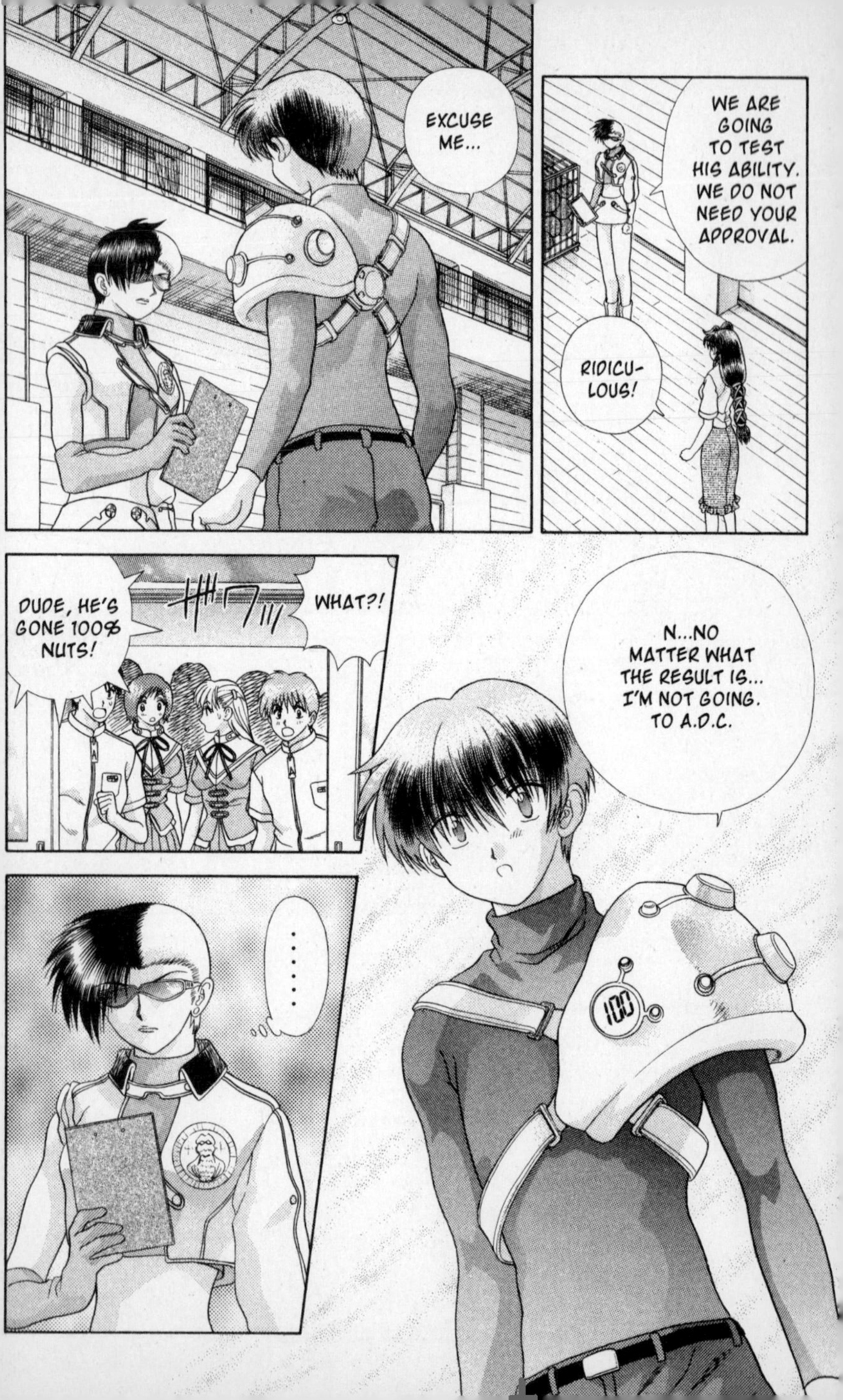
WE ARE GOING TO TEST HIS ABILITY. WE DO NOT NEED YOUR APPROVAL.
RIDICU-LOUS!
EXCUSE ME...
N...NO MATTER WHAT THE RESULT IS... I'M NOT GOING. TO A.D.C.
WHAT?!
ザワッ
DUDE, HE'S GONE 100% NUTS!
......
100

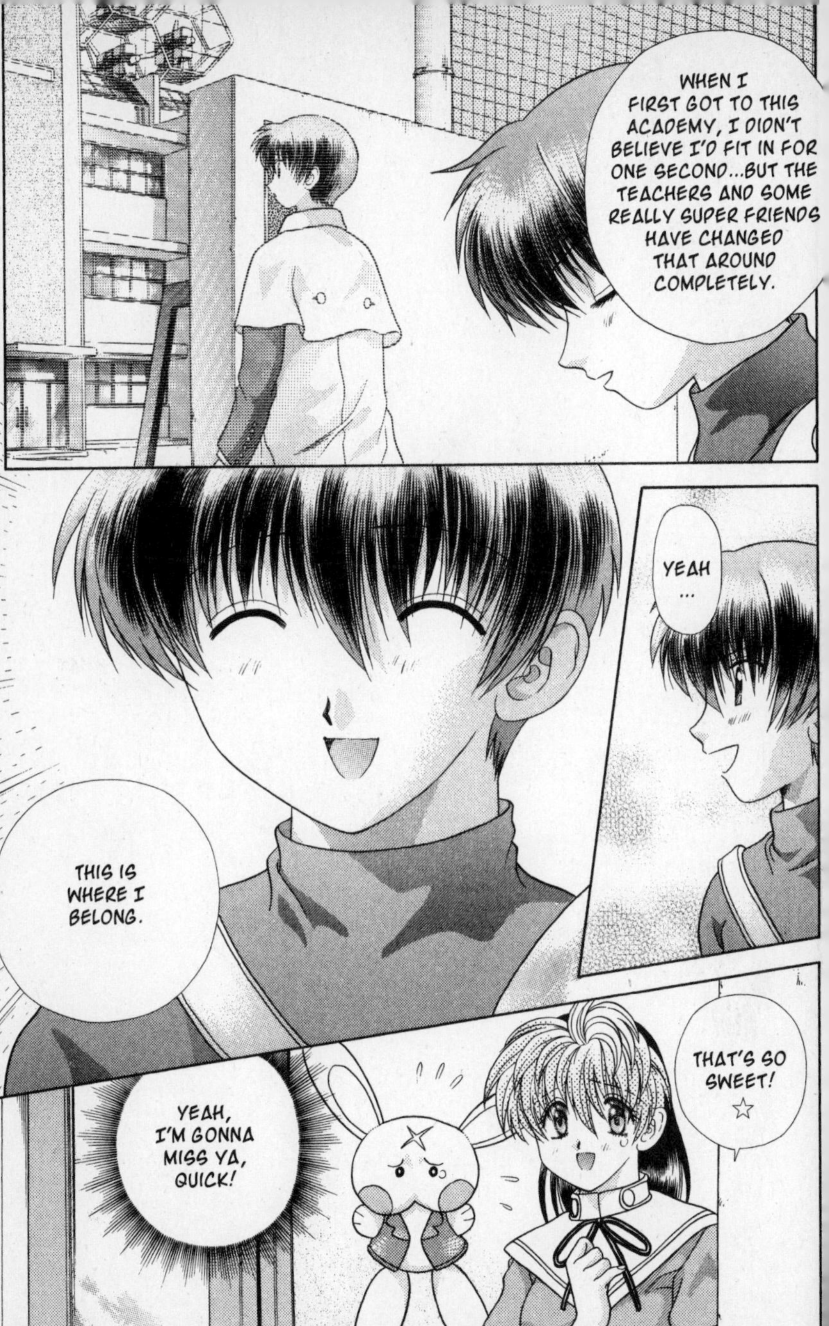
WHEN I FIRST GOT TO THIS ACADEMY, I DIDN'T BELIEVE I'D FIT IN FOR ONE SECOND...BUT THE TEACHERS AND SOME REALLY SUPER FRIENDS HAVE CHANGED THAT AROUND COMPLETELY.
YEAH ...
THIS IS WHERE I BELONG.
THAT'S SO SWEET! ☆
YEAH, I'M GONNA MISS YA, QUICK!

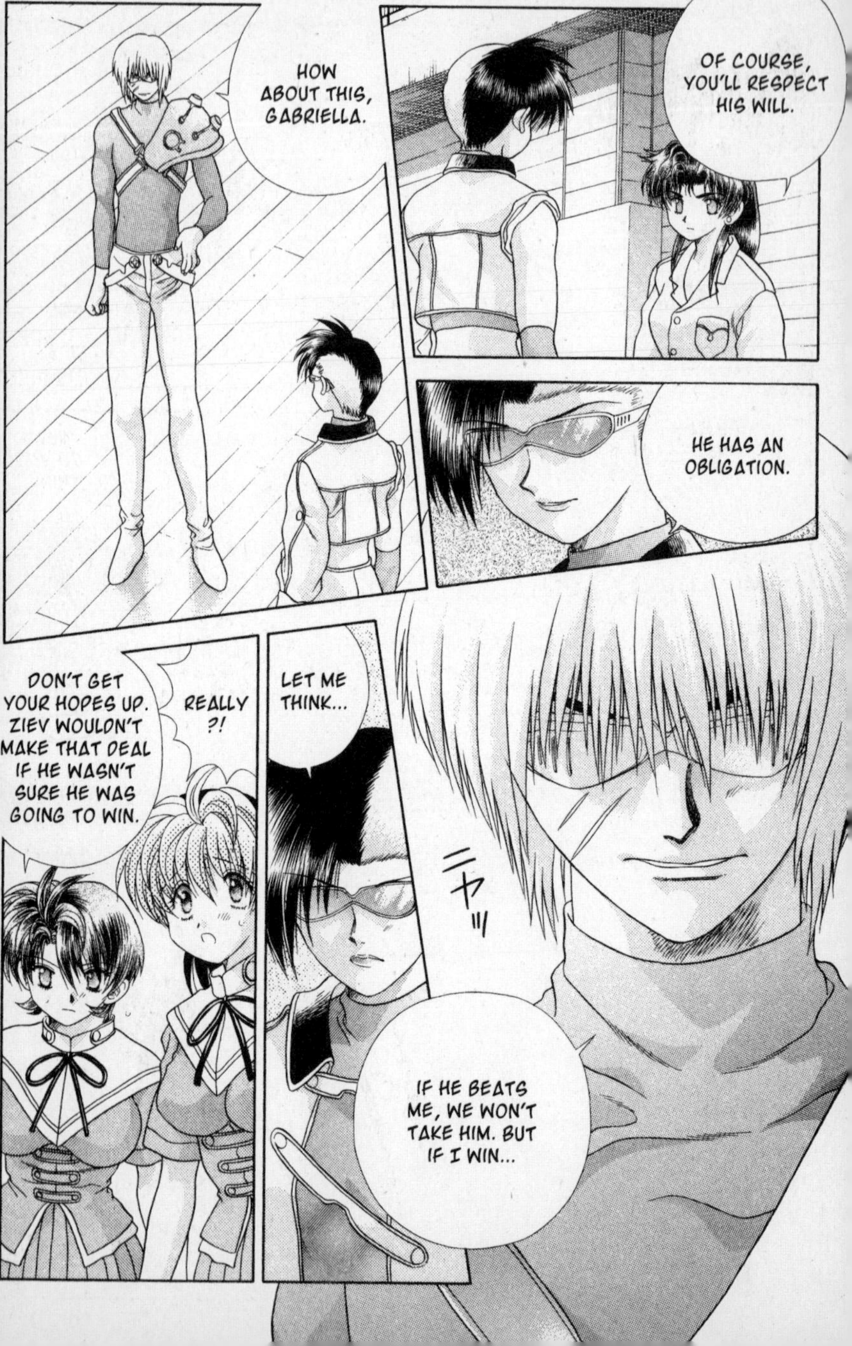
OF COURSE, YOU'LL RESPECT HIS WILL.
HE HAS AN OBLIGATION.
HOW ABOUT THIS, GABRIELLA.
ニヤッ
IF HE BEATS ME, WE WON'T TAKE HIM. BUT IF I WIN...
LET ME THINK...
REALLY ?!
DON'T GET YOUR HOPES UP. ZIEV WOULDN'T MAKE THAT DEAL IF HE WASN'T SURE HE WAS GOING TO WIN.

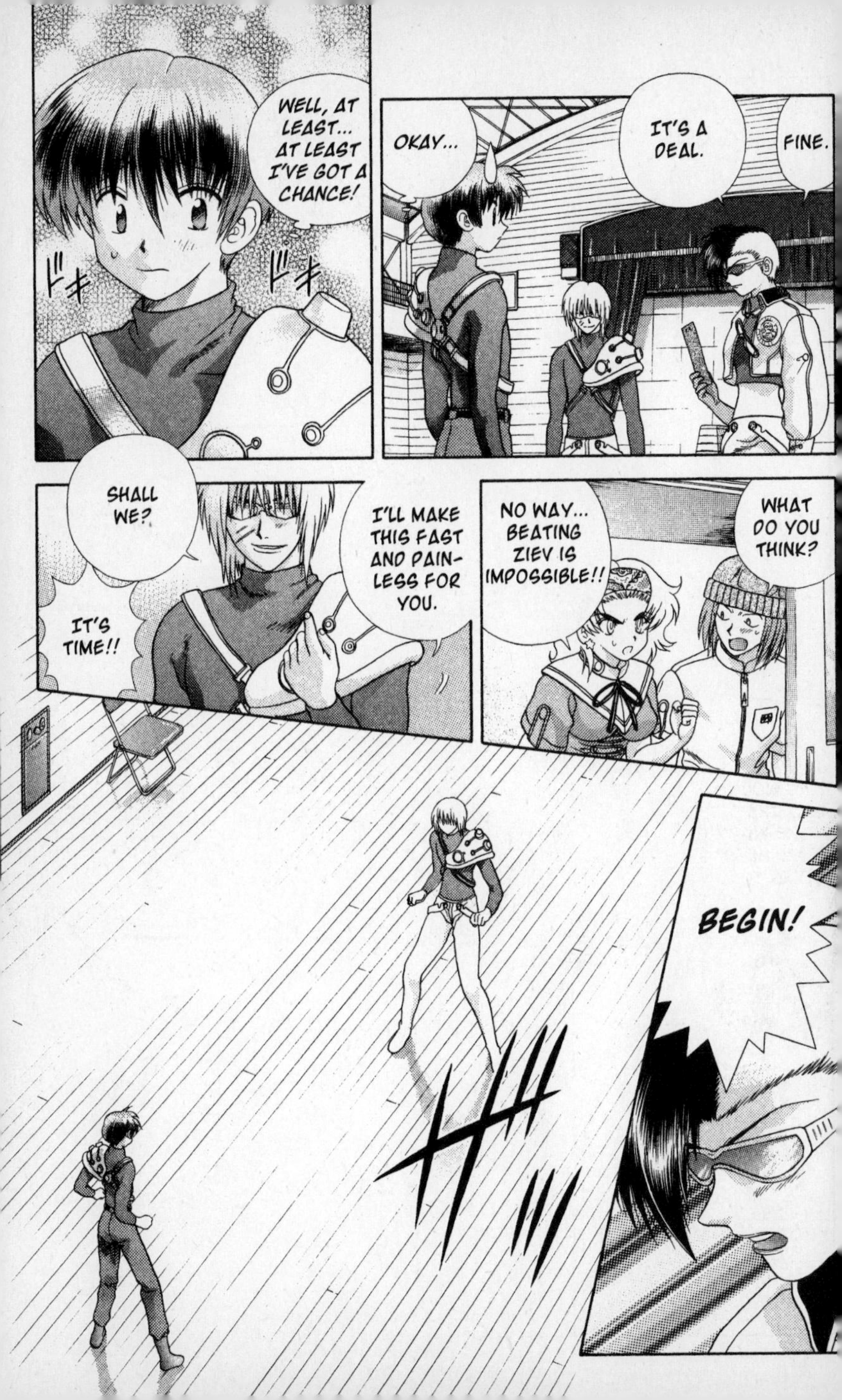

FINE.
IT'S A DEAL.
OKAY...
WELL, AT LEAST... AT LEAST I'VE GOT A CHANCE!
ドキ ドキ
WHAT DO YOU THINK?
NO WAY... BEATING ZIEV IS IMPOSSIBLE!!
I'LL MAKE THIS FAST AND PAIN-LESS FOR YOU.
SHALL WE?
IT'S TIME!!
BEGIN!

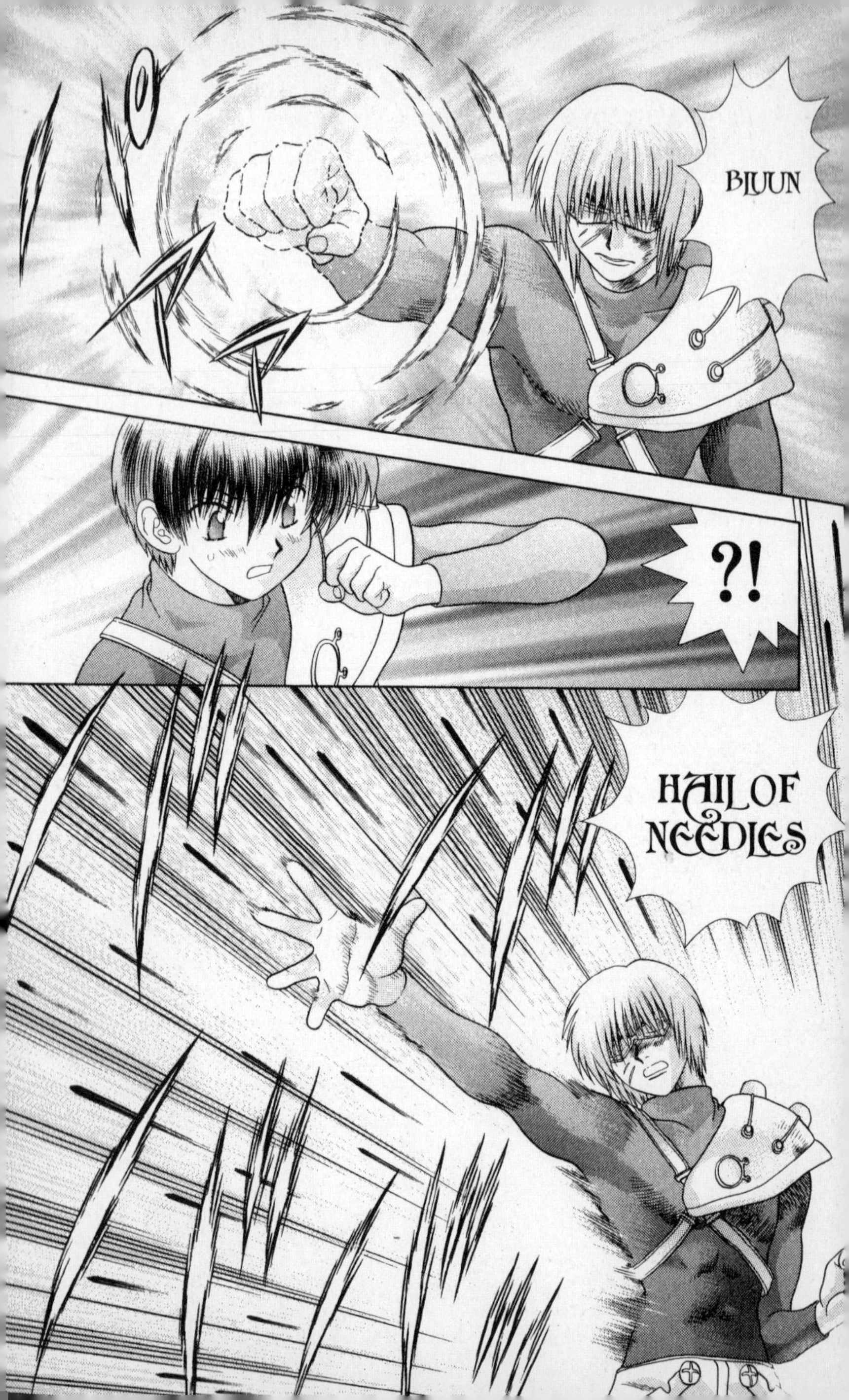
BLUUN
?!
HAIL OF NEEDLES

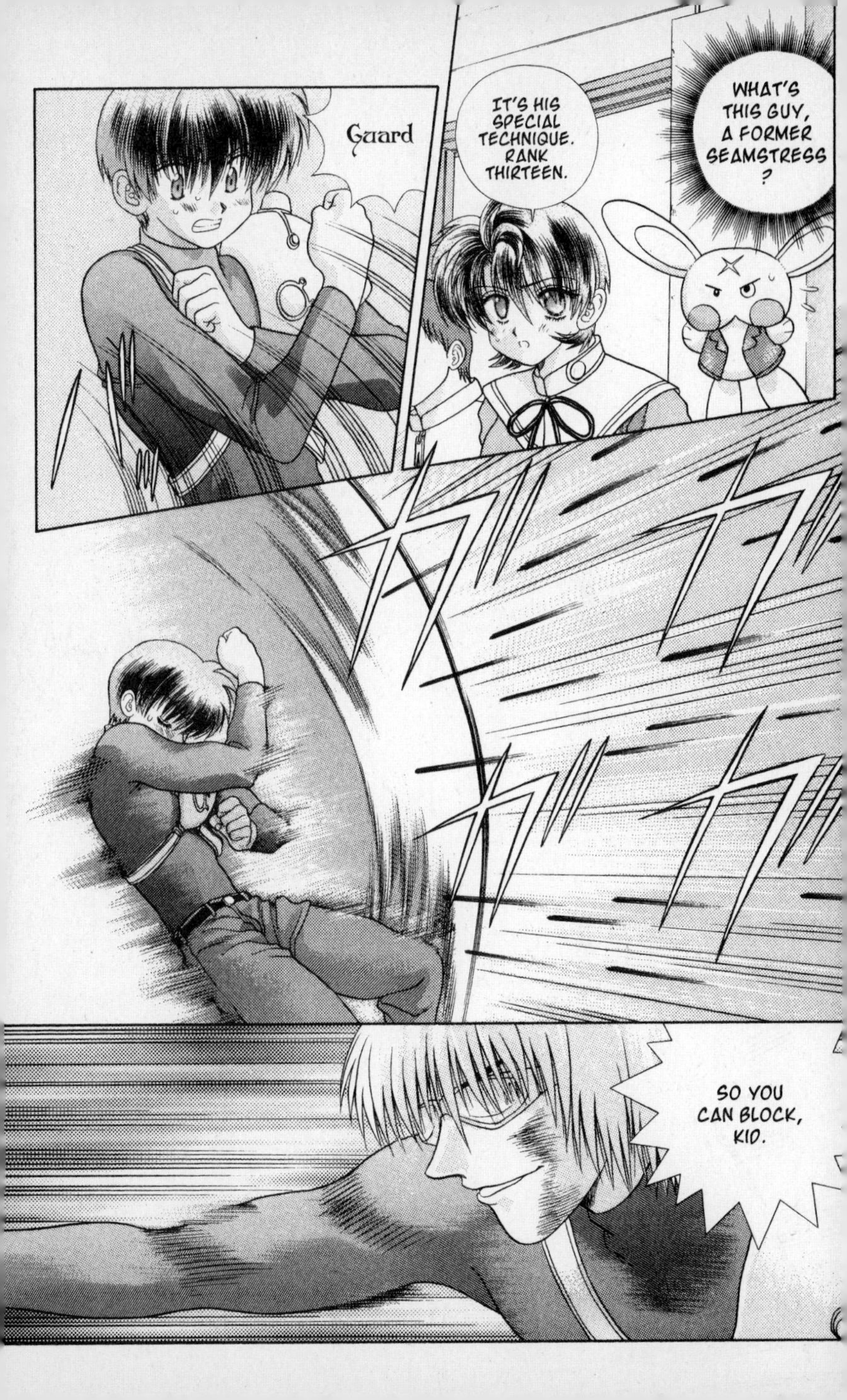
WHAT'S THIS GUY, A FORMER SEAMSTRESS?
IT'S HIS SPECIAL TECHNIQUE. RANK THIRTEEN.
Guard
SO YOU CAN BLOCK, KID.

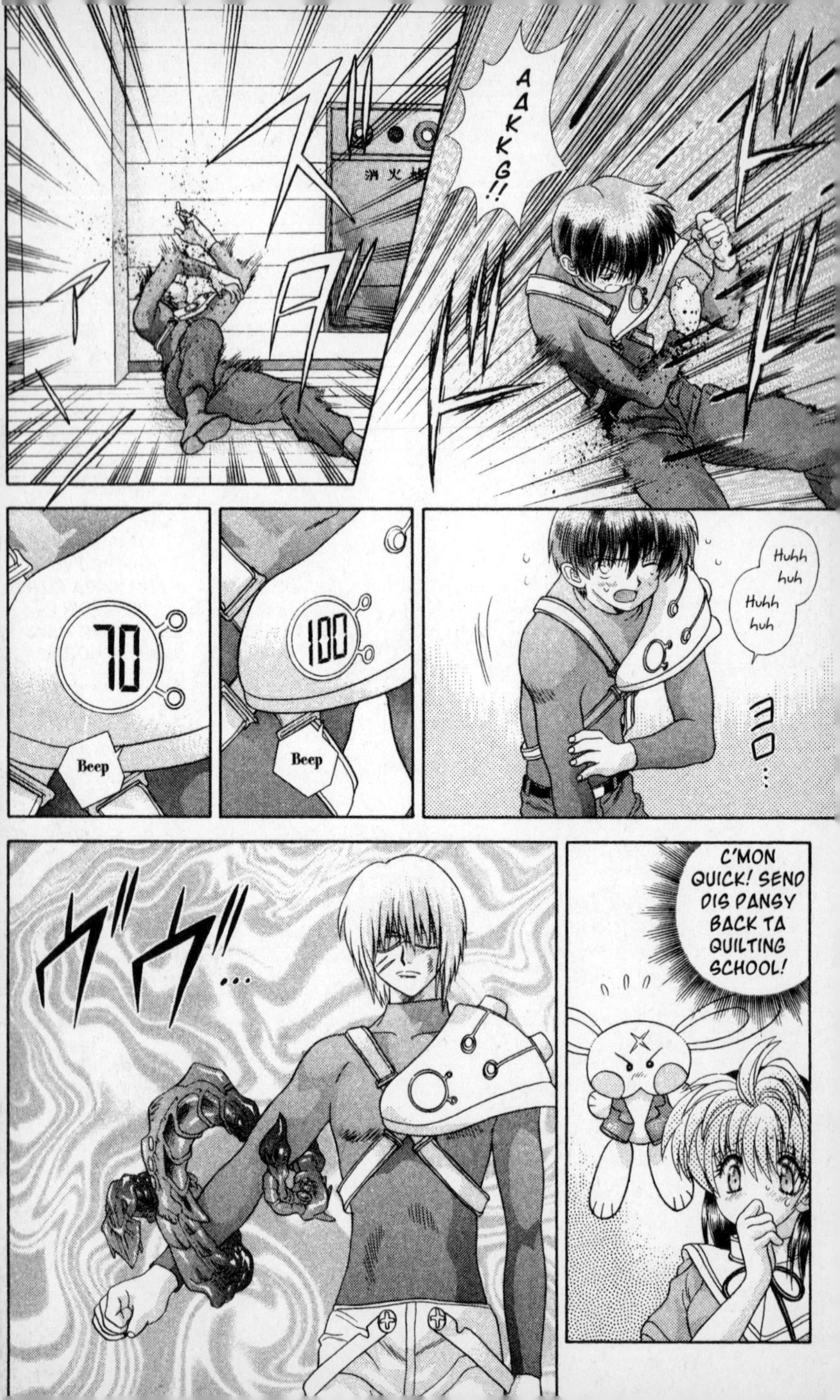
AAKKG!!
Huhh huh
Huhh huh
ヨロ…
100
Beep
70
Beep
C'MON QUICK! SEND DIS PANSY BACK TA QUILTING SCHOOL!
...

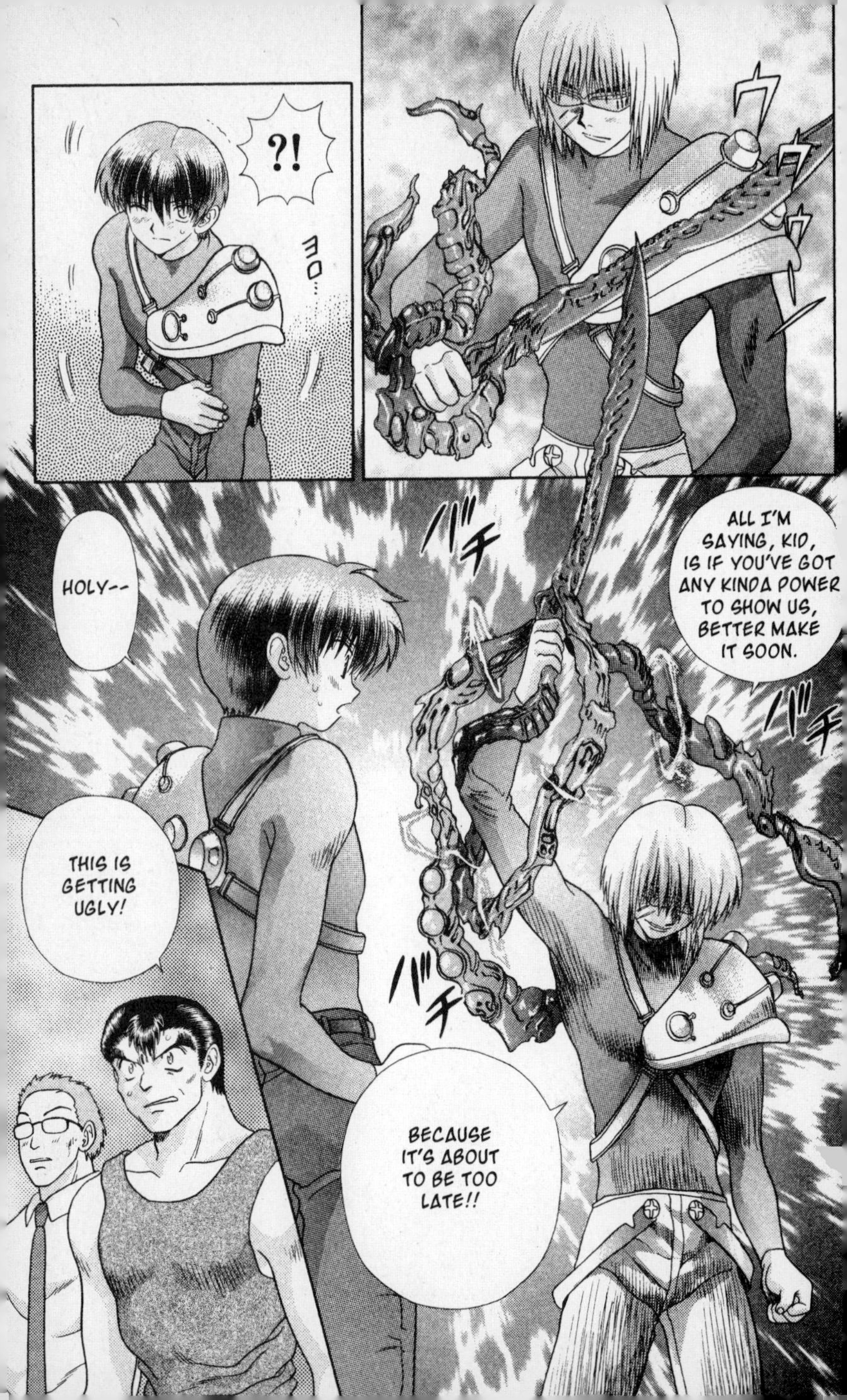
?!
ヨロ…
ALL I'M SAYING, KID, IS IF YOU'VE GOT ANY KINDA POWER TO SHOW US, BETTER MAKE IT SOON.
バチ
バチ
HOLY--
THIS IS GETTING UGLY!
バチ
BECAUSE IT'S ABOUT TO BE TOO LATE!!

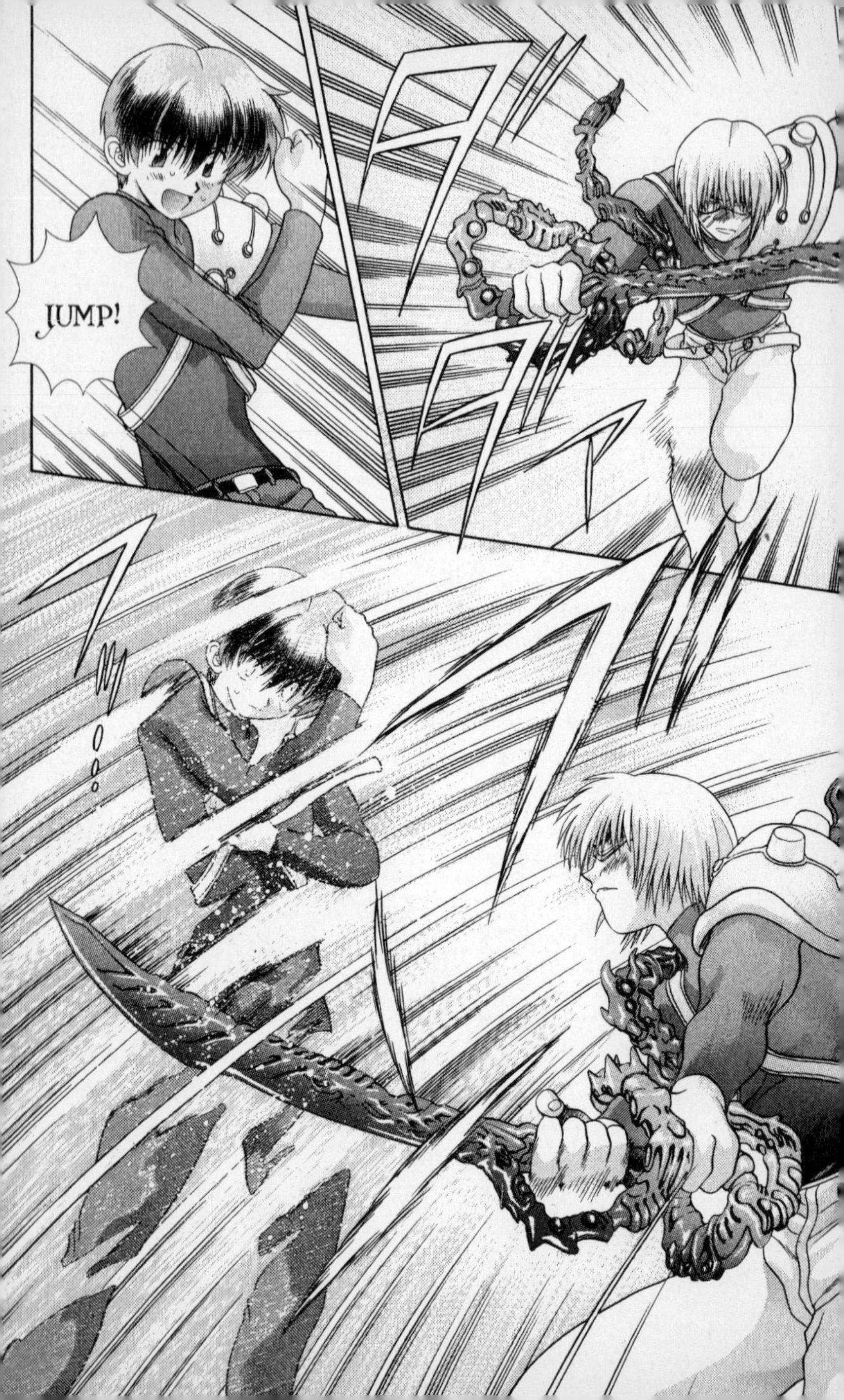
JUMP!

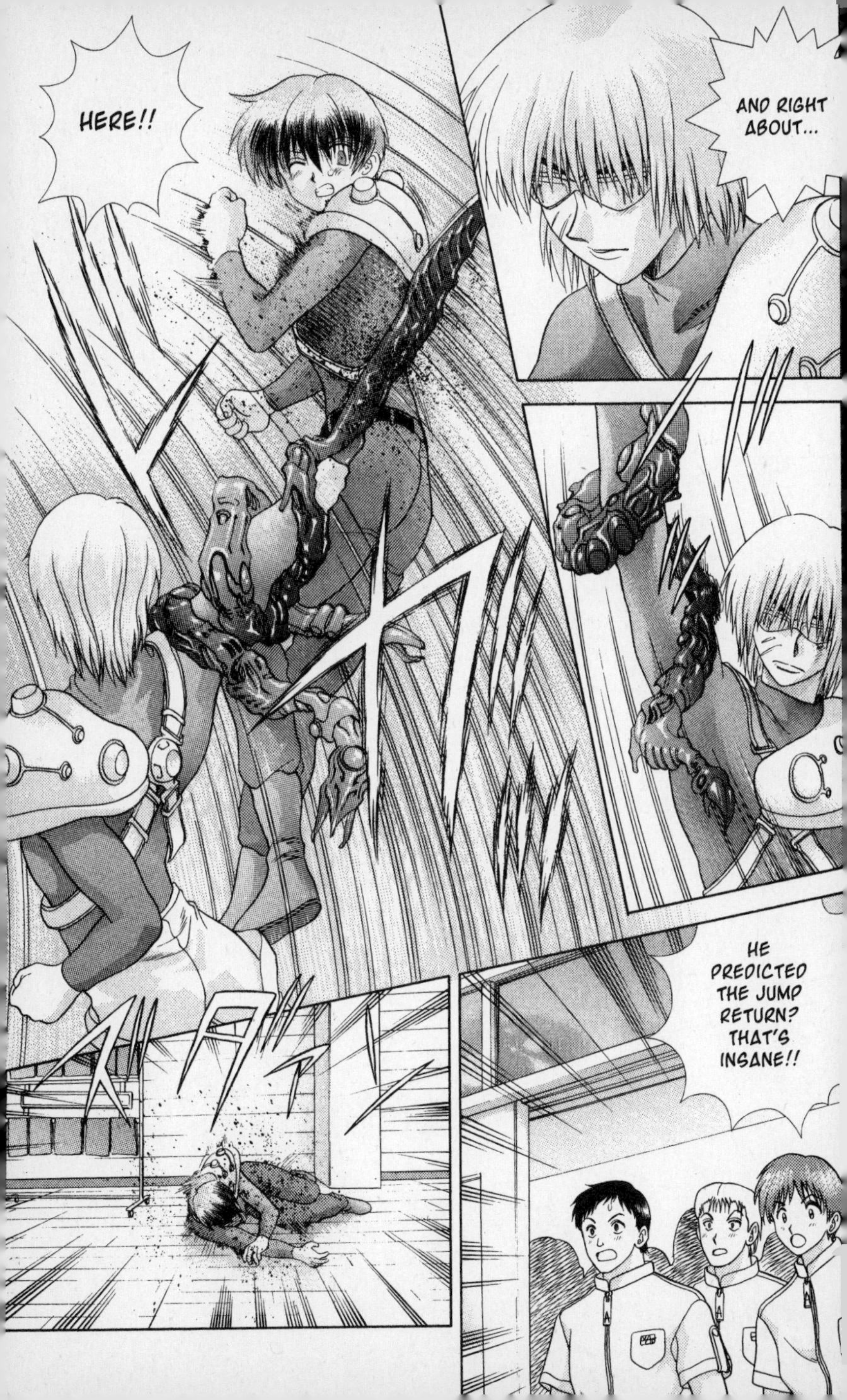
AND RIGHT ABOUT...
HERE!!
HE PREDICTED THE JUMP RETURN? THAT'S INSANE!!

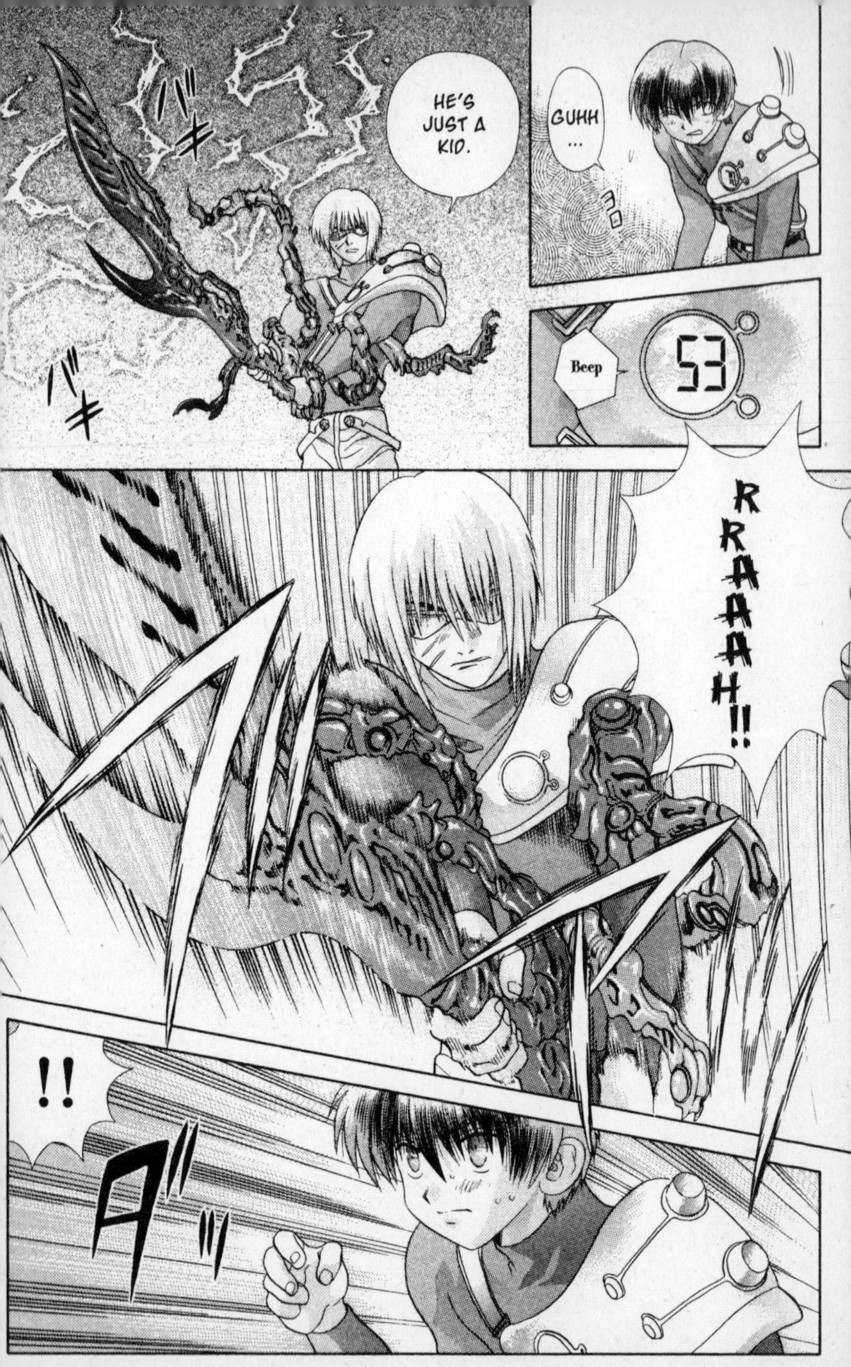

GUHH ...
Beep
53
HE'S JUST A KID.
バキ
バキ
RRAAAAH!!
!!

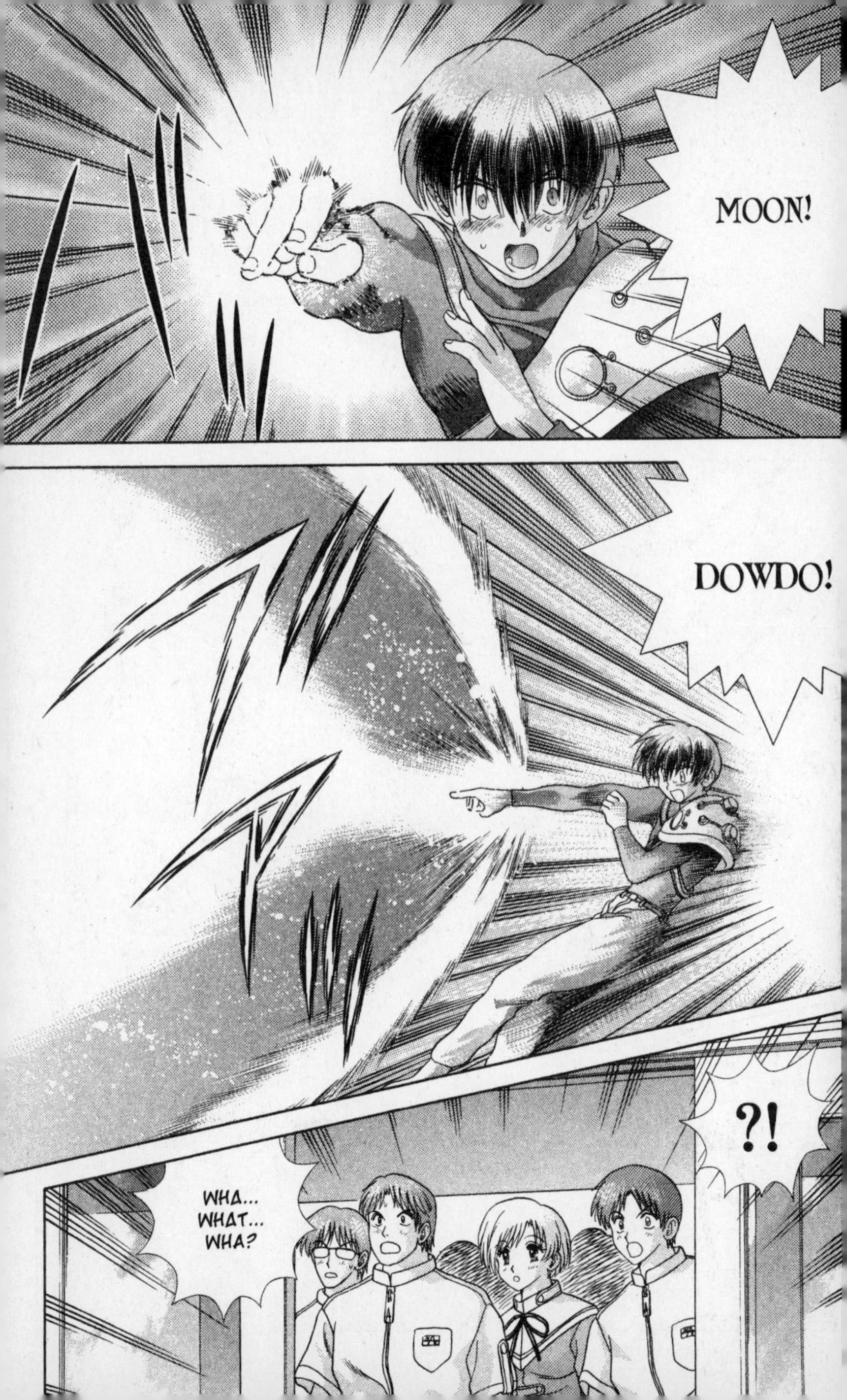
MOON!
DOWDO!
?!
WHA... WHAT... WHA?

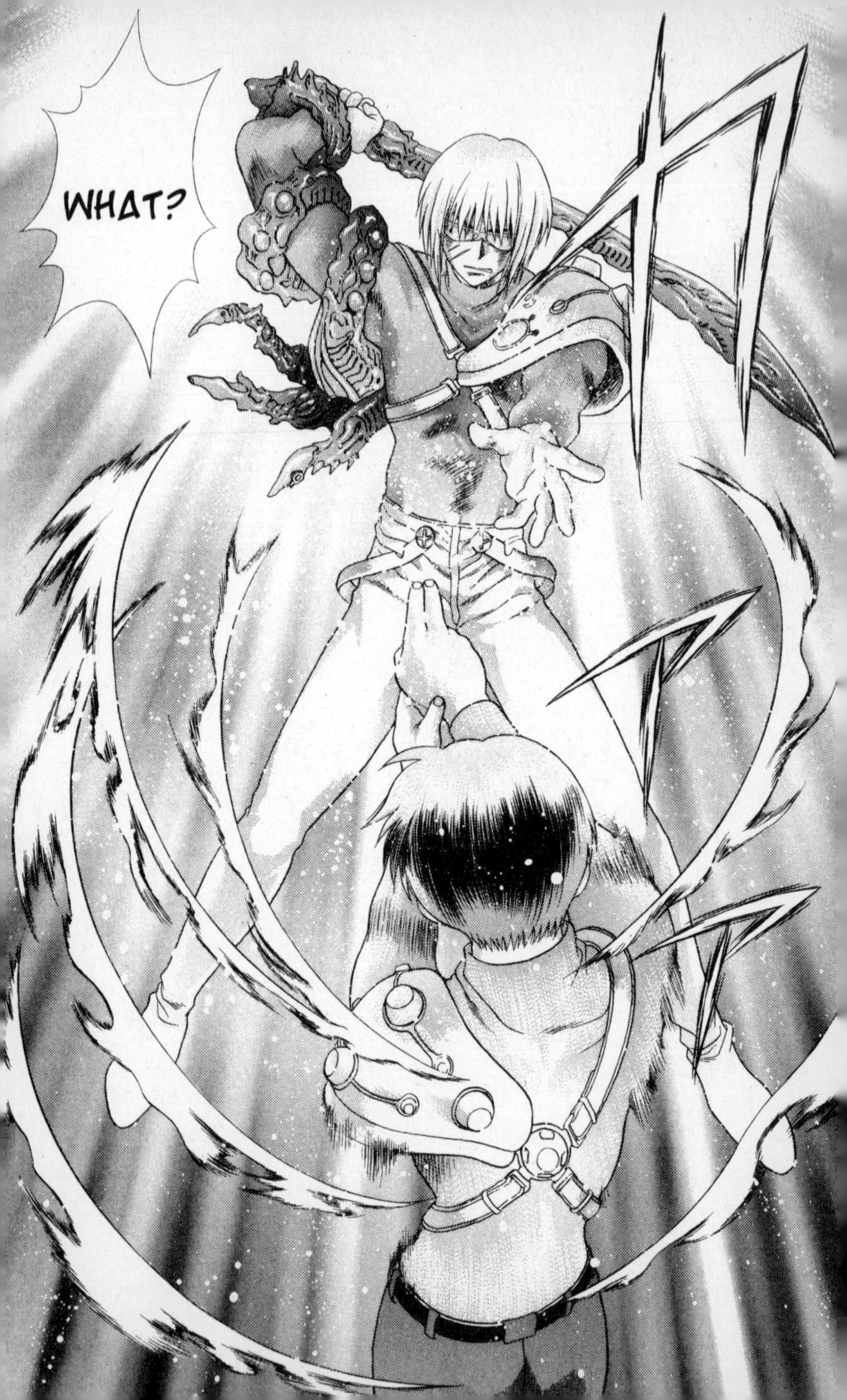
WHAT?

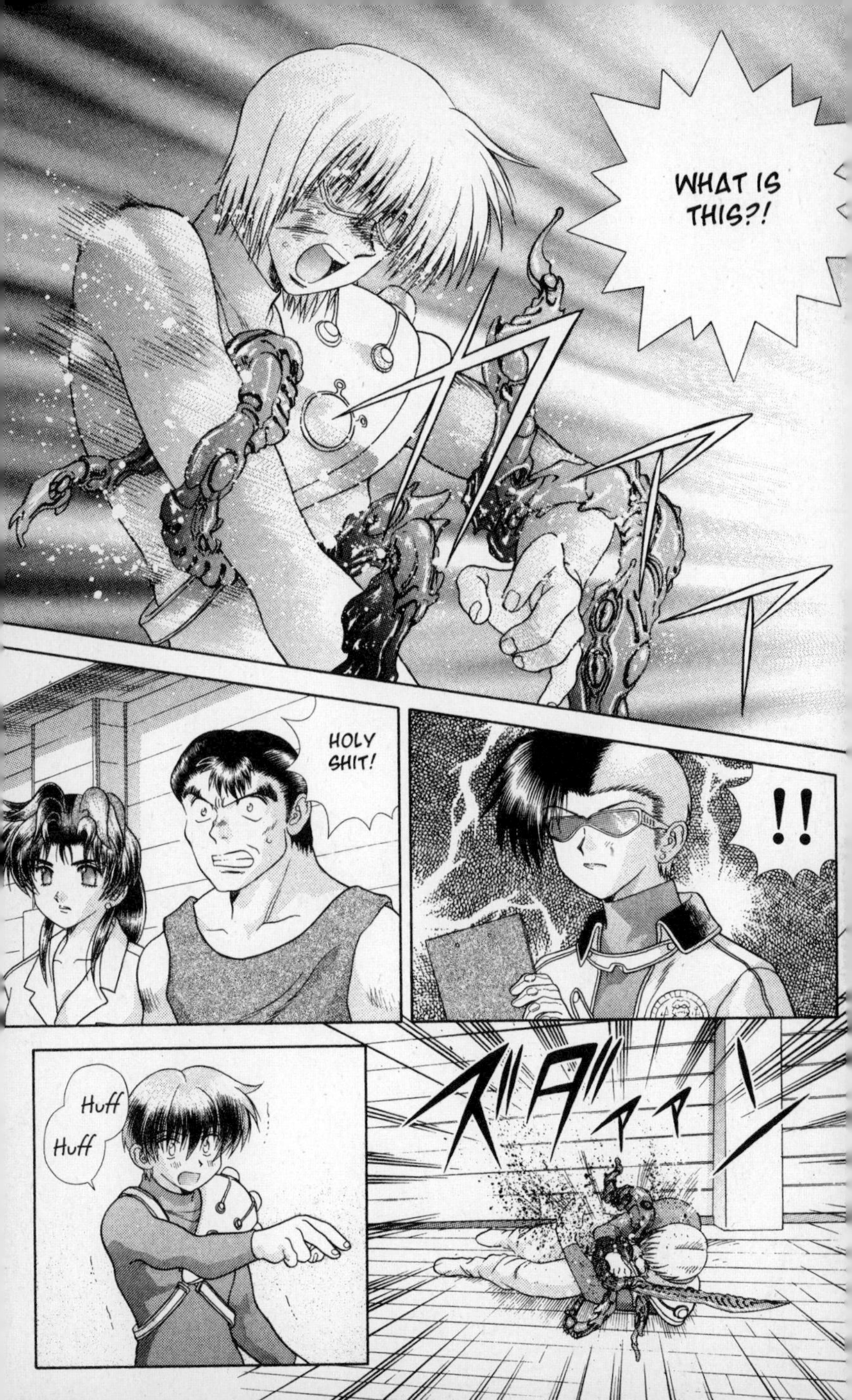
WHAT IS THIS?!
!!
HOLY SHIT!
Huff
Huff

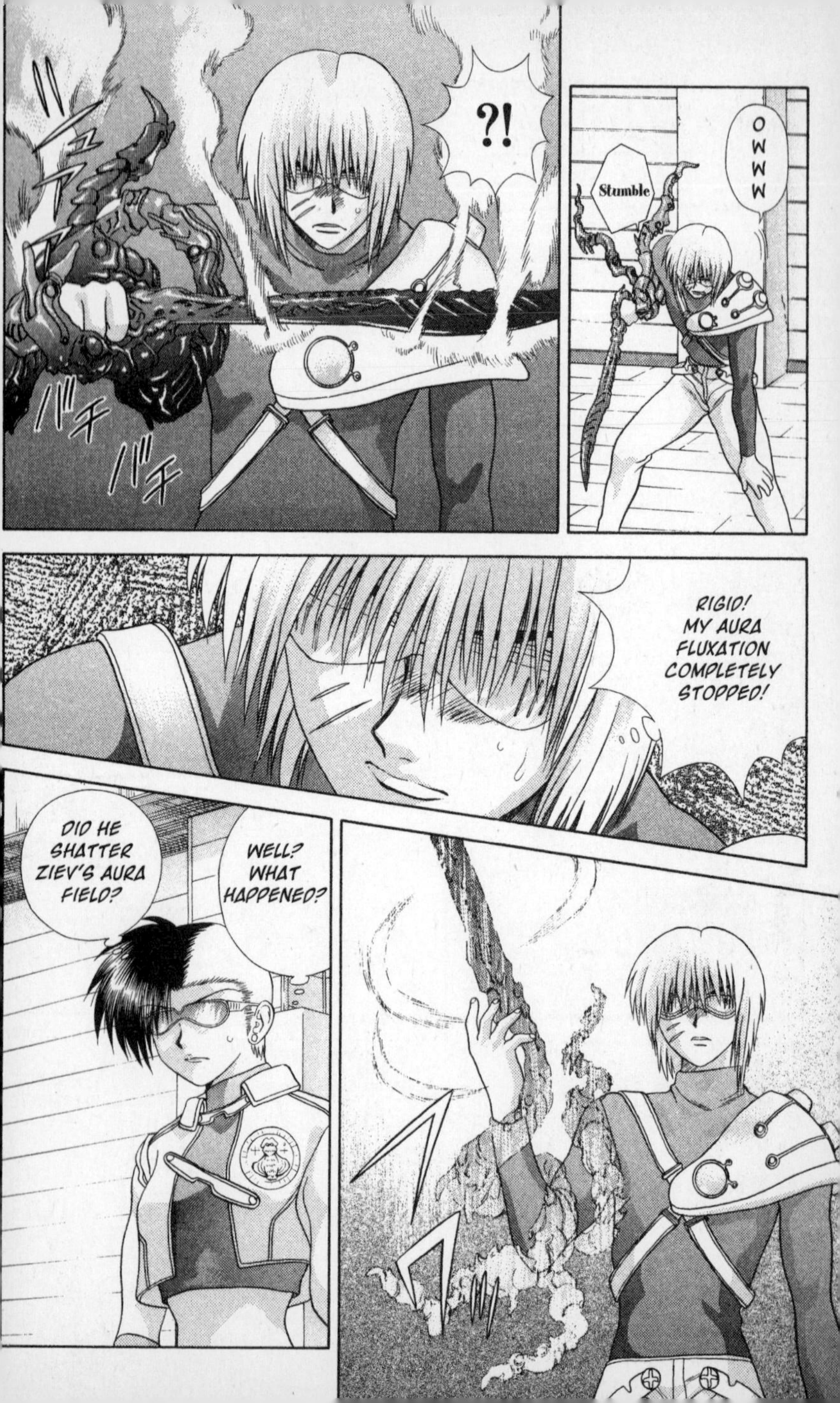
OWWW
Stumble
?!
バチ
バチ
RIGID! MY AURA FLUXATION COMPLETELY STOPPED!
WELL? WHAT HAPPENED?
DID HE SHATTER ZIEV'S AURA FIELD?

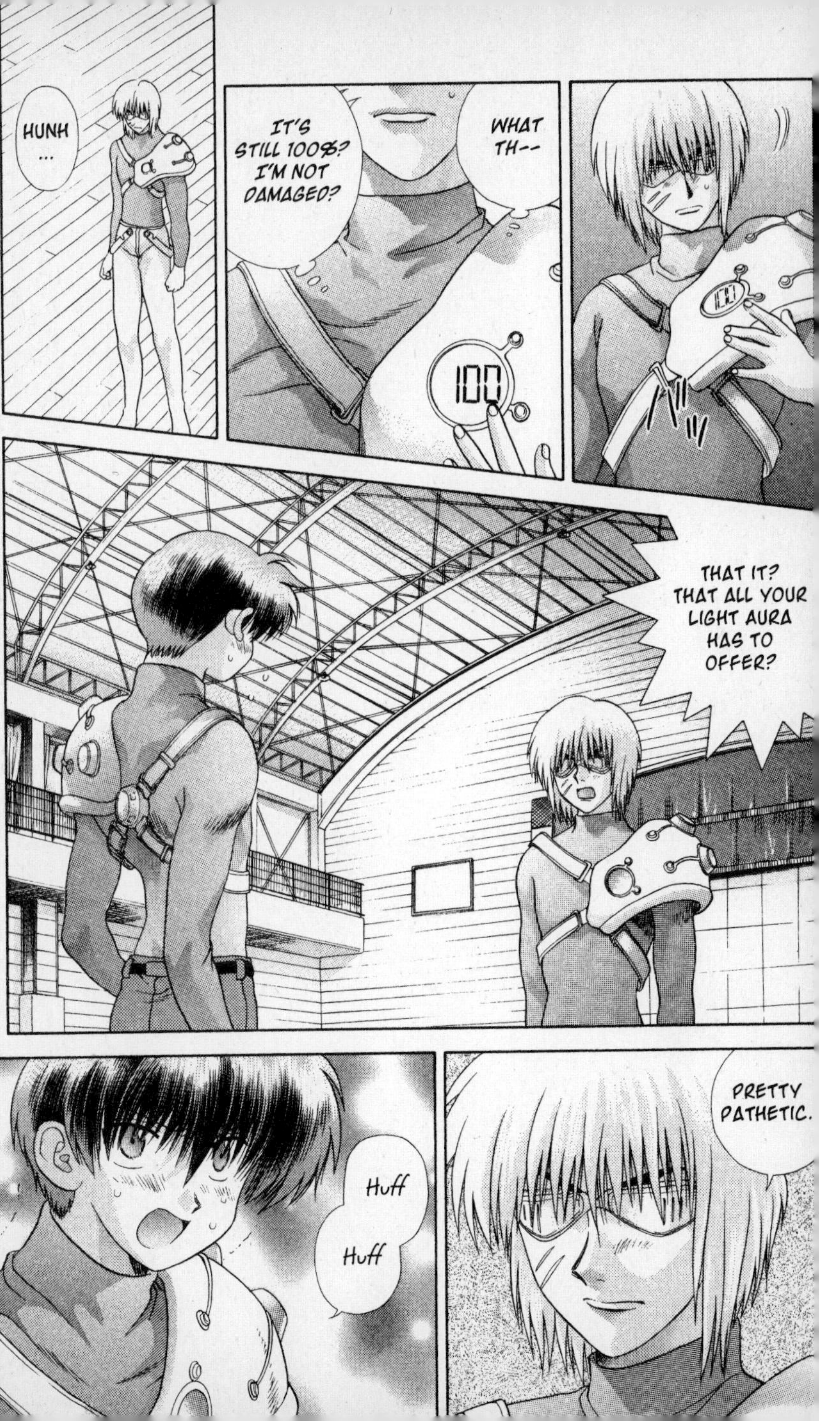
WHAT TH--
IT'S STILL 100%? I'M NOT DAMAGED?
100
HUNH ...
THAT IT? THAT ALL YOUR LIGHT AURA HAS TO OFFER?
PRETTY PATHETIC.
Huff
Huff

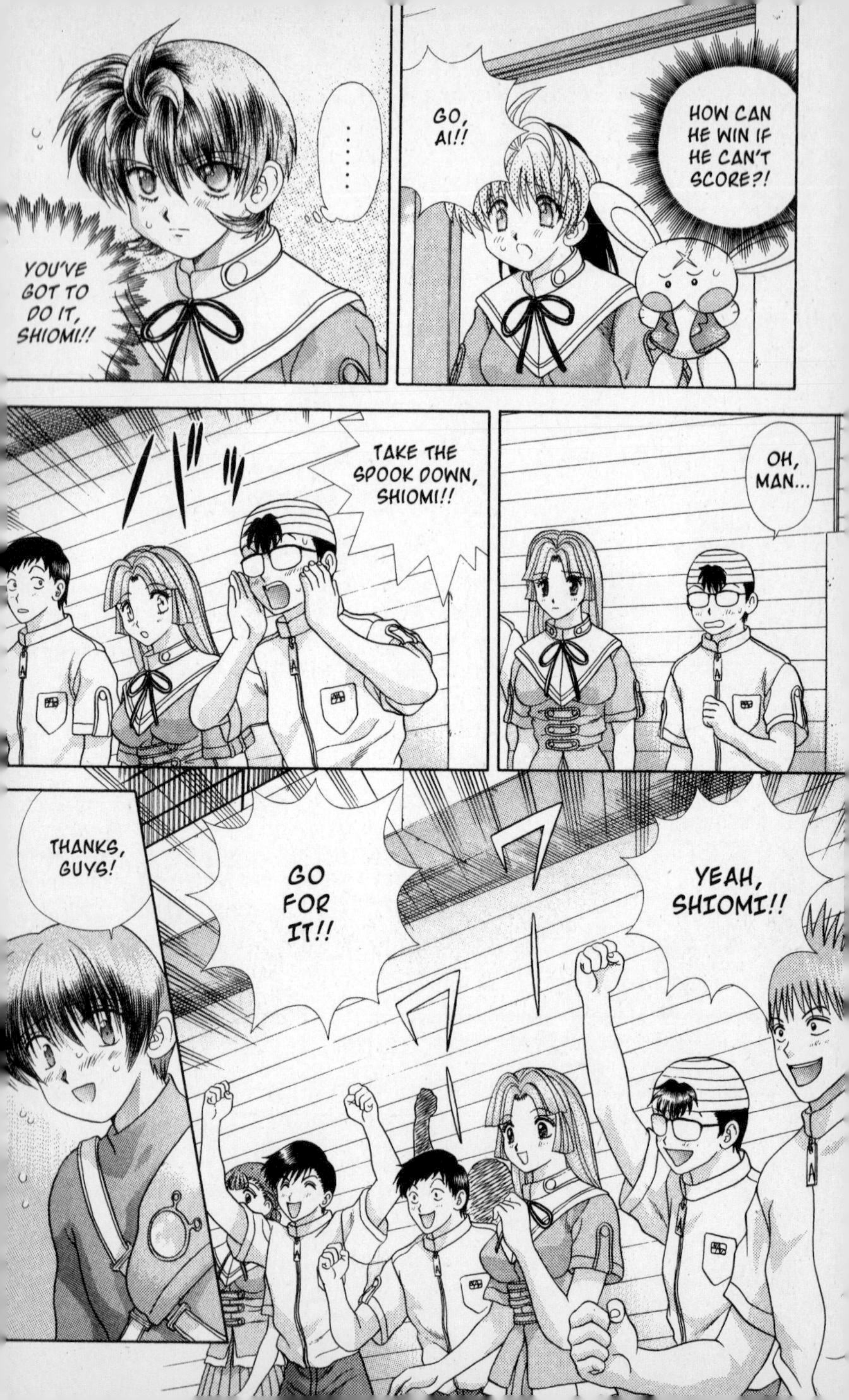
HOW CAN HE WIN IF HE CAN'T SCORE?!
GO, AI!!
......
YOU'VE GOT TO DO IT, SHIOMI!!
OH, MAN...
TAKE THE SPOOK DOWN, SHIOMI!!
YEAH, SHIOMI!!
GO FOR IT!!
THANKS, GUYS!

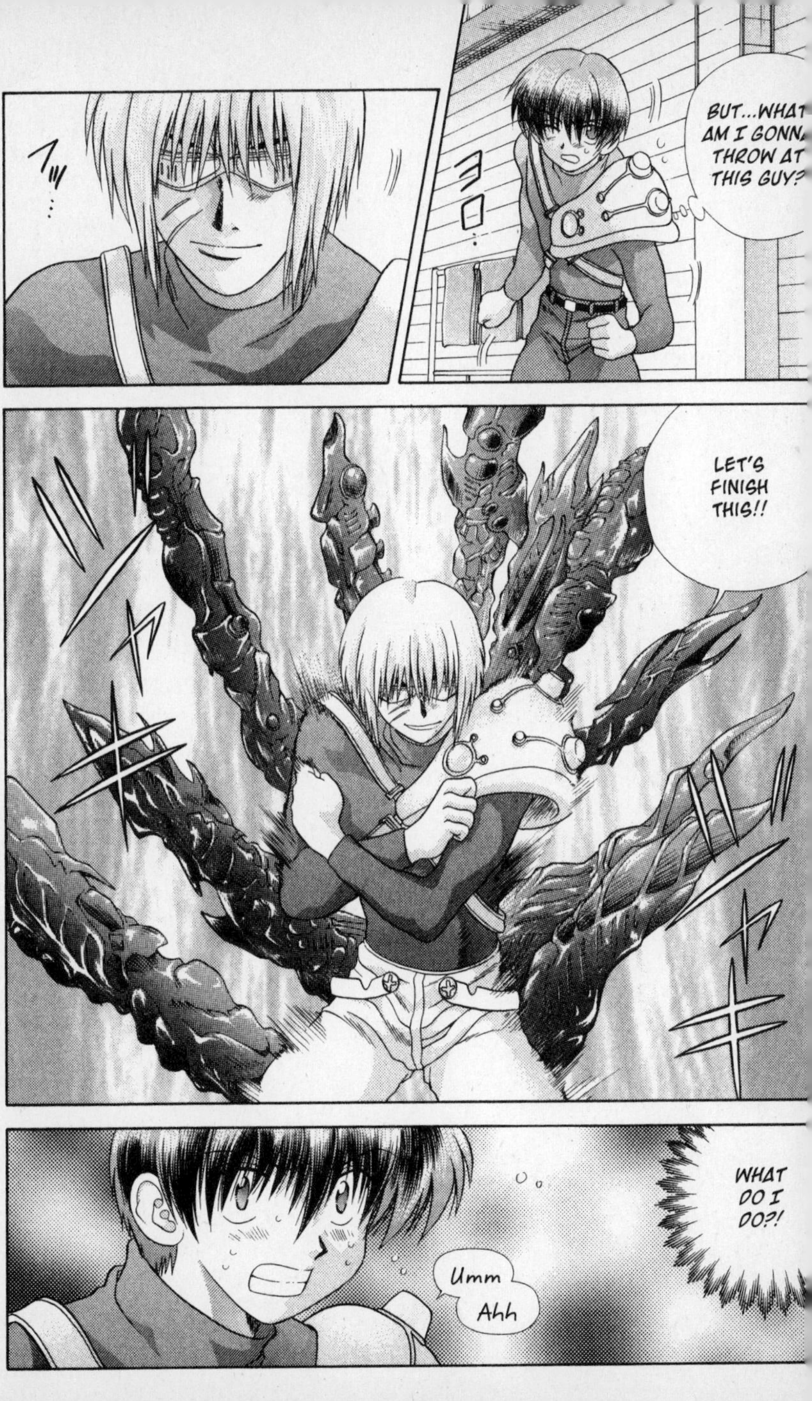

BUT...WHAT AM I GONNA THROW AT THIS GUY?
ヨロ…
LET'S FINISH THIS!!
WHAT DO I DO?!
Umm
Ahh

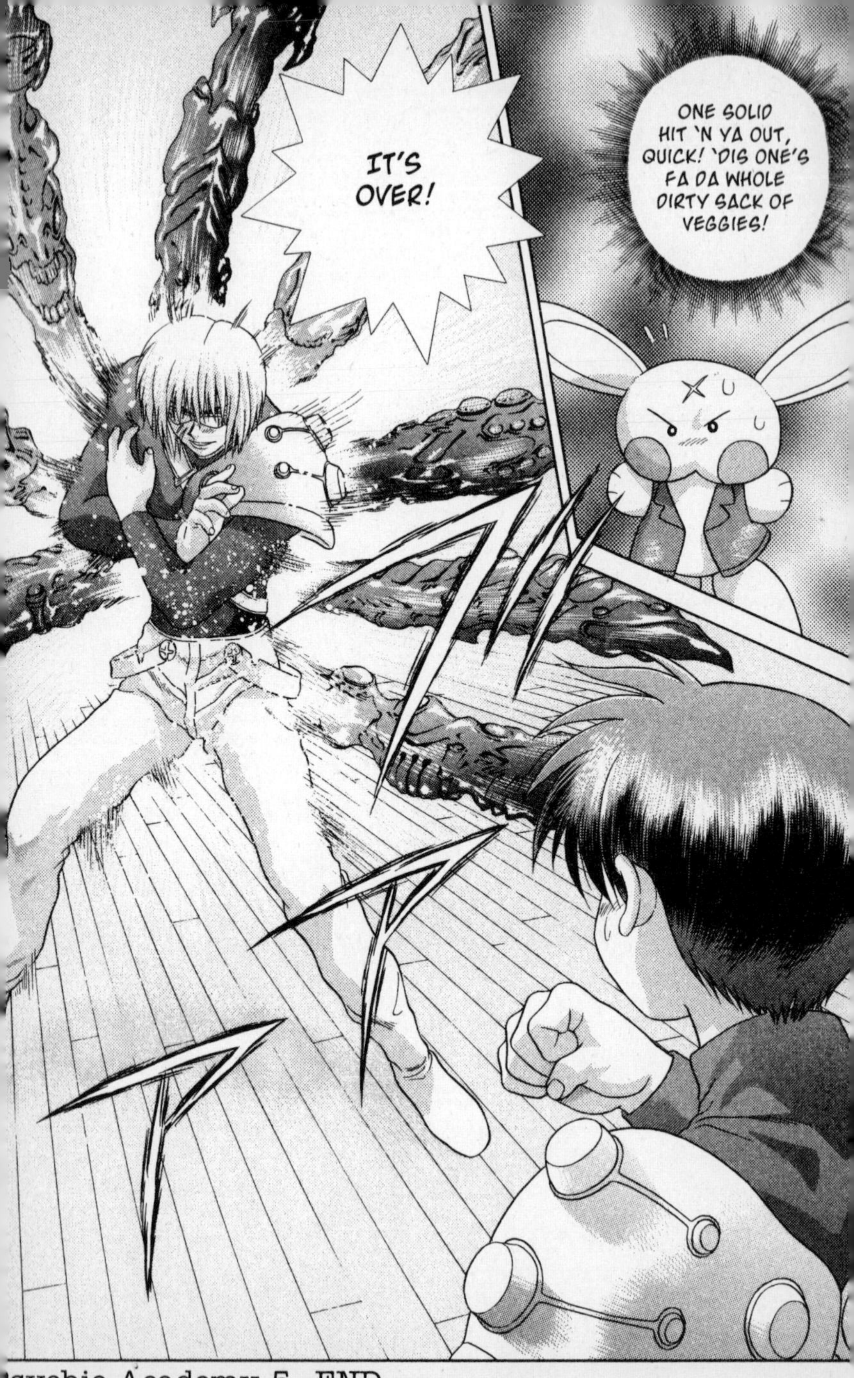
ONE SOLID HIT 'N YA OUT, QUICK! 'DIS ONE'S FA DA WHOLE DIRTY SACK OF VEGGIES!
IT'S OVER!

'sychic Academy 5 END

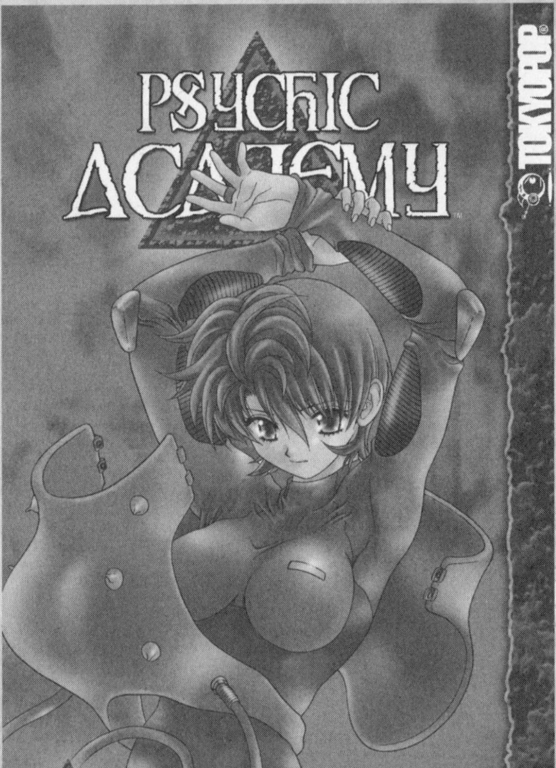
PSYCHIC ACADEMY
TOKYOPOP
6
KATSU AKI

In the next volume...

If Ai doesn't beat a highly trained, extremely powerful, master psychic, he gets whisked away to California to be a study subject for the A.D.C. What will he do? What will Sahra do? What will Mew do? What's worse...what will Zero–who has already confessed to his adopted parents that Ai is his responsibility–do? But what's the point if a new A.D.C. center ends up being built Japan? The Psychic Academy may lie directly in the ominous building's shadow. And when a bunch of middle schoolers go on a hunt to prove their might against the mighty Ai Shiomi, will he have to kick little kid butt?

ALSO AVAILABLE FROM TOKYOPOP®

08.20.04T

ALSO AVAILABLE FROM  TOKYOPOP®

MANGA

.HACK//LEGEND OF THE TWILIGHT
@LARGE
ABENOBASHI: MAGICAL SHOPPING ARCADE
A.I. LOVE YOU
AI YORI AOSHI
ALICHINO
ANGELIC LAYER
ARM OF KANNON
BABY BIRTH
BATTLE ROYALE
BATTLE VIXENS
BOYS BE...
BRAIN POWERED
BRIGADOON
B'TX
CANDIDATE FOR GODDESS, THE
CARDCAPTOR SAKURA
CARDCAPTOR SAKURA - MASTER OF THE CLOW
CHOBITS
CHRONICLES OF THE CURSED SWORD
CLAMP SCHOOL DETECTIVES
CLOVER
COMIC PARTY
CONFIDENTIAL CONFESSIONS
CORRECTOR YUI
COWBOY BEBOP
COWBOY BEBOP: SHOOTING STAR
CRAZY LOVE STORY
CRESCENT MOON
CROSS
CULDCEPT
CYBORG 009
D•N•ANGEL
DEARS
DEMON DIARY
DEMON ORORON, THE
DEUS VITAE
DIGIMON
DIGIMON TAMERS
DIGIMON ZERO TWO
DOLL
DRAGON HUNTER
DRAGON KNIGHTS
DRAGON VOICE
DREAM SAGA
DUKLYON: CLAMP SCHOOL DEFENDERS
EERIE QUEERIE!
ERICA SAKURAZAWA: COLLECTED WORKS
ET CETERA
ETERNITY
EVIL'S RETURN
FAERIES' LANDING
FAKE
FLCL
FLOWER OF THE DEEP SLEEP, THE
FORBIDDEN DANCE
FRUITS BASKET

G GUNDAM
GATEKEEPERS
GETBACKERS
GIRL GOT GAME
GRAVITATION
GTO
GUNDAM SEED ASTRAY
GUNDAM WING
GUNDAM WING: BATTLEFIELD OF PACIFISTS
GUNDAM WING: ENDLESS WALTZ
GUNDAM WING: THE LAST OUTPOST (G-UNIT)
HANDS OFF!
HAPPY MANIA
HARLEM BEAT
HYPER RUNE
I.N.V.U.
IMMORTAL RAIN
INITIAL D
INSTANT TEEN: JUST ADD NUTS
ISLAND
JING: KING OF BANDITS
JING: KING OF BANDITS - TWILIGHT TALES
JULINE
KARE KANO
KILL ME, KISS ME
KINDAICHI CASE FILES, THE
KING OF HELL
KODOCHA: SANA'S STAGE
LAMENT OF THE LAMB
LEGAL DRUG
LEGEND OF CHUN HYANG, THE
LES BIJOUX
LOVE HINA
LOVE OR MONEY
LUPIN III
LUPIN III: WORLD'S MOST WANTED
MAGIC KNIGHT RAYEARTH I
MAGIC KNIGHT RAYEARTH II
MAHOROMATIC: AUTOMATIC MAIDEN
MAN OF MANY FACES
MARMALADE BOY
MARS
MARS: HORSE WITH NO NAME
MINK
MIRACLE GIRLS
MIYUKI-CHAN IN WONDERLAND
MODEL
MOURYOU KIDEN: LEGEND OF THE NYMPHS
NECK AND NECK
ONE
ONE I LOVE, THE
PARADISE KISS
PARASYTE
PASSION FRUIT
PEACH GIRL
PEACH GIRL: CHANGE OF HEART
PET SHOP OF HORRORS
PITA-TEN
PLANET LADDER

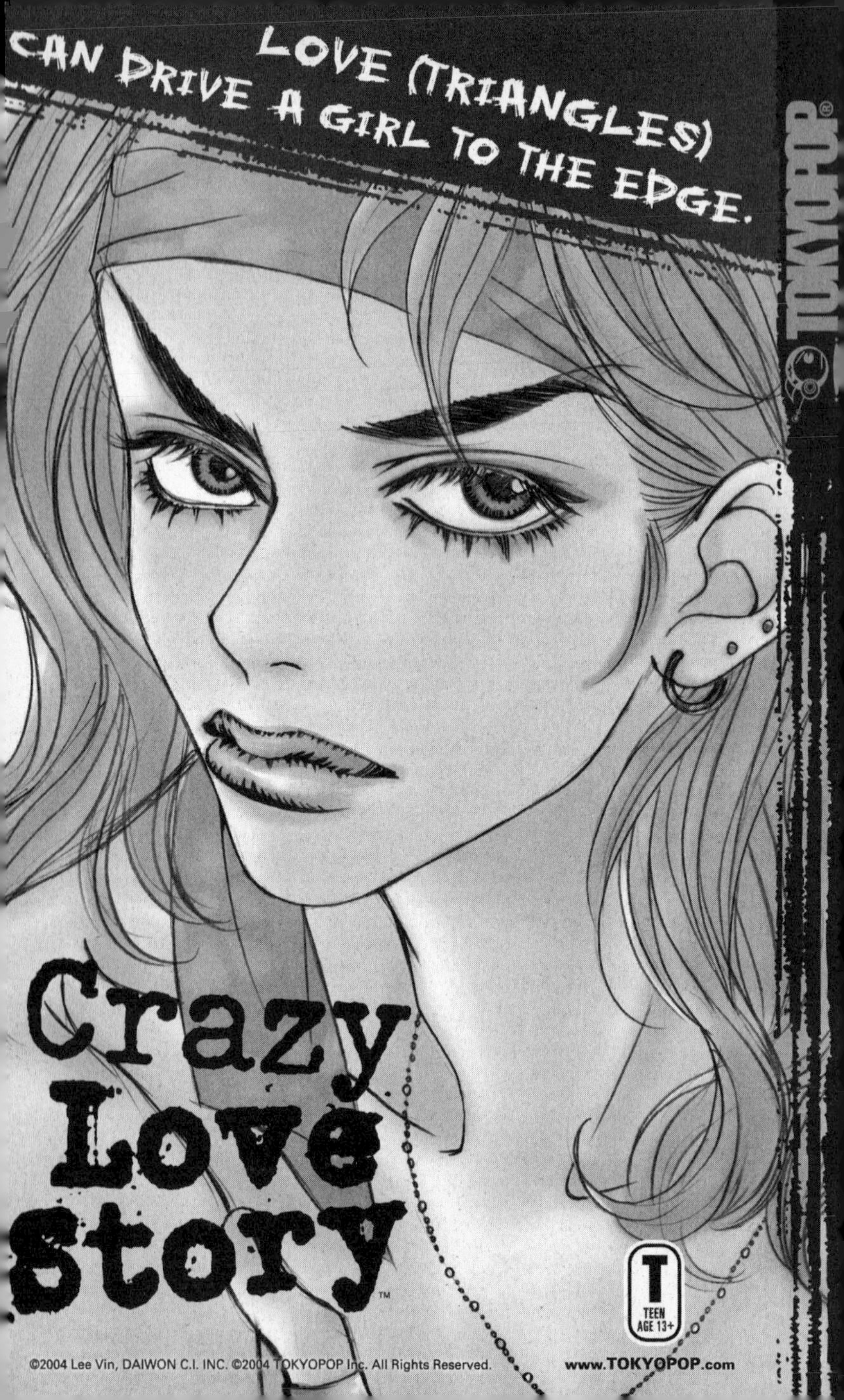
LOVE (TRIANGLES)
CAN DRIVE A GIRL TO THE EDGE.
TOKYOPOP
Crazy Love Story™
T TEEN AGE 13+
©2004 Lee Vin, DAIWON C.I. INC. ©2004 TOKYOPOP Inc. All Rights Reserved.
www.TOKYOPOP.com

LEGAL DRUG™

When no ordinary prescription will do...

STOP!

This is the back of the book.
You wouldn't want to spoil a great ending!

This book is printed "manga-style," in the authentic Japanese right-to-left format. Since none of the artwork has been flipped or altered, readers get to experience the story just as the creator intended. You've been asking for it, so TOKYOPOP® delivered: authentic, hot-off-the-press, and far more fun!

DIRECTIONS

If this is your first time reading manga-style, here's a quick guide to help you understand how it works.

It's easy... just start in the top right panel and follow the numbers. Have fun, and look for more 100% authentic manga from TOKYOPOP®!